State and Local Government

State and Local Government

2005–2006

Edited by Kevin B. Smith
University of Nebraska–Lincoln

CQ PRESS

A Division of Congressional Quarterly Inc., Washington, D.C.

CQ Press
1255 22nd Street, NW, Suite 400
Washington, DC 20037

Phone: 202-729-1900; toll-free, 1-866-427-7737 (1-866-4CQ-PRESS)

Web: www.cqpress.com

Cover design by Auburn Associates, Inc., Baltimore, Maryland

♾ The paper used in this publication exceeds the requirements of the American National Standard for Information Sciences—Permanence of Paper for Printed Library Materials, ANSI Z39.48-1992.

Printed and bound in the United States of America

09   08   07   06   05   5   4   3   2   1

ISSN 0888-8590
ISBN 1-56802-971-3

Contents

Preface

At the beginning of the twenty-first century, state and local governments are facing changes across the board: in relationships between and within governments, in their roles and responsibilities, in their policy priorities and in those holding office. Officeholders are searching for new solutions to the wide range of challenges they must address; they are tackling budget deficits while adapting to new technologies. In the meantime, their constituents are voting for change through ballot initiatives that alter the structure of government, determining who is elected to office—and how long they can stay.

One of the most notable changes is in the relationship between state and national governments, the relationship that is at the heart of the U.S. federalist political system. In the 1990s there was a growing bipartisan consensus in Congress to shift more policy power and responsibility to the states. However, in recent years, this movement has been abandoned even by its erstwhile advocates. The federal government has continued to pass unfunded mandates despite promises not to do so and has even begun to encroach upon the traditional jurisdiction of states and localities by significantly extending its power over education.

Traditional state governments are also being challenged by considerable changes generated by internal forces. Over the past decade, citizens have increasingly used ballot initiatives to take policy directly into their own hands. Voters at the ballot box have, among other things, limited the number of terms that state legislators may serve, committed California to spending billions on stem cell research, increased the minimum wage in Florida, required

Nevada's legislature to fund primary and secondary education before dealing with any other part of the state budget, and passed constitutional amendments banning gay marriage in a number of states.

The impact of such ballot initiatives is beginning to be felt with full force as hundreds of legislators have had to leave office because of term limits. These forced retirements are making way for a new breed of legislator—the inexperienced kind, not necessarily the sort of citizen-representative whom advocates of term limits had in mind. Term limits seem to have done little to discourage careerism in politics, but they have succeeded in eroding the level of experience among legislators and, subsequently, the degree of influence yielded by legislative party leaders and committee chairs. As a result, influence seems to be shifting toward the executive branch, not just to governors but also to state bureaucracies.

This turnover in state legislators is coming at a time when experienced hands might prove useful in finding solutions to serious problems. One of the most unwelcome changes state governments are grappling with these days is budgetary turmoil. States spent much of the 1990s in the enviable position of having high revenues and low taxes, and they were hit hard by the economy's rough landing at the turn of the century. Many are struggling to balance the books and are revisiting the way they think about how the government gets its money and what it spends it on.

Local governments are far from immune from all this change. They too are struggling with their own budgets, which have suffered as the result of state-level fiscal crises. In the good economic times of the 1990s, many state governments capped property taxes—in effect, placing limits on the major revenue source for local governments. The state governments promised to ease the burden of these revenue limits by giving local governments more money from state coffers, but such promises are being broken in these times of fiscal stress. Local governments thus are also being forced to change how they do business in order to stay in business.

All of these changes, and many more, are detailed and explored in the readings throughout this book. One of the intended purposes of *State and Local Government* is to serve as an annual survey on the health, direction and performance of states and localities. The readings show that despite less than ideal circumstances on these fronts, state and local governments are doing what they have historically proven to be very good at: adapting to change.

Although some of the solutions are painful, both to those who make the decisions and to those who deal with the consequences, they also reflect the vibrancy and vitality of state and local governments. Undoubtedly, these are times when tough choices have to be made. Yet state and local governments are stepping up to the challenge, making those choices and surviving—even thriving, in some cases.

It is also important to note that amidst all these changes, some constants remain. Paramount among these is the central role that state and local governments continue to play in virtually all aspects of political, economic and social life in the United States. The readings in the 2005–2006 edition of *State and Local Government* show that these levels of government remain closest to the day-to-day lives of citizens.

Parts 1 through 3 of this edition address the general political context of state and local governments, with readings on federalism and intergovernmental relations, elections and political environment, and political parties and interest groups. After setting the basic context, Parts 4–7 contain readings on the basic institutions of these governments: legislatures, governors and executives, courts and the bureaucracy. Part 8 looks specifically at local government, and Parts 9 and 10 examine readings on bugets and taxes and the current major policy challenges state and local governments are facing.

Thanks are owed to numerous people for making this volume possible. First and foremost, I would like to salute Thad L. Beyle, the founder of this series and until this year its editor. Thad set very high standards, and taking over the "franchise" and living up to those standards provided the motivation for what follows. I would also like to thank all the good folks at CQ Press, especially Charisse Kiino, who made sure that *State and Local Government* continued after Thad stepped down. Finally, I'd like to thank an overworked teaching assistant of mine—Tyler White. For every article you read in the volume, I read at least twenty others. Tyler read twice that number. I hope you find this volume informative and thought provoking, and I am already looking forward to the next edition.

State and Local Government

Federalism and Intergovernmental Relations

I t's improvised, it's partisan, and it's undermining traditional allegiances to strong state and local governments. Welcome to the "new" New Federalism.

New Federalism is the notion that states should be more independent of federal policymaking and less dependent on the federal treasury, and it has been an article of faith for conservative Republicans at least since the Nixon administration. New Federalism is an expression of the core conservative philosophy that power should be decentralized, and that the best government is the government closest to the people.

Given the sweeping electoral triumphs of conservative Republicans in recent years, one might expect a strong New Federalism agenda to be in place, a concentrated effort to push power back to state capitals. As a former governor, President George W. Bush came to office knowing all too well the federal government's encroachments on state sovereignty and pledging his help to ensure state governments did not take their marching orders from Washington, D.C.[1] The stars seemed to align behind such a policy objective. Conservative Republicans ascended to leadership positions in both houses of Congress, many of whom had long called for a "devolution revolution" to take power away from the federal government and give it back to the states. Given this, we should be witnessing a new golden age of state governments emerging from the federal shadow, right?

Wrong.

As the readings in this section will show, in many ways state governments are finding themselves ever deeper in that shadow. This is not simply frustrating to those who want stronger and more independent state and local governments—it has policy consequences that affect the day-to-day lives of citizens. For example, when the federal government mandates new programs at the state and local levels but does not cover the costs, state and local governments must choose to raise taxes, cut spending, or do both.

What we have witnessed over the past few years is half of the New Federalism formula being put into effect. States are increasingly expected to make do with fewer federal dollars, but the federal government has shown little restraint in bossing states around. Unfunded mandates—federal laws ordering state action that provide no financial support for that action—continue to be a central source of friction between state and federal governments. A few members of Congress do remain committed to the cause of states' rights with their votes as well as their words, but, as Alan Greenblatt puts it in one of the articles that follows, these officials are a relatively lonely and isolated bunch.

How did the party and ideology most committed to states' rights in the 1990s shift course so dramatically once they actually came to power? The answer to that question tells the story of the most important trend in federalism of recent years.

THE SLOW RISE AND QUICK FALL OF NEW FEDERALISM

Federalism is the central organizational characteristic of the American political system. In federal systems, national and regional governments share powers and are considered independent equals.[2] In other words, states are independent sovereign governments. They must obey the mandates of the U.S. Constitution, but with that caveat, they are free to do as they wish. State governments primarily get their power from their own citizens in the form of their own state constitutions. At least in theory, they are not dependent on the federal government for power, nor do they have any obligation to obey federal requests that are not mandated by the U.S. Constitution.

In practice, the federal system established by the U.S. Constitution left the federal and state governments to figure out for themselves who had to do what, and who had to foot the bill for doing it.[3] Initially the federal and state governments tried to keep to themselves, pursuing a doctrine of dual federalism, or the idea that federal and state governments have separate and distinct jurisdictions and responsibilities. Dual federalism was dead by World

War II, a victim of the need to exert centralized economic and social power to fight two world wars and deal with the Great Depression.

These needs, and the general acknowledgement that the state and federal governments had shared and overlapping interests in a wide range of policy areas, gave rise to cooperative federalism. The core of cooperative federalism is the idea that both levels of government must work together to address social and economic problems. The basic division of labor that emerged under cooperative federalism was for the federal government to identify the problem, establish a basic outline of how to respond to the problem, and then turn over the responsibility of implementation to state and local governments along with some or all of the money to fund the programs.

Cooperative federalism defined and described the basic relationship between state and federal governments for much of the twentieth century. This arrangement, though, always had critics who feared that the transfer of money at the heart of the relationship allowed the federal government to assert primacy over the states. The basic argument was that by becoming a central source of money for programs run by the states, the federal government would become a living embodiment of the golden rule: he who has the gold gets to make the rules.

This became true enough. The federal government began putting strings on its grants to state and localities, requiring them to pass and enforce certain laws or meet certain requirements as a condition of receiving the money. States and localities didn't like this much, but were faced with an uncomfortable choice. They could refuse to go along—as they were allowed to as sovereign governments—but then they lost the money. Things got really bad as the federal government began passing unfunded mandates in the 1970s and 1980s, essentially ordering the states to establish programs and policies while providing either a fraction of their cost or no financial support at all.

Conservatives were pushing against cooperative federalism's tendency to centralize power at the national level more or less from the start, but it wasn't until Ronald Reagan was elected president in 1980 that the movement against the excesses of cooperative federalism became a sustained New Federalism policy agenda. Reagan cut and consolidated grant programs, and generally slowed the flow of federal dollars to states and localities. He also boldly proposed divvying up social-welfare responsibilities, offering to have the federal government assume full responsibility for Medicaid if the states would take on welfare (a deal that seemed risky and was rejected at the time, but in retrospect states largely regret not taking—see Donald F. Kettl's article in this section).

It was not until the 1990s, however, that New Federalism finally seemed to be poised to replace cooperative federalism as the new way of doing business between the federal government and the states and localities. Following the first Gulf War, the United States enjoyed much of a decade of relative peace and prosperity. A former governor—Bill Clinton—was in the White House, and with his support the federal government radically transformed welfare, turning over much of the responsibility to the states, and passed the Unfunded Mandate Reform Act, designed to stop the federal government from passing obligations on to the states without funding them.

When George W. Bush became president, it seemed as if New Federalism was about to hit a threshold moment. With conservative Republicanism ascendant, the stage was set for the federal government to step back and let the states take the lead on a wide range of policy initiatives. However, as a serious policy movement, New Federalism arguably began to crumble almost immediately after Bush moved into the White House.

At the beginning of the twenty-first century, powerful forces aligned to slow, and even reverse, the trend of decentralizing power that had emerged in fits and starts during the previous two decades. The peace and prosperity that marked much of the 1990s disappeared with the bursting of the market bubble in high technology stocks and the terrorist attacks of Sept. 11, 2001. At the dawn of the new century, the United States faced a soft economy and a global effort to combat terrorism that soon included invasions and extended guerilla conflicts in Afghanistan and Iraq.

Political scientists and historians have long noted that power tends to flow toward the states during times of peace and prosperity and back toward the federal government during times of war and economic stress (this is sometimes called the cyclical theory of federalism). The reason for power accumulating at the federal level during such times is simple: the federal government is simply better positioned to coordinate and implement responses to problems whose causes and consequences are beyond the borders of the states. The past few years have once again show this to be true: The dominant pol-

icy concerns have been stimulating the economy and prosecuting the war in Iraq. These mean the federal government, not the states, is making the key policy decisions of the day.

NEW FEDERALISM BECOMES AD HOC FEDERALISM

The fading of New Federalism is not simply a product of unforeseen national and international events. The Bush administration has pushed for federal primacy across a wide range of policy areas, many of which are traditionally the jurisdiction of state and local governments. In the past few years there has been enthusiastic support for a stronger federal role in areas such as education and regulation of marriage. Once they controlled the federal government, conservative Republicans seemed to be just as willing to impose unfunded mandates on state and local governments as their Democratic and more liberal predecessors.

Federal laws such as the No Child Left Behind and the Help America Vote acts require states and localities to set up expensive new programs with little financial help (see the article by Molly Stauffer and Carl Tubbesing in this section). These are examples of the federal government, in effect, having and eating its political cake. Both laws were popularly supported (at least initially), and by passing them federal lawmakers got to take credit for addressing high-profile issues the public considered important. After taking the credit, they passed much of the costs on to states and localities. These costs run into the hundreds of millions of dollars and come at a particularly bad time for state and local governments, which spent the past few years struggling with severe budget difficulties.

Those budget difficulties are made even more difficult by the federal government's taste for tax cuts. Many states link their tax systems in some fashion to the federal government's tax system, which means that federal cuts shrink the bottom line for states. To make matters worse, the federal government has become increasingly willing to tell state and local governments what they can and cannot tax (see the article by Jonathan Walters in this section).

Thus the federal government has been squeezing the finances of states and localities in two ways: on the one hand forcing them to spend more by passing unfunded mandates, and on the other limiting the amount of tax revenue they can collect. The federal government can get away with expenditures exceeding revenues because it is under no legal obligation to balance its budget. Most state and local governments, in contrast, are legally bound to produce balanced budgets, an obligation that is harder to accomplish given recent decisions made by the federal government.

Rather than the maturing of New Federalism, some scholars argue that what we are currently witnessing is the beginning of a new direction of the relationship between the federal government and the states and localities. Rather than a commitment to a core philosophy about the proper role of different levels of government and their relationship to each other, what seems to be driving current developments in federalism is the political advantage to be gained from the issue at hand. This has been labeled "ad hoc federalism," which describes the process of picking a state- or federal-centered perspective on the basis of whatever best supports a partisan or ideological preference on a given issue.[4] A good example is the recent controversy over same-sex marriage (detailed in the article by Joseph F. Zimmerman in this section). Decisions at the state level to legalize or consider legalizing same-sex marriage have prompted a number of conservatives—traditionally defenders of states' rights—to push for federal laws preventing states from passing marriage laws they oppose.

This section contains a series of readings that highlight key areas of the most recent developments in state/local and federal relations. Most tend to support the argument that ad hoc federalism is replacing, and may have already replaced, any commitment to New Federalism. The article by Joseph F. Zimmerman uses the provisions of the U.S. Constitution regulating relations between the state governments, and between state governments and the federal government, to examine trends in interstate relations. As the article explains, states cooperate on a broad range of programs and policy areas, often as a means to head off preemptive actions by the federal government. Although states do a good job of forging cooperative agreements to address issues of mutual concern, this sort of interstate coordination has achieved mixed success in fending off federal intervention. The article by Donald F. Kettl shows that the New Federalism revolution started by Reagan continues, but in ways not predicted by states and localities. The pieces by Jonathan Walters and by Molly Stauffer and Carl Tubbesing detail the painful impact of federal tax cuts and unfunded mandates on state and local governments. The Alan Greenblatt article provides a good overview of the most recent developments in federalism, including the insider's view on Capitol Hill. In broad perspective, Greenblatt's article highlights a general decline in the commitment to the principles of New Federalism, a development that does not bode well for the independence and financial well-being of state and local governments.

Notes

1. Rueben Morales, "Federalism in the Bush Administration," *Spectrum: The Journal of State Government* 75, no. 2 (2001): 5–6.

2. Kevin B. Smith, Alan Greenblatt, and John Buntin, *Governing States & Localities* (Washington, D.C.: CQ Press, 2004), 26.

3. The U.S. Constitution does lay down a basic set of responsibilities for federal and state governments. See Lee Epstein and Thomas G. Walker, *Constitutional Law for a Changing America: Institutional Powers and Constraints,* 5th ed. (Washington, D.C.: CQ Press, 2004), 323.

4. Barton Aronson, "The Rising Tide of Federalism," CNN.com, February 1, 2001, www.cnn.com/2001/LAW/02/columns/fl.aronson.federalism.02.01 (accessed November 25, 2002).

1

Trends in Interstate Relations

Joseph F. Zimmerman

States can get along with each other, but can they get along with the federal government?

From *Spectrum: The Journal of State Government*, Fall 2004.

The drafters of the U.S. Constitution included in the fundamental document five most important clauses—full faith and credit, interstate commerce, interstate compacts, privileges and immunities, and rendition—governing relations between sister states.

FULL FAITH AND CREDIT

This clause (Art. IV, §1) stipulates: "Full Faith and Credit shall be given in each State to the public acts, records, and judicial proceedings of every other State." Congress by general law is authorized to "prescribe the manner in which such acts, records, and proceedings shall be proved, and the effect thereof." This authority was exercised in 1790, 1804, 1980, 1994, 1996 and 1999. The 1996 clarification was prompted by the Hawaiian Supreme Court's 1993 decision in *Baehr v. Miike* (852 P.2d 44 at 57–72) holding that the statutory denial of a marriage license to same sex couples violated equal protection provision and equal rights amendment to the state constitution and remanding the case for a trial. On December 3, 1996, trial judge Kevin S.C. Chang ruled same sex couples had the constitutional right to marry. Implementation of the decision was delayed until the state legislature had an opportunity to act. Voters on November 3, 1998, reversed the decision of the Supreme Court by ratifying a legislatively proposed constitutional amendment (Art. I, §23) granting the legislature "the power to reserve marriage to opposite sex couples."

Congress responded to the Hawaiian Supreme Court's decision by enacting the Defense of Marriage Act of 1996 (110 Stat. 2419, 1 U.S.C. §1) defining a marriage as "a legal union between one man and one woman as husband and a wife" and the term "spouse" as

5

"a person of the opposite sex who is husband or a wife" and authorizing states to deny "full faith and credit to a marriage certificate of two persons of the same sex." Currently, 39 states have enacted a state defense of marriage act, and Maryland, New Hampshire, Wisconsin and Wyoming have statutes or court decisions banning same sex marriages. Missouri voters on August 3, 2004, and Louisiana voters on September 18, 2004, ratified a proposed defense of marriage constitutional amendment. Georgia, Kentucky, Mississippi, Oklahoma and Utah will vote on the question of prohibiting same sex marriages on November 2, 2004.

The controversy over same sex marriages was re-ignited on November 18, 2003, by the 4 to 3 decision of the Massachusetts Supreme Judicial Court in *Goodridge v. Department of Health* (440 Mass. 309, 798 N.E.2d 941) holding unconstitutional a statute denying "the protections, benefits, and obligations conferred by civil marriage to two individuals of the same sex who wish to marry." The decision immediately raised the question whether same sex nonresidents could marry in the Commonwealth. The answer is found in a 1913 Massachusetts statute disqualifying individuals from marrying if they are ineligible to marry in their home state.[1]

The Massachusetts Senate requested an advisory opinion from the Court whether a civil union statute would comply with the court's decision. The answer rendered on February 4, 2004, was no (440 Mass. 1201, 802 N.E.2d 565), but indicated the General Court (state legislature) had the option of not calling a same sex civil union a marriage if the term was dropped for heterosexual marriages.

The General Court, convened in 2004 as a constitutional convention, proposed a constitutional amendment reversing the Supreme Judicial Court's decision. This proposal will not appear on the referendum ballot unless the General Court approves the proposal for a second time in 2005. Should the proposition appear on the 2006 ballot and voters approve it, same sex

> *"Currently, 39 states have enacted a state defense of marriage act, and Maryland, New Hampshire, Wisconsin and Wyoming have statutes or court decisions banning same sex marriages."*

couples who married between May 17, 2004 and November 7, 2006, will be in a legal limbo as they were legally married, but their marriage will be illegal after adoption of the constitutional amendment. Furthermore, same sex married couples arc not entitled to federal health care and nursing home benefits, or authorized to obtain a divorce in other states.

A number of courts in sister states have commenced to receive petitions for dissolutions from persons united in a civil union in Vermont since July 2000. To be eligible for dissolution of a civil union in Vermont, one party must be a resident of the state for one year. Courts in other states have to wrestle with the question whether they have authority to dissolve a union. In 2002, a Connecticut judge dismissed a petition for a dissolution on the ground the state docs not recognize a civil union, but in 2003, a Sioux City, Iowa, judge granted a dissolution petition. On March 24, 2004, Essex County Probate and Family Court judge John Cronin granted a petition for dissolution of a Vermont civil union, the first such dissolution in Massachusetts.

INTERSTATE COMPACTS

The U.S. Constitution (Art. 1, §10) authorizes a state to enter into a compact with one or more sister states with the consent of Congress. The U.S. Supreme Court in 1893 (148 U.S. 503 at 520) opined the consent requirement applies only to political compacts encroaching upon the powers of the national government. A compact may be bilateral, multilateral, sectional or national in membership, and may be classified as advisory, facility, flood control and water apportionment, federal-state, promotional, service provision, and regulatory. There are 26 functional types of compacts administered by a commission or by regular departments and agencies of party states.[2]

Recent developments include congressional consent (116 Stat. 2981) for an amendment to the New Hampshire-

Vermont Interstate School Compact authorizing incurring debts to finance capital projects when approved by a majority vote at an annual or special district meeting of voters conducted by a secret ballot. The newly drafted Interstate Compact for Juveniles was enacted first by the North Dakota Legislative Assembly on March 13, 2003, and its lead has been followed by 20 additional state legislatures in 2003 and 2004. Arkansas is dissatisfied with the Interstate Compact on the Placement of Children because each of the 50 member states have individual laws pertaining to participation in the compact, thereby causing bureaucratic delays. The American Public Human Services Association established a task force to review the compact and the American Bar Association's Center on Children and the Law is also reviewing possible compact amendments.

The Registered Nurses (RNs) and Licensed Practical or Vocational Nurses (LPN/VNs) Interstate Compact dates to 1998, when Utah Gov. Michael O. Leavitt signed Senate Bill 149 adopting the compact subsequently enacted by 20 additional state legislatures. The National Council of State Boards of Nursing (NCBN) on August 16, 2002, approved an Advanced Practice Registered Nurses (APRNs) Interstate Compact. The Utah Legislature on March 15, 2004, became the first state to enact this compact.

The business of insurance was regulated by state legislatures until 1944 when the U.S. Supreme Court (322 U.S. 533) opined the business was interstate commerce. Congress overturned this decision by enacting the McCarran-Ferguson Act of 1945 (59 Stat. 33, 15 U.S.C. §1011) devolving to states authority to regulate the insurance industry. Continuation of nonharmonious state regulation of the industry encouraged firms to lobby Congress to preempt specific areas of slate regulatory authority. The Gramm-Leach-Bliley Financial Reorganization Act of 1999 (113 Stat. 1353, 15 U.S.C. §6751) preempted 13 specific areas of state regulation of insurance and threatened to establish a federal system of licensing insurance agents if 26 states did not establish a uniform licensing system by November 12, 2002. This threat was averted when 35 states were certified as having such a system on September 10, 2002. Recognizing the danger of preemption, the National Association of State Insurance Commissioners drafted the Interstate Insurance Product Regulation Compact creating a commission with regulatory authority and the Utah Legislature in 2003

enacted the compact and its lead has been followed by eight other state legislatures.

The U.S. Supreme Court on May 19, 2003, settled an original jurisdiction dispute—*Kansas v. Nebraska and Colorado* (538 U.S. 720, 123 S.Ct. 1898)—involving the Republican River Interstate Compact and failure of Nebraska to deliver water to Kansas by issuing a decree approving the final settlement stipulation executed by the parties and filed with the special master on December 16, 2002. It provides "all claims, counterclaims, and cross-claims for which leave to file was or could have been sought . . . prior to December 15, 2002, are hereby dismissed with prejudice . . ." Kansas had anticipated Nebraska might have to pay up to $100 million in damages.

Other developments relating to the interstate compact device include continuing pressure for restoration of the Northeast Dairy Compact that became inactive on October 1, 2001, when Congress refused to extend its consent for the compact U.S. Sen. Charles Schumer of New York in 2003 proposed an expansion of the original compact to include Delaware, Maryland, New Jersey, New York, Pennsylvania and West Virginia. A number of certified public accountants (CPA) are advocating a CPA interstate licensing compact and the section on Administrative Law of the American Bar Association in 2003 established a committee to draft a administrative procedure for interstate compact commissions. Currently, commissions rely upon a 1981 model administrative procedures act drafted by the National Conference of Commissioners on Uniform State Laws (NCCUSL) or the federal administrative procedure act. Both have disadvantages for interstate compact commissions.

In a related development, 13 state legislatures have enacted the Uniform Interstate Enforcement of Domestic Violence Protection Orders *Act* drafted by the NCCUSL. In 2004, South Carolina added the U.S. Postal Service electronic postmark to the *Uniform Electronic Transactions Act* as an alternative to certified or registered mail. Forty-six states, the District of Columbia, and the U.S. Virgin Islands have enacted the uniform act.

INTERSTATE ADMINISTRATIVE AGREEMENTS

State legislatures have delegated broad discretionary authority to department heads to enter into administrative agreements with their counterparts in sister states. Numerous such agreements, formal written and verbal, are in effect, but it is impossible to determine the precise number.

The 39 states operating lotteries became aware that the larger the jackpot, the larger the ticket sales. In consequence, 27 states, the District of Columbia, and U.S. Virgin Islands by administrative agreement are members of the Multi-State Powerball Lottery, 11 states participate in the Mega Millions Lottery, seven states operate the Big Game Lottery, three states are members of the Tri-State Megabucks Lottery, and three states are participants in Lotto South. Recent developments include the 2003 decision by the Texas Lottery commissioner to become a member of the Mega Millions Lottery, the 2004 decisions of Maine and Tennessee to join the Powerball Lottery, and in 2003, the newly established Tennessee Lottery Board termination of negotiations with the Georgia Lottery Corporation to form a joint operation because of fears lawsuits would reduce the amount of money available for scholarships.

Attorneys general continue to form cooperative administrative partnerships to conduct investigations and file lawsuits against companies. Their greatest success in terms of a settlement was the recovery of $246 billion in Medicaid costs from five tobacco companies. The settlement does not require manufacturers of other brands, often sold at a major discount, to contribute to the escrow account in each state. In consequence, 35 states by 2004 established directories of brands approved for sale.

Other recent developments include legal actions in May 2004 by the attorneys general of Connecticut, New Jersey and New York and the Pennsylvania secretary of Environmental Protection against Pennsylvania-based Allegheny Energy, Inc., for emitting air pollution causing smog, acid rain, and respiratory problems in Pennsylvania and the other suing states. The action was initiated in response to a decision by the U.S. Environmental Protection Agency to change its clean air enforcement policy in late 2003 and terminate 50 investigations. Joint actions by attorneys general in 2004 also resulted in Medco agreeing to pay $29.3 million to settle complaints by 20 states the company violated consumer protection and mail fraud statutes by switching patients to more expensive drugs and a group of rare stamp dealers agreeing to create a $680,000 restitution fund to settle a lawsuit brought by California, Maryland and New York charging them with a 20-year conspiracy to rig stamp auctions.

New Hampshire, Vermont and Rhode Island in 2004 formed the New England Compact Assessment Program to establish a common system for measuring student achievement and saving money. The U.S. Department of Health and Human Services in 2004 approved plans by five states—Alaska, Michigan, Nevada, New Hampshire and Vermont—to pool their purchasing powers in order to obtain larger discount on prescription drugs for their Medicaid recipients. Illinois, Indiana, Maine, New Hampshire and Virginia have joined the E-Zpass consortia, an electronic toll network for motor vehicles extending from the Canadian border to the mid Atlantic States and the Midwest. And Arizona and New Mexico signed the first interstate homeland security agreement.

The Pacific Northwest Economic Region (PNER), a statutory public-private organization, was created by the state legislatures of Alaska, Idaho, Montana, Oregon and Washington, provincial legislatures of Alberta and British Columbia, and the legislature of the Yukon Territory. In 2001, PNER organized the Partnership for Regional Infrastructure security to develop and coordinate action to protect all types of infrastructure.

One interstate administrative agreement—Multistate AntiTerrorism information Exchange (MATRIX)—appears to be dissolving. Utah on March 25, 2004, became the eighth state to drop out of the agreement. Florida, Michigan, Ohio and Pennsylvania remain members. MATRIX promoters were convinced the computer-driven program would integrate data and information from various sources including criminal records, driver's licenses, vehicle registrations, etc. Concerns over privacy were expressed by the American Civil Liberties Union, Electronic Privacy Information Center, and Electronic Frontier Foundation.

THE EXCISE TAX PROBLEM

Each state is free to determine the amount of excise and sales taxes (if any) to be levied on various products. The wide variation in excise taxes on alcoholic beverages and tobacco products results in buttlegging and bootlegging which often involve organized crime. Recent sharp excise tax increases for cigarettes in a number of states offered new incentives for buttleggers and are responsible for the dramatic increase in the number of domestic and foreign online sellers of cigarettes which are required by law to report sales to state tax officials, but who seldom do so and cite the Internet Nondiscrimination Act of 2001 (115 Stat. 703, 47 U.S.C. §151). Cigarette sales and excise tax revenues in Delaware and New Hampshire also increased dramatically as nonresidents make purchases in these states to avoid high excise taxes in their home states.

Congress enacted the Jenkins Act of 1949 (63 Stat. 844, 15 U.S.C. §375) prohibiting use of the postal service to evade excise tax payments, but a violation is only a misdemeanor. U.S. attorneys prefer to prosecute violators under the Mail Fraud Act of 1909 (35 Stat. 1088, 18 U.S.C. §1341) as a violation is a felony. In 2004, the U.S. Bureau of Immigration and Customs Enforcement arrested 10 persons and charged them with trafficking in a multi-billion dollar black market in counterfeit major brands of tobacco products made in Asia.

SUMMARY AND CONCLUSIONS

Court legalization of same sex marriages in Massachusetts and same sex civil unions in Vermont will continue to result in controversies in states lacking a defense of marriage act relative to enacting such an act. It will also raise questions whether courts in sister states possess authority to dissolve a Massachusetts same sex marriage or a Vermont same sex civil union.

Interstate cooperation generally continues to be excellent as additional states enact interstate compacts and enter into interstate administrative agreements on a wide variety of subjects. Compacts and enactment of harmonious regulatory laws have been promoted as a means to discourage Congress from exercising its powers of preemption removing regulatory authority completely or partially in specified fields from states. Nevertheless, disparate state regulatory statutes, increasing globalization of the domestic economy, international trade treaties, lobbying by interest groups, and technological developments will result in Congress enacting preemption statutes in addition to the 499 enacted since 1789.

Notes

1. *Massachusetts Laws of 1913, chap. 360, §2, and Massachusetts General Laws,* chap. 207, §11.
2. Joseph F. Zimmerman, *Interstate Cooperation: Compacts and Administrative Agreements,* (Westport, CT.: Praeger Publishers, 2002) and Ann O'M. Bowman, "Trends and Issues in Interstate Cooperation," *The Book of the States, 2004* (Lexington, KY: The Council of State Governments, 2004), 34–40.

2

Radical Federalist

Donald F. Kettl

When it comes to relations between the states and Washington, the Reagan era is still going on.

Ronald Reagan's funeral stirred some remarkably warm reflections about his life and legacy. But amid the retrospectives, analysts largely ignored his impact on federalism, where he tore down a wall every bit as imposing as the one in Berlin.

Until the Reagan administration, federal spending for grants to state and local governments had been steadily growing in America for decades. As a share of the economy, federal aid had increased from 1.6 percent of the Gross Domestic Product in 1965 to 3.4 percent in 1980. Reagan's tight budgets stopped that growth. By the end of his two terms, federal spending for intergovernmental aid had shrunk by almost a fifth (after accounting for inflation). As a share of the economy, grants fell by a third.

Even more important than Reagan's decrease in spending was the change in the way the federal government distributed the money. In the 1950s, the federal government began big grant programs for urban renewal and interstate highways. In the 1960s, Lyndon Johnson's Great Society expanded these categorical programs dramatically. Richard Nixon, succeeding Johnson as president in 1969, believed that the categorical programs relied too much on federal control, so he replaced the old job training, community development and social service programs with block grants—money distributed by formula with relatively few strings. Local governments loved them, but critics increasingly questioned what value the nation got for the money spent.

Reagan and his team came to office wanting to go much further: They were convinced that the existing federal aid system was broken. They transformed old categorical programs and some of the newer block grants into still broader programs, which coupled even

From *Governing,*
August 2004.

more administrative flexibility with less money. Reagan's argument: With a greater ability to fit federal programs to local needs, state and local governments did not need as much cash.

By the time he left office in 1989, Reagan had eaten away at a large part of the Great Society's core. To be sure, the federal aid bureaucracies remained in existence and billions of dollars continued to flow. But the Reagan presidency put a cork in the steady growth of spending and ended the federal government's long "big brother" tradition of dominance in the intergovernmental system.

Even more fascinating is a bold move that failed but nevertheless shook the system. In his 1982 State of the Union address, Reagan stunned congressional Republicans and governors alike with a plan to swap responsibility for Medicaid and welfare. The federal government would assume the burden for Medicaid, while the states would take over welfare programs, including food stamps and Aid to Families with Dependent Children.

The plan seemed too risky for almost everyone. The states worried they would end up on the short end. Members of Congress worried they would spend enormous political capital in exchange for uncertain gain. No one but Reagan and his staffers seemed very enthusiastic about the swap, and within weeks Reagan's dramatic proposal died.

With his radical plan, however, the conservative president had tapped into the emerging issue of federal-state fiscal relations. In backing away from the deal, the states ended up with prime responsibility for both welfare and Medicaid. The rising caseload swelled their welfare costs. In response, some states—notably Wis-consin and Michigan—tried creative experiments that eventually produced the revolutionary 1996 welfare reform block grant.

Meanwhile, Medicaid costs started to soar at an even more alarming rate. By the turn of the 21st century, Medicaid was the fastest growing item in many state budgets. Faced with the biggest fiscal crunch in generations, governors looked to Washington for help. They got little in return.

More than one state official looked wistfully back at the Reagan swap proposal and concluded that the states should have taken the deal when they had the chance. Had they done so, states could have pursued the Wisconsin welfare reform strategy and ridden welfare costs down, while passing Medicaid, their biggest budgetary nightmare, to the feds. And with the federal government in control of both Medicaid and Medicare, the nation would have been a step closer to a system of national health insurance.

Johnson's Great Society brought the federal government into more programs than ever before, and on a scale and scope previously unimagined. Reagan ended the Great Society era by capping the size of the federal government's commitment. He shaped the new generation of grants, highlighted by welfare reform, that define the basic administrative relationships of 21st-century federal grant programs. And with the welfare-Medicaid swap proposal, he identified the nastiest issue in the fiscal relationship.

Johnson stretched the fabric of American fiscal federalism into its modern form. Reagan tailored it to the clothing we wear today.

3

House of Loopholes

Jonathan Walters

The more tax cuts Congress passes, the more trouble states and localities will have making ends meet.

Probably the simplest way to describe the relationship of inter-governmental tax systems is to use the balloon analogy: Squeeze revenue-raising capacity at one level, and it's going to bulge out somewhere else. Absent truly drastic cuts in programs, somebody has to find the money to pick up the tab.

President George W. Bush and this Congress have proved themselves to be world-class balloon squeezers. In September, the president signed legislation to make the existing "middle-class tax cuts" permanent—locking in place a reduced income tax rate for millions of Americans, eliminating the marriage penalty and codifying a higher per-child deduction. All this will eventually cost the U.S. Treasury an estimated $164 billion.

Meanwhile last month, members of the House and Senate were hustling to finish work on a different tax bill that only a corporate lobbyist could love. Initially intended to make a narrow fix in the revenue code to satisfy a World Trade Organization ruling, the bill instead did what many tax bills in Washington do when organized business catches wind of the chance to meddle: It became a $136 billion giveaway to oil and gas explorers, timber companies and consulting firms, among other interests.

How Congress and the president can give away so much money so guiltlessly isn't such a hard question to answer. They don't have to balance the books. Far from the front lines of actual service delivery, it's much easier to treat money as some vague abstraction. But to flip Senator Dirksen's famous adage, you chop $100 billion here and $100 billion there and pretty soon you're talking real cuts.

It is a worn-out lament that the place fiscal reality looms largest is at the state and local level. But it's true. For years, states and localities

From *Governing*, November 2004.

have gamely stepped into the fiscal breach—or at least tried to—in an effort to make up for the fiscal folly of their governmental partners in Washington. Lately, however, a new and more troubling trend is emerging, directly related to the balloon theory of revenue raising. Congress is beginning to insert itself more aggressively and directly into state and local fiscal policy, so that when Washington squeezes the balloon, state and local governments are less able to raise the kind of revenues they need to deal with the bulge.

The practice started several years ago with the federal ban on state and local taxation of the Internet and its sales transactions. The argument in favor of that law was simple: The Internet is a fledging form of commerce that needs nurturing. It was also wrong: Companies doing business electronically are profitable and just as capable of meeting their tax responsibilities as those doing business the traditional way.

But what was most troubling about this decision was the possibility that it would set a precedent for new federal interference in tax debates to follow. It suggested a belief among many in Congress that the federal government—while hamstringing its own ability to raise revenues—is also well within its rights to commandeer state and local tax policy.

That belief was on display most clearly this year with the introduction of a bill known officially as the "Business Activity Tax Simplification Act." That's an accurate title—if creating yet another dubious loophole can be considered simplification.

BATS (an appropriate acronym if there ever was one) carries significant bipartisan support and dozens of influential sponsors in the House. Under its provisions, states and localities would be deprived of the authority to raise billions of dollars that they're currently collecting in business franchise taxes. If it becomes law, Congress will have moved beyond denying these governments the right to new revenue—it will be preempting state and local tax codes in the collection of existing revenue.

It is hard to make much of a case that state and local tax authorities are gouging corporations under the current system. State corporate taxes have been declining for more than a decade, and now make up just 5 percent of all state revenues, according to the Federation of Tax Administrators. All the other taxes—and the individual taxpayers who must pay them—contribute the other 95 percent. At a moment of extreme fiscal distress for state and local governments almost everywhere in the country, it's hard to see what sensible public purpose this could possibly serve.

The bottom line is that states and localities now find themselves in the position of having to fight just to protect what they already have, when the conversation should really be about rationally redesigning tax policy in the face of the revolutionary changes that have converted the industrial economy of the 20th century into the service-based economy of the 21st.

More and more, Congress and the Bush administration seem to suffer from the delusion that the balloon squeeze can go on forever. Governments will just have to do more with less. And perhaps with practice, they'll find they can do even more with even less. If they perfect it, one supposes, they can do everything with nothing. Either that, or the balloon goes bang.

4

The Mandate Monster

Molly Stauffer and Carl Tubbesing

Unfunded federal mandates are back, and they are costing states billions.

In the late 1980s, state legislators were "mad as hell" and they weren't going to take it anymore. They were angry about unfunded federal mandates. Democrats and Republicans alike railed against specific mandates, such as elements of the Safe Drinking Water Act and crumb rubber requirements in the highway law. And, more fundamentally, they viewed unfunded mandates as a sign of a troubling one-size-fits-all, top-down imbalance in the federal system.

For several reasons, including passage of the federal Unfunded Mandate Reform Act (UMRA) in 1995, the firestorm of complaints about unfunded mandates largely abated during the latter half of the 1990s. Less than a decade later, however, unfunded mandates are back with a vengeance.

A new study released by the National Conference of State Legislatures in March indicates that state governments in the current fiscal year are confronting at least $29 billion in cost shifts from the federal government—almost 6 percent of state general fund budgets. The figure is projected to rise close to $34 billion in FY 2005. The study confirmed what many legislators know from personal experience. The federal government is imposing numerous requirements, standards and conditions on the states, but is not providing adequate funds to cover the costs.

"Even in good economic times," says Pennsylvania Representative David Steil, "costs like these are insidious. They cause state and local officials to cut services and to steal funds from worthy state programs to pay for federal ones. In bad economic times, these mandates are intolerable."

The NCSL study found that the bulk of the $29 billion in cost shifts are in eight areas. Education programs are the two with by

From *State Legislatures,*
May 2004.

far the largest price tags. For years, state legislators have complained about the federal government's failure to live up to its promise to fund 40 percent of the costs of special education. The NCSL research notes that there is a $10 billion shortfall between the promise—the amount authorized in the Individuals with Disabilities Education Act—and the money appropriated for FY 2004.

Similarly, current fiscal year appropriations for the new No Child Left Behind Act are $9.6 billion under the amounts authorized in the law for mandated state activities.

State officials hoped that the new Medicare prescription drug law would relieve states of the financial responsibility for "dual eligibles"—individuals who receive both Medicaid and Medicare benefits. Congressional negotiators failed to ease this burden for FY 2004. States continue to absorb the $6 billion in annual costs needed to provide prescription drug coverage for these people.

STILL WAITING

As of April 1, states have not received $2.4 billion that Congress appropriated to implement provisions of the Help America Vote Act, the federal election reform law passed in 2002. In this unique case, the money has been appropriated, but has not been delivered to the states. This is primarily because Congress and the president were slow to agree on membership of the four-person federal Election Assistance Commission, which is charged by law with distributing the funds.

Environmental programs account for $1 billion in the FY 2004 shortfall. "Over the past seven years, seven rules have imposed costs of more than $100 million per year on state, local and tribal governments," says a recent report by the U.S. Office of Management and Budget.

Appropriations for the State Criminal Alien Assistance program, which reimburses states for the costs of incarcerating illegal aliens, are $350 million below the amount originally authorized. A cap on federal contributions to states for administering the Food Stamp program costs states $227 million. And Colorado, Delaware, Minnesota and West Virginia face $19 million in sanctions in FY 04 for not adopting the federal .08 blood alcohol content as the standard for drunk driving.

BUDGET BUSTERS

One way to understand the effect of these cost shifts, according to Gary Olson, director of the Senate Fiscal Agency in Michigan, is to compare them to state budget gaps for FY 04.

In November 2003, the Michigan fiscal staff projected a $505 million gap in the state's FY 04 budget. NCSL's mandates study estimates that Michigan has absorbed at least $812 million in unfunded mandates and other cost shifts this fiscal year.

Olson is quick to point out that there are many explanations for Michigan's severe budget woes. "Yet," he says, "these federal cost shifts have clearly compounded our broader fiscal problems. Not having this $812 million unfunded liability clearly would have given the Legislature some desperately needed breathing room."

The situation is similar in other states. NCSL's last fiscal survey in February 2003 showed Indiana facing a $1 billion FY 04 budget gap. More than $480 million could be attributed to federal mandates. Connecticut had a $65 million shortfall, which could have been a $243 million surplus without the federal cost shifts. Kentucky confronted a $302 million gap with $395 million in federal mandates.

"These mandates have a corrosive effect on our federal system," says Utah Speaker Martin Stephens, NCSL president. "Federal policy priorities supplant state priorities.

The 8 Worst Offenders	
	Minimum FY 2004 Gap (in millions)
Individuals with Disabilities Education Act (IDEA)	$10,087
No Child Left Behind (NCLB)	9,600
State Drug Costs for Dual-Eligibles	6,000
Help America Vote Act (HAVA)	2,400
Environment	1,000
State Criminal Alien Assistance Program (SCAAP)	350
Food Stamps	197
Transportation Sanctions	19
Total	$29,303

Source: www.ncsl.org/programs/press/2004/pr040310.htm

Legislatures' spending options are handcuffed by federal decisions." Frequently, he says, a legislature's only choice is to cut funding for local governments. And they may be facing even tougher decisions about services and taxes.

"In other words, officials furthest removed from the voters are making budget decisions for state legislators and city councilmen," Stephens says. "But that's not easy to explain when all the voter wants to know is why the library had to cut its hours."

WHAT WENT WRONG?

A decade ago, state legislators, galvanized by their own budget and federalism frustrations, united with governors and local officials to win passage of the Unfunded Mandate Reform Act. Using information and procedural mechanisms, the law is widely acknowledged to have curtailed the use of unfunded mandates by Congress and executive agencies. In fact, the Congressional Budget Office, which is charged with developing fiscal notes for bills with potential unfunded mandates, has identified only three laws passed since 1995 that qualify under the reform law as unfunded mandates.

How is it then that the NCSL study finds so many more unfunded mandates with such high price tags? The answer lies in the strict definition of an "unfunded mandate." Many legislators look at the No Child Left Behind Act and say: There's not enough money here. It's an unfunded mandate. The mandate law, though, looks at No Child Left Behind and says: No Child Left Behind is a grant condition. States don't have to participate. Grant conditions aren't, according to UMRA, unfunded mandates. Therefore, No Child Left Behind isn't an unfunded mandate.

Legislators look at the discrepancy between the amount authorized for special education and the funds actually appropriated and say, that's an unfunded mandate. UMRA doesn't apply to appropriations bills, so, technically, the IDEA shortfall isn't an unfunded mandate, either.

Legislators look at a section in the new Medicare law that requires states to conduct eligibility studies for the new low-income subsidy of the prescription drug program. They discover the law doesn't provide funding for upgrading computer systems or training staff to make the eligibility determinations. They conclude that it is an unfunded mandate. The 1995 mandate law, though, excludes entitlement programs from its definition. The

The Cost to the States of Selected* Unfunded Federal Mandates

State	Total State Gap (FY 2004 in millions)
Alabama	$359
Alaska	69
Arizona	332
Arkansas	219
California	3,160
Colorado	302
Connecticut	309
Delaware	72
DC	62
Florida	1,425
Georgia	650
Hawaii	82
Idaho	91
Illinois	1,040
Indiana	480
Iowa	212
Kansas	211
Kentucky	395
Louisiana	421
Maine	125
Maryland	396
Massachusetts	666
Michigan	812
Minnesota	403
Mississippi	282
Missouri	522
Montana	75
Nebraska	141
Nevada	123
New Hampshire	98
New Jersey	743
New Mexico	167
New York	2,191
North Carolina	687
North Dakota	60
Ohio	927
Oklahoma	267
Oregon	273
Pennsylvania	992
Rhode Island	107
South Carolina	344
South Dakota	67

(*continued*)

The Cost to the States of Selected* Unfunded Federal Mandates (Continued)	
State	**Total State Gap (FY 2004 in millions)**
Tennessee	433
Texas	1,830
Utah	152
Vermont	72
Virginia	526
Washington	456
West Virginia	158
Wisconsin	424
Wyoming	57
Totals	**$24,400**

*Does not include mandates in environmental programs, SCAAP and some programs authorized in the NCLB Act.

Sources: Federal Funds Information for States and the National Conference of State Legislatures, Washington, D.C., March 2004.

low-income subsidy program is an entitlement, so the additional administrative costs aren't considered unfunded mandates.

A RENEWED FIGHT

In retrospect, these exclusions and exemptions are major loopholes in the law. To leaders in the fight for UMRA's passage, such as former New York Senator James Lack, these exclusions were "concessions that we had to make to get the bill passed."

Speaker Stephens hopes that the time is ripe to secure additional safeguards against unfunded mandates. He used the release of the new NCSL mandate report to launch a renewed campaign against federal cost shifts.

"NCSL believes in the Unfunded Mandate Reform Act. We hope that Republicans and Democrats in Congress will join with us in exploring revisions to the law that will make it even more effective in stemming this new flood of unfunded mandates and other cost shifts."

5

The Washington Offensive

Alan Greenblatt

Republicans may be suspicious of federal power, but they're imposing it on states and localities every chance they get.

Lamar Alexander, who served two terms as governor of Tennessee and twice ran for president, came to the U.S. Senate a couple of years ago hoping to advance the cause of devolution and states' rights. It has been a lonely occupation. "I've been disappointed," Alexander admits, "to find so few voices in the United States Senate who respect the prerogatives of governors and mayors to make their own decisions. The conservatives are just as bad as liberals at passing new programs and expecting someone else to pay for it."

That's not a bad description of politics in Washington as George W. Bush's second term opens. Federalism is being treated these days a little like the burgeoning federal deficit: It's important—but not as important as six or eight other things that policy makers care more about. Even diehard devolution advocates such as Alexander concede that the ability of states and localities to shape domestic policy—or even to preserve their existing leverage over local spending and taxation priorities—is on the downhill slide.

Four years ago, the picture looked considerably different. In the 1990s, states had taken the lead in dealing with critical policy issues that Congress discussed but didn't address, such as health care and utility regulation. A governor who decried federal power grabs was about to take office as president, joined by a Republican Congress whose members were fond of asserting that the most effective levels of government were those closest to the people—states, counties and cities.

That seems like a long time ago, in more ways than one. In the years that have passed since the September 11, 2001, terrorist attacks, more and more Americans have come to see centralization

From *Governing,*
January 2005.

of government as the best route to future security. As a result, federal standards have been imposed on state and local activities, major and minor—including, in the most recent session of Congress, the provision of driver's licenses. "The trend is absolutely toward less respect for state initiatives, rather than more," says Douglas Kendall, of Community Rights Counsel, a public interest law firm, and co-author of a new book on federalism.

Even beyond security-related issues, however, the first half of the current decade has seen an unusual amount of aggressive federal intervention. The No Child Left Behind Act, signed into law in 2002, may be the most prominent case, imposing strict federal penalties on local school systems whose pupils are unable to pass standardized tests. But there have been many others, in central areas such as health care, the environment and social issues.

Remarkably, all of these and other centralizing federal initiatives have been launched by a conservative Republican president and Congress whose previous rhetoric tended to support devolution and states' rights. "The ardor for devolution and federalism among Republicans has cooled considerably," says Michael Greve, director of the Federalism Project at the American Enterprise Institute. "People don't even pay lip service to it anymore."

Not too many years ago, Congress was full of subcommittees devoted specifically to the subject of intergovernmental affairs—the relations among the national, state and local governments. Today, it's hard even to find individual members who take these concerns seriously.

There's not much institutional support for federalism outside of Congress, either. The old U.S. Advisory Commission on Intergovernmental Relations in its heyday attracted senators and cabinet secretaries to its meetings—even the president on occasion—but the organization became politicized and, after it died in 1996, nothing emerged that could take its place. The National Academy for Public Administration has just launched a forum for federalism discussions, but it's very much in the early stages.

SIGN UP—OR ELSE

Increasingly, the people whose job it is to lobby for states and localities in Washington feel that when the Republican majority decides something has to be done about an issue, such as homeland security, education or safe drinking-water standards, state and local governments have lit-

tle choice but to get on board in some fashion or other. They can't remain significant players if they simply oppose any federal role. "We try to protect things we've been protecting for 20 years," says Ray Scheppach, executive director of the National Governors Association. "The world is shifting, and we have to recognize that. There are not a lot of people on the Hill recently who have shown a lot of interest in federalism. We're on the defensive now."

The biggest fights loom in the area of taxes. Many state rates are tied to the federal code, so states will be losers assuming, as everyone in Washington does, that the biggest recent cuts in income and estate taxes are made permanent. And there is major buzz around the idea of saving the federal government money by eliminating or reducing the federal deduction for state income tax. "There's very serious sentiment in the Republican Party for doing that because it has the incidental benefit of hammering mostly high-tax, Democratic states and that can't be unwelcome," says the AEI's Greve.

On the spending side, the 1995 law barring Congress from imposing new mandates on the states without committing to pay for them remains on the books. But it has had minor practical effect, especially in the past several years. Congress has found it remarkably easy to structure laws that force lower levels of government to do things without creating a mandate in a technical sense. Most of the time, these create programs in which states and localities are asked to participate voluntarily—but at the risk of losing large amounts of federal funding if they decline. Or new federal programs carry with them the promise of future funding to defray state and local costs but the money does not appear.

To help pay for the No Child Left Behind requirements, the feds upped their share of total education spending, to about 8 percent, but with the law just three years old, they're already more than $25 billion behind in their payments to states and local school districts. Similar shortfalls are bedeviling special education, despite passage of a new law promising full funding. "Under the new federalism," says Donald Borut, executive director of the National League of Cities, "you have new mandates where a small amount of money is defining and leveraging how the larger amount of money is being spent."

More arrangements of this sort seem inevitable in the near future, given the massive deficits that exist at the federal level. Federal revenues, measured as a share of the gross domestic product, have reached their lowest point since the 1950s. Given President Bush's stated desire to cut the federal deficit in half, coupled with his desire for more tax cuts, enormous pressure is going to fall on those domestic programs that are largely carried out in the form of grants to state and local governments. There is hardly an area of their budgets—on either the revenue or the spending side—that will not be adversely affected by upcoming decisions in Washington.

Intergovernmental aid formulas drawn up by Congress in more generous times have kept the number of federal dollars flowing to states and localities high by historical standards during the past couple of years. But the rate of growth in funds for domestic programs other than entitlements has slipped during every year of the Bush presidency, and the flow of dollars in absolute terms has already slowed in many parts of the fiscal 2005 budget. The one entitlement that Congress can turn to for major budget savings is the one where cuts stand to cost states the most money: Medicaid. The joint state-federal health care program will soon surpass education as the largest single expenditure at the state level, even though more than half the program's cost currently comes out of federal accounts. The Bush administration proposed in 2003 to convert Medicaid into a block grant, with more flexibility for states but limited funding, and while that proposal went nowhere, the administration may try again. Failing creation of a block grant, significant targeted cuts in Medicaid seem inevitable.

Similar shortfalls may soon befall welfare programs, which were turned back to the states in 1996 (in what was seen as a landmark achievement of the devolution era), with Washington sending block grant funds. The welfare law has been extended eight times since expiring in 2002 and will come due again in March. Whenever a new law finally makes it through, the block grants are virtually certain to shrink.

With federal assistance to the states decreasing, and increasing portions of state budgets going to make up for the absent federal dollars, it is inevitable that states will re-examine policies toward their own local governments as a way of saving money. Aid to local government has already been reduced more than any area of state budgets in recent years, aside from higher education.

And cities and counties certainly can't count on much direct help from the feds. The Bush administration has already attempted to phase out several programs that assist urbanites, such as Community Development Block Grants and the Section 8 and Hope VI housing programs. Aid to poor families through the tax code is likely to taper off as well. "It's hard to think of urban constituencies to whom the Republicans owe anything," says Greve. "If you figure there's only so much money to go around and attention to be lavished, even without someone saying let's go out and punish Chicago and Manhattan and L.A. and San Francisco, the lack of attention is enough to have that effect."

THE URGE TO PREEMPT

As worrisome as the coming round of budget austerity may be to state and local advocates, it does have a cyclical quality to it. Federal deficits rise and fall; federal formulas are stingier in some years than they are in others. The 1960s and '70s were periods of relative generosity toward states and localities; the '80s were a period of retrenchment; the prosperity of the '90s loosened things up again. Eventually, situations do change. What is more worrisome for the long run is the increasing interest of federal governing majorities in preempting state power altogether: lifting whole areas of policy out of the hands of state governments and centralizing them at the national level. This is a strategy that much of the business community and its lobbying organizations have come to endorse.

It used to be a given that many industries preferred to be regulated in state capitals, where their political influence was greater and the assertiveness of legislators was much weaker. But that has changed. In the past couple of decades, many state legislators, governors and other officials have turned into activist regulators across a broader range of policy, from health care to finance to pollution. New York Attorney General Eliot Spitzer is only the most prominent among a whole new generation of state policy makers imposing demands on corporations and industries that used to enjoy relatively lenient treatment at the state level.

As a result, business groups—which are themselves increasingly national or global in reach—are turning to Congress for relief from state-level regulation that not only tends toward strictness but also differs from one jurisdiction to another in its details. And Congress, although dominated by Republicans nominally suspicious of federal power, has been quicker than in the past to preempt state regulation, often arguing that national uniformity is necessary.

This has been happening whether it's a major issue, such as time limits on welfare, or a relatively minor one, such as blocking unwanted telemarketers. The fiscal 2005 budget passed by Congress, for example, preempts any state or local requirement that hospitals, insurance companies or health providers provide abortion services or referrals. (California's attorney general plans to challenge these strictures in court.) The Bush administration, meanwhile, regularly has challenged state authority on other social issues, from medical marijuana to assisted suicide.

These trends are accelerating fast, in part because rapid communication among activists can quickly move an idea that blossoms in one state—a ban on state contractors sending work overseas, say—to legislatures in 30 or 40 capitals. Almost as quickly as new state regulations are passed, businesses and trade associations are in Washington arguing that they can't comply with a chaotic flurry of regulatory legislation whose fine print may not be the same in any two states. The bottom line is that much of organized business now prefers to deal with a single 800-pound gorilla, rather than 50 monkeys.

A prime example of the change in strategy is insurance regulation. Insurance companies have always been regulated solely by the states, but most now argue that they need a regulatory framework in Washington to compete with banks and other financial service entities that have been given more flexibility by the feds.

There are two proposals on Capitol Hill right now. One would set up a dual charter, similar to what banks have, under which an insurance company could choose whether to be regulated by states or the federal government. The other would keep the states as primary regulators—but only if they change their rules to satisfy congressional demands within three years. "It's a very interesting debate as to whether that is more of a jab at states' rights than an optional federal charter," says Gary Hughes, of the American Council of Life Insurers.

Hughes adds that states have tried to be responsive to his industry, but that it's still a cumbersome process for any insurer to win multi-state approval quickly enough to move new products to the market in competition with other financial services. "Even if you get 50 state regulators to agree on a course of action," he asks, "can you get their 50 state legislatures to agree to do the same thing?"

It's possible that no insurance bill will move through Congress anytime soon, given the abuses in the industry recently exposed by Spitzer in New York—but it's also possible that proponents of centralization will use the controversy as proof that the federal government needs to step up its role. Regardless, this question of differing state policies is a factor in an increasing number of areas. The governors and the American Association of Motor Vehicle Administrators led a cooperative effort to get state DMVs to agree to a uniform policy of driver's license security requirements, in order to stave off a federal intervention. More than 40 states quickly got on board, but the handful of stragglers left a big opening for the feds to fill with new standards included in the intelligence reform bill passed last month.

Despite the difficulties, it's possible that such voluntary efforts offer the best strategy for state and local governments to use at a time of increasing pressure to centralize. All the major state and local groups met with telecommunications companies last month in hopes of arriving at a mutually agreeable set of tax rates for that industry, before Congress takes away states' telecom taxing authority altogether.

Scheppach of the governors' association says that in some areas states should be pushing for hybrid models, in which the feds would set regulations but states would enforce them. A model could be the Streamlined Sales Tax Project, under which 21 states have agreed to standardize their sales tax codes in hopes of being allowed to collect taxes on electronic purchases. The U.S. Supreme Court has ruled in the past that the diversity of state sales tax codes would present an unreasonable burden on electronic and catalog sellers. A standardized code might lead to the relaxing of this restriction—although states still need congressional approval before they can make any tax mandatory on interstate commerce.

It's also possible that, in the end, the streamlined sales tax will merely serve as a prelude to a national sales tax. Federal officials have found that they like flexing their muscles in areas where state and local governments used to dominate. Taxes are unlikely to be different. And once the feds do move in, it's difficult to imagine a future in which they might choose to move out, whether the subject is taxes, education, public safety or the environment. "Whether Bush thinks he's doing it or not, he's redefining federalism," says Bruce Katz, director of the Brookings Institution's metropolitan policy program. "Cities and states will have to deal with the consequences. What they're going to hope for is, 'You're going to cut our budgets, but please don't tie our hands.'"

II

Elections and Political Environment

Turnout is high. Competition is low. Voter falloff is falling. Constituent e-mail volume is climbing. The appetite for ballot initiatives is increasing or decreasing depending on the issue. Political participation at the state and local level is an up-and-down story these days.

The 2004 electoral cycle was dominated by news of close, competitive races. There was the presidential election, of course, with George W. Bush and John Kerry battling through a seesaw fall campaign where Bush came out the winner by a few percentage points. Yet as a race, the presidential campaign was a snoozer compared with the Washington State gubernatorial race between Democrat Christine Gregoire and Republican Dino Rossi, which came down to a few votes. Rossi was initially reported to have won the election by a few hundred votes, but that margin shrank in a recount. It disappeared altogether in another recount. The final tally, a product of a manual third recount, declared Gregoire the winner by a little more than a hundred votes out of the nearly 2.8 million cast.[1]

Gregoire and Rossi were not the only gubernatorial candidates locked in a tight battle. Five of the eleven governorships up for election in 2004 were won with less than 51 percent of the vote.[2] State legislatures were balanced so closely that, in some cases, a switch of just a few seats made the difference between a Republican or Democratic majority. Yet while close gubernatorial races and the battle for partisan control got most of the headlines, perhaps the most notable trend in state elections—one that is not limited to the 2004 campaign cycle—got little ink at all. The dirty secret of state elections is that in most races for state-level office, there is not much competition. Of the roughly 6,000 state legislators who faced the voters in 2004, most did so with token opposition or no opposition at all. There are a number of reasons for this, though much of it has to do with the built-in advantages of incumbency and the willingness of state legislatures to gerrymander districts for partisan advantage (see the article by Alan Greenblatt in this section).

Although tight races are much rarer than the headlines might imply, a horserace between two evenly matched candidates is not necessary to get voters out to the polls. Ballot initiatives continue to provide a major forum for deciding controversial issues ranging from same-sex marriage to stem cell research (see the article by Jennifer Drage Bowser in this section). Once they have been enticed to the polls by a series of controversial ballot issues, voters are willing to support other candidates and measures. Voter falloff is the process of voting for one issue or for a candidate in one race, but not voting on other issues or for candidates in other races on the same ballot. There is evidence to suggest that falloff between ballot initiatives and other races and issues is declining (see the article by Mathew Manweller in this section).

Political participation, however, is about more than voting. Participation also includes everything from writing a check to a campaign fund to calling a city council member to complain about a pothole. Technology is making some of these forms of participation easier and more common. E-mail, for example, is a quick, low-cost way to let your representative know exactly what you think of his or her stand on a particular issue. Legislators are getting the message—quite literally. More and more state legislators are using e-mail as an important communications tool to respond to and contact constituents and interest groups (see the article by Antoinette Pole in this section).

What all this means is that there is no single trend in political participation in the states—there are trends. This section seeks to highlight some of the more important trends and their implications for state politics and policy.

DIRECT DEMOCRACY CONTINUES: POLICY AND THE INITIATIVE

Roughly half of the states allow some form of direct democracy, where citizens get to make major policy decisions themselves rather than electing representatives to make those decisions on their behalf. The most common method is the ballot initiative, which puts proposed laws to popular vote.

The 2004 election cycle once again showed a wide variety of groups willing to use ballot initiatives to bypass legislatures for pet issues. Probably the most high-profile issue state voters were asked to decide on was whether to ban same-sex marriage. Such bans proved to be overwhelmingly popular—they were on the ballot in eleven states and passed with strong majorities. These ballot issues had implications for the presidential race because they were seen as a way to mobilize social conservatives, who tended to favor incumbent President George W. Bush over Democratic challenger John Kerry (see Jennifer Drage Bowser's article in this section).

Other ballot issues covered a broad range of proposals ranging from California's Proposition 71 authorizes up to $3 billion in spending on stem cell research, to Colorado's Amendment 36, which proposed altering how the state allocated its Electoral College votes (Proposition 71 passed, Amendment 36 did not). Political analysts have long been concerned about using ballot initiatives to make such significant policy changes. There tend to be two primary fears about ballot initiatives. The first is that they are becoming less a vehicle of popular control and more a tool of well-heeled special interest groups, who run sophisticated marketing campaigns to spin proposals that favor their agendas as being in the public interest. The second is that people are making huge decisions with little idea about the consequences. For example, it's one thing to be in favor of stem cell research, but it's quite another to come up with $3 billion. That's a lot of money for a state to guarantee, especially a state like California that is already struggling with deficit problems.[3]

In terms of political participation, however, ballot initiatives may have some positive effects. If you believe that higher voter turnout is good for democracy, ballot initiatives may be a good thing. Controversial ballot proposals motivate people to go to the polls, and once in the voting booth they may cast a vote for other races and issues. Once of the more interesting trends political scientists have observed in recent years is that voter falloff is decreasing in ballot-initiative states. There are at least some preliminary signs that voters are not being overwhelmed by large numbers of initiative proposals, nor are they showing up at the polls just to vote on their pet issues. Ballot proposals seem to be increasing voter turnout for all races, not just for particular issues (see Mathew Manweller's article in this section).

E-PARTICIPATION

Changes in information technology are having a noticeable impact on political participation, both in terms of how and when citizens participate. The vast majority of state agencies and most local agencies have Web sites. These are often interactive, allowing citizens to send e-mails and use site-based search engines.[4] Candidates for office are also recognizing that an Internet presence is an important way to connect with voters; such Web sites are becoming a common part of the electoral environment of state and local politics.

While voters are increasingly turning to electronic forms of communication to connect with their representatives, government officials are adjusting accordingly. Many state legislators now use e-mail as a regular tool for communicating with constituents, interest groups, and others in government. E-mail makes it easy for a constituent to connect with a representative. Maybe too easy—some legislators are finding their in-boxes inundated. Still, the rate of participation through electronic means is undoubtedly rising and will continue to do so for the foreseeable future. E-participation, however, will move in fits and starts. As Antoinette Pole's article in this section shows, some officials are adapting to the electronic trend more quickly than others.

These readings on political participation offer a mixed set of insights. Political participation can be considered in many ways to be healthy and increasing. Information technology is providing new avenues to connect representatives and the represented. Drawn by a competitive presidential race, as well controversial ballot proposals in many states, people went to the polls in large numbers in 2004. Yet once in the voting booth, they found that there was a distinct lack of competition for many state offices. Depending on new information technology and direct democracy to boost political participation is fine as far as it goes. Democratically speaking, however, offering meaningful choices in competitive elections might be a better option.

Notes

1. Washington Secretary of State, "Manual Recount Results," December 23, 2004, vote.wa.gov/general/recount.aspx (accessed March 18, 2005).

2. CQ Press, "2004 Gubernatorial Elections, All States," www.cqpress.com/docs/2004Elections/2004 Gov.htm.

3. For a broad overview of the problems with direct democracy in states and localities, see David Broder, *Democracy Derailed: Initiative Campaigns and the Power of Money* (New York: Harcourt, 2000).

4. Rob Gurwitt, "Behind the Portal," *Governing*, August 2001, 66.23.131.98/archive/2001/aug/egweb.txt (accessed March 17, 2005).

6

Whatever Happened to Competitive Elections?

Alan Greenblatt

Nearly 6,000 state legislators will be elected next month. Most of them face little or no opposition.

Florida looks very close for president again this year. Perhaps not as close as in 2000, the year of the hanging chads and butterfly ballots, but competitive enough that President Bush and John Kerry will each have campaigned there numerous times before the contest ends. And Florida's battle for a U.S. Senate seat seems destined for a close finish as well.

When it comes to the legislature, however, it's a very different story. Republicans are a mortal lock to retain control of the state House and Senate, because Democratic voters have been jammed into so few districts that there is no way for them to break out of minority status. In what is otherwise one of the most exciting campaign years in modern Florida history, the legislature is nothing but a big, lopsided snooze.

How lopsided? Of 22 contests for the state Senate, only six feature candidates from each of the two major parties, and just 34 of the 120 House races will have two-party competition. Even where there is nominal competition, it doesn't amount to much. Two years ago, the average margin of victory in both House and Senate races was 21 percent. Incredibly, the winning margins were, on average, even higher in open districts, showing more clearly than anything how much the districts themselves favor one party's chances.

"In the old days, under the former Soviet Union, they held elections and we belittled them because Communists would run unopposed," says Scot Schaufnagel, a University of Central Florida political scientist. "Here in Florida, 90 percent of the time we don't have any meaningful competition. It's tough to pin that all on redistricting, but clearly meaningful competition is very difficult to find and it starts with redistricting."

From *Governing,*
October 2004.

There is nothing anomalous about Florida. All over the country this fall, elections for state legislatures are largely non-events. This is just as true where Democrats have the upper hand as it is in Republican states. California's politically bifurcated map may be the most prominent example, but Democrats have worked their advantage wherever they can. Indiana, for example, is likely to vote for the Bush-Cheney ticket next month by a wide margin. But Democrats aren't particularly worried about holding their majority in the state House, no matter what the overall voting trend may be. Recent history is on their side. Two years ago, Republicans took 56 percent of the statewide House vote, and went to bed on election night believing they had recaptured the chamber. But Democrats had drawn the individual districts carefully enough to thwart those ambitions, and when all the votes were counted, there was a one-vote Democratic advantage.

What the Democrats had done was to implement classic gerrymandering strategy, as it has been practiced for the past 200 years. They conceded a third of the districts to Republicans, packing those districts full of huge GOP majorities and rendering thousands of GOP votes superfluous. They then carved up the rest of the state to link Democratic precincts together and create a legislative majority.

The map is likely to work its same magic this year. There aren't more than a half-dozen serious House contests out of 100 seats, and the few that are in play tend to favor the Democrats. "As a result of redistricting, there are so many noncompetitive seats," says Ed Feigenbaum, editor of Indiana Legislative Insight. "Republicans say '54 in 04,' but I think the Democrats will come out of this with 51 seats and maybe 52."

POLITICAL ILLUSION

Nearly 80 percent of all state legislative seats are up for election around the country this year. On paper, legislative politics look as close as they could possibly be. In 2002, Republicans pulled ahead of Democrats in the total number of seats held nationally for the first time in half a century, but by the narrowest of margins—only about five dozen, out of 7,400 total across the 50 states. This year, there are 23 legislative chambers where a switch of three seats or fewer would change the party that holds the majority.

Looking at the country district by district, however, the reality is that true competition exists in only a tiny fraction of places. Even where political strength is closely balanced in the aggregate, the vast majority of individual districts are lopsidedly drawn in favor of one party or the other, engendering no real contest at the polls.

Ohio, Pennsylvania, Wisconsin and Michigan are all battleground states in presidential voting, but they are not battlegrounds in the contest for legislative power. Republicans control them; Democrats haven't a prayer of gaining a majority in any of the chambers in those states. The redrawing of the lines that followed the 2000 Census is the primary culprit.

The ability to create the desired political effect increases every decade with advances in technology, making it easier for legislators and advocacy groups to target partisan precincts and predict their likely voting behavior for years to come. "Dummymanders"—sociologist Bernard Grofman's term for overly greedy gerrymanders that backfire—have become increasingly rare as sophistication about redistricting grows.

Good redistricting software and powerful databases were available during the 1990s—and partisan gerrymanders certainly took place well before the dawn of the computer age—but this time around, mapmakers benefited from a technological advance that at first glance seems trivial: high-quality color printing. The subtly shaded maps that were possible in the latest redistricting round allowed legislative staff to cycle quickly through dozens of permutations until their legislative bosses were perfectly satisfied and the gerrymanders were airtight. One more traditional element of uncertainty was thereby removed.

AFTER THE VOTING

The new gerrymandering has political significance that goes far beyond the fall campaign. To an increasing extent, it governs the relations between the two parties when the legislature is in session. "You have more and more non-competitive and very liberal or very conservative districts where the only threat comes in a party primary," says Larry Sabato, a University of Virginia government professor. "Therefore, there is simply less centrism, less moderation and less encouragement for legislators to compromise, just as we've seen in Congress."

In the musical *Annie,* Daddy Warbucks instructs his secretary to "phone Al Smith and find out what Democrats eat." That joke doesn't even apply to many of today's legislatures. In Wisconsin, for example, Mark Pocan, who represents a liberal Assembly district in Madison, says that after a Republican friend was elected to the body and they dined out together, he "was called into the leadership office and told, 'You don't eat dinner with Democrats.' "

Wisconsin's Republican House speaker has taken over from the nonpartisan chief clerk the duty of signing off on staff hires. Republican requests are fulfilled first. Out of the hundreds of bills passed this year in that state, only a handful were sponsored by Democrats. Typically, if a Democrat wants her bill to win consideration, she has to try to find a friendly Republican to put his name on it. (Democrats were just as partisan when they were in control; some of their former leaders are now under indictment on charges stemming from a corruption scandal.)

When one-party legislative dominance becomes an accepted fact of life, the fight for power takes place entirely on that party's side. That was the case this year in Virginia, where internecine warfare broke out among GOP majorities in both chambers. Some Republicans broke with their party to support a tax increase originally proposed by the Democratic governor. As a result, opposing wings of the party are already gearing up for next year's elections, preparing and financing separate slates of candidates to do battle for the all-important GOP nominations.

The only legislative elections that matter now in Virginia are the primaries in the spring, not the general elections in November. As in Florida, about one third of Virginia's legislative contests weren't even challenged when the entire legislature came up for election last year. "It is a Republican state, but not by a 2-to-1 advantage," says Democratic state Representative Brian Moran. "Redistricting has clearly created disproportionate Republican representation."

In some states, redistricting has left the two parties roughly even in their battle for control of a legislative

Who Controls the Legislature?

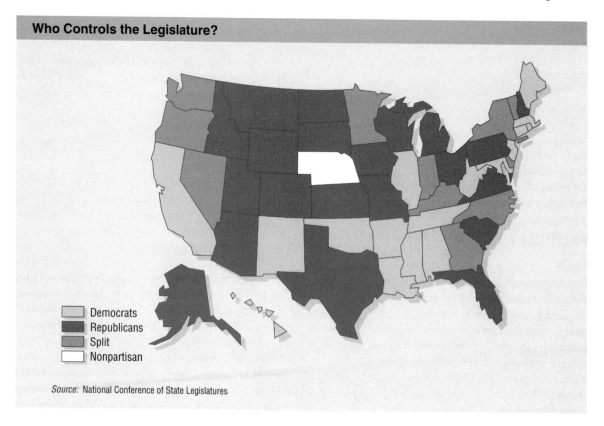

- Democrats
- Republicans
- Split
- Nonpartisan

Source: National Conference of State Legislatures

chamber but created so many safe districts that virtually all the competition still takes place over a handful of seats. That's the case in Maine, where Democrats control the state Senate by just one vote, but the vast majority of districts remain safe for one party or the other.

As a result of redistricting, Maine state Senator Michael Brennan, a Democrat who initially won his Portland seat in a special election hotly contested by both parties, now sits in a district that's going to give him an easy ride. Meanwhile, up the road in Augusta, Republican Karl Turner represents a redrawn district that's more certain to support the GOP. "Both of us had districts that could have been considered swing districts but are now solidly Democratic, in my case, or Republican in his," Brennan says. "Both parties are putting all their efforts into just a few districts."

In cases such as these, redistricting doesn't stifle competition by changing the partisan advantage but by essentially freezing it: creating safe seats for incumbents of both parties. The legendary example is New York's legislature, which has featured a Democratic Assembly and a Republican Senate for the past 30 years. Redistricting at the start of each decade merely serves to protect incumbents, bolstering the Democratic majority in one chamber and the Republican majority in the other, and maintaining the underlying division of power. That will be the case again this year.

SOMETHING PECULIAR

What's interesting is that among the few legislative chambers that seem to be genuinely in play this fall (the Senate in Maine, the House in Vermont, Nevada and North Carolina, both chambers in Washington State), nearly all had their maps drawn by courts, commissions or divided governments—somebody other than legislators of a single party enjoying a free hand. "In every one of those cases, you've got clearly some sort of compromise of the redistricting process," says Michael McDonald, a visiting fellow at the Brookings Institution, "something peculiar to that state that pushed it into the toss-up column."

The Georgia House of Representatives has a chance to change hands this year largely because a court created a more competitive set of districts. Georgia Democrats haven't won a majority of legislative votes since 1996, but they have been able to preserve their power up to now through redistricting. Even in 2002, when a strong Republican voting trend swept GOP candidates to victory

in elections for governor and for the U.S. Senate, Democrats won a majority of the legislative contests.

Party defections by individual members later tilted Senate control to the Republicans, but the House remains in Democratic hands. A new court-ordered map imposed earlier this year has undone much of the Democratic gerrymandering. "The map that it replaced was a classic partisan gerrymander drawn by the Democrats," says University of Georgia political scientist Charles Bullock. "They were trying to take a 45 or 47 percent share of the vote and turn it into a majority."

Even under the new map, however, it's not clear that the GOP can erase the Democrats' current advantage in one election, because more than 15 seats would have to change hands, and a fair number of Democratic incumbents may be able to win reelection at least once even in GOP-tilting districts. After they retire or are beaten, Republicans should reign in Georgia for quite a while (perhaps with the help of a map they'll draw themselves in time for the 2012 elections).

Turning to a court or commission to draw legislative districts is no guarantee of a nonpartisan approach. That point was underscored last year in Montana. The rules mandated a five-member commission to draw the lines, with each party allowed to choose two members, and a tie-breaking fifth member selected by the other four. But the commissioners couldn't agree on who the tie-breaker should be, and so the state Supreme Court intervened, appointing a fifth member who, it turned out, favored a Democratic-leaning map.

As a result, Republican districts are now overpopulated and Democratic districts are underpopulated, meaning Democrats used fewer people to make more districts favorable to their own side. "Every substantive vote was party line on the commission, and the Democrats just ramrodded the thing through," complains Chuck Denowh, executive director of the Montana Republican Party. "They did everything they could—I've got to tip my hat to them." The bottom line is that Democrats have a strong chance of taking over at least one of the Montana chambers this year.

THE BIG SORT

As much havoc as gerrymandering has caused in the current election process, some political scientists suggest that there is a less mischievous factor in the general decline of competition: natural demographic realignment. Voters, they say, are clustering together in partisan enclaves that make it difficult even for fair-minded mapmakers to draw many competitive districts.

Despite the rising number of registered independents, surveys indicate that voters are more partisan than they were 20 years ago—less likely to split their votes among candidates of different parties and also less likely to switch party preference from one election to the next. And, while the media characterization of "Republican red" and "Democratic blue" states may be simplistic, there is evidence that within smaller geographic areas, one party or the other is increasingly likely to be the dominant attraction.

Demographers are starting to refer to this phenomenon as "the big sort," in which people move to live among like-minded individuals. It's not that liberals or conservatives ask their real estate agents for printouts of precinct voting data when they're shopping for houses, but they do make lifestyle choices that place them among people who tend to live—and vote—much the way they do.

Political analyst Charles Cook likes to joke that Democratic candidates have trouble carrying any district that doesn't include a Starbucks. Rural areas are strongly Republican, cities are Democratic and the two parties fight their major turf wars in the suburbs, with fast-growing outer suburbs favoring the GOP. Such generalizations have long carried an element of truth, but some experts think the truth grows more compelling with each passing election year.

"Even if you drop below the broad regional level, you find that neighborhoods and communities are looking more homogenous than they ever have before," says James Gimpel, a government professor at the University of Maryland. "You have Republicans settling in around Republicans and Democrats settling around Democrats."

The more that partisan votes cluster together, the less room there is for creating districts that are compact and contiguous and still competitive between the parties.

> *"Voters, some say, are clustering together in partisan enclaves that make it difficult even for fair-minded mapmakers to draw many competitive districts."*

This creates an interesting dilemma. Good-government activists have long considered it desirable to protect communities of interest by keeping geographical jurisdictions or neighborhoods with historic identities together within legislative districts. But the "big sort" means there are more and more areas where the only way to create a competitive district is to lump two conflicting communities together, which is a scenario that creates new problems most sensitive mapmakers want to avoid.

Then there is the question of racial minorities. Under the law, they comprise a community of interest all their own. Federal courts spent much of the 1990s limiting race as a factor that can be allowed to dictate the makeup of political districts, but there are still Voting Rights Act requirements to avoid discriminating against minority interests, including preserving most of the majority-minority districts drawn during the 1990s.

In the most recent round of mapmaking, this caused serious problems for Arizona. That state used a ballot initiative to establish a redistricting commission with a mandate to create competitive districts as part of its charter, but the commission found it difficult to do so once it took into account the need to create districts to favor the state's Hispanic population. "There's a real tension between the Voting Rights Act and drawing competitive districts in a Republican-leaning state," says Michael McDonald of Brookings. "Once you've drawn minority districts, you've really whitewashed the rest of the state."

That doesn't always have to be the case. In New Jersey's most recent round of redistricting, a commission driven by a nonpartisan academic pushed legislative staff not only to create record numbers of Asian and Hispanic districts but to create a higher number of competitive districts as well. The commission kept asking for maps to be tweaked until they contained the highest number of competitive districts possible. One result was a Democratic takeover of the legislature in 2001, but the maps are such that a modest swing in public opinion could allow Republicans to take back the legislature next year.

Given all the complications, is there any way the current wave of gerrymandering could be brought under constitutional control? In theory, yes. Last spring, the U.S. Supreme Court left the door open to the possibility that it might find a partisan gerrymander unconstitutional. But the court, in rejecting a challenge to a Pennsylvania gerrymander, said there were as yet no workable standards for identifying such an illegal gerrymander. Barring a greater degree of judicial consensus on this issue, that means that redistricting for strictly political purposes is going to be with us for the foreseeable future.

In response to the Supreme Court's demand for a way of judging excessive partisanship, political scientists are trying to quantify competitiveness, joining with politicians such as former Vermont Governor Howard Dean in pushing for reforms. There's talk of an initiative in Florida to create an Arizona-style commission.

But, as in past decades, the 10-year redistricting calendar is certain to slow any reformer's momentum. "Because we're in the middle of the decade, there's no urgency to it," says Tim Storey, of the National Conference of State Legislatures. "On the heels of redistricting, there's gnashing of teeth and complaints that we have to do something about it, but then the energy dissipates because it's six or eight years until the next round of redistricting."

7

The People's Choice

Jennifer Drage Bowser

From stem cell research to electoral college reform, citizens have their say.

W hen voters are asked to pass laws directly, they often are quite selective. This year was no different. The people in 34 states considered 162 ballot measures in November. Some of them were high-profile and drew national attention—same-sex marriage bans, stem cell research and immigration, for instance. But most dealt with the nuts and bolts of state policy—how elections should be conducted, funding essential programs like education, health care and energy policy.

OF NATIONAL INTEREST

Banning same-sex marriage was the issue of the day. On the ballot in 11 states, it passed with large margins in every one of them. Oregon was the only state where opponents believed it might fail, but it garnered about 56 percent of the vote.

Other issues that received national attention included two in California—stem cell research and the "three-strikes" law, an anti-immigration measure in Arizona, and Colorado's proposal to change the way it allocates its electoral votes.

California's Proposition 71 passed comfortably. It will provide $3 billion over the next 10 years for embryonic stem cell research, making California the first state to allocate public funds for such study. A second California measure in the national spotlight was Proposition 66, which would have relaxed the state's three-strikes law, requiring that the third strike be a serious or violent crime. The people agreed with Governor Arnold Schwarzenegger, who opposed the proposition.

Colorado's Amendment 36, which would have changed the state's procedure for allocating electoral votes, went down in flames.

From *State Legislatures,* December 2004.

It received just 34 percent of the vote. Had it passed, five of Colorado's electoral votes would have gone to George Bush and four to John Kerry. Because it failed, Colorado continues to use its winner-take-all system for allocating electoral votes, and this year George Bush received all nine.

Arizona's anti-immigration measure, Proposition 200, proved popular. It will require that everyone registering to vote in Arizona prove their U.S. citizenship, and that state and local workers verify the eligibility of all people who apply for public benefits, mainly welfare. If someone who isn't eligible applies, government employees are required to report it to federal authorities or face a four-month jail term.

TORT REFORM ACROSS-THE-BOARD

Voters in six states considered tort reform measures, with mixed results. California voters passed a measure limiting who can sue for unfair business practices, while Colorado voters declined to repeal limits on suits by homeowners against builders for construction defects.

The tort reform measures in Florida, Nevada, Oregon and Wyoming centered on medical malpractice. Florida voters passed a package of three measures dealing with malpractice. One gives patients the right to access doctors' records of malpractice, another prohibits licensing doctors who have committed three acts of malpractice, and the third limits how big a chunk attorneys can take from medical malpractice awards. Nevada voters passed a measure limiting noneconomic damages in malpractice cases, but another measure that would have punished attorneys who file frivolous lawsuits failed to pass. Wyoming's results on this issue were mixed too—voters passed a measure requiring alternative dispute resolution or a medical panel review before a malpractice suit may be filed, but failed to pass a measure that would limit noneconomic damages in malpractice cases.

UP AND DOWN ON GAMING

Gaming measures also had mixed results. Two measures on California's ballot failed. One would have expanded tribal casinos, the other non-tribal gaming. A Florida initiative that would have paved the way for slot machines at race tracks in Miami-Dade and Broward counties was too close to call at press time, but looked to be failing.

Michigan voters passed a measure requiring voter approval for any new gaming. Oklahoma voters agreed to a new lottery, dedicating its revenues to education. Washington voters took the unheard-of step of turning down a tax decrease because it was tied to an expansion of gambling. Initiative 892 would have allowed non-tribal entities to operate slot machines, and dedicated the revenue to offsetting property taxes.

Nebraska voters faced a confusing array of four gambling measures on their ballot, one from the legislature and three initiatives. The legislature's proposal failed. Results on the initiative proposals were close at press time, but all looked likely to fail by a very narrow margin.

EDUCATION FUNDING MIXED

The dilemma over how to adequately fund public education spilled over to the ballot in five states this year. A property tax increase to fund education failed to pass in Arkansas. And Washington voters said no to a state sales tax increase that would have gone to education.

North Carolina voters approved a proposal allowing the legislature to dedicate revenues from civil fines and penalties to education. Oklahoma voters agreed to dedicate lottery revenues to education. Maine voters turned down a property tax decrease that would have taken a big bite out of education funding.

Nevada voters approved an initiative requiring the legislature to fund K-12 education before addressing any other part of the state budget. Before it can take effect, it has to be approved again in the 2006 general election.

BIG THREE RETURN

Drug policy, animal rights and term limits, three of the regulars of the initiative process over the past decade or so, made brief appearances on the ballot this year. Alaska voters turned down an initiative that would have legalized marijuana for all adults, and Oregon voters decided not to expand their existing medical marijuana program. Montana voters passed a new medical marijuana law.

It was a bad day for animal rights activists. Measures restricting bear hunting failed to pass in Alaska and Maine, while measures protecting the right to hunt and fish passed in Louisiana and Montana.

The two legislative proposals that would have relaxed term limits in Arkansas and Montana failed to pass.

MINIMUM WAGE AND HEALTH CARE

The minimum wage will be going up in Florida and maybe in Nevada, thanks to successful ballot measures. In Florida, voters agreed to establish a minimum wage of $6.15 per hour. And if Nevada's Question 6 passes for a second time on the 2006 ballot, employers there will have to pay an extra dollar per hour ($6.15) if they don't provide health insurance for employees.

Coloradans, Montanans and Oklahomans agreed to increases in tobacco taxes to fund health care programs. California voters had the chance to affirm a new law requiring employers to provide health insurance for their employees, but it failed.

YES TO RENEWABLE ENERGY

Colorado energy providers will have to produce or purchase 10 percent of their energy from renewable sources by 2015. Voters said yes to this initiative 53 percent to 47 percent. Look for more renewable energy measures on the ballot in 2006, as advocates were watching this first-ever initiative effort closely.

NO BULLET TRAIN

Florida voters changed their minds on the high-speed bullet train, taking back their demand of four years ago that it be built between the state's five most populated areas. The

Legislature struggled to find a way to fund the very high price tag, and went back to voters this year to ask if they really wanted it. In Colorado, Denver-area voters passed a $4.7 billion transit expansion which will add light-rail and diesel-powered commuter rail lines and other improvements. It calls for an increase in the Regional Transportation District's sales tax in the metro area to 1 percent from 0.6 percent. And Maricopa County voters in Arizona approved a half-cent-per-dollar sales tax for 20 years that will bring in $4.8 billion for freeways, light-rail lines and expanded bus service in the fast-growing Phoenix area.

CHANGING THE PROCESS

In Arizona voters refused to shorten the deadline to file initiative petitions, but said OK to a proposal that requires that initiatives specify funding sources that don't affect the general fund. Opponents said the measure will seriously limit the power of voters to set public policy.

Nebraska voters passed an initiative that will make it more difficult for the legislature to amend or repeal any law passed by initiative. A legislative referendum passed in Florida will set an earlier filing deadline for proposed initiative constitutional amendments. Alaska set the requirement for petition signatures a little higher, requiring they be gathered from more parts of the state.

Examining Decreasing Rates of Voter Falloff in California and Oregon

Mathew Manweller

8

How do ballot initiatives shape voting behavior? A scholarly analysis.

When people go to the polls, they are asked to vote on a variety of candidates and issues. It is common for most people who go to the polls not to vote for every contested position or proposed initiative. The difference between how many people go to the polls and how many people actually vote on a specific candidate or issue is called voter falloff. For example, if a million voters cast ballots for at least one position or ballot measure, but only 800,000 votes are cast specifically for a particular measure, then the falloff is 200,000 votes, or 20 percent. The level of falloff varies from position to position and issue to issue. Although most people vote for a presidential candidate, some choose not to vote for candidates running for "lesser" positions. It is also quite common for people to vote for a presidential candidate but fail to vote for one or several proposed state ballot measures.

Voter falloff on ballot measures may occur for a variety of reasons. Some measures, especially bond issues or legislative referrals of mundane administrative issues, have little political salience because it is rare to encounter political advertising, newspaper editorials, or voter guide arguments about administrative or bond measures.[1] Another possible reason for voter falloff is information costs (Downs 1957). Overwhelmed by the number of initiatives on a ballot (Oregon had 26 initiatives on the 2000 ballot), voters may have a difficult time acquiring sufficient information about a ballot measure and, feeling uninformed, may simply skip down the ballot to the next issue. Or, some voters may not have an

From *State and Local Government Review*, Fall 2004.

The author thanks Eric Lindgren and Jerry Medler of the University of Oregon for their assistance with the statistical analysis.

interest in the topic of a specific ballot measure and not vote on that particular issue.

PREVIOUS RESEARCH

Measuring voter falloff offers insight into the legitimacy of the initiative process and the willingness of the public to participate in forms of direct democracy. If the data show that falloff is relatively high, one might have to question the "democratic" nature of the process. Feeney and Dubois (1998) question whether initiatives, which have the same validity as statutes passed in the legislature, have political legitimacy if they are being enacted by a small percentage of the populace. Conversely, if falloff is relatively low, such data might suggest that members of the public are able and willing to be more politically active. In fact, there is some research to indicate that states that have the initiative system tend to have higher voter turnout than do states that do not have the process (Magleby 1984; Southwell and Paaso 2001).

In a study of "voter fatigue" using 1976 data, Magleby (1984) noted that initiative falloff averages around 6 percent.[2] Moreover, he found that falloff fluctuates among types of initiatives. Bonds and legislative referrals suffer much higher falloff rates than do citizen-sponsored initiatives.

Cronin (1988) used data from the early 1980s to examine voter falloff. He found that falloff ranges between 5 percent and 15 percent and that where an issue appears on a ballot does not affect falloff. Falloff only occurred between voting for candidates and voting for ballot measures: "On balance, then, there is little evidence that position on the ballot influences either the amount of participation on ballot measures or their success or failure.... The only real voter falloff or fatigue that occurs, then, is that between the number who vote for partisan candidates and those who vote on issues in general" (Cronin 1988, 70).

Most of the research on ballot measure voter falloff took place before the explosion of the initiative process in the late 1980s and early 1990s. Bowler, Donnovan, and Happ (1991), used data from 1974 to 1988 to examine falloff as a function of several variables (i.e., length of the measure, spending, placement on the ballot, and type of initiative). Since their study, the use of the initiative system has grown significantly (Tolbert 2002). It is now common to see ballots in California and Oregon that include over 20 measures. Although Feeney and Dubois (1998, 153) note that there is "very little scientific research concerning how many issues voters can absorb at a given time," Bowler, Donovan, and Happ (1991) found that falloff has been decreasing over time, which suggests that voters are becoming comfortable with increasing information costs.

In this article, I examine how voters react to increasing information costs being created by large numbers of ballot measures, specifically the trend toward increased use of ballot measures in the western states. My research looks at voter falloff over a 20-year period in California and Oregon. The model shows that, with periodic and explainable exceptions, falloff has been decreasing since 1976 but that the rate of decrease has slowed since 1988. After analyzing the findings, I suggest three possible explanations for the trend. . . .

RESULTS AND ANALYSIS

The summary statistics highlighted in Tables 1–3 indicate that falloff has been declining over a 20-year period. Oregon's average falloff rate for 1976 was 11 percent but fell to 3 percent in 1992 and then jumped back to 6 percent in 1996 (see Table 1). In California, average falloff in 1976 was 14 percent but steadily fell to 8 percent by 1996 (see Table 2). When the data were pooled, average falloff declined from 13 percent to 7 percent (see Table 3).

There are two slight interruptions in the declining trend of ballot measure voter falloff. In California, falloff basically held constant between 1984 and 1988. In Oregon, there was a slight jump between 1992 and 1996. In California in 1988 there were 29 measures on the ballot, and in Oregon in 1996 there were 26 measures on the ballot. These numbers represent a one election-cycle

Table 1. Average Falloff in Oregon

Year	Mean	N	Standard Deviation
1976	.1118	12	4.637E-02
1980	.0711	8	2.278E-02
1984	.0666	9	2.032E-02
1988	.0489	8	2.638E-02
1992	.0358	9	1.252E-02
1996	.0618	23	2.160E-02
Total		**69**	**3.496E-02**

Table 2. Average Falloff in California

Year	Mean	N	Standard Deviation
1976	.1451	15	4.168E-02
1980	.1337	11	4.722E-02
1984	.1047	16	2.909E-02
1988	.1088	29	3.196E-02
1992	.0983	13	2.633E-02
1996	.0838	15	1.727E-02
Total		**99**	**3.744E-02**

increase of 14 and 13 initiatives per ballot, respectively. Given that information costs affect the "cost" of voting (Downs 1957), these significant increases in the number of ballot measures may account for the brief interruptions in the decline in voter falloff. . . .

An alternative explanation for decreasing voter falloff is the possibility that ballot measure issues have recently come to address more controversial and salient issues. . . . Issues relating to social policy attract more voters, and mundane issues pertaining to administrative issues increase falloff. Given the high salience of abortion and gay rights issues and the relative lack of salience for bond and administrative issues, these results make intuitive sense. Nevertheless, falloff continues to decrease even after controlling for the effects of ballot measure salience. . . .

Table 3. Average Falloff in California and Oregon (Pooled)

Year	Mean	N	Standard Deviation
1976	.1303	27	4.614E-02
1980	.1073	19	4.948E-02
1984	.0910	25	3.185E-02
1988	.0958	37	3.943E-02
1992	.0727	22	3.799E-02
1996	.0705	38	2.255E-02
Total		**168**	**4.230E-02**

CONCLUSION

Political scientists who study the initiative process have noted that voter participation rates for ballot measures are less than those for candidates (Cronin 1988; Magleby 1984). However, this study indicates that the phenomenon of voter falloff is decreasing and has been decreasing for some time. Lower falloff rates suggest that people are no longer simply ignoring initiatives that appear on the ballot.

Voters may be acting this way for several reasons. It is possible that the public is becoming more comfortable with the initiative process. Although the initiative process has been part of western politics since the early 1900s, it was not until after California's Proposition 13 in 1978 that ballot measures began to deal with salient political issues on a regular basis (Waters 1998).[7] In the mid 1970s, voters may simply have been ignoring a political process about which they were not comfortable or knowledgeable. However, as ballot measures became increasingly common, voters' comfort levels increased.

It is also possible that voters are putting more effort into obtaining information about ballot measures. This explanation may be the result of a "lag effect" that initiatives have on public policy. For example, when voters first passed tax limitation measures such as California's Proposition 13, Oregon's Measure 5, or Colorado's "TABOR" Measure 1, the benefits were immediately noticeable in the form of lower taxes and a sense of "voter rebellion" against the state.[8] However, the fiscal effects of these measures were not felt until some time after the election. It was not until some years later, after schools and other social services felt the crunch of these tax limitations, that voters felt the true effects of the passed initiative. It may be that the delayed shock effect of these ballot measures encouraged voters to pay attention to—and participate in—the ballot measure process to a greater degree than they had in the past. Closely tied to this explanation is the possibility that the public has come to realize that ballot measures have a significant impact on public policy, and opting not to vote on them has serious ramifications.

There is also the effect of money on the initiative process. Several scholars have highlighted the increase in spending on ballot measure campaigns during the past decade (Smith 2001; Gerber 1999). In fact, Garrett and

Gerber (2001) note that over half a billion dollars was spent on California initiatives alone in the period between 1992 and 1998. Gerber (1999) also provides a glimpse of the growth in spending. Her data show that spending for all initiatives in all states in 1992 was $147 million. However, by 1998, spending had increased to over $400 million. In their examination of California's experience, Bowler, Donovan, and Happ (1991) showed that falloff for a specific initiative decreases when there is an increase in campaign spending for or against the initiative.

Decreased falloff suggests that voters are engaged in the initiative process. It can be assumed that when voter falloff rates were as high as 20 percent in the early 1970s, voters were being excluded from the system—even if the exclusion was voluntary. However, the results of this study suggest that voters are being presented with a host of complicated policy issues, but they are choosing to participate in direct democracy anyway.

Notes

1. Many states that vote on ballot measures send voters a voter guide a few weeks before election day. The voter guide contains arguments for and against each measure. These arguments can be filed by anyone who wishes to pay the nominal fee. However, interest groups who have a stake in the outcome of the vote typically file them. Both states in this study (California and Oregon) send out voter guides.

2. There is little consistency among scholars regarding the concept of voter falloff. "Falloff," "dropoff," "rolloff," and "ballot fatigue" are all used to describe what I refer to as voter falloff. To further confuse the situation, voting behavior scholars also study the effects of ballot position on voter participation. Some (Magleby 1984) have argued that the more information voters have to read on a ballot, the less interested they become in the ballot issues and the less likely they are to vote. To describe this phenomenon, scholars have used the same terms noted above.

3. Waters (1998, 127) writes, "In 1978, with the passage of California's Proposition 13, people began to realize the power of the initiative process once again and its use began to rise. Indeed, the last two decades have seen the most widespread use of initiative in the nation's history."

4. Proposition 13 and Measure 5 both rolled back property taxes in California and Oregon. Proposition 13 rolled back property taxes 60 percent. Measure 5 limited taxes to $15 of every $1,000 of assessed value for school levies and $10 for every $1,000 of assessed value in nonschool tax levies. In Colorado, the Taxpayers Bill of Rights, or TABOR, requires the public to approve through referendum any new tax increase that the legislature passes.

References

Bowler, Shaun, Todd Donovan, and Trudi Happ. 1991. Ballot propositions and information costs: Direct democracy and the fatigued voter. *Western Political Quarterly* 54, no. 2: 559–68.

Cronin, Thomas. 1988. *Direct democracy.* Cambridge: Harvard University Press.

Downs, Anthony. 1957. *An economic theory of democracy.* New York: Harper and Row.

Feeney, Phillip, and Floyd Dubois. 1998. *Lawmaking by initiative: Issues, options and comparisons.* New York: Agathon Press.

Garrett, Elizabeth, and Elisabeth Gerber. 2001. Money in the initiative and referendum process: Evidence of its effects and prospects for reform. In *The battle over citizen lawmaking,* edited by Dane Waters. Durham, NC: Carolina Academic Press.

Gerber, Elisabeth. 1999. *The populist paradox.* New Jersey: Princeton University Press.

Magleby, David. 1984. *Direct legislation.* Baltimore: Johns Hopkins University Press.

Smith, Daniel. 2001. Special interests and direct democracy: An historical glance. In *The battle over citizen lawmaking,* edited by D. Waters. Durham, NC: Carolina Academic Press.

Southwell, Priscilla, and Pamela Paaso. 2002. The relationship between voter turnout and ballot measures. *Journal of Political and Military Sociology* 29, no. 2: 275–81.

State of California. various years. *Statement of votes.* Sacramento.

State of Oregon. various years. *Oregon blue book: Oregon election history.* http://wwwbluebook.state.or.us/state/elections/elections06.htm.

Stimson, James. 1985. Regression in space and time: A statistical essay. *American Journal of Political Science* 29, no. 4: 914–47.

Tolbert, Caroline. 2002. Public policy and direct democracy in the twentieth century: The more things change, the more they stay the same. In *The battle over citizen lawmaking,* edited by Dane Waters. Durham, NC: Carolina Academic Press.

Waters, Dane. 1998. A century later—The experiment with citizen-initiated legislation continues. In *America at the polls 1998.* Storrs, CT: Roper Center Publications.

9

Trends in E-Representation: The Vermont and New York Legislatures

Antoinette Pole

Information technology is changing how state legislators talk to each other and their constituents.

E-mail and Internet use have become commonplace in the United States. Just under one-half of all adults reported using the Internet in 2000 and almost 59 percent of adults indicated that they used the Internet by the end of 2002.[1] While several studies examine the use of e-mail and the Internet among adults in the United States, the extent to which state legislators have used these technologies is largely unknown. It appears that most state legislatures obtained Internet access in the mid to late 1990s, while many state legislatures had e-mail—albeit internally—in the early 1990s. Still, there is significant variation in terms of how e-mail and the Internet are used across state legislatures and by individual state legislators.

Prior research on information technology and government can be divided into two camps, the optimists and the pessimists. Authors in the former camp, Dahl, Grossman, Browning, Rosenthal, Bennett and Fielding, assert that information technology is beneficial. They maintain that information technology will increase political participation and democratization and ultimately lead to better representation. The latter camp, Davis, Barber, Abramson, Arterton, and Orren and Bimber, argues that technology will not necessarily improve the prospects for political participation and democratization. Instead the pessimists state, e-mail and the Internet may result in less deliberation and government by opinion polls. They suggest that those who already wield media power will also monopolize new technologies, minimizing any perceived benefits that e-mail and the Internet may have yielded.

Though these debates outline the merits and dangers concerning the nexus between information technology and government, largely from a theoretical perspective, none examine whether and

From *Spectrum: The Journal of State Government*, Summer 2004.

how legislators are using these technologies. Using survey data and in-depth interviews, this article examines how representatives in the Vermont and New York state legislatures use e-mail and the Internet to conduct legislative business. This article will investigate how information technology has influenced communicating with constituents, responding to policy and attending to individual and group needs, crucial aspects of representation.[2]

FINDINGS

Representation and E-mail

One might think that e-mail use in state government, state legislatures in particular, is a given. While many state legislators have had e-mail for about 10 to 15 years, it has not been employed with any regularity until the last five years. Survey data show that 23 percent of Vermont and New York state legislators (20 out of 88) still do not use e-mail. More encouraging, 38 state legislators (100 percent) in Vermont and 27 state legislators in New York (55 percent) indicated that they use e-mail for legislative business and casework. Of the 20 New York state legislators (41 percent) who do not use e-mail, 17 have staff (85 percent) that use e-mail for legislative business and casework, creating an environment where over 95 percent of state legislative offices (85 out of 88) access e-mail.

To assess how state legislators use e-mail, survey recipients were asked to indicate for what purposes or how they use e-mail. There are considerable differences between the two states, with the exception of *contacting constituents* in which state legislators act similarly. State legislators in Vermont use e-mail to contact other state legislators and to schedule meetings. For example, 32 Vermont state legislators, or 100 percent, use e-mail to contact other state legislators. Twenty-four respondents (100 percent) indicated that meetings are scheduled through e-mail. The rural composition and the non-professional nature of the state legislature contribute to a dependence on e-mail. During in-depth interviews many committee chairs suggested that e-mail makes it infinitely easier to schedule committee meetings and a minority of respondents admitted that they use e-mail to strategize politically. E-mail is also used by state legislators to communicate with their constituents. The data show that 33 out of 38 Vermont state legislators (47 percent) and 39 out of 50 New York state legislators (53 per-

cent) e-mail constituents. Though the percentage of state legislators who indicated that they e-mail constituents is the same across the two states, the similarities end there. A scant 14 respondents (100 percent) in New York reported e-mailing another state legislator. During interviews most respondents said that they only forward information via e-mail. New York is not rural, but it is considerably larger than Vermont. What accounts for the reason why fewer state legislators in New York e-mail their colleagues? Culturally, e-mail has not taken hold among state legislators in New York, perhaps because state legislators spend more time in Albany, though this alone is unlikely to explain why e-mail is so infrequently used between state legislators. Though they do not use e-mail to communicate with each other, 41 state legislators (100 percent) in New York reported sending or receiving attachments through e-mail and another 36 state legislators (100 percent) use e-mail to request information or documents.

According to scholars who study representation, creating policies that will benefit one's constituents is an important component of representation. The survey asked state legislators to indicate whether e-mail and the Internet helped them to gauge what issues were important to constituents. The data show that 37 percent of state legislators (13 out of 35) in Vermont find e-mail to be *very helpful*, while 46 percent (16 out of 35) said e-mail is *somewhat helpful* in gauging the policy preferences of constituents. In New York fewer state legislators, 25 percent (12 out of 48), find e-mail to be *very helpful,* though a similar percentage of individuals indicated that e-mail is *somewhat helpful* in gauging the policy preferences of constituents. Even though e-mail is only somewhat helpful in terms of gauging policy preferences, this is arguably still significant, especially if it aids in policy formulation. In interviews, state legislators in both states said they frequently receive constituent e-mail on policy issues indicating that constituents favored or opposed a particular policy. While only 25 percent (9 out of 37) of state legislators in Vermont reported tallying e-mail, 64 percent (32 out of 50) of state legislators in New York indicated that they tally e-mail from constituents. New York state legislators indicated in interviews that they track constituents' policy preferences that they receive via e-mail, often converting the e-mail to a hard copy and filing the printed version in the appropriate policy folder, then tallying the e-mails.

Table 1 E-mail Use of State Legislators and Staff in Vermont and New York

	State legislators		Staff members	
	Yes	No	Yes	No
Vermont	100%	...	31%	...
	(38)	...	(10)	...
New York	55%	41%	94%	6%
	(27)	(20)	(47)	(3)

Question: Do the following individuals in your office use e-mail for legislative business or casework?

Note: Numbers in parentheses denote sample size.

State legislators were also asked to indicate what percentage of constituent e-mail addressed casework versus legislation. The modal values show that responses are divided evenly between casework and legislation. Constituents e-mail state legislators on issues ranging from less serious concerns like a pothole or a broken street light to more serious matters such as proposed budget cuts for particular state programs. One interviewee said,

> "At times it feels like you are running triage in an emergency room. I'm checking e-mail several times a day. Of course, the biggest load of e-mail is received in the morning. So we want to prioritize. For example, this lady who e-mails us about her house going into foreclosure and is about to be put out on the street, [we're] going to give her a call and try to get to the bottom of that first, rather than responding to an e-mail that extends an invitation to a Little League reception. We prioritize."

Representation and the Internet

While e-mail has been around for 10 to 15 years, access to the Internet, albeit limited, has only been available since 1995 in both legislatures. The survey asked state legislators whether they used the Internet and if they used the Internet for casework or legislative business. Eighty-three percent or 28 out of 34 state legislators in Vermont indicated that they use the Internet for casework or legislative business. Dramatically fewer state legislators in New York reported using the Internet. It is suspected that this is because New York is a professional legislature in which state legislators rely heavily upon their staff to perform tasks related to constituent services and policy formulation. Only 48 percent (23 of 48) of New York state legislators use the Internet, though 98 percent (48 out of 49) of staff indicated that they use the Internet for casework and legislation.

State legislators and staff used the Internet to complete a variety of tasks related specifically to casework and policy formulation, and more generally for research on a wide range of issues. Over 95 percent of respondents in both states indicated that they use the Internet to *perform research or to check pending legislation* and a large number of respondents in New York (46 out of 50) reported using the Internet *to obtain news.* In contrast, fewer state legislators and staff use the Internet *to respond to constituent requests or concerns or to draft legislation.*

The Internet has had mixed effect in terms of whether it has helped representatives to gauge the policy preferences of constituents. According to the data, a plurality of state legislators in Vermont indicated that the Internet has a neutral effect in terms of helping them to gauge the policy preferences of constituents, while 25 percent of legislators (9 out 35) asserted that the Internet is somewhat helpful and 14 percent of legislators (5 out of 35) said *very helpful.* Forty percent of New York state legislators (19 out of 48), however, indicated that the Internet is somewhat helpful in terms of helping them to gauge the policy preferences of constituents compared to 33 percent (16 out of 48) who reported that the Internet has a neutral impact. While New York state legislators viewed the Internet as having a more favorable impact on their ability to respond to the policy preferences of constituents than did Vermonters, it should be noted that a sizable percentage of state legislators in Vermont, 20 percent (7 out of 35), indicated that the question was *not applicable,* perhaps accounting for the difference between the two states.

State legislators were asked what impact they felt their state legislature's Web site had on state politics. In both states, legislators indicated that their state legislative site is an excellent way to disseminate information. Legislators also asserted that not only did the state legislature's site serve constituents and various organizations but it also allows them to obtain information on bills. Information posted to the state legislature's site can be accessed in a more expedient manner than if it were necessary to obtain a hard copy. The Web site essentially facilitates access to state legislative information, and according to one member, makes the Vermont legislature more transparent. In both Vermont and New York, state legislators stated that they feel more constituents contact them because of the state legislature's site. An overwhelming majority of respondents in New York reported that the state legislative site definitely contributes to increased contact as well as improved access to information. One staff member in New York further explained that,

> "If you want access to government, there's no excuse now. You can go right to the Internet. You can watch it [session] happen on tv [the Internet]. A lot of the e-mail that we get, you can see that people have visited the Assembly Web site because they are very specific about a bill. Prior to the development of the state legislature's Web site, only staff knew about bill numbers. This has enabled these people to have information so that they can better communicate their concerns to us."

Clearly state legislative Web sites have played an important role in terms of expanding access and contact, while providing a host of information. This in turn improves state legislators' ability to represent their constituents and to formulate and pass laws.

CONCLUSION

In general, there is a growing tendency to use e-mail in both legislatures, though New York state legislators have been much slower to embrace e-mail. Vermont state legislators are clearly more comfortable using e-mail than representatives in New York. This might be attributed to the fact that New York state legislators are slightly older than Vermont state legislators and that legislators in New York can rely upon staff to e-mail on their behalf. Despite the fact that New York state legislators do not vigorously use e-mail, almost all staff in New York indicated using e-mail. This is especially noteworthy because constituents may unknowingly reside in a district with a state legislator who devalues or refuses to use e-mail.

While state legislators do not employ e-mail for the same tasks in both states, almost all state legislators indicated that they responded to e-mail sent by constituents. E-mail was especially useful to disseminate information and to respond to questions that were not too complex or overly complicated. Furthermore, state legislators indicated that e-mail did in fact help them to better gauge the policy preferences of their constituents, though only a quarter of representatives in Vermont actively tracked or tallied constituent e-mail compared to a majority of New York state legislators.

Internally, state legislators in Vermont were more likely to e-mail one another. Without staff, legislators in Vermont must contact their fellow colleagues directly. In contrast, few state legislators in New York e-mailed another state legislator. Representatives in New York have perhaps resisted using e-mail because staff facilitate communications, placing a phone call to another member's office on their representative's behalf. Locating a colleague is likely to be difficult in Vermont because state legislators lack offices and they usually return home rather than staying overnight in Montpelier, whereas state legislators in New York have offices and they spend as many as three consecutive days in Albany.

Despite the fact that over 80 percent of state legislators in Vermont and over 95 percent of staff in New York indicated using the Internet for casework and legislative business, the data show that respondents typically did not use the Internet to respond to constituent requests. Instead, the Internet was more frequently used to perform research and to check on pending legislation. Diverging responses as to whether the Internet helped legislators to better gauge the policy preferences of their constituents

Table 2 How State Legislators and Staff Use E-mail

	Vermont	New York
To send or	39%	61%
receive attachments	(26)	(41)
To request information	46%	55%
or documents	(30)	(36)
To schedule meetings	65%	35%
	(24)	(13)
To contact other state	70%	30%
legislators	(32)	(14)
To contact constituents	47%	53%
	(33)	(39)
To contact interest groups	64%	36%
or lobbyists	(21)	(12)

Question: How, or for what purposes, does your office use e-mail?

Note: Numbers in parentheses denote sample size.

might be attributed to the fact that in addition to the New York state legislature's Web site, state legislators also have individual Web sites. Members in New York can upload information on issues or policies and they can analyze activity on their Web sites, enabling them to determine whether information on issues or policies is being accessed, whereas most Vermont state legislators do not have individual Web sites. Despite disagreement over whether the Internet helped legislators to gauge policy preferences, state legislators in both states lauded their state legislature's site, asserting that it had dramatically improved communication and information dissemination.

In light of the findings from this study, coupled with the permanence and widespread use of these technologies, it behooves state legislators to examine how they are using e-mail and the Internet to provide constituent services and to formulate legislation. Hence, legislators should take note of the following recommendations:

- Log or track policy preferences received via e-mail;
- Respond to constituent e-mail in a timely manner;
- Use e-mail to communicate with other state legislators strategically or otherwise;
- Develop individual web sites where district news and important policy issues can be advertised; and
- Track and analyze what information is accessed and who visits individual and state legislative sites.

Clearly e-mail and the Internet provide state legislators and their constituents with an additional means for communicating and disseminating information, which has tremendous potential to enhance representation if used vigorously.

Notes

1. Tom Spooner, "Internet Use by Region in the United States," August 27, 2002, http://www. pewinternet.org.

2. Malcolm E. Jewell, *Representatives in State Legislatures,* (Lexington, KY: University of Kentucky Press, 1982).

References

Abramson, Jeffery B., F. Christopher Arterton, and Gary R. Orren. 1988. The *Electronic Commonwealth: The Impact of New Media Technologies on Democratic Politics.* New York: Basic Books.

Barber, Benjamin R. 1984. *Strong Democracy: Participatory Politics for a New Age.* Berkeley: University of California Press.

Bennett, Daniel and Pam Fielding. *The Net Effect: How Cyberadvocacy is Changing the Political Landscape.* 1999.

Bimber, Bruce A. 2003. *Information and American Democracy: Technology in the Evolution of Political Power, Communication, Society and Politics.* Cambridge, UK; New York: Cambridge University Press.

Browning, Graeme. 1996. *Electronic Democracy: Using the Internet to Influence American Politics.* Information Today, Inc.

Dahl, Robert. 1989. *Democracy and Its Critics.* New Haven, CT: Yale University.

Davis, Richard. 1999. *The Web of Politics: The Internet's Impact on the American Political System.* New York; Oxford: Oxford University Press.

Grossman, Lawrence. *The Electronic Republic.* NY: Viking, 1995.

Kurtz, Karl. "Understanding the Diversity of State Legislatures." Boulder, CO: Center for the Study of American Politics, Department of Political Science, University of Colorado-Boulder. 1992.

Nicholson-Crotty, Sean and Kenneth J. Meier. "The Practical Research Size Doesn't Matter: In Defense of Single-State Studies." *State Politics and Policy Quarterly,* 2 (4) (Winter 2002): 411–22.

Przeworski, Adam and Henry Teune. 1970. *The Logic of Comparative Social Inquiry.* NY: Wiley Interscience.

Rosenthal, Alan L. 1998. *The Decline of Representative Democracy.* Washington, D.C.: CQ Press.

Political Parties and Interest Groups

What a difference a century makes. A hundred years ago, political parties dominated political and economic life in vast stretches of urban America and even whole states. In many states and cities the public sector was governed by the disciplined—and often corrupt—hand of party machines. Some states were virtually partisan fiefdoms, with one party dominating politics from top to bottom.

These powerful party organizations were run by relatively small groups of party insiders, a set of "bosses" who controlled who would get to wear the party label in the next election, and what that candidate would be expected to deliver in return once in office. Political parties in those days were as much about money as power. The bosses wielded enormous influence over public-sector jobs and contracts, which made the political party a crucially important part of millions of people's lives. Your job or your business might be tied to your party loyalty, and how you cast your vote might determine not just the quality of your public services, but whether you got any public services at all.[1]

Fast forward to today. Political machines are a thing of the past; in most states both major parties are competitive for at least some major offices. Public-sector jobs and contracts are no longer controlled by a handful of party insiders, and candidates now need only the blessing of voters—not the party elites—to gain the right to carry the party label into a general election. Success in a job or failure in a business has almost nothing to do with whether you vote for a Republican or a Democrat, and the mayor is expected to get potholes filled even in the neighborhoods that vote for the opposition.

What happened to the power of political parties?

In some ways, the parties were victims of their own success. Corruption and naked partisan self-interest created a backlash of reform. Public-sector jobs were shifted to a civil service system, meaning government employees were hired and fired on the basis of merit and job performance—and insulated from the political fortunes and preferences of party bosses. Some of the most powerful bosses of all, people like William Marcy "Boss" Tweed of New York's famous Tammany Hall machine, ended up as convicted criminals and died broken men.[2]

Perhaps the most important contributor to the decline of party power was the institution of the direct primary, an election to determine party nominees for offices in the general election. Primaries took power away from the party bosses and empowered rank-and-file party members to determine who could run under the party label in a general election. If the party bosses decide who gets to be the party nominee, that nominee is beholden to the bosses if he or she wins. If the voters decide in a primary election, the candidate is beholden to the voters, not the bosses. Primary elections, in short, helped break the power of party machines.[3]

Does this mean political parties are no longer central forces in state and local politics? No, they are still an important influence. Political parties have proved to be remarkably adept at reinventing themselves. There may no longer be a few insiders in a smoke-filled room doling out patronage and deciding who gets which office. But some group still has to organize government, package coherent policy agendas for consideration by voters and policymakers, recruit candidates, and mobilize voters. Political parties do this and much more: they also raise campaign funds, provide logistical support for their candidates, and connect voters with their government.[4]

Although political parties remain important, other organizations like special interest groups do many of the same things as the parties, such as mobilizing voters, promoting particular policies, and raising campaign funds. Special interest groups are more commonly thought of as trying to influence the federal government, but organized special interest group activity has grown considerably at the state, and even the local, level during the past few decades. The reason for this growth is fairly easy to fathom—state governments are independent policymakers and their decisions have a broad impact on many aspects of social and economic life. Beer, for example, is

regulated by state governments, not the federal government. It thus makes sense for a big brewing company like Anheuser-Busch to have lobbyists in state capitals, and it does. States also license and regulate professionals in more than one thousand occupations, ranging from doctors and lawyers to art therapists and barbers. It seems natural that professional organizations would have organized lobbying efforts directed at state governments, and they do.

Virtually every interest group imaginable, from a pharmaceutical company to the National Rifle Association to the Motion Picture Association of America, has a state-level presence. State government decisions affect their interests, and in turn interest groups try to shape those decisions. Special interest groups spend hundreds of millions of dollars every year trying to persuade state legislators to support their favored agenda.[5]

This section takes a brief tour of the latest trends and developments related to political parties and special interest groups, two of the most important forces driving state and local politics. As the readings that follow show, what's most notable about political parties these days is not their centralized grip on power, but the seesaw battle between Republicans and Democrats for control of the major institutions of state government. Money remains a big concern, though it is the regulation of campaign contributions and lobbying that occupies reformers, not clamping down on patronage. Today public interest advocates are less concerned with public-sector patronage and more concerned with private-sector patronage in the form of wealthy individuals who are willing to use their fortunes to support public-sector projects.

POLITICAL PARTIES AND SPECIAL INTEREST GROUPS: WHAT'S THE DIFFERENCE, AND WHAT SHOULD WE DO ABOUT THEM?

At what point does a political party stop being a political party and become a special interest group? For many people, the distinction is a little blurry, and it's no wonder. As already noted, political parties and special interest groups do lots of the same things, including supporting each other. They both raise money, endorse candidates, and try to get government to support their favored policies.

They are, however, fundamentally different. Here's how to tell them apart: Political parties run candidates for office under their own label, and they help organize government. Special interest groups do not. Candidates might vie for the endorsement and campaign support of the National Rifle Association, but they run as Republicans and Democrats, not as nominees of the National Rifle Association. Once in office politicians organize government into the majority and minority parties, with the majority controlling the key leadership posts in the legislature. Even in governments that are nonpartisan by law, such as many city councils and Nebraska's unicameral state legislature, candidates are often not shy about declaring their partisan credentials and seeking party endorsements. In effect, informal party systems can exist even where they are formally prohibited. Political parties are virtually impossible to keep out of politics. The same might be said of special interest groups. Although special interest groups do not run their own candidates for office or organize government, they most definitely try to influence the decisions government makes.

The scramble to win elections, control the key offices and institutions of government, and influence the decisions of policymakers tends to create a negative image of political parties and special interest groups. In some cases, the public's skepticism, or even outright cynicism, is justified. Sometimes political parties do enter into a win-at-all-costs mentality, and special interest groups have been known to try to engage in checkbook democracy.

Yet there is a flip side to this that often gets left out of such judgments. First, political parties and special interest groups usually take care to stick with lawful activities—stories of graft, kickbacks, and other forms of outright corruption get so much attention because they represent the exception rather than the rule. Second, political parties and special interest groups represent the fundamental democratic rights of citizens in action.

As citizens, Americans have the right to band together with people of similar interests to support a common cause. That, in a nutshell, is why political parties and special interest groups are created, and also what they do. Many people are cynical about special interest groups, but make an exception for their own group. Mention "special interest" and most people do not think of teachers, police officers, or firefighters. Yet all three professions have an organized lobbying presence in virtually all states and many localities. The point is that one person's narrow-minded, selfish special interest is another person's noble cause.

Most states regulate political parties like public utilities—they view them as providing a necessary public service and seek to ensure that the service does not unduly profit, benefit, or exclude certain people or groups. Many regulations are explicitly aimed at preventing antidemocratic, antimajoritarian activities such as "boss" control of political parties.[6]

In contrast, special interest groups are relatively lightly regulated. State law (not to mention the First Amendment of the U.S. Constitution) recognizes that individuals and organizations have the right to petition government and make their preferences known. The regulatory machinery is thus often aimed at registration and public reporting of activities rather than actually dictating what special interest groups can and cannot do.

RECENT TRENDS

At the state level, the most notable recent trend of importance to political parties is the struggle for partisan control of legislatures. The readings in part 2 highlighted the fact that most state legislators face little competition when they run for office. It is somewhat ironic, then, that the competition between the parties over legislatures is fierce and increasing.

The 2004 election cycle left the two major parties pretty even. Democrats cut the existing Republican edge slightly; after the state ballots were all counted, the GOP controlled twenty state legislatures and the Democrats nineteen, leaving ten states with split party control and one nonpartisan legislature (Nebraska). Underlying this back-and-forth battle are regional trends: Republicans are gaining steadily in the South, but Democrats are offsetting their Southern losses with gains in the Northeast and West. How these regional partisan trends play out will continue to determine partisan fortunes in many states (see the article by Tim Storey and Nicole Casal Moore in this section).

Political parties in the states are also struggling to deal with the implications of the Bipartisan Campaign Reform Act (better known as the McCain-Feingold act). Congress passed the law in 2002, and the Supreme Court upheld most of its provisions a year later. Its primary purpose is to strictly limit campaign financing, which has created some difficulties for state political parties. Prior to the McCain-Feingold act, state parties served as the primary handlers of vast amounts of "soft money" that was largely unregulated by federal campaign finance law. Compliance with the McCain-Feingold act requires more than a shift in accounting for state political parties; the law is forcing them to change some of the ways they do business (see the article by Alan Greenblatt in this section).

For special interest groups, notable recent trends include a growing interest in creating publicly accessible databases of interest group activity, such as the Wisconsin State Ethics Board's "Eye on Lobbying." In Wisconsin any organization that employs a lobbyist now has to identify its interest in a proposed law as soon as it starts to try to influence decisions on that law. This information is available online to anyone with access to the World Wide Web. Policymakers and lobbyists alike can look at individual organizations to see what bills they are trying to influence, or look at the bills and rules being considered by the legislature to see who is trying to influence them (check it out at ethics.state.wi.us/LobbyingRegistration Reports/LobbyingOverview.htm). For a more in-depth discussion, see Roth Judd's article in this section.

Finally, this section considers another emerging trend: the growing awareness of—and sometimes unease about—billionaire benefactors of local government. Some of the super-rich are channeling their wealth into things like revitalizing local downtown districts. Others are spending large amounts to influence elections or ballot proposals. Such individuals are acting as a special interest group of one. John Buntin explores this phenomenon in his article on sugar daddy government.

Notes

1. David R. Mayhew, *Placing Parties in American Politics: Organization, Electoral Settings and Government Activity in the 20th Century* (Princeton, N.J.: Princeton University Press, 1986).

2. Kenneth D. Ackerman, *Boss Tweed: The Rise and Fall of the Corrupt Pol Who Conceived the Soul of Modern New York* (Berkeley, Calif.: Carroll and Graf, 2005).

3. David E. Price, *Bringing Back the Parties* (Washington, D.C.: CQ Press, 1984).

4. John F. Bibby and Thomas Holbrook, "Parties and Elections," in *Politics in the American States,* 7th ed., ed. Virginia Gray, Russell L. Hanson, and Herbert Jacob (Washington, D.C.: CQ Press, 1999), 108.

5. Robert Morlino and Leah Rush, "Hired Guns," Center for Public Integrity, www.publicintegrity.org/hiredguns/report.aspx?aid=165 (accessed March 27, 2005).

6. Malcolm E. Jewell and Sarah M. Morehouse, *Political Parties and Elections in American States,* 4th ed. (Washington, DC: CQ Press, 2001), 76.

10

Perpetual Parity

Tim Storey and Nicole Casal Moore

Just when it looked like state legislatures couldn't get any closer, they did.

November's state legislative elections did little to change the political landscape that shows a divided electorate. Democrats and Republicans find themselves stuck as they try to squeeze through the door to control America's legislatures. The 2004 election gave each party hope, but ultimately they remain locked in political parity.

IT'S ALL KNOTTED UP

Before the election, America's two major political parties were in an historic gridlock for control of the states. Republicans held a majority of the 7,382 legislative seats by just over 60 seats. In terms of the overall control of states, Republicans had 21 compared to 17 controlled by the Democrats. Eleven states were divided with neither party claiming both chambers. (The Nebraska Legislature is not only unicameral, but also elected on a non-partisan basis.)

But just when it looked like it could not get any closer, it did. With a handful of recounts still pending in key races that could swing control in a couple of chambers, Democrats appear to have regained the majority of all legislative seats, but by only about 10. That's about a 0.1 percent advantage. In terms of the big picture, the difference in overall state legislative control also shrunk. Republicans continue to hold more legislatures, but by only a one state margin—20 Republican, 19 Democratic and 10 split.

Parity is not unique to state legislatures. The president garnered just 3 percent more of the popular vote than did Senator John Kerry. Congress is close in both houses.

From *State Legislatures,*
December 2004.

49

"America is divided, more divided than ever," said Bill Schneider, senior political commentator at CNN. "And the division persists, even though the Republicans had a good year. I would have imagined they'd have bigger breakthroughs in state legislatures."

Experts predict this division to be more than a passing fad. Here's a closer look at how the state legislative results of election 2004 shook out, why they did in such a fashion and what they say about this nation.

MODEST GAINS FOR DEMOCRATS

Roughly 80 percent of state legislative seats were up for election in 44 states this year. In just over 35 percent of those races, one party's nominee got a pass by not having opposition from the other major party. In the others, the competition was fierce. In 23 states, there were 28 chambers where a slight shift of only five House seats or three Senate seats would reverse the party in power.

Party control switched in 12 chambers which is the average in every two-year election cycle. A new party is in power in eight of the top 10 state legislative election battlegrounds that NCSL identified in July, as well as four more chambers that weren't considered that close.

On the whole, the Democrats can claim a small victory in 2004 on the legislative front. They picked up seven chambers, compared with the GOP's four. An additional chamber the Republicans controlled before the election is now tied.

Democrats won both Colorado chambers (for the first time in 40 years), the Montana Senate, the North Carolina House, the Oregon Senate, the Vermont House and the Washington Senate. They managed a tie in the Iowa Senate, which Republicans had by an eight-seat margin before Election Day.

"Democrats at the state level exceeded national trends," said Michael Davies, executive director of the Democratic Legislative Campaign Committee. "While we did pick up seats in states where we did well presidentially, we also picked up seats in states where the Democrats lost in the presidential election. I think we did well in both blue and red states because the Democrats in those states did a really good job of localizing their races."

The GOP, however, also claimed prizes on Election Day with some historic pick-ups. Republicans grabbed the Georgia House, the Indiana House, the Tennessee Senate and the Oklahoma House. In Georgia and Tennessee, new Republican majorities are the first since Reconstruc-

Legislative Control		
Republicans	**Democrats**	**Split**
Alaska	Alabama	Delaware
Arizona	Arkansas	Iowa
Florida	California	Kentucky
Georgia	Colorado	Minnesota
Idaho	Connecticut	Montana
Indiana	Hawaii	Nevada
Kansas	Illinois	New York
Michigan	Louisiana	Oklahoma
Missouri	Massachusetts	Oregon
New Hampshire	Maryland	Tennessee
North Dakota	Maine	
Ohio	Mississippi	**Nonpartisan**
Pennsylvania	North Carolina	Nebraska
South Carolina	New Jersey	
South Dakota	New Mexico	
Texas	Rhode Island	
Utah	Vermont	
Virginia	Washington	
Wisconsin	West Virginia	
Wyoming		

tion. In Oklahoma, Republicans have not held the House in more than 80 years.

"We are thrilled about our historic victories in places like Tennessee, Georgia and Oklahoma," said Alex Johnson, executive director of the Republican Legislative Campaign Committee. He added that many of the states where Democrats gained were very close going into the election. "We lost some chambers that were real tight, but they are still very close, and we'll try to win them back next time."

REGIONAL TRENDS

Republicans continue their gains in the South. In less than 15 years, the GOP has gone from having not one single legislative chamber in the South to controlling 13 out of 26, a quite remarkable realignment in a relatively short time span.

Alan Rosenthal of Rutgers University believes the trend toward the Republicans started in the mid-1990s and was fueled by the popularity of Newt Gingrich. The cham-

State Where One Party Controls Legislature and Governorship

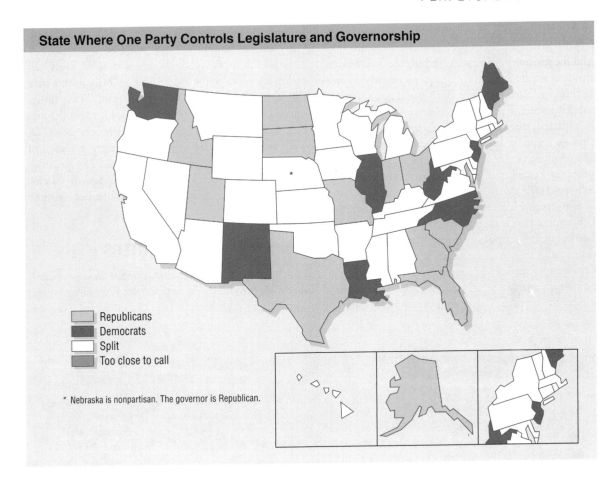

Republicans
Democrats
Split
Too close to call

* Nebraska is nonpartisan. The governor is Republican.

bers that turned red in 2004 appear to be part of this movement. "Gingrich was trying to get the Republicans to become the majority party at a time when the South was ready to become more conservative. They had been electing conservative Democrats. Now, the Republicans were giving them conservative Republicans instead," Rosenthal said.

After factoring in November's results, Republicans have added a net of 67 seats in the South in the past two years. In 2004, the Democrats offset those gains by doing well in the Northeast and West. The net gain for the Democrats in the East since 2002 is 57 more seats and 26 additional seats in the West. In the Midwest, it is essentially a draw with Democrats netting a mere three seats.

SOME CHAMBERS SWING BIG

Large numbers of seats changed hands in many states. In certain chambers, including houses in Minnesota, Georgia and Vermont, party gains and losses were in double figures.

Though the Democrats didn't overtake the Republicans in the Minnesota House, they picked up a slew of seats—14 to be exact. Before the election, Republicans held a comfortable 30-seat majority. Now it's down to a claustrophobic two. Minnesota narrowly went for Kerry in the presidential race.

In the Georgia House, Democrats held a 27-seat majority before the election. Now it's the Republicans with an eight-seat majority. This large-scale swing can be attributed to several factors including a new, court-drawn redistricting plan that gave the Republicans a golden opportunity for gains. Republicans also raised and spent record amounts of campaign money in Georgia this year. And President Bush had a good showing with 58 percent of the popular vote.

"Coattails made a huge difference in Georgia," said Charles Bullock, political science professor at the University of Georgia. "There was a massive surge of voters, and the Republican get-out-the-vote machine really paid off."

The presidential race may have also had a major impact in Vermont House races. Republicans controlled that chamber by five seats before the election. The Democrats picked up 14 seats to secure a 23-seat majority. Kerry won 59 percent of the vote in Vermont. In addition to Vermont, it appears that Kerry's coattails helped swing a large number of seats to the Democrats in a number of states like Minnesota, Iowa, Oregon and even in Colorado where Kerry lost, but ran stronger than past Democrats.

The Oklahoma House also saw seats shift. The GOP picked up nine, giving it a 13-seat majority in this state that went for Bush by a large margin. Term limits opened the door to Republican control here for the first time in 80 years. Of the chamber's 101 legislators, 28 were forced to retire. Term limits were a factor in Michigan and Arkansas this year as well. The Arkansas House lost 36 percent of its membership and the Michigan House lost 34 percent. Neither chamber changed hands.

MORE PEOPLE, MORE VOTERS

Headed into the 2004 election, pundits were predicting that voter turnout might swell to over 125 million voters. Some even said it could be up 25 million from the last

On the Way to Congress

So you want to be a member of Congress? You might start by serving in a state legislature. For several decades, one of the most common shared experiences among members of Congress has been that they once served in their state legislature. In fact, since the 1998 elections, just over half the members of the national legislature served previously in a state legislature. The new 109th Congress will continue that tradition.

When Congress convenes in January, 50.6 percent of the membership will have come from state legislatures—exactly the same percentage as the past biennium.

There will be 47 first-termers in the 109th—nine in the Senate and 38 in the House. Of these, 24 are former state legislators—three in the Senate and 21 in the House. Among them are three who have been in the leadership of the National Conference of State Legislatures. Newly elected California Congressman Jim Costa will become the third former NCSL president to serve in the U.S. House. (He joins Minnesota Congressman Martin Sabo, who was NCSL president shortly after its formation in the mid-1970s. Missouri Congresswoman Karen McCarthy, the other NCSL president to serve in Congress, did not run for re-election this fall.)

Michigan Congressman-elect Joe Schwarz was a member of the NCSL Executive Committee in the mid-1990s. Newly elected Pennsylvania Congresswoman Allyson Schwartz served on the Executive Committee in 1999 and 2000 as a state senator. (A fourth recent member of the NCSL governing body, Larry Diedrich, lost his bid in November to represent South Dakota in the U.S. House.)

The new class of former legislators contains 13 Republicans and 11 Democrats. Only one, celebrated Illinois Senator Barack Obama, moved directly from his state legislature to the U.S. Senate. Three of the four Georgia newcomers held leadership positions in their legislatures. Senator-elect Johnny Isakson once was Georgia House minority leader. Congressman-elect Tom Price was the state's Senate majority leader in 2002–03 and his colleague Lynn Westmoreland has just concluded his stint as the House minority leader.

Other former state legislative leaders in the new class include Congresswoman-elect Cathy McMorris, who recently served as the minority leader in the Washington House of Representatives, Congresswoman-elect Gwen Moore, who was the pro tem of the Wisconsin Senate in the late 1990s, and Congressman-elect Schwarz, a former pro tem of the Michigan Senate.

—Carl Tubbesing, NCSL

presidential election. There were more voters, but in the modest range of just over 15 million.

Experts say that those new voters broke pretty evenly between the two parties. In addition, the two parties embarked on massive get-out-the-vote efforts that in the end wound up canceling each other out. "There was as much Republican new turnout as Democratic new turnout. The mobilization efforts basically negated each other," said University of Virginia Professor Larry Sabato.

NEARLY DEAD EVEN

While a few chambers shifted dramatically and a few shifted slightly, most remained relatively stable, solidifying this American parity. The Republican and Democrat numbers first evened out in 2000. Before that, the Democrats led in chamber numbers and total legislators for 50 years. The 2004 elections may mark the beginning of an era with neither party dominating legislatures, but rather perpetually sharing power.

What's causing this even division? Schneider, of CNN, says, "It has to do more than anything else with values: religion, personal values, cultural values. It has to do with whether you own a gun, whether you support Iraq. What it does not have to do with is social class anymore."

Virginia's Sabato agreed when asked about what issues motivated voters when they chose state legislators. He says it's the issues that get people to pound the table when they argue—the issues that people feel intensely about. "Intensity generates coattails, and it's the social and cultural issues like abortion, the death penalty, gun control and morals that generate that intensity. Polarization continues across the board on issues like this and it translates down the ballot to races for state legislature."

Experts don't predict a return to decades of party monopoly. "For the immediate future, we've got a very

competitive political party system," Rosenthal said. "It's competitive for president, for the Senate and the House. It's competitive for every state governor, and in probably 60 percent of the 98 state legislative bodies. And I think competitiveness on a systemic level can be good. It's good in that it offers a choice."

Candidates for state office aren't just competitive on the campaign trail. Once they get elected, they must contend with each other, and the other branches of state government. The 2004 election results show that when the governor's party is taken into account, Republicans control both legislative chambers and the governor's mansion in 12 states. Democrats do in seven states. And control is divided between the parties in 29 states with Washington still pending and Nebraska not included due to its nonpartisan elections for the legislature.

TIME TO GOVERN

Even though legislatures remain closely divided between the two parties, it is time to start focusing on lawmaking now that the election is over. The big question is whether legislators in the many close chambers will be able to work together to address the needs of voters.

Davies, of the Democratic Legislative Campaign Committee thinks these splits and the 50–50 nature of the country will call for more compromise. "Especially with the state budget crises, there's a need for more bipartisanship in more chambers," Davies said. "We've got a lot of chambers that are very close, and a lot of states that have some great challenges. We're going to have to see a level of bipartisanship that is much more congenial than what we've seen at the national level."

Former Republican Governor Jim Edgar of Illinois said the election gives state lawmakers a chance to do just that.

"Let's take advantage of this new start," he said. "It's imperative that we find common ground to solve the problems the American people want solved."

11

Eye on Lobbying

Roth Judd

Wisconsin's "Eye on Lobbying" allows anyone with Internet access to check on special interest group activity in the state legislature.

Wisconsin's "Eye on Lobbying" combines new technologies with the spirit and principles of Wisconsin's progressive lobbying law to shine a bright light on efforts to influence the development of public policy, and it is winning praise and support from legislators, lobbyists, editorial writers and reporters.

"Eye on Lobbying" permits anyone with access to the Internet to learn the legislative agenda of every organization that employs a lobbyists and, for any legislative proposal, who is trying to influence it. This is possible because now every business and organization that tries to influence a bill identifies its interest in a bill when it starts to lobby, and that information about who is lobbying on what is updated every business day on the Internet.

The effects are many, concrete, dramatic and significant. As the first step in undertaking a program audit of a state agency, the state auditor consults "Eye on Lobbying" to identify the organizations with special interest in the agency's actions. When preparing the fiscal analysis required of every bill and budget provision, analysts turn to "Eye on Lobbying" to identify affected groups that can explain the bill's financial implications. As a bill is passed, the governor, before deciding whether to sign the bill, may consult "Eye on Lobbying" to identify which interests are affected and how. "Eye on Lobbying" has become so important to decision-makers that the Wisconsin legislature has linked its internal computer system directly to the "Eye on Lobbying" web page so that as elected representatives on the floor of the legislative chamber discuss and vote on a specific bill they have displayed before them the names of the organizations trying to influence it.

From *Spectrum: The Journal of State Government*, Winter 2003.

HOW IT WORKS

Prior to or within two weeks after a lobbyist's first communication with a legislator, legislative staff or agency official about a bill, administrative rule, budget item, or subject of potential legislative activity, an organization retaining a lobbyist identifies its interest in the bill or rule to the Ethics Board. The organization reports the information by keying it into a form available on the Ethics Board's web site. Multiple times every business day the Board updates its web site, http://ethics.state.wi.us, to display the information that organizations have reported over the course of the day.

"Eye on Lobbying" can be searched:

- By bill or rule, to determine the organizations trying to affect it as well as its text, its status, and its history.
- By organization represented by a lobbyist, to learn the bills and rules it is trying to influence.
- By keyword of lobbying interest, to identify the businesses and organizations lobbying on a topic.
- By key word or phrase in a bill, to identify legislation affecting a matter.
- By subject in budget bill to learn which groups are trying to affect an agency's budget or operation.

NOT ONLY FOR LEGISLATORS

Businesses and organizations use "Eye on Lobbying" for knowledge of the legislative proposals that competitors and kindred interests are trying to affect so that the organizations can decide how or whether to offer support or countervailing arguments. And an organization can readily spot and address a conflict arising from its lobbyist's retention by another organization with a different and antagonistic interest in a bill.

Reporters, editorial writers, and commentators have an on-line display of all the organizations trying to affect each bill and rule along with the name and telephone number and e-mail address for each organization's spokesperson.

Government agencies receive daily notice of the interests trying to modify agencies' programs and budgets and notice of the interests trying to promote, stall or modify administrative rules agencies have proposed.

The public has direct access to information about the many voices participating in and trying to affect the legislative process.

ANYONE CAN DO IT

"Eye on Lobbying" is eminently replicable. Although now one of a kind, it possesses potential to become the norm. This program does not require: significant cost, unusual or complicated programming, computer hardware or software other than those commonly found in most offices, or additional employees (if a jurisdiction already has even a small office with lobbying responsibilities).

The Wisconsin Ethics Board inaugurated its initial version of "Eye on Lobbying" for about $20,000 using readily available off-the-shelf software, and has found it can administer the program without significant increase of costs.

The implementing legislation could not have been simpler. All that was needed for the program's start was legislation requiring an organization that employs a lobbyist to identify to the Ethics Board the number of any bill about which the organization's lobbyist communicated with a legislator or legislative employee. The Ethics Board, without requirement or prompting, was eager to post the data to a web site as the Board received it.

The Wisconsin experience is instructive because it demonstrates how quickly and completely the affected parties coalesced to promote the innovation—even in spite of initial misgivings. After initial resistance "Eye on Lobbying" was endorsed by the Association of Wisconsin Lobbyists and by Common Cause in Wisconsin, has the enthusiastic support of every interest it has touched, and was approved by the unanimous vote of the Republican Assembly and Democratic Senate.

Enforcement and Compliance

Compliance has been high. And why shouldn't it be? First, this web site, much visited by legislators, is a lobbyist's dream. It is an opportunity for an organization to express its support or opposition to a bill or to recommend an amendment. Moreover, the legislator sees the organization's position when that bill has the legislator's attention and is seeking information about it, perhaps to make a decision affecting its scheduling or passage. Second, noncompliance carries not only a legal penalty, but perhaps even more significantly, the risk of being discredited and shunned by his or her colleagues in the lobbying corps if the lobbyist is discovered to be engaged in stealth lobbying.

WHO USES "EYE ON LOBBYING"?

Traffic to the Ethics Board's web site has surpassed expectations. However measured—average number of visits each day: 375; unique visitors per month: 4500; average number of pages viewed each day: 8,000; or hits per month: 425,000—use of "Eye on Lobbying" has been impressive.

Legislature's Acceptance and Support

So enthusiastic has been the Wisconsin legislature's acceptance and support of "Eye on Lobbying" that the legislature, for the benefit of its members, has linked the "Eye on Lobbying" web page directly to the legislature's own home page. Moreover, the Assembly has linked the Ethics Board's lobbying information to the Assembly's in-session page that Representatives use in the legislative chamber to follow a day's proceedings.

Further evidence of the legislature's enthusiasm arrived during the first legislative session of the program's operations. Initially, lobbyists were obliged to identify only proposed rules and bills that had been introduced and assigned a number. Soon, however, legislators were asking for information about the nature of all those meetings and hallway conversations, not about bills already before the legislature, but about bills that might be offered and about items that might be included in the budget bill by amendment. Even before the legislature had completed its first session with "Eye on Lobbying," the legislature had refined the initial legislation to say that when a lobbyist communicates with a legislator or legislative employee about a legislative proposal that has not yet been assigned a number, the lobbyist must describe the topic of the lobbying communication with reasonable specificity, sufficient to identify the lobbying communication's subject matter.

By the time that legislators arrived at the capitol to be sworn into office for the following term, lobbyists had already identified to the Ethics Board and had posted on the "Eye on Lobbying" web site nearly 1000 proposals for legislation. "Eye on Lobbying" revealed the extent and nature of lobbying that went on when it appeared to many that the legislature was not in session. More importantly, it had permitted legislators, opinion leaders and the 650 organizations employing lobbyists to know the legislative agendas of various lobbying interests and to participate in the shaping of legislation even before the first bill of the session had been introduced.

WHAT'S NEXT?

The Ethics Board is now offering to anyone interested in the legislative agenda the ability to receive notification by e-mail whenever new lobbying activity on a topic or bill of special interest is reported to the Ethics Board. For example, a legislator might receive an e-mail alerting him whenever an organization registers its intention to affect a bill that the legislator has authored. A lobbyist tracking a bill will receive an e-mail whenever an organization starts to lobby on that bill or an organization changes its position or updates its comment on the proposal. The e-mail will identify the new or changed information. A transportation company might receive a notice whenever a bill is introduced referring to "highway," "gasoline tax," "trucking" or other keyword that the organization selects.

Many states register lobbyists and collect information about how much a business or organization spends to influence legislators. Wisconsin does that too; but the Wisconsin Ethics Board has overthrown the traditional system of collecting information about how much money organizations spent to lobby last month or last year and has rededicated its efforts to disseminating information about the issues and efforts in the legislature today, next week and next month.

The American Society for Public Administration, the Council on Governmental Ethics Laws, the International City/County Management Association and The Council of State Governments conferred the 2002 Public Integrity Award on the Wisconsin Ethics Board for its conceiving and implementing this innovative program.

12

The Soft-Money Crackdown

Alan Greenblatt

There's a lot that state political parties still don't know about the new campaign finance law. They need to learn fast.

From *Governing,* March 2004.

Mitch Daniels is the leading Republican candidate for governor of Indiana, and he has spent the winter doing the things all such candidates do: attending Lincoln Day dinners (more than three dozen at last count), showing off his made-in-Indiana RV and extolling his own virtues and those of President George W. Bush.

The link with the president is a natural connection for him to make. The 54-year-old Daniels has had a long career in government and in the pharmaceutical business, but he is best known for his stint as Bush's budget director, a post he gave up last year to run for the top job back home. Bush's operatives helped clear the GOP field for Daniels, and the president himself has already made an early campaign appearance for him.

And Daniels, in return, praises Bush to the skies. "Providence was smiling on the United States of America," he told nearly 300 party faithful at a Lincoln dinner in Shelby County, "on that night when George Bush finally became president of the United States." Nearly all Republican regulars agree that sticking close to Bush will be a big help in November. "Around here, Bush is a shoo-in," says Rob Nolley, a Shelbyville city councilman. "Daniels' experience working for him is a big deal."

But Daniels' stamp of approval from the White House has suddenly become a lot harder for him to show off. On the day of the Shelbyville dinner, the Federal Election Commission ruled that Bush cannot appear in endorsement ads proclaiming his fondness for Daniels—or any other Republican—unless Bush's campaign pays for the ad itself. Under the new rules, if Daniels pays for or approves a TV spot that features Bush or even mentions his name, he will technically be making an illegal donation to the Bush campaign. "Absurd is not strong enough a word," Daniels fumes. "If anything we contemplate is really proscribed by that law, it ought to be amended immediately."

The statute Daniels refers to derisively as "that law" is the Bipartisan Campaign Reform Act, known more widely as McCain-Feingold, after its two sponsors in the U.S. Senate. The law was passed by Congress in 2002 and was, for the most part, upheld by the Supreme Court last December. Political professionals are generally familiar with its effects on fundraising by federal candidates and its restrictions on advertising by outside interest groups. But state and local officeholders and party officials are only beginning to sort through the effects the law will have on parties and anyone running for office at the lower levels of the American political system.

Those effects will be profound. All the nuts-and-bolts party work that takes place within 120 days of a federal election—general or primary—such as identifying voters, registering them or bringing them to the polls, has been reclassified as "federal election activity." It is subject to federal regulation and must be paid for with so-called hard money (donations that are limited in amount and require federal disclosure). It doesn't matter whether a local party seeks merely to support its local sheriff. If there is a federal candidate on the ballot, the party's contacts with voters are considered federal activity and subject to the new regulations. "State and local parties can't get around the law by avoiding the mention of a federal candidate's name," warns Donald Simon, counsel to Common Cause and a leading campaign finance lawyer.

"You could interpret this law so broadly that if I tell people to 'vote for the Republican team,' that could trigger federal disclosure and reporting requirements," says Indiana state Representative Mike Murphy, the newly-installed chairman of the Marion County (Indianapolis) Republican Party. "The whole psyche of how people identify with political parties would be damaged if state and local candidates have to put up a Chinese wall between themselves and federal candidates."

CRIMINAL OFFENSES

It's not only going to be harder for state and local parties to help federal candidates—it's going to be difficult for them to promote state and local candidates in federal election years. The law creates new categories of money

and makes it much more complicated for parties at various levels—local, state and national—to transfer money among themselves. In California, for example, the Republican Party contracts with its 58 county central committees to handle the work of registering voters. The state party has to explain to the county organizations that it can no longer reimburse them for those costs—or, if it does, the local party becomes ineligible for receiving other types of financial help from the state or national party, according to Chuck Bell, an attorney for the California GOP.

"The unfortunate consequence of the law, at least in the short term, is that it strains our relationship with the county party committees," says Bell. Even if the county parties manage to raise adequate operating money on their own, they will have to file complex monthly forms with the FEC if they spend just $5,000 a year on registering voters or calling them on Election Day to remind them to turn out. These rules may not be easy to enforce, but there are criminal penalties for violation, and few party officials will want to risk going to jail in order to test the boundaries of the law.

Over the past year, former party officials have been setting up quasi-party organizations known as 527s, after a section of the U.S. tax code. There are legions of these groups, including traditional names such as the Republican Governors' Association and new ones called America Coming Together (pro-Democrat) and Americans for a Better Country (pro-Republican). The 527s were planned as a way to skirt McCain-Feingold's restrictions on parties by spending hundreds of millions of dollars during this campaign year.

But the FEC ruled in February that the restrictions on "federal election activity" during even-numbered years apply to 527s as well as parties. So there appears to be no chance that the 527s will supersede the parties entirely. "I would rather see parties get money rather than outside groups," says Sarah Morehouse, a University of Connecticut political scientist, "because I see the parties as having the ability to broker interests or moderate interests, rather than groups that are single interests and have one ax to grind and can give a lot of money to their candidates."

American political parties are nothing if not adaptable. Once the dominant force in American politics—deciding who would get to run for what office and with how much support—they have found a new role as support organs, offering consulting and fundraising services to self-selected aspirants. Now, with those functions under legal restriction, the parties may be forced into still another role: as clearinghouses of legal advice for avoiding the law's many minefields. "The bottom line," says Wayne Hamilton, a senior adviser to the Texas GOP, "is we tell our local parties to stay completely away from any type of federal activity unless they have the money to hire attorneys that specialize in FEC regulation and federal campaign laws."

Many state parties are currently hosting seminars for local party officials, trying to help them understand the shifting world created by the new law. "It doesn't seem plausible that Congress could regulate bumper stickers for local sheriffs," says state Representative Luke Messer, executive director of the Indiana GOP. "One of the unfortunate consequences of this law is that it weakens parties."

MACHINE POLITICS

Indiana, more than most states, has a powerful party tradition. The Marion County (Indianapolis) Republicans, in particular, operated a formidable political machine, coordinating thousands of volunteers, dominating local offices, running up the score for statewide candidates and providing Richard M. Nixon the solace of knowing there was one big city where he remained popular even during the latter years of his presidency. As state Senator Lawrence Borst recalls in his memoir of 40 years in Indiana politics, the Marion County party used to screen and recruit candidates from county treasurer (still a rich source of patronage jobs) all the way up to the U.S. Senate. The local GOP was instrumental in creating a unified city-county government, which gave Republicans a 30-year lock on the Indianapolis mayor's office—a lock that was broken only four years ago by Democrats, aided by the fact that thousands of Republicans had moved beyond Marion to outer suburban counties such as Shelby, Hendricks and Hamilton.

> *"It doesn't seem plausible that Congress could regulate bumper stickers for local sheriffs. One of the unfortunate consequences of this law is that it weakens parties."*
>
> —State Representative Luke Messer

It wasn't until the 1970s that Indiana did away with the practice of nominating candidates by party convention, rather than open primary. It wasn't until the 1980s that it abolished the custom of entrusting the parties with the lucrative job of running the county vehicle license bureaus. Even now, Indiana's parties receive funds from the sale of vanity license plates—about $750,000 a year for each party, much of which trickles down to county organizations. That may "not be enough money to wad a pop gun," as former Marion County GOP Chairman John Sweezy says, but having three-quarters of a million dollars to start with, even in non-election years, has established a steady income stream that has allowed some party officials to make six-figure salaries and has created more stable careers in politics than are possible in places where parties close up shop in odd-numbered years.

Even in an era of candidate-centered politics, there's been plenty of work for the parties in Indiana to do. During the last gubernatorial campaign, the state Democratic Party and its incumbent, Governor Frank O'Bannon, split the political chores. O'Bannon's team took care of the big money activities, such as polling and media buys. The state party handled direct mail, absentee ballot applications, phone banks, bumper stickers, posters and yard signs. It was a formula that worked very well.

But it cannot be easily repeated this year. Under McCain-Feingold, party activities that once could be split on a prorated basis between federal and state accounts will now have to be paid for entirely with federally regulated dollars (dollars that can come only from individuals in limited amounts). Local parties and candidates for state offices, who can raise large amounts from corporations and unions, have not been in the habit of soliciting strictly limited individual donations or having to account for them. "What will be the reaction of governors and state legislators when they realize state parties can't use funds the way they used to for get out the vote, voter identification and voter mobilization?" asks

Benjamin Ginsberg, counsel to the Bush-Cheney campaign and numerous state parties.

Those who believe in the McCain-Feingold approach think the critics are exaggerating the problem. Even under the strictures of the new law, parties will still raise and spend more for candidates this year than any of the outside groups that have sprung up in response to the changing rules. "Party operatives tend to have a worldview that very little regulation is good but even less regulation is better," says Simon, the Common Cause counsel. "The new law doesn't say to them that they can't do any of these activities or work with federal candidates. The law just regulates what kind of money they can use for these activities."

What they can't use is the funding known ubiquitously as "soft money"—contributions that until now have been largely unregulated and could be collected in unlimited amounts from corporations, unions and wealthy individual donors. Under the old system, state parties became conduits for soft money that was spent, sometimes surreptitiously, to support candidates at the federal level. Prior to McCain-Feingold, the rule was that state parties could use soft money for anything that qualified as "party-building activities." But the soft-money exemption grew into an enormous loophole, stretched to the point where national parties were using state parties as conduits for millions of soft-money dollars spent mostly to pay for TV ads.

During the 2000 and 2002 election cycles, the two major national parties gave $472 million in soft money to state parties around the country. In 2002, according to Anthony Corrado, a campaign finance scholar at the Brookings Institution, state parties spent only about $52 million on genuine party-building expenses such as voter registration, buttons and yard signs. Most of the rest went to produce and broadcast advertisements— ads that were essentially immune to regulation or accountability for their cost or content.

LEVIN BUCKS

In cracking down on the abuse of soft money, the authors of McCain-Feingold didn't intend to weaken state parties. They actually tried to help the parties in a couple of ways. One was to double the amount of money they could receive in hard-dollar contributions. Secondly, they created a new category of contributions: the so-called Levin

funds. If state law permits, state and local parties can raise Levin funds (named for their Senate sponsor, Carl Levin of Michigan) in chunks of up to $10,000 per year from individuals, PACs, corporations and unions. Levin dollars can be used only for certain expenses related to federal election activity. They can't be used for ads or other communications with the public, and they come with numerous restrictions that lawyers will make a lot of money explaining to parties in the coming months.

Despite the complications, not everybody—even within state party organizations—thinks the parties will necessarily suffer as a result of the new law. As a state senator in 1998, George Jepsen sponsored Connecticut's first-in-the-nation state ban on soft money. "Short of public financing," he says, "if you're looking for ways to restore some sanity to the process, a ban on soft money sort of jumps out at you." Now that Jepsen is chairman of the state Democratic Party, he has to live with that ban. But he says it hasn't been so bad: His fundraising was up by more than a third in 2003, compared with 2001. His party has hired a full-time field director and is providing professional services such as enhanced voter files to town committees and candidates.

In the past couple of years, Connecticut Democrats have made major inroads into traditionally Republican territory, including the affluent suburbs of Fairfield County. Democratic mayors and first selectmen now preside over 70 percent of Connecticut's population. Jepsen attributes these gains at least in part to the Democrats' ability to adjust to the new rules and take advantage of them. "We're turning the party," he says, "from an organ that really just convened conventions and stamped people on the foreheads as Democratic candidates, into a party that actively provides services and reaches out to constituencies."

BAYH-IN

When it comes to national politics, Indiana is a reliably Republican state. Not only does it support the GOP candidate for president every four years but because of its early poll-closing time, it is nearly always the first state to be colored Republican red on network TV maps. Still, Hoosier Republicans have lost the governorship four times in a row, in large part because of Evan Bayh, the popular moderate Democrat who captured the statehouse in 1988 and 1992, then passed it along to his lieutenant governor, Frank O'Bannon, who won in 1996 and 2000. (O'Bannon died last year and his replacement, Joe Kernan, will be the Democratic nominee against Mitch Daniels.)

Bayh's strength not only boosted O'Bannon into the governor's mansion but also has helped Democrats control the state House of Representatives for all but two of the past 16 years. Bayh is in the U.S. Senate now, and he continues to maintain favorability ratings around 70 percent. Indiana Democrats running for lesser offices routinely associate themselves with him to get elected. "Why wouldn't you want to hitch your wagon to somebody like that?" asks Dan Parker, executive director of the state Democratic Party.

But because of McCain-Feingold, that is not so easy anymore. The new law imposes restrictions on using the images of federal candidates, so Bayh probably won't be featured on any of the party's posters in 2004. Merely including the senator's name on an invitation to a party event, Parker says, now requires a disclosure so long and complicated that some traditional donors mistakenly think they're not allowed to give money to the party at all.

Nothing frustrates Parker more than the prospect of losing Bayh's presence in state and local campaigns. Last November, for example, the senator agreed to appear in an ad endorsing Jonathan Weinzapfel, the Democratic nominee for mayor of Evansville. But Bayh knew that McCain-Feingold had changed the rules, so he asked for an advisory opinion from the FEC on whether it was permissible for him to appear on TV on behalf of a local candidate.

In the end, the ad was approved because Bayh wouldn't be on any ballot for more than 120 days (the period of time before a federal election during which most of the new restrictions apply). Candidates who want to use Bayh's image this year—or Republicans such as Daniels who want to feature Bush—can do so only between May 5 (the day after the state's primaries) and July 4, when the 120-day period before the November election opens up.

And even during the brief window in which the ads are legal, any federal office-holder who appears in them can't mention his job title or talk about himself in any way. "I was happy to abide by the new law," Bayh says. "It did, however, make a traditional, innocuous activity more cumbersome and expensive."

As candidates and party officials sort through McCain-Feingold's permutations, many worst-case scenarios are being trotted out. Campaigns for Congress might become legally segregated from state and local officials in ways that could cripple intraparty communication. Zealous local prosecutors may seize on violations for use as political weapons. Campaign consultants worry about having to incur the expense of producing ads far in advance, as Weinzapfel did, to allow the FEC to rule on them—thereby telegraphing strategy to their opponents in the process. Some states are even talking about moving their state elections to odd-numbered years in order to avoid the law's encumbrances.

In the end, none of these things may happen. Bayh is confident that, as the campaign season wears on, the law's complexities will get sorted out. The decision in his case, after all, set the precedent for the new restrictions on ads featuring President Bush. As the FEC's thinking becomes clear, there will be less need for parties and candidates to consult with lawyers on every move they make. Rules that are now unsettling may soon become second nature.

But the most certain outcome of the law, which was designed to limit the influence of money in politics, is still likely to be a perverse one. There will be more money raised than ever—not only by the new 527 groups but also by parties and candidates at different levels of government who previously worked together but now can't rely on each other to make sure the party's message is getting out. "We can't share plans, and we can't coordinate the way we used to," says Don Morabito, executive director of the Pennsylvania Democratic Party. "We're either going to be duplicating our efforts in significant areas, or we might be ignoring important areas. We may be wasting resources or not doing what we need to do."

13

Sugar Daddy Government

John Buntin

A new generation of billionaires is remaking American cities. The cities are better off; the democratic process sometimes suffers.

From *Governing,*
June 2004

A dozen blocks north of downtown Seattle, the neighborhood adjoining Lake Union is in the midst of transformation. Alongside the car dealerships, sign stores and furniture markets that line Westlake Avenue, there's a new biomedical research laboratory, a bioinformatics facility for Merck, the drug company, and new labs for the University of Washington. All told, more than 3 million square feet of new development is underway in a little pocket of the city.

This is happening in the midst of Seattle's worst recession in 30 years. So it's no wonder that local officials look to the laboratories and biotech businesses as a form of economic salvation. Mayor Greg Nickels says it's as important to the city "as the day Bill Boeing started to build airplanes."

The official name of this neighborhood is South Lake Union. But some residents have another name for it: Allentown. That's because it started as the private vision of one man, Paul Allen, the co-founder of Microsoft. Thanks to Allen's wealth (about $21 billion, according to Forbes magazine), the development of South Lake Union has been able to proceed regardless of business cycles.

It's not his only project in Seattle. Over the course of the past seven years, Allen has orchestrated the construction of a new football stadium, redeveloped the old train station, financed two museums (a shrine to rock-and-roll and a science fiction museum), refurbished a classic movie palace and contributed generously to new libraries at the University of Washington and downtown. In the process, he has emerged as Seattle's most important civic figure—more important than anyone in elected office. Allen's idiosyncratic vision and passion for development are literally reshaping the city.

There is only one Paul Allen. But there are billionaires doing roughly similar things, if on a generally smaller scale, in quite a few cities around the country these days. Some, such as New York Mayor Michael Bloomberg, have used their wealth to win power the old-fashioned way—by getting elected. Others find running for office unnecessary, even irrelevant. Instead, with major cities starved for funds, they are simply using their private fortunes and the skills that made them rich to change their hometowns.

In Madison, Wisconsin, businessman Jerry Frautschi's Overture Foundation is spending $100 million to transform the dated Civic Center into the hub of a thriving arts district. The oil-rich Bass brothers have refashioned once-decrepit downtown Fort Worth into Texas' liveliest urban center. Nor are the wealthy limiting their activities to economic development. In Los Angeles, Eli Broad, a businessman who had the good sense to establish two Fortune 500 companies, has become not just the city's most generous benefactor but its most powerful private citizen, deeply involved in controversial issues that range across the policy spectrum. Not since mid-century, when David and Nelson Rockefeller operated in New York, the Chandler family ruled Los Angeles and Amon Carter rode herd on Fort Worth, have wealthy individuals held such sway and had such impact on the official apparatus of government.

For mayors and civic activists accustomed to the negative effects of corporate consolidation and the loss of local business leaders, the appearance of a new generation of activist-tycoons sometimes seems like a godsend. "The fact they are out there enables the city government to think boldly," says David Brewster, executive director of the Seattle arts group Town Hall, "because the bold thought will appeal and the bold thought might be funded. We all walk around with much bigger ideas in our head."

Not everyone is so sanguine, however. The same qualities that make someone successful in business—decisiveness, self-confidence, the relentless pursuit of a distinctive vision—can be a recipe for conflict in the public realm. For politicians who cross their paths or for citizens who reject their visions, power-wielding billionaires can be frightening. "No matter how benevolent the actor may be," insists John Fox, the head of a group called the Seattle Displacement Coalition, "it is inherently undemocratic."

AFTER THE VAULT

There is nothing new about rich people being involved in urban planning. To a great extent, it is the way planning has traditionally been done. But it used to be done largely through organizations. In Boston, there was "The Vault," an informal but powerful group named after the bank meeting room where the city's business elite met to plot downtown developments. Los Angeles had the "Committee of 25." In Seattle, it was the Rainier Club, in Cleveland, the Union Club. The names were different, but the purposes were much the same: These were the associations of local decision makers, and they wielded enormous—if often hidden—clout behind the scenes of formal city government.

Then came the upheavals of the late 1960s and early '70s. By the end of that time, private corporate power in most (although not all) American cities was in retreat. Seattle was typical: Its city council enacted a flurry of reforms designed to open meetings and development proposals to public scrutiny and limit the role of private wealth in politics.

To much of the electorate, and to many local officials, this was good news—a sign that influence at the community level was finally being democratized. But cities soon discovered that an anemic business community could be worse than the old overbearing ones. As local retailers and hometown banks disappeared, replaced by national chains, local corporate leadership withered. Even the biggest cities were not immune from these trends. By the late 1990s, Los Angeles, the nation's second-largest city, was virtually devoid of Fortune 500 home offices. "You've got to look hard to find a major corporation headquartered here," says L.A. School Superintendent Roy Romer. "It's hard to call in a key group and say, 'You represent the structure and leadership of the community, let's get this done together . . .'"

But the same processes that were displacing local companies were creating vast new fortunes for entrepreneurs shrewd enough to harness them—people such as Paul Allen, Michael Bloomberg and Eli Broad. The relationship of these new business tycoons to their hometowns was very different from that of the old business elites. The wealth of the old business leaders had often been tied directly to the health of their hometowns. The new tycoons are in business around the world; the precise economic condition of Seattle or Los Angeles isn't crucial to their fortunes, even though they may live there. And they are more loners than joiners. When they invest their money in the city, it's a personal choice—a way to pursue an individual passion. That offers both opportunity and danger.

MAN OF MYSTERY

Paul Allen is something of a mystery even in his hometown. "It's hard to get much of a fix on him," says David Brewster. "He doesn't grant interviews. There's this kind of, 'Why are you so reclusive?' But on the positive side, people feel he is what you might call an original."

Allen is 51 years old. He and Bill Gates first met as high school students in suburban Seattle. Both were computer hobbyists, and they soon found they shared the dream of making a living writing commercial software. Eventually, they both dropped out of college (Allen from Washington State, Gates from Harvard) to join forces and start a company called Microsoft. Soon thereafter, Allen purchased the rights to the operating system that would become DOS. When IBM selected DOS to run its first consumer PCs, Microsoft's explosive growth began.

A battle with cancer forced Allen to drop out of Microsoft in 1983, but he held on to his Microsoft stock. As a result, by the early '90s he was one of the world's richest men. He invested in high-tech start-ups, bought Ticketmaster and the Portland Trail Blazers basketball team, and in 1995 stepped into local politics by supporting a plan to transform South Lake Union, a gritty commercial neighborhood with a smattering of low-income housing, into a grand urban park.

Allen came late to this effort, but after he purchased 11 acres of neighborhood land for what was called the "Commons" project, he became closely identified with the effort. Opponents denounced it as a ploy to "yuppify" Seattle, and Allen soon emerged as a central figure in Seattle's nastiest class battle in many years. Despite the project's unanimous support from the city council, the electorate rejected it twice.

After the Commons defeat, Allen was left with 11 acres of undesirable land. But his public involvement escalated. In 1997, he bought the Seattle Seahawks football team, demolished its stadium, the Kingdome, and bankrolled a referendum campaign that persuaded state taxpayers to finance a new facility. He started buying even more property in South Lake Union. It soon became clear that he had a new vision for the neighborhood: He wanted to transform it into a mixed-use, environmentally sustainable biotech center. In 2002, he found an unexpected ally in Greg Nickels, Seattle's newly elected mayor.

In many ways, it was an unlikely partnership. During the mayoral campaign, most of the city's "cyber-riche," including Paul Allen himself, had sided with Nickels' opponent, incumbent Paul Schell. Nickels, a former King County councilman, had relied on labor unions and neighborhood activists for most of his support. Nickels and Allen were not exactly buddies; they had met a handful of times, and then only at social functions or sporting events. Yet soon after taking office, Nickels decided to embrace Allen's vision for South Lake Union.

After talking with researchers at the University of Washington, the mayor concluded that the next big thing was biotech—and that South Lake Union was the place to do it. There was just one problem. South Lake Union was a grungy, low-income neighborhood cut off from the rest of the city by two freeways. Nickels proposed spending nearly $500 million in state and local funds to upgrade the area's infrastructure and make South Lake Union into a desirable neighborhood.

Nickels knew that one of the effects of such massive investment would be to further enrich Paul Allen, who owns about 40 percent of South Lake Union through his Vulcan development company. However, the mayor argued that Seattle and the state of Washington stood to benefit even more. A study commissioned by the city's Office of Policy and Management estimated that developing South Lake Union could generate as many as 23,000 new jobs and $1.3 billion in new revenues for the state and city. A third of those jobs would come in the field of biotechnology.

"I was elected eight weeks to the day after September 11," Nickels says. "Boeing was laying off thousands of people, the hospitality industry was on its knees. We have since then been in the top five in unemployment as a state and our part of the state is particularly hard hit. So the question I was facing was how to build a strong economic future."

LINGERING DOUBTS

Not everyone accepts the job-creation forecasts for South Lake Union as solid.

Local critics argue that Nickels is asking for a big public investment in pursuit of an uncertain payoff. "The projections for growth are highly speculative and rest on assumptions that Seattle will capture this inordinate share of national biotech market," says John Fox. "We could take a fraction of what we are spending"—about $30,000 per job—"and generate more jobs."

Councilman Nick Licata, Allen's toughest questioner on the council, talks in similar terms. "I think in some ways Mayor Nickels is more under the influence of Paul Allen than Paul Allen is under Mayor Nickels," he says.

Others focus on the close connection between the city administration and Vulcan, Allen's development company. "They have extraordinary access to this government right now," says Peter Steinbrueck, the head of the city council's urban development and planning committee. "I haven't seen this administration raise a single objection to anything that Vulcan has proposed. Sometimes it comes out as not Vulcan's plan but the city's or the mayor's, but much of it behind the scenes is really being directed by Vulcan." In short, there is growing fear that Allen is changing Seattle from a city where neighborhoods, activists and elected officials set the vision into a place where an unelected but immensely wealthy individual does. "It inherently works to distort policymaking and planning," John Fox complains, "to reflect the vision of the individual as opposed to the many."

BROAD AGENDA

Other cities exhibit similar ambivalence toward their current billionaire benefactors. Los Angeles is feeling it about Eli Broad, the city's second-richest man, who led the homebuilders Kauffman and Broad (now KB Homes) and the annuity giant Sun America. Broad, 71, is a native New Yorker, the son of staunchly Democratic lower-middle-class parents who, in his words, "was raised on this rhetoric of the poor workers and the big bad bosses."

While Broad made much of his fortune building suburban tract houses, he has also made a major effort to strengthen central Los Angeles, arguing that "no city in world history has been great without a center." In the late '70s, he took the lead in creating the Los Angeles Museum of Contemporary Art. More recently, he stepped in to rescue the faltering downtown Disney Concert Hall project, and adjudicated a longstanding dispute between the city and Los Angeles County over development plans for Grand Avenue, a downtown boulevard that Broad is determined to transform into Los Angeles' Champs-Elysées.

Meanwhile, Broad has used his money to alter the course of city electoral politics. Two years ago, when communities in the San Fernando Valley considered seceding from Los Angeles, he attempted to reconcile the warring camps. When that effort failed, he contributed handsomely to a successful media campaign aimed at defeating the secession movement in a referendum.

At the same time, he has emerged as an often-controversial power behind the scenes in the city's school policy decisions. In 1999, Broad helped engineer a takeover of the L.A. school board. Along with Mayor Richard Riordan, he created a new school pressure group, the Coalition for Kids, and contributed more than $200,000 to its slate of candidates. The Coalition's slate swept into office, defeating three incumbents. Two years later, Broad and Riordan pressured one board member to scale down a teacher salary increase, and then, when she refused, contributed to a candidate who ousted her in the next election. Broad is said to have dangled $10 million before the president of Occidental College in an unsuccessful effort to persuade him to run against another school board member.

All this involvement in local politics has generated a backlash, notwithstanding the general good feeling about Broad's charitable efforts. Broad has become a target for criticism not only from teachers' unions but also from the Los Angeles Times, which has published accusations that Broad profited from school board construction decisions and improperly lobbied the school board to build yet another Broad project: a fancy new arts high school downtown.

SUNDANCE ADVENTURES

To the extent that Eli Broad's involvement in civic affairs is a problem, however, it's a problem many other cities would love to have. In an era in which cities compete fiercely to attract new residents among the "creative class," large donations to the arts or to downtown redevelopment can be community-defining events. That certainly has been the case in Fort Worth, where the billionaire Bass brothers have spent most of the past 20 years putting their personal stamp on the city's central core.

Heirs to the estate of legendary oilman Sid Richardson, the brothers hold the largest family fortune in

Texas. Since the early 1980s, they have been committed to using some of it to bring the center of Fort Worth back to the glory days they remembered as children, when they had gone downtown to visit their Uncle Sid.

Perhaps the most committed was Ed Bass, who had studied architecture at Yale and was determined to transform downtown into a vibrant, mixed-used area. In 1983, when Ed Bass opened a nightclub in downtown Fort Worth, with an apartment for himself on top, the area was in serious decline. "The curbs were just crumbling," says Bill Boecker, who now oversees development on the 40 blocks of Bass property downtown. "Storefronts boarded up as far as you can see." There was nothing to indicate that downtown Forth Worth would escape the fate of other declining urban centers.

Bass selected an area of low-slung buildings around Main Street and named it Sundance Square, in honor of the outlaw who had frequented the area at the turn of the century. When a natural gas explosion damaged four city blocks in 1986, Ed Bass bought much of the bombed-out property, built luxury apartments, and persuaded a theater chain to put a Cineplex downtown. To run Sundance Square, the Basses brought in a manager from the Rouse Company, developers of Boston's Quincy Market and many other urban commercial projects. To ensure the safety of their developments, they created their own private police force, reportedly the fourth largest in Tarrant County. Some locals called it, jokingly, the Basstapo.

STRAINED RELATIONS

Even when activist billionaires steer clear of local politics, their dealings with civic leaders can be fraught with difficulty. In Cleveland, Peter Lewis, chairman of the Progressive Insurance Co., has repeatedly clashed with local officials and with the hometown establishment. In the mid-1980s, Lewis approached then-Mayor George Voinovich about relocating the company's corporate headquarters to a Frank Gehry-designed skyscraper downtown. Lewis' idea wasn't exactly embraced by the establishment. At the party to unveil his plan, the head of the city's most powerful law firm turned to Lewis and asked him where he worked.

To Lewis, it was a vivid demonstration of his outsider status, a sign that the insular Cleveland establishment wasn't interested in him. The deal eventually fell apart under conditions both sides still refuse to discuss, depriving Cleveland of a landmark building. Stung by this defeat, Lewis decided to focus his philanthropic activities on Case Western Reserve University and nearby University Circle, only to watch with dismay as, he says, the university mismanaged a $36 million gift. In 2001, an angry Lewis denounced the school, describing it as "a diseased university that is collapsing and sucking Cleveland into a hole with it." To protest the establishment's supposed stranglehold over the city, Lewis suspended all of his local giving.

The moratorium remained in effect until last fall, when Lewis invited cultural institutions in University Circle to request funding for plans that would remake the area into a multi-use, "must-experience" 24/7 neighborhood. In the meantime, however, New York and other cities benefited from large gifts that might otherwise have gone to Cleveland.

Lewis may be more eccentric than any of his fellow billionaire activists. He's brutally candid about saying what's on his mind. At age 48 (he is now 70), Lewis announced he was getting divorced because he would no longer go along with the pretense of monogamy. He admits to enjoying marijuana and has bankrolled ballot initiatives across the country to legalize the use of marijuana for medical purposes. But he continues to insist on what Jennifer Frutschy, his philanthropic adviser, calls "the challenge of excellence and always doing better than what was there before."

Peter Lewis shares with Allen, Broad and the Bass brothers a zeal to break with established institutional processes—to create, as Broad puts it, "new things that don't exist, rather than presiding over the status quo." Lewis' admirers applaud him for giving Cleveland's political establishment a kick in the pants, just as Allen's supporters applaud the Microsoft tycoon for prodding city leaders to think in more ambitious terms.

If the new generation of politically active billionaires is a threat to liberal democratic values, not every liberal seems to realize it. "These guys are probably more creative partners to work with than the traditional local bank executive or chamber of commerce president," says historian Walt Crowley, the founder of historylink.org and a person known throughout Seattle for his left-leaning views. "They're definitely more fun."

Crowley should know. Paul Allen is historylink.org's most generous private donor.

IV

Legislatures

L egislators get little sympathy from citizens. From Congress to City Hall, elected representatives are more likely to be viewed with mistrust and cynicism than praised for doing the grunt work of democracy. However, these days one could be forgiven for sparing a charitable thought for legislators. They face tough decisions, institutional shake-ups, personnel turnover, new policy challenges, tighter budgets, and citizens who not only demand the impossible, but want it accomplished quickly.

State legislators have been struggling with something of a perfect storm during the past couple of years. Many states are dealing with the fallout of term limit initiatives, which are forcing as much as 70 percent of a legislature's incumbents out of office in a single electoral cycle.[1] Most people would balk at the thought of getting open-heart surgery from a committee of surgeons who had never been in an operating room before or actually cut open a patient. Yet, metaphorically speaking, that's what is happening in a number of state legislatures. Inexperienced legislators find themselves in charge of multibillion dollar budgets, running public programs that millions rely on, and facing touch decisions about how to balance the two in times of fiscal stress. That's a tall order for veteran legislators, let alone for rookie representatives who are still learning the ropes.

The fiscal stress is no laughing matter. States have been dealing with soft economies coupled with rising health care and education costs. You may know from personally painful experience that public universities are jacking up tuition rates. One of the reasons for the raises is that state legislatures are finding it all but impossible to cover their funding obligations. The result? Well . . . check your tuition bill.

As the arm of state government that raises public money and authorizes its expenditures, legislatures have had to face some tough trade-offs: Cut funding for higher education or secondary education? Split the difference and cut both? No, the federal government's No Child Left Behind Act requires new programs the states have little choice but to fund. So the states look for ways to raise a buck or save a penny: Ease back on law enforcement? Make some adjustments to welfare eligibility? Bite the bullet and raise taxes? These sorts of choices virtually ensure that legislators are going to be viewed as villains by just about everybody.

The readings in this section provide a glimpse into the challenges state legislatures, and state legislators, have been grappling with in the past year or two. What the readings make clear is that state legislatures are in an era of changes—some good, some not so good, and some very much in the eye of the beholder.

WHAT LEGISLATURES (AND LEGISLATORS) DO

State legislatures do three basic things: they pass laws, they represent the people, and they oversee public agencies in other branches of government. This sounds simple, but it involves a lot of work. A state legislature can deal with more than 20,000 proposed laws in a single year. Even the most sedate state legislature deals with more than 1,000 bills.[2] It is not easy to ensure the interests of all citizens get represented while managing that volume of lawmaking. Consider that California has a population of about 35.4 million. The California state legislature consists of eighty members in the House and forty members in the Senate,[3] which works out to about 295,000 citizens for every state legislator. Have you ever tried to keep 295,000 people happy? Most legislators would say don't bother—it can't be done. Overseeing public agencies in other branches of government is no picnic either. Most college deans will tell you it is hard enough to keep track of a single department with less than 20 faculty members. Try keeping an eye on the 2.7 million people employed in public higher education, the 1 million cops enforcing state laws, the 430,000 state utility workers, and the 714,000 corrections employees.[4]

You might say this sounds like a full-time job, but it isn't, at least not in many states. Even some huge states—Texas, for example—have part-time legislatures. Americans have long been suspicious of professional politicians, and at the state level a common way to avoid creating a professional class of elected representatives has been to make sure the legislature meets on a part-time basis and that legislators only get part-time pay. Even in states with full-time legislators, the term limits movement has tried to make sure legislators do not settle into careers as elected representatives. Politics is one of the few careers where experience can be a job disqualification. In recent years, however, there has been something of a shift in these sorts of attitudes, a change that can be most clearly seen in the latest developments in the term limits movement.

TERM LIMITS

The term limits movement, which has had an enormous impact on who serves in state legislatures, may have finally reached its high-water mark. There seems to be less enthusiasm for adopting new term limit laws, and in some states there are even the beginnings of a backlash. Although the spread of term limits may have slowed or even come to a stop, the impact of term limits is in some ways just now being felt with full force.

—Twenty-one states have adopted term limit laws. Term-limited legislators started to leave office in California and Maine in 1996, and there has been a steady stream of term-limited incumbents on their way out of office ever since. The term limits movement was primarily driven by voters, evidenced by the fact that most term limit laws were enacted through ballot initiatives (term limits are rare in states without the ballot initiative). There was support, though, from a number of legislators, especially Republicans who were frustrated with entrenched Democratic incumbents in state government. The push for expanding term limits, however, lost much of its momentum in 2004. Indeed, the current trend seems to be heading in the other direction.

There are a number of reasons the term limits movement may have peaked. There are few states left where term limit proposals stand a chance of becoming law. Most states with ballot initiatives have already passed term limit laws, and legislators in the other states show little inclination to impose term limits on themselves.

It has also become clear recently that term limits have a downside. Political analysts point out that legislators in states with term limits are less knowledgeable about issues, less in touch with their constituents, and generally less effective compared with legislators in states without term limits. Even some voters who supported term limit initiatives have changed their minds, and legislators in a number of states are actively pushing to amend or repeal term limit restrictions.[5] It is unlikely that there will be a wholesale repeal of term limit laws because they remain too popular with broad sections of the electorate. As the drawbacks of term limits become clearer, however, it seems that support for term limits is already past its all-time high (see the article on term limits by Mary Lou Cooper in this section).

CHALLENGES FOR STATE LEGISLATORS

States are facing some of their biggest policy challenges in two decades. The strong economy of the 1990s is long gone, and with it the happy times when legislators could spend more and still cut taxes. These days the challenge is not deciding which programs get more money and which taxes get cut, but which programs get cut and what or who can be squeezed for more money.

States are caught in a dilemma: a soft economy means revenues are flat or down, yet costs are increasing as are the demands for new and more expensive programs. The big culprits on the expenditure side include health care and education. Medicaid alone accounts for about 20 percent of state spending. Education is one of the single biggest expenditures of state and local governments, and many of the resources for primary, secondary, and higher education come from state government coffers (about seven cents of every dollar collected by state governments goes to higher education).[6] Just as state governments are finding it harder to fill those coffers, there is more pressure to drain them. For example, the No Child Left Behind Act, a federal law designed to increase the accountability and performance of public schools, is forcing states to help pay for costly monitoring and testing systems (see the article by Ed Fouhy in this section).

Health care and education are traditional concerns of state legislatures. State legislators increasingly have to grapple with nontraditional concerns such as international trade and immigration. Although these issues are considered more the province of the federal government than state legislatures, the states have little choice but to get more involved: the globalization of the economy affects local job opportunities; increasing immigration strains the social services provided and funded by states and localities; the war on terrorism creates a new and more integrated role for first responders like firefighters, paramedics, and police officers; and the war in Iraq has put enormous pressure on National Guard units, who are as likely to find themselves engaging in combat in the Middle East as helping deal with natural disasters in their home states. Again, legislators face tough choices on such matters. They can be passive and hope for the best (and face the wrath of voters if things turn out for the worst), or they can at least try to be proactive and shape the social and economic destiny of their states. Increasingly, legislators are opting for the latter approach; more than 800 bills dealing with international issues were introduced into state legislatures in the 2001–2002 biennium (see the article by Timothy Conlan and Joel Clark in this section).

The readings in this section illustrate the broad range of challenges and changes state with which legislatures are currently grappling. They include Ed Fouhy's extended interview with six prominent state legislators, Mary Lou Cooper's article on the decline of civility within legislative chambers, and Joel Hadfield's examination of calls to shake up the process used to draw state legislative districts. The latter issue has nearly the same potential as term limits to dictate who runs for office. These readings may not make you any more sympathetic toward legislatures or legislators, but they may give you a greater understanding of how tough the job of legislating truly is.

Notes

1. Kavan Peterson, "Term Limit Movement Is Running Out of Steam," *State Legislatures,* April 2004, 15–16

2. Kevin B. Smith, Alan Greenblatt, and John Buntin, *Governing States and Localities* (Washington, D.C.: CQ Press, 2005), 178.

3. National Conference of State Legislatures, "Current Number of Legislators, Terms of Office and Next Election Year," www.ncsl.org/programs/legman/about/numoflegis.htm (accessed April 15, 2004).

4. *The Book of the States 2003* (Lexington, Ky.: Council of State Governments, 2003), 459.

5. Peterson, "Term Limit Movement Is Running Out of Steam," 15–16.

6. U.S. Census Bureau, Table 274 in *Statistical Abstract of the United States: 2004–2005,* www.census.gov/prod/2004pubs/04statab/educ.pdf.

14

Life with Term Limits

Mary Lou Cooper

Term limits are bringing big changes to state legislatures—and not all of them are good.

From *State News,*
August 2004.

Here's how state Sen. Shane Broadway, former speaker of the Arkansas House, tells the story: A new legislator encounters a veteran staff member in the men's room at the statehouse. "How's it going?" asks the staff member. "Let's put it this way," the legislator says. "This is the only room in the Capitol where I know what I'm doing."

Versions of this story are told in term-limited states across the nation. Since they first took effect in 1996, term limits have forced out nearly a thousand legislators. As these lawmakers walked out the door, they took with them institutional memory, policy expertise and hundreds of years of collective experience, shifting the balance of power away from the legislature.

DID TERM LIMITS ACCOMPLISH WHAT THEY SET OUT TO DO?

First and foremost, term limits accomplished what former Michigan Speaker and term limits supporter Chuck Perricone calls the movement's "dirty little secret." The push for term limits, he says, was led by people who wanted to change the parties then controlling the legislatures. He thinks term limits succeeded in his state and believes that extending term lengths will iron out any wrinkles in the current system.

When it comes to throwing out incumbents and increasing turnover in the legislature, term limits are an unqualified success. Researchers report that House turnover in term-limited states increased on average about 10 percent after they were implemented in the 1990s. California went from an average House turnover of only 16 percent in the 1980s to a whopping 40 percent the following decade.

While replacing incumbents with newcomers may have brought a fresh perspective, new research indicates that term limits also led to serious and perhaps unintended consequences along the way, especially loss of power by legislative leadership and committee chairs.

In April 2004, leading academics and legislative practitioners joined forces to tackle questions about the impacts of term limits. At a conference at the University of Akron hosted by the Bliss Institute of Applied Politics, academics reported on the latest findings from a 50-state survey and from in-depth case studies in selected states. Seasoned legislative leaders added practical insights from their perch as the ultimate insiders. Here's what they found.

The Churning Power of Term Limits
Percent Turnover in the House, 1981–2000
(in states that enacted term limits)

States where term limits are in effect	1981–1990	1991–2000
Arizona	25	37
Arkansas	14	32
California	16	40
Colorado	30	34
Florida	22	32
Maine	25	37
Michigan	20	30
Missouri	20	22
Montana	30	35
Ohio	17	26
South Dakota	28	39
AVERAGE	**22**	**33**
States where term limits were enacted, but not yet in effect		
Louisiana	29	29
Nevada	35	29
Oklahoma	28	17
Average turnover in all 50 state Houses	**24**	**25**

Source: Time, Term Limits and Turnover: Trends in Membership Turnover in U.S. State Legislatures, 2003, excerpt from Table 1, Moncrief, Niemi and Powell.

A NEW BREED OF LEGISLATOR?

- The people who run for and win state legislative seats after term limits look very much like they did before in terms of gender, ethnicity, ideology, age, religion, professional background and socioeconomic status.
- Term limits didn't discourage "professional politicians." Newcomers in term-limited states were more likely than any other group to have held public office prior to their election to the legislature.

DO TERM-LIMITED LEGISLATORS BEHAVE DIFFERENTLY?

- Lawmakers in term-limited and non-term-limited states "self report" that they spend about the same amount of time studying and developing proposed legislation, specializing in policy, campaigning and fundraising.
- Legislators in term-limited chambers say they spend less time keeping in touch with constituents than those in non-term limited states, and this is especially true in states where the limits are fully implemented, not just enacted.
- Legislators in states with term limits in effect also say that when they must choose between following their own conscience or the needs of the state versus the views of their district, they are more likely to choose state and conscience above district needs.
- Term-limited lawmakers say they spend less time securing government spending or projects for their districts.

HAS POWER SHIFTED AWAY FROM TERM-LIMITED LEGISLATURES?

- The national legislative survey reveals no measurable change in the power of lobbyists after term limits. Some things get better for them and some get worse. On the one hand, lobbyists may have more information than neophytes. On the other hand, long-term lobbyist relationships with incumbents have been disrupted.
- Limited evidence suggests that if staff influence has increased, the boost applies only to personal and partisan staff, not nonpartisan staff.

- The big winners in the post-term-limits power struggle appear to be members of the executive branch—the governor and administrative agencies.
- The big losers in most cases are party leaders and committee chairs. Party leaders lose influence from the moment term limits hit the books. Committee chairs retain power by virtue of their issue expertise until they are forced from office.

ARE TERM LIMITS HERE TO STAY?

Since the movement's heyday in the 1990s when 21 states adopted term limits, the number of states with state legislative term limits has dropped to 15. However, in none of these states did voters initiate the overthrow of term limits.

State supreme courts in Massachusetts, Oregon, Washington and Wyoming overturned term limits, while state legislatures did so in Idaho and Utah. Legislative term limits remain in place in Arizona, Arkansas, California, Colorado, Florida, Louisiana, Maine, Michigan, Missouri, Montana, Nebraska, Nevada, Ohio, Oklahoma and South Dakota.

Whether or not term limits are here to stay, voters still love them. According to the advocacy group U.S. Term Limits, the average "yes" vote for term limits adopted at the ballot box was 66 percent.

Recent surveys of Michigan and Florida voters show that support for term limits is still strong and widespread among voters regardless of party, race, gender or socio-economic status. In Michigan, 71 percent of voters still support term limits, and in Florida 72 percent approve of them.

A mere 13 percent to 14 percent of Florida and Michigan voters would like to extend the length of legislative terms. Only in two states did voters say "no" to term limits when confronted with a clear ballot choice—Mississippi (55 percent voted against) and North Dakota (53 percent). Idaho voters supported the Legislature's action to overturn term limits on a referendum. Some experts, however, believe a confusing ballot question affected the outcome.

Despite overwhelming public support for term limits, many of the term-limited lawmakers interviewed said they should be repealed entirely or at the very least extended. Once in office these legislators find that it takes more than a few terms to master the job. Limited time in office forces legislators to focus on short-term issues rather than long-term, complicated matters like transportation, budgets and water. Term limits, said one termed-out leader, don't encourage a body of work from legislators, but rather produce a series of hit-or-miss issues.

Perhaps the biggest impact of term limits is the revolving door pattern for legislative leaders. Said one former speaker, "The minute I was selected, the race began to succeed me."

All of that makes running a term-limited legislature a very tough job. One former Senate president summed it up this way: "Managing the Legislature under term limits is like fielding a baseball team of free agents."

15

The New Legislative Reality: How Leaders See It

Ed Fouhy

Five prominent lawmakers examine the challenges facing state legislatures.

T hese are difficult times for lawmakers. The economy for the past three years has caused severe budget shortfalls. Health care costs continue to rise; education money is scarce and it's exacerbated by the No Child Left Behind Act. Public colleges and universities are struggling to maintain affordability as state aid is cut. Manufacturing jobs are being lost; other jobs are moving. Legislators are criticized by a skeptical press and a disengaged public. Five legislative leaders met in Washington, D.C., recently with Ed Fouhy, executive director of the Pew Center on the States, to talk about life on the job and this new legislative reality.

Ed Fouhy

Tax collections are up, but growing health care costs will make it tough for most states to balance their books. Thirty-two states expect to end FY 2004 with a modest surplus, but 33 states expect to have budget gaps for Fiscal 2005. You've all had tough budget choices to make over the last three years. Where do you go from here?

Senator Carolyn Allen

Voters have passed a large number of initiatives in our state that take an enormous amount of money right off the top of our budget. We need tax reform—we need tax reform desperately.

Representative Joe Hackney

The fiscal situation in our state is similar to that of many. We have a three-legged stool in North Carolina with state and local

From *State Legislatures,* July/August 2004.

taxation. We have sales taxes, income taxes and property taxes. Over the years, by virtue of effective political pressure, corporate income taxes have gone down as a proportion of the budget. And sales taxation has gone up because the public seems to have more tolerance for it. We have collected significant owed but unpaid taxes through aggressive collection, including out-of-state efforts. We've gone against corporate offshore or out-of-state loopholes. We have high hopes for the streamlined sales tax. We're trying to keep the state moving forward through the hard times.

Assemblyman Paul Tokasz

We're going to have our first $100 billion budget in New York this year. If you look back to the last three budget cycles, we were successful in sustaining the first difficult budget because we had tons of rainy day funds. This last budget cycle, we did broad-base taxes. Right now we have a huge issue, which is equitable funding for education.

Senator Robert Garton

Sales tax is a big income producer for our state. I think one of the major problems is we cannot collect sales tax on Internet or catalog sales. It may be as high as a $300 million loss in Indiana.

Senator Steve Rauschenberger

A logical increase in our sales taxes is to tax services. Publicly that's unacceptable, however. It is simply not going to happen.

Fouhy

Any thought of cutting programs?

Senator Allen

We're in budget negotiations now. The public does not want to be taxed, but they also continue to want certain programs that they believe are necessary.

Senator Garton

Indiana has a structural deficit of $1 billion at the end of this biennium. If you take K-12, higher ed, property tax reductions and Medicaid, you're at 80 percent of our budget. You're not going to get a billion dollar reduction out of the remaining 20 percent. But I've been saying for two years the economy is going to

improve, and now I may be right. Housing starts are up, the stock market is much better, employment is coming back, companies are hiring again, tourism is up. I think we may work our way out of it without having to increase taxes.

Fouhy

But there's an 800-pound gorilla sitting in the corner, and that's Medicaid. It's consuming 20 percent of state spending and growing 8 percent a year. What do we do?

Senator Rauschenberger

We're running Medicaid and Medicare programs that were designed in the late '60s. Their model of benefit delivery has very little to do with the structure of medical delivery today or the real needs of constituents. If the federal government wants to improve Medicaid and prevent the 800-pound gorilla from continuing to distort our medical delivery system, it has to grant states flexibility with block grants or give a lot more waivers. In Illinois, we pay for 70 percent of all long-term care beds with state Medicaid dollars. The federal government walks out the door in 61 days. Long-term care is the next gorilla. And the third piece of the puzzle is pharmaceuticals. This year, Medicaid expenditures for pharmaceuticals will exceed the budget of every single state university in Illinois.

Assemblyman Tokasz

When you look at the money we spend on health care from all sources—state programs, federal programs, insurance carriers—it's just astounding. Yet we have 44 million people with no health insurance. That's an indictment of the process. The solutions have to be borne in Washington, D.C., by people who have the political will to take on the special interests in a way that produces a better system. But I'm very pessimistic.

Senator Rauschenberger

There's a tremendous opportunity out there to experiment with improving the system without putting it all at risk. The biggest problem with wanting D.C. to do it is, if they get it wrong, we lose the best medical system in the world. That's why I would much rather see Illinois and Arizona try and learn from it.

Senator Garton

We're similar to Illinois. We have only seven public institutions of higher education. But the state appropriation for them is very close to the state's appropriation for Medicaid. Both are slightly over $1 billion. Where's the future of your state if you want to talk about setting priorities? But we're compassionate people. We are going to take care of those who qualify for Medicaid. You cannot cut a service once it's established. It seems to me if you're really dedicated to providing the service for those who need it the most, you could do it by keeping the poverty line where it was originally intended.

Fouhy

Let's talk about No Child Left Behind and its unintended consequences.

Senator Allen

In Arizona, we have precious little time to teach because we're always testing. It's putting enormous pressure on our children. There is a great deal of hostility because of the "no child with no money." Frankly, as a Republican, the idea that this administration is mandating how we will run our education system is well-meaning, but not well received in Arizona.

Senator Rauschenberger

I think No Child Left Behind is symptomatic of the public distrust and dissatisfaction with public education. We're doing an abysmal job in the K-12 system for our kids across the country. We continue to fall behind competitively with other countries. States have been custodians of Harry Truman's educational system for almost 50 years. We're running Harry Truman's calendar, Harry Truman's school day. We're teaching in a Socratic method more than 2,000 years old. No Child Left Behind is absolutely one of the worst things that Congress has done in the last two decades. Some well-intended, 27-year-old education staffer on the Hill wrote a 1,200-page bill that attacks the very core and fiber of American public education.

Representative Hackney

No Child Left Behind represents a failure of federalism. The problems it's created are far more severe than any benefit we are going to see. The federal government is too far from the schoolroom to be making the kinds of rules it's made in No Child Left Behind. Those should be left to the state or local school boards. I do think financial participation by Congress is in the national interest. We have a global marketplace, and we have to train people to work in it. But micromanagement is the problem.

Assemblyman Tokasz

No Child Left Behind is an attempt to system manage from Washington, D.C. The people who brought us the Pentagon are now trying to write a one-size-fits-all regulatory statute that works on 50 state systems that have different local origins, different political cultures, different funding bases. I agree it's a failure of federalism.

Representative Hackney

There's no single, best answer. What works on an Indian reservation in Arizona probably isn't what works in Chapel Hill. You have to have experimentation, and you have to have the flexibility to allow successful experiments to work. By all accounts the two states that have done a good job with student test improvement are Texas and North Carolina. But now we have to retrofit our program to No Child Left Behind. I don't see the wisdom in that.

Fouhy

Do you hear from your constituents when a school is labeled as a failing school?

Senator Rauschenberger

Every place I go in Illinois, there's frustration with the schools. Property taxpayers are frustrated with the state. Parents are frustrated with their school boards and superintendents. With all due respect, I think we're rearranging the deck chairs on the Titanic. We know a lot about how kids learn, but I don't see any innovations. When John F. Kennedy was president, 85 out of 100 school kids had a parent at home to serve them lunch. Today we have single-parent families and two-income families, but our schools have not adapted their hours or their calendars.

Representative Hackney

I agree there are some serious problems in public education. But I disagree that there isn't innovative thinking. Former Governor Jim Hunt spent a career in North Carolina directing funds to early childhood education based on the latest research out of the Frank Porter Graham Child Development Center, which is in my district. We have allocated money to put technology into schools, which we didn't used to do. So there are some positive changes. Teacher pay remains a serious problem in all of our states. In my state, we can't recruit enough teachers because of the salaries we pay.

Senator Garton

I'm not sure we've determined if education is a process or a product. Is it the process of conveying, receiving and understanding or is it a product that measures our schools—testing. We really ought to get more into the process and how you teach individual kids and how they learn.

Fouhy

What about the university system? In some states they're saying we're cutting back on our support of the university. It's burning up too many dollars. We're going to give the citizens who need it state scholarships, and let them go wherever they want.

Senator Allen

The universities have been one of the favorites to attack in Arizona because we don't have a lot of other areas where we can cut. We have people in our legislature who don't like large universities. This year one of the bigger fights is do we give another $25 million to the universities for higher enrollment or do we go to all-day kindergarten?

Representative Hackney

In North Carolina, we have continued to fund universities through the hard times. We value our universities as one of the primary engines of our economic growth. Looking to the future with biotechnology and genetics initiatives and all kinds of new knowledge-based initiatives, we think the universities are very important.

Fouhy

Outsourcing jobs overseas is an issue facing many of your states. What do you think the implications of job creation are in the current economy?

Senator Rauschenberger

Outsourcing is an emotional issue. It's made legislators very aware of policies that affect corporate decisions on where they locate. Probably two-thirds of the outsourcing that has been talked about in Illinois is actually not outsourced overseas. It's outsourced to states that have more attractive business climates, have better work rules, tort reform and have done more proactive things. I think American higher education is not meeting the challenge or the expectation of future job markets. If you're going to win in a skills-based economic race, you're going to have to keep notching up the credibility and the skill level of our workforce.

Assemblyman Tokasz

Much of the discussion about outsourcing is political, and we are all guilty of that. What legislators can do is look at the tax breaks we give businesses, but ensure that the total job creation goal is met by the company. Enforcement of environmental standards internationally in places that are producing our steel and enforcement of human rights issues in countries that are taking a lot of our manufacturing jobs—that's where the trade policy nationally has to be looked at, and that's where the pressure must be brought to bear.

Senator Garton

We just made Indiana's research development tax credit permanent. It gives certainty to business. We need to look at preferences for in-state companies for in-state government work. Why are we contracting for state government work overseas? The business community is constantly on us to invest more in education, to improve the quality of life. I don't think businesses take quality of life and education into consideration when they move to Mexico or India or wherever.

Representative Hackney

We're a high growth state, so we need more teachers than we can train, more medical personnel. Biotech same thing. We're trying to train people through our community college and university systems. We've seen the exacerbation of the difference between high-income and low-income work populations. Somebody calculated that it takes $13 an hour for a single parent and child to live in an urban area in North Carolina, and people in tourism jobs aren't making $13 an hour. So training is very important.

What Is the New Legislative Reality?

"It's a cynical press, cynical public—we can do nothing right. However, as long as you try to create a perception, particularly among the members, of fairness and civility, you're going to work through it."

—*Senator Robert Garton*

"Constituents want quick solutions to very difficult problems and that's driven by the media demanding those solutions. I'm a believer that legislative bodies should move slowly. You need to build consensus. Consensus is not easy. Consensus takes time. We have to resist that impulse to try to do a quick fix and understand the broader ramifications of what we're trying to do."

—*Assemblyman Paul Tokasz*

"With term limits in my state, there's less stability. There is no respect for institutional memory. There's very little respect for the institution itself. People come in and

immediately run for leadership, but they have virtually no real understanding of the process or how you build coalitions. They tend to be very party faithful, which isn't helpful in trying to break gridlocks."

—*Senator Carolyn Allen*

"Partisan divisions are going up, money in politics is going up, party discipline is going down. And our tax structures are really not designed for today's economy. In my caucus and in my chamber, the people who are successful are respectful of other members. They're the people who listen, as well as talk. They have trust across party lines. They're the people who have a strong local base and a good, sound footing in their districts as opposed to a single-issue candidate. Those are the kinds of legislators that make the place work. I think in this new climate, those factors become increasingly important."

—*Representative Joe Hackney*

We have done three things in terms of public works that have helped our economy. We passed a massive capital bond issue for our 16 public universities. We adopted a clean smokestacks environmental initiative to retrofit coal-fired plants with scrubbers. That's being paid for by the utilities and rate payers. Huge numbers of people are employed in that project. We also have a big transportation public works initiative under way.

Fouhy

What do you see as the biggest change in the legislature, whether it's the institution or the public policy? Change that has happened or is happening?

Senator Allen

Lack of civility.

Assemblyman Tokasz

The public demanding an immediate solution.

Senator Allen

Term limits.

Representative Hackney

The impact of big money in politics.

Senator Rauschenberger

The explosion of information in communication.

Senator Garton

The status and the significance of state government. Within the last 30 years, legislatures have become important. We have been ahead of the federal government on welfare reform, school reform, environmental reform. We have been the where the action is.

Senator Rauschenberger

That's why we have the stablest democracy in the world, because we have a shared dispersal of power.

16

The International Activities of State Legislatures[1]

Timothy J. Conlan and Joel F. Clark

Globalized trade and the war on terriorism have created an international role for state legislatures.

O ver the past 30 years, American state governments have become increasingly active in the international arena.[2] Most states now view international trade as an integral component of their economic development strategies. By 1999, state governments had opened over 240 offices in 34 foreign countries to promote exports of state products, and most pursued foreign direct investment with similar energy and creativity.[3] Governors and other state leaders routinely travel the globe in pursuit of markets and investments. States along the southern and northern borders of the United States have increasingly engaged with their counterparts in Mexico and Canada over common policy concerns, from immigration to environmental protection. State public colleges and universities attract thousands of international students each year, while state departments of Natural Resources and Environmental Protection have formed environmental partnerships with countries around the world.

To date, our understanding of these developments has stemmed mainly from high profile executive initiatives, such as gubernatorial trade missions and the development of executive branch offices and programs to promote trade and investment in the global economy. But, state legislatures also have participated in the globalization of state government, drawing upon their fiscal and legislative powers and their expertise in the practice of representative democracy. Although there is wide variation in state legislative involvement in the international arena, reflecting differences in state resources and priorities, legislatures as a whole have joined with the rest of state government to become increasingly active participants in the global arena of the 21st century.

From *Spectrum: The Journal of State Government,* Spring 2004.

In order to explore the international activities of state legislatures in more detail, this article draws upon three sets of data. First, a questionnaire was mailed to directors of state legislative research support agencies.[4] Second, the authors conducted computerized searches of bills and resolutions introduced and passed in all 50 states, covering a period from 1991–2002. Finally, case studies were conducted in five regionally diverse states, allowing for in-depth interviews with legislators and staff.[5]

STATE LEGISLATIVE INVOLVEMENT IN INTERNATIONAL AFFAIRS

The core function of legislative bodies is to draft, debate and adopt new laws. Thus, the most important indicator of global involvement by state legislatures is their willingness to consider and adopt internationally-directed legislation. A comprehensive analysis of state legislative activity across the 50 states shows that, on the whole, legislatures have indeed been active in this area, considering and adopting hundreds of bills and resolutions with significant international content during the past decade.

The Scope of International Lawmaking. Measuring the level of international activity among the 50 state legislatures is a complex task. To accomplish it, this study relied on multiple searches of the Lexis/Nexis state legislative database. Using a combination of search terms such as "international trade," "human rights," "Kyoto Treaty," and specific country names (Cuba, China and Mexico), bill titles and abstracts were analyzed in multiple waves of searches. Where ambiguities about bill content were evident, a search of the complete bill text was conducted. In some cases, a state's own legislative database was searched to supplement the results of the Lexis/Nexis search.

This search process identified approximately 823 bills and resolutions with significant international content introduced in the 2001–2002 legislative sessions of the 50 states.[6] These range from resolutions memorializing Congress and the president to take—or refrain from taking—a specific foreign policy action to substantive laws utilizing the powers of state governments to affect immigration, international trade, environmental protection, border relations with Canada and Mexico, and national defense. Approximately 270 of these bills and resolutions were enacted into law or, if simple resolutions, passed by the requisite legislative chamber.[7]

The Substance of International Legislation. The subject matter of state international legislation is varied and evolving. In the 2001–2002 legislative session, anti-terrorism legislation was the single most common focus of legislative action. This clearly reflected the impact of the September 11, 2001 terrorist acts, and it makes that legislative session distinct from earlier sessions examined. State bills and resolutions considered to have a focus on international terrorism included such proposed and adopted legislation as a Minnesota bill establishing new procedures for declaring national security health emergencies and providing criminal penalties for bioterrorism,[8] a Texas resolution memorializing victims of the terrorist attack on the U.S.S. Cole,[9] and a Virginia bill that expands the state law on wiretaps to enable a wiretap when terrorist activity is suspected.[10]

As Table 1 indicates, trade related legislation was the second most common form of international legislation introduced in the 2001–2002 period. Examples here include such legislation as a New Jersey bill to establish a foreign trade zone incentive program,[11] a Minnesota resolution urging state and local government authority be protected in international trade agreements,[12] and a California bill to establish a position of California liaison to the WTO.[13] Antiterrorism and trade legislation were followed in frequency by country-specific bills and resolutions, border policy issues and defense-related legislation. Examples of these types of bills and resolutions are: a concurrent resolution in North Dakota urging that the trade embargo with Cuba be lifted, a bill to establish a Border Trade Advisory Commission in Texas,[14] and a West Virginia resolution urging the state's congressional delegation to work to implement a National Missile Defense System.[15] The "other" legislation category includes items ranging from humanitarian resolutions, environmental issues, special tax provisions for overseas activities, reciprocal education agreements, and other diverse issues. A Massachusetts bill to provide for the protection of tropical rain forests by restricting state purchases of certain wood products[16] represents one example that falls into the "other" category.

Non-Legislative Activity. State legislative involvement in international affairs extends beyond legislative activity. For example, according to the survey of state legislative research staffs, approximately half of all state legislatures received at least one delegation of foreign leaders or parliamentarians during the 2001–2002 period, and about

Table 1 Substantive Makeup of International Legislation, 2001–2002

	Trade	Human Rights	Defense	Anti-Terrorism	Environment	Country-Specific	Border Issues	Other	Total
Bills Introduced									
Number	218	27	46	297	19	87	50	92	836
Percent	26%	3%	6%	36%	2%	10%	6%	11%	100%
Bills Passed									
Number	71	5	7	92	8	40	14	33	270
Percent	26%	2%	3%	34%	3%	15%	5%	12%	100%

half of all responding legislatures sent at least one delegation of members to a foreign country. Overall, about 50 different foreign countries were involved, either sending or receiving delegations. The largest number of visits came via delegations from East Asian countries, followed by Eastern Europe and the former Soviet Union, Western Europe and Africa. U.S. legislators who went abroad most frequently visited countries in East Asia, followed by Western Europe, Latin America and Africa.

The creation of new institutional structures and procedures for dealing with international affairs represents another area of state legislative activity. Twenty-six percent of responding legislatures had created a committee or subcommittee with major responsibility for dealing with issues of international trade or international affairs. Examples include the Alaska Senate Special Committee on World Trade and State/Federal Relations, the California Senate Select Committee on International Trade Policy and State Legislation, the Oklahoma Joint Special Committee on International Development, and Washington State's Task Force on International Trade

Agreements and the Role of the State. As more state legislatures have become engaged internationally, they have also begun to institutionalize their procedures for international protocol. Twenty-three of the states responding to the international survey (57 percent) had designated a legislator or staff person with major protocol responsibilities for the legislature.

TRENDS IN LEGISLATIVE INTERNATIONAL ACTIVITY

In order to examine trends in state international lawmaking over time, this study examined international legislative activity during three periods: 1991–1992, 1995–1996 and 2001–2002.

As Table 2 shows, there was a clear pattern of increased activity over time. The number of international bills and resolutions introduced increased 17 percent between 1991–1992 and 1995–1996, and the number of bills and resolutions passed during this period increased 15 percent. The increase was even more substantial in the latter period. Between the 1995–1996 session and 2001–2002, the number of international bills and resolutions introduced grew by a whopping 105 percent and the numbers passed increased by 225 percent. This rapid pace of growth is illustrated in Figure 1.

Along with overall growth, the composition of state international legislation has also changed over

Table 2 The Growth of International Legislation, 1991–2002

	2001–2002 TOTALS		1995–1996 TOTALS		1991–1992 TOTALS	
	Introduced	Passed	Introduced	Passed	Introduced	Passed
Total	823	270	402	83	343	72

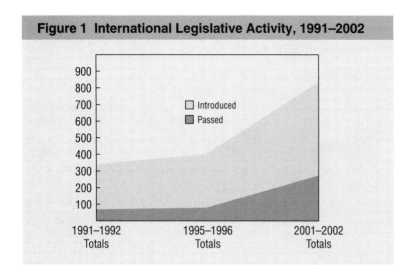

Figure 1 International Legislative Activity, 1991–2002

agenda in the early and mid-1990s, when approximately 60 percent of all international bills introduced were trade related. About 15 percent of all international bills and resolutions in these earlier periods were connected to specific countries-resolutions concerning Israel and the Middle East, Cuba, Armenia, and the like. The remainder of the legislation introduced dealt with a broad range of other topics, from human rights and the environment to border issues and defense. As noted earlier, and as Figure 2 makes clear, the composition of international legislation changed dramatically in 2001–2002, reflecting a new and pronounced concern with issues of terrorism. As noted earlier in Table 1, about 36 percent of international bills and resolutions introduced in 2001–2002 dealt with issues of terrorism, while trade related legislation comprised about 26 percent.

time. Figure 2 shows the changing composition of international bills and resolutions introduced during the three time periods examined in this study. Trade-related bills and resolutions clearly dominated the states' international

As Figure 3 shows, a very similar pattern emerges when looking at the trends in international bills and resolutions that were passed by state legislatures. Again, the dramatic growth in legislation adopted in the most recent period was driven mainly by the proliferation of new terrorism-related laws and resolutions adopted after September 11, 2001. About one-third of all legislation passed in this period was terrorism related. Trade-related bills and resolutions remained the next most popular form of legislation passed in the 2001–2002 period, constituting one-quarter of all adoptions. In percentage terms, this was a steep decline from the 1995–1996 period, when 70 percent of bills and resolutions adopted were trade related. However, it is important to note that, even with that percentage decline, slightly more trade legislation was passed in 2001–2002 than in 1995–1996—71 versus 58 bills and resolutions. The shrinking percentage is simply a reflection of how greatly the overall number of bills and resolutions increased in the recent period.

When interpreting these trend data, it is important to remember that data were collected

Figure 2 Numbers and Types of International Bills Introduced, 1991–2002

	1991–1992	1995–1996	2001–2002
Other	61	51	184
Border	28	25	50
Country	53	65	87
Terrorism	4	28	297
Trade	197	232	218

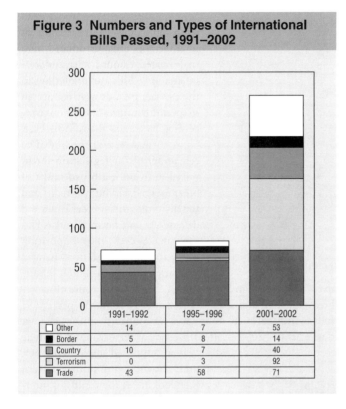

Figure 3 Numbers and Types of International Bills Passed, 1991–2002

	1991–1992	1995–1996	2001–2002
Other	14	7	53
Border	5	8	14
Country	10	7	40
Terrorism	0	3	92
Trade	43	58	71

increased substantially in the aggregate. For example, in the 2001–2002 period, international legislative activity varied from zero bills and resolutions introduced or passed in four states to highs of 93, 81 and 66 bills or resolutions introduced in Texas, Virginia and Minnesota respectively. Overall, the 50 state legislatures averaged 16.7 bills and resolutions introduced and 5.4 bills and resolutions passed.

International travel and the reception of foreign delegations also varied widely. Fifteen states reported receiving no foreign delegations, although many may have received international visitors on a less formal basis. At the opposite extreme is California, which reported a high of 637 foreign dignitaries from 67 different countries in 2001. Other states also reported significant numbers of foreign delegations. Minnesota, for example, reported receiving 77 foreign delegations over a two-year period from 2000–2001, with over 400 foreign visitors. Texas reported receiving 260 delegations over this same period.

Similar variations existed in state legislators' travel abroad. Sixteen states reported sending no legislative delegations abroad during the 2001–2002 period, or they lacked data on the subject. Fifteen states reported legislative travel to 18 different countries. Indiana, for example, reported legislative visits to eight countries in Europe and Asia during this period.

for only six of the 12 years between 1991 and 2002. This is helpful for gaining an overview of general tendencies over time, but it means that issues that arose and faded quickly in one of the non-sampled years may not be captured in this data. One example of such an issue involves state laws and resolutions regarding global warming. There were relatively few pieces of legislation addressing this issue in the 2001–2002 session, but during the period from 1997 to 1999, 75 bills and resolutions addressing the Kyoto protocols were introduced in the various state legislatures, and 21 of these were adopted. By 2002, approximately one-third of all states had adopted policies through legislation or executive order to reduce emissions of greenhouse gases.[17]

VARIATIONS IN STATE INTERNATIONAL ACTIVITY

States vary widely in their policies, and state international activities are no exception to this pattern. The international activities examined in this study vary considerably from state to state, even though they have

MOTIVATIONS BEHIND STATE INTERNATIONAL ACTIVITY

What motivates state legislators to become involved with international issues? States have modest powers in the field compared to the national government, and constituents express far more interest in domestic policy issues, such as education and transportation. Yet, many legislators do become involved with international issues. The reasons for this are as numerous as the legislators themselves, but several motivational patterns are apparent from the questionnaire and interviews with legislators and legislative staff.

Legislative Sponsorship. In both the survey questionnaire and interviews, the most commonly cited motivation for sponsoring international bills and resolutions involved constituency influence and requests. This was mentioned as a major motivating factor by 86 percent of the survey respondents. As one legislative aide put it: "An individual legislator typically gets contacted by a constituent active with an organization, and we have large immigrant populations in this state." For example, legislators and staff in several states related sponsorship of resolutions on human rights in China to the presence and activities of Chinese Americans and recent Chinese immigrants. African-Americans were leading supporters of bills and resolutions relating to Africa in many states.

Direct constituency involvement is supplemented on many issues by lobbying campaigns orchestrated by organized groups. Far more interest groups are now engaged in lobbying at the state level than in the past, and this expansion of state level lobbying is evident on international issues as well as domestic ones.[18] For example, the Armenian National Institute in Washington, D.C. has worked nationwide to secure the passage of state resolutions commemorating the genocide of Turkish Armenians in 1915–1923.[19] Agricultural groups have lobbied states to encourage lifting the U.S. trade embargo with Cuba, while environmental groups have lobbied states to address global warming.[20] Even foreign governments have been involved in formal or informal lobbying efforts. The Mexican foreign ministry has worked to persuade states, as well as local governments and private firms, to accept the Mexican *matricula consular* as a valid form of ID in the United States.[21]

Legislators' own substantive policy concerns are another important motivation for sponsoring international bills and resolutions. This factor was mentioned as a major motivation by 59 percent of the survey respondents. One Minnesota legislator, who has been active sponsoring resolutions concerning international trade agreements, National Missile Defense, and trade with Cuba, put it this way: "I grew up in an era when international issues were vitally important—in the 1960s and 1970s—so it just seems natural. People tease me about wanting to chair the [nonexistent] State Foreign Relations Committee." Personal policy concerns were mentioned as the driving force behind New Jersey and California legislators' efforts to address the preemption of state authority by international trade agreements as well.

Legislative policy activists often belong to networks and organizations that link legislators across state boundaries and that aid in the diffusion of policy ideas from state to state. Many conservative legislators are members of the American Legislative Exchange Council, which has taken positions on several international issues, including trade sanction legislation and state greenhouse gas initiatives. On the left are organizations like the Center for Policy Alternatives and the State Environmental Resource Center, which develop model state legislation on issues ranging from immigration to labor and energy issues. Non-partisan organizations representing state governments and legislators, such as The Council of State Governments and its regional affiliates and the National Conference of State Legislatures also play an important role in policy diffusion.

Mass media were a third motivating factor of significance. Media attention to issues and problems, whether in the mass broadcast and print media or in more specialized policy newsletters, were identified as a major source of inspiration for international activities and a source of policy ideas by 59 percent of survey respondents. The most telling example of this media role is apparent in anti-terrorism policy, which went quickly from a secondary to a leading focus of state policy initiatives in the wake of the September 11 terrorist attacks.

FEDERAL INVOLVEMENT IN STATE INTERNATIONAL POLICYMAKING

Because foreign policy is primarily a national government responsibility, one might expect to find a high degree of federal involvement when state legislatures engage in international activities. This is often not the case, however. Although there have been high profile cases of federal-state conflict over state involvement in foreign policy—as in the case of state efforts to sanction firms doing business in Burma/Myanmar—such cases of conflict and close intergovernmental interaction appear to be the exception rather than the rule.

For example, according to our international activities survey, federal officials generally do not testify on international issues before state legislative committees. Eighty-nine percent of survey respondents indicated that this rarely occurs. Similarly, 80 percent of respondents indicated that federal officials rarely lobby behind the scenes on such issues. Trade and environmental protection were identified as the issues most likely to generate federal efforts to lobby or influence state government, and officials with the departments of Agriculture and Commerce were considered to be the most likely to testify before the legislature. Finally, only two states (Washington and Maryland) reported state legislative consultations with the office of U.S. Trade Representative.

The survey of legislative research directors also uncovered only modest levels of concern about the preemptive effects of international trade treaties, although such apprehension appears to vary considerably over time and from state to state. For example, 20 percent of state respondents did not consider federal preemption of state authority via international trade treaties to be a major policy concern at this time. The largest number—slightly over 50 percent—described such preemption as an occasional concern.

About one-quarter of legislative respondents did describe trade-based preemption as a major concern, although none put it in the category of highest policy priorities. Illustrative of these concerns, at least two states have established legislative committees or task forces to monitor the effects of international trade negotiations on state legislative prerogatives,[22] and legislators in various states have sponsored resolutions memorializing the president and Congress to respect state authority when negotiating and ratifying international treaties.[23] According to questionnaire respondents, the policy areas where legislators are most concerned about federal preemption are environmental protection, labor regulations and transportation.

Overall, state legislators mirror broader social divisions about the costs and benefits of international trade. Some emphasize the positive dimensions of trade for economic growth; they tend to support new treaties to open markets and expand trade, including state resolutions urging Congress to support presidential "fast track" authority in trade negotiations. Others are more concerned about negative effects of globalization, especially on declining industries and the environment. Depending on the nature of the local economy, some legislatures may be dominated by one of these positions, while others, such as California, are divided.[24]

THE FUTURE OF STATE LEGISLATIVE INVOLVEMENT IN INTERNATIONAL AFFAIRS

State involvement in the international arena has grown significantly over time, though often in fits and starts.

On the executive side, earlier research of state trade agencies found surprising volatility in their budgets, staffs, and overseas offices, often in response to changing state fiscal conditions and gubernatorial priorities.[25] This study finds a similar pattern on the legislative side of state government. Legislative concern with international issues increased substantially during the 1990s, but the pace of change and the issues of concern were subject to rapid shifts.

In part, this variability reflects changes in the issue environment. National debates over the negotiation and ratification of new international treaties can generate a burst of state legislative concern with international issues, as was evident during the 1990s with the NAFTA and Kyoto treaties and during 2002 with international terrorism and homeland security. The condition of the economy and the state fiscal climate can also shift legislators' attention. As one California Assembly staffer observed: "In a time of state education and health care crises, how important are these international trade issues in comparison?"

Despite some volatility, state legislatures are likely to grow increasingly concerned with international issues. Globalization makes it harder and harder to carve out distinct, autonomous realms of state policy that are untouched by international affairs. Law enforcement, education, emergency preparedness and economic development have all become increasingly intertwined with international forces. At same time, the federal government relies increasingly on state and local authority and resources to deal effectively with many problems and issues in these areas. Thus, we are likely to see international affairs become increasingly intergovernmentalized in the future, creating pressures and opportunities for expanded state legislative involvement in the international arena. The real question for the future may be, not whether legislatures are actively involved with international issues but whether the federal-state relationship in international affairs is predominantly cooperative or conflictual in nature.

Notes

1. This article grows out of a report sponsored by The Council of State Governments, with funding and support provided by the U.S. Agency for International Development. Special thanks go to Chris Whatley and Magdalena Mook of CSG, and to

Richard Sheppard, formerly with U.S. AID. The authors would also like to thank Suzanne Blagg and Kristina Dorville, both graduate students at George Mason University. Each devoted enormous energy to assisting with the collection and assimilation of state legislative data. The authors also express their deepest appreciation to all of the state legislators, legislative staff, and other government officials who gave generously of their time to respond to our questionnaires and participate in the interviews that made this report possible. The authors are grateful for their candor and willingness to help give us a better understanding of state international activities. Very special thanks are due to Kevin Donahue, Patrick Flahaven, Chris Kuykendall, Christine Sasseville, Clarke Straughan and Nick Vucinich.

2. See Michelle Sager, *One Voice or Many? Federalism and International Trade* (LFB Scholarly Publishing, 2002); and Earl H. Fry, *The Expanding Role of State and Local Governments in U.S. Foreign Affairs* (Council on Foreign Relations Press, 1998).

3. David Naftzger, "The States' Role (if any) in Foreign Affairs," *State Legislatures,* 26 (Dec 2000): 24.

4. After two rounds of mailings and follow-up calls, questionnaires were received from 40 states.

5. The states were California, Texas, Virginia, New Jersey and Minnesota.

6. Three states, Mississippi, New Jersey and Virginia, hold their legislative elections in off-years, so the period under study includes portions of two different legislative sessions for these states.

7. These totals of 823 bills and resolutions introduced and 270 passed should be taken as close approximations rather than precise estimates, however. Although they were carefully compiled, the exact numbers can vary according to several different factors, such as the treatment of companion and substitute bills, definitions of international content, and the search engine employed.

8. House Bill 3031, 2002.

9. HR 143, 2001.

10. House Bill 38, 2001.

11. Assembly bill A880, 2002.

12. HF3733, 2002.

13. SB 945, 2001.

14. Senate Bill 195, 2001.

15. House Concurrent Resolution 37, 2002.

16. House Bill 2261, 2001.

17. Barry Rabe, *Greenhouse and Statehouse: The Evolving State Government Role in Climate Change* (Pew Center on Global Climate Change, 2002), 7.

18. Clive Thomas and Ronald Hrebnar, "Interest Groups in the States," in Virginia Gray, Russell Hanson, and Herbert Jacob, *Politics in the American States,* 7th ed. (CQ Press, 1999).

19. Armenian National Institute, International Affirmation of the Armenian Genocide, www.armenian-genocide.org.

20. See Elizabeth Benjamin, "Activists Air Plans to Fight Warming," TimesUnion.com, November 21, 2002; and Rabe, *Greenhouse and Statehouse.*

21. "ID cards offer peace of mind," CalifornianOnline.com, November 26, 2002.

22. California Senate Select Committee on International Trade Policy and State Legislation and Washington State's Task Force on International Trade Agreements and the Role of the State.

23. See, for example, Minnesota S.B. 3468, "Memorializing the President, Congress and the Governor to ensure that international trade agreements respect the traditional authority of state and local governments to protect the public interest," which passed the state Senate in 2002.

24. See the appendix case study of the California legislature.

25. Timothy J. Conlan and Michelle Sager, *International Dimensions of American Federalism: State Policy Responses to a Changing Global Environment* (Washington: U.S.—Asia Environmental Partnership & Council of State Governments, 1997).

17

Mind Your Manners

Mary Lou Cooper

Can legislative civility survive
polarized voters and
contentious politics?

I t's really no surprise that elected officials hold sharply divergent
views. So do their constituents.

That was the message from Shawnta Watson Walcott, director of
communications for polling firm Zogby International, when she
spoke at the combined 2004 *CSG-WEST* and CSG State Trends
and Leadership Forum last September.

But does dissent have to mean disrespect? State officials and academics discussed that question during a forum on legislative civility
convened by *CSG-WEST's* Western Legislative Futures Forum. Alaska
Rep. Lesil McGuire, chair of the committee, asked participants: Can
legislative civility survive polarized voters and contentious politics?

WHY ARE PEOPLE SO CRANKY?

Political and personal civility are hot topics for the 21st century,
McGuire said, and she pointed to a growing number of popular
magazine articles with titles like "The Rude Age" and "Why is
Everyone So Cranky?"

In the 2004 presidential election, voters were bombarded by
political commentators who talked endlessly about conservative-
leaning "red states" and liberal-leaning "blue states." According to
Walcott, not only are voters polarized on the big issues of Iraq, gay
marriage, gun control, the environment and abortion, we are a
nation divided on the small stuff too.

When Zogby pollsters looked at undecided voters (about 10 percent of all voters), they found disagreement over preferences in ice
cream, soft drinks, TV stations, coffee, movies and more. Undecided

From *State News*,
January 2005.

voters in "red" states, for example, preferred Haagen-Dazs to Ben & Jerry's ice cream and liked to get their news from Fox TV. Undecided voters in blue states drank Starbucks' coffee and got their news from CNN.

These political, social and cultural divisions seem to be increasingly accompanied by a lack of tolerance in the legislative process. But political incivility isn't new, McGuire noted. When Thomas Jefferson ran for president, John Adams' supporters called him an atheist, an anarchist, a demagogue, a coward and a trickster. Andrew Jackson was accused of adultery, gambling, cockfighting, bigamy, drunkenness, theft, lying and murder.

Elected officials need to be concerned about civility or lack of it, said McGuire, because "all of us who run for office must eventually turn to governing."

> *"Legislatures are adversarial forums where strong disagreements flourish. The trick is to disagree without being disagreeable."*
>
> —Nevada State Sen. Carl Dodge, 1981

WHY CAN'T LAWMAKERS BE MORE CIVIL?

University of Maryland professor and national political civility expert Eric Uslaner shared his insights with forum participants. Uslaner is the author of *The Decline of Comity in Congress.* When he first began looking at the subject of civility, Uslaner said, people attacked each other across party lines and within party lines. He recalled that in 1985, Newt Gingrich called Sen. Bob Dole, then Republican Senate leader, the tax collector for the welfare state and that by today's standards that would almost be a compliment.

More recently, attacks have become far more partisan and far more personal—in both Congress and in state legislatures. Uslaner noted that in Wisconsin, a state with a long tradition of civility, lawmakers started calling each other Nazis on the floor. One member banged a microphone into a desk, breaking the desk.

So what brought about all this incivility? Uslaner disagreed with those who think that structural reforms that took power away from central leaders are to blame. Incivility exists not just in the "reformed" U.S. House of Representatives, but also in the U.S. Senate that never reformed itself, in many state legislatures, on the U.S. Supreme Court and in "every little city council you can imagine."

Neither does Uslaner attribute incivility to divided government where one party controls the legislature and another controls the executive branch. He pointed out that Dwight Eisenhower actually preferred to deal with Democratic leaders of Congress. Uslaner also disagrees that "the media did it." Despite the outlandish mike grabbers like former Democratic Congressman Jim Traficant, viewers get their impressions of Congress from leaders, who still get the bulk of face time on TV. Uslaner also disputed the idea that incivility is the fault of newcomers, such as those in term-limited states. Even lawmakers who stick around a long time primarily talk to colleagues with whom they agree.

More important than all these things, said Uslaner, is our polarized party system. "The reason why our legislatures are so polarized is that our citizens are so polarized." In the past, conservative Democrats and moderate Republicans bridged some of the gaps created by partisan differences. Now there's no such thing as a loyal opposition. Instead of seeing someone who disagrees with us as someone who just has a different world view, it's now an "I'm right and you're morally defective" world.

Uslaner said that this distrust between people who think differently is not just a political phenomenon, but also a social and cultural phenomenon. He pointed to research from 1960 that found 58 percent of Americans agreed that most people can be trusted. By 2002 and 2003, only 33 percent felt this way.

Long-time legislative observer and political author Alan Rosenthal with the Eagleton Institute of Politics at Rutgers University agreed that the most important cause of legislative incivility is partisan competition. And that competition doesn't stop after the election is over.

Rosenthal suggested that the legislative session is part of the campaign, and that more than ever before, campaigning and governing are totally intermixed. "When you're targeting members of the other party in a chamber, it's difficult to maintain friendships or civility. It's not only that you campaign in a guy's district, but you're killing him in the legislative process as well."

In addition to partisanship, Rosenthal said that outside interest group advocacy, particularly on ideological and social issues, contributes heavily to legislative incivility. "They do believe the other side is the enemy and is evil."

Ironically, said Rosenthal, tougher ethics laws also contribute to incivility in legislative chambers. "The lobbyists used to bring members together across parties," he reported. But that doesn't happen as much now, and the legislature is probably better in some ways for it. However, when lawmakers never get together socially, it's tougher to build consensus across the aisle.

Are there consequences to incivility? Yes, says Rosenthal: the legislature as an institution suffers when there is no recognition that the other side has a legitimate point of view. The lack of civility feeds the public's negative perception of legislatures, according to the scholar.

Legislators themselves had a few things to say about the consequences of incivility. They mentioned gridlock in getting the work done, lack of respect for the institution, and lack of trust in the process. Incivility, some said, leads to an atmosphere of retaliation and gamesmanship. Good public policy and constituent service suffer, and the public's confidence in the legislature goes down.

IS THERE A CURE?

Can anything be done to reverse this apparent growing incivility in many state legislatures? Forum participants offered a wide variety of solutions. Uslaner asked lawmakers to declare their own unilateral cease fire—to call off their dogs first. Stop legislative procedures that obstruct what the majority does or run roughshod over the minority. He also asked legislative leaders to quit leading campaigns against incumbents of another party. If you fail to defeat these incumbents, it's not easy

> *"Now there's no such thing as a loyal opposition. Instead of seeing someone who disagrees with us as someone who just has a different world view, it's now an 'I'm right and you're morally defective' world."*

to work together. Campaign instead for open seats, he advised.

Uslaner suggested that interfaith summits are one way to build bridges in a society where the biggest conflicts are religious and cultural. Further, leaders from across the political spectrum need to have a national discourse so we remember that despite our differences. we have a shared faith in our country. "I'm asking more people to be like Bob Dole who is truly a man of the Senate and . . . could work with people on both sides," Uslaner said. You have to accept the legitimacy of all or at least 97 percent of your colleagues, he told the audience.

Rosenthal offered his own remedies for incivility. Retreats that encourage members and families to get to know each other as human beings make it more difficult for legislators to be uncivil. Including all members in orientation and other training sessions would give people an opportunity to get together. He mentioned that in Maryland new members and some senior members take a bus trip around the state. The speaker sponsors the trip, which allows members to see other parts of the state beyond their district and to talk to each other.

Rosenthal implored legislators, especially incumbents, not to bash or run against their own institutions. He also argued that it is the legislature's job to explain to citizens—and to school kids in particular—about representative democracy and the legislature's role in it.

Legislators offered each other practical advice on reducing incivility, including the following suggestions:

- Senior lawmakers should mentor newer lawmakers.
- Set clear standards for what behavior is acceptable and what is not.
- Leadership must set a tone of civility from the beginning.
- Hold retreats and outside activities like basketball games or bowling tournaments where members of both parties can get to know one another.

- Have regular lunches with members of the opposite party to promote bipartisanship.
- Consider shared committee leadership by both parties to promote comity.
- Attack ideas; don't attack people.
- Encourage training and professional development activities to build trust and benefit the legislature as a whole.

After more than 30 years as a student of state legislatures, Rosenthal cut to the heart of why legislative civility matters. "Members will become more civil when they learn to appreciate the overriding importance, not only of their bills, not only of their parties, not only of their agendas, not only of their careers, not even of their constituencies, but of the legislature, which is the engine of democracy."

18

Arnold Takes On the Gerrymander

Joe Hadfield

After a status quo election in 2004, the governator calls for change.

With 100 of 120 seats in the California legislature up for election last fall, Gov. Arnold Schwarzenegger hoped to see at least some Democratic state lawmakers—whom he once called "girlie men"—replaced by fellow Republicans.

Despite his stumping on behalf of GOP candidates, Schwarzenegger's high approval ratings did not rub off enough to change California's status quo politics. In each state legislative contest in 2004, the party in power stayed in power. Not a single seat shifted sides. The same was true for California's 53 U.S. congressional contests on the November ballot.

Rather than accepting the many Republican defeats, the governor soon made it known that he was exploring the possibility of a voter initiative that would transfer redistricting control to an independent commission of retired judges. What's more, Schwarzenegger's post-election musings hinted at the prospect of another California-style special election, instead of waiting and tacking the proposition on to the 2006 statewide ballot. This proposal could be coupled with a proposal to make the legislature part-time, rather than full-time, as it has been since the late 1960s.

"The governor believes one way to make politicians more responsive to voters is by changing redistricting," said Ashley Snee, the governor's deputy press secretary.

Already one organization has taken Schwarzenegger's cue and set out to gather 600,000 signatures by an April 29 deadline. The group, People's Advocate, also spearheaded efforts to recall former governor Gray Davis.

California Democrats consider this new push nothing more than a case of sour grapes.

From *Campaigns & Elections,* February 2005.

"I think he [Schwarzenegger] needs a pacifier," said Art Torres, state Democratic Party chair. "This is what happens when he loses things. Now he's trying to threaten the legislature with making them part-time and changing reapportionment."

On the one hand decrying a need for a special election, Torres also applauded Democratic legislators' recently announced intentions to form a review committee to analyze the adoption of a commission. In doing so, state Assembly speaker Fabian Nunez said ultimate authority over redistricting should remain with the legislature.

DEMISE OF THE GERRYMANDER?

Why any majority party would be reluctant to let redistricting slip out of their hands is obvious: legislators get a chance to choose their voters before voters choose their legislators. The strategy has been a part of American politics ever since the late 18th century, when Massachusetts Gov. Elbridge Gerry drew a plan that included a district resembling a salamander, hence the term gerrymander.

Gerrymander strategies are becoming increasingly effective thanks to the use of geographic information systems. California's current map sports a few oddly shaped districts of its own, such as the 23rd Congressional District, drawn after the 2000 census. Represented by U.S. Rep. Lois Capps (D), this 200-mile ribbon of coastline leeches inland every so often, reeling in tracts of Democratic voters.

The stack-and-crack philosophy of legislative redistricting—when the weaker party is stacked heavily into a few districts and then cracked among all the rest—produces uncompetitive races in both directions. The California Republicans who win do so in a big way, but Democrats remain the overall victors. In 2004, just eight of the 100 state legislative contests saw a margin of victory of less than 10 percent.

A handful of states have already done what Schwarzenegger has proposed for California. Iowa relies on a state agency to draw a fair map, and six other states use independent commissions to manage reapportionment from start to finish without legislative oversight.

In 2004, states using an independent approach produced more than twice as many competitive races for state legislatures than did gerrymandered states such as California, Florida and Texas. The percentage of uncon-

tested races is also higher overall for states where legislatures draw the political boundaries.

Making the case for an independent commission may prove easier than making the case for a special election.

"It just boggles my mind that anybody would call for a $60 million special election when we hear Republican cries for fiscal maturity," Torres said, noting the 2003 gubernatorial recall election cost California an estimated $90 million.

ARIZONA FOLLOW-UP

The situation unfolding now in California played out in 2000 in neighboring Arizona, with a few exceptions, of course. Instead of a Hollywood star leading the charge, a wealthy commercial developer sunk around $1 million in support of a proposition to create an independent redistricting commission.

The party stances were also reversed, with the Republican majority fighting against the idea of a commission. In all, the Arizona GOP spent $130 million against Proposition 106, with a little financial help from their counterparts in the Nevada state party.

Arizona voters passed the measure by a margin of 54 to 46 percent. The requirements of competitive redistricting plans went into the state constitution. That wealthy developer, Jim Pederson, soon after became the Arizona Democratic Party chair. The Arizona Independent Redistricting Commission (AIRC) formed with the nominations of two Republican commissioners, two Democratic commissioners, and a fifth independent commissioner.

Five years later there seems to have been some hitch in Arizona Democrats' comeback story. They control no more state legislative seats than they did before Proposition 106 passed. They gained a single U.S. House seat, but that partially came by default with the census awarding two more representatives to the state.

"If we had gone by the old method, we would have gotten the same thing," Pederson said.

Pederson added his party fell behind in the rush to staff the AIRC, resulting in its contracts going to conservative consultants. The final redistricting plan divided Arizona into 30 political districts for state senators and representatives. Only four, Pederson says, fit his definition of a competitive district.

Thanks to new constitutional language, Pederson says state courts are now capable of striking down maps that could reasonably be made more competitive. Already some Democratic legal challenges have been successful and will presumably find their way before the state Supreme Court by summer.

Despite these early frustrations, Pederson still considers the commission system an improvement.

"Now we have remedies," Pederson said. "This is new, and it will go through a trial and error process, but it's in our Constitution now."

ARNOLD'S CAMPAIGN LESSON

In California, Schwarzenegger has his work cut out for him if he continues to pursue changes to redistricting in California. For starters, the issue is technical, process-oriented and boring to many voters.

Consequently, voters likely would follow the rule of thumb to vote against an initiative they either do not understand or do not care about.

In Arizona, Pederson boiled down the Proposition 106 campaign to themes supportive of citizen involvement and critical of self-serving leaders. Some ads used the slogan "Let the People Draw the Lines," and others depicted a smoke-filled room of politicians in the basement of the state capitol alongside headlines about the 1990 redistricting.

In addition to presenting a clear message, the Proposition 106 team lined up endorsements from the state's major newspapers and public interest groups.

Although the California governor's office remains tight-lipped about where they plan to take the redistricting issue, the governor's early statement specifically mentioned retired judges as the pool from which commissioners would be drawn. Having managed Arizona's campaign for redistricting change, Pederson thinks getting into such details is a mistake.

"Don't get involved in all the details or try to explain the method," Pederson said. "Go with the general theme."

Whether or not the push for an independent redistricting commission succeeds in California, Pederson believes the now spotty movement will see a flurry of activity across the country in the elections preceding the 2010 census.

"I think it is a movement that is catching a little steam," Pederson said. "People don't look with approval on this gerrymandering process."

PART

V

Governors and Executives

During the administration of President George W. Bush the federal government has regulated business with a relatively light hand. Yet while federal regulatory agencies such as the Environmental Protection Agency (EPA) and the Securities Exchange Commission (SEC) might be more sympathetic to big business these days, New York Attorney General Elliot Spitzer is not.

Spitzer put together a group of northeastern states to sue polluting utility companies. He went after Wall Street companies that had been less than honest in their business dealings, getting ten of the biggest stock brokerages in the nation to pay $900 million in fines and to agree to change the way they do business. He's sued drug companies for failing to disclose the potential side effects of their products, mutual funds for treating customers unfairly, and grocery stores for failing to pay their delivery employees minimum wage.[1] Spitzer's influence extends beyond the borders of New York State and has made him a rising star in the Democratic Party.

Spitzer is perhaps the most extreme example of a new breed of twenty-first century state-level executives. They're smart and ambitious, and they see expanding expectations and increasingly complex challenges as opportunities to build a record that provides a platform for greater political success.

These executives do not have to look far to find occasions to exercise the authority of their office. Indeed, executives in state—and often local—government are expected to be proactive multitaskers of the highest order. Governors, for example, are required to be the key policymaker, head bureaucrat, party leader, commander-in-chief of the National Guard, and general all-around cheerleader for their state. They also serve as the natural point of contact for relations between states, and between their state and the national government.

This multiplicity of roles, a result of four decades of reform in state government, gives governors and other state-level elected executives, such as attorneys general, an increasingly important role in the nation's political system. Spitzer is a good example, but he is far from the only one. The governor's office is a prime training ground for future presidents. Since 1980 only one president—George H. W. Bush—has not served as a state governor. He is also the only president in the past twenty-five years span not to be elected to a second term.[2] Former governors are also showing up in a wide variety of the top jobs in the federal government. George W. Bush has called on them to head up federal agencies including the Department of Homeland Security, the EPA, and the Department of Agriculture.

There has been a similar revolution in the role and importance of executives at the local level. Mayors of large urban communities, for example, often are expected to take on a variety of responsibilities that are roughly analogous to those expected of a governor. Sitting at the head of a city government like New York's is not a job for the faint of heart, nor is it a career for those who do not like to put in long hours or cannot get along with others in what can be tense and contentious situations (see the article by Christopher Swope in this section).

The readings in this section provide insight into the people who serve in the most important elected executive offices in state and local government. What these readings reflect is the culmination of a lengthy reform process that has increased the importance—and expectations—of state and local executives.

THE ORIGINS AND DEVELOPMENT OF ELECTED EXECUTIVES

State and local governments differ from the federal government in the number of executive positions that are elected offices. With the exception of the president and vice president, all important executive offices at the federal level are appointed rather than elected. Filling the top jobs in the executive branch through the appointive powers of the president gives the chief executive more control over government, because the president has the power to hire and fire the heads of the key bureaucracies.

This is not the case at the state and local levels, where many executive offices are elected and thus have a measure of independence from the governor or local-level equivalent. Elliot Spitzer (a Democrat), for example, does not serve as attorney general of New York because Governor George Pataki (a Republican) necessarily wanted him in that position. He is attorney general because he got the most votes in a general election. If Pataki doesn't want Spitzer running investigations of Wall Street brokerage companies, there's not much he can do about it. But it's not just the state's chief lawyer who is often elected. Everyone from the insurance commissioner to the head of the state's education bureaucracy may be elected. In many states, the executive branch of state government consists of a group of independent electoral fiefdoms, not a strictly hierarchical system where the chief executive has the power to hire and fire as he or she sees fit.

Explaining how and why this system came to be requires a little history. Governors represent the oldest executive office in the United States, predating the founding of the country. Early colonial governors were agents of the monarch rather than officials elected by the people. They nonetheless often wielded considerable power, including the ability to veto bills passed by colonial legislatures or even to dissolve these legislatures outright.

After winning its independence, the newly formed republic was understandably suspicious of concentrations of power in executive office. Accordingly state governments were typically organized so that governors occupied a comparatively weak position. Some states had plural executives—essentially the governor's job was done by committee—and in other states the governor was little more than an honorary position. Most governors had no veto power, had very short term limits (often only a year), little appointive power, and no real budgetary power. Real power belonged to the legislature.[3]

Executive power became even more fragmented during the 1800s by the implementation of the "long ballot." The aptly named long ballot was a reform designed to give citizens the final say in who held a wide variety of public offices—not just governor and lieutenant governor, but treasurer, attorney general, and, at the local level, county executive, sheriff, and county treasurer. All of these offices, and many more, were put onto the ballot, making the process of selecting executives at the state and local levels as much elective as appointive.

In time there was something of a countermovement against this executive fragmentation, mainly as a response to corruption in the legislature. In the late nineteenth and early twentieth centuries, a number of states pursued reforms designed to centralize more power in the hands of chief executives. Few states actually trimmed the long ballot—by shifting elective offices back to appointive offices—but many undertook reorganizations of the executive branch that included creating line-item veto powers, granting greater discretion in hiring and firing personnel, increasing the length of terms, and providing increased budgetary authority.[4]

For much of the first half of the twentieth century, however, the executive branches of state government did little to change or modernize. Events such as the Great Depression, World War II, and the Cold War shifted citizens' expectations and attention to the federal government. In addition, the malapportionment of state legislatures allowed state government to be dominated by rural interests, which were content to stick with the organizational status quo.

THE DEVELOPMENT OF THE MODERN EXECUTIVE

The most significant reforms in the executive branches of subnational government did not begin to gain momentum until the 1960s and 1970s. Malapportionment ended in the 1960s with the "one-man, one-vote" ruling of the U.S. Supreme Court. This radically reshaped the nation's legislatures, by shifting them from institutions focused on rural interests to institutions more oriented toward urban interests, where the population was concentrated. In urban areas there was strong demand for the public services that fell under the jurisdiction of the executive branch. Therefore one outcome of the shift in legislative emphasis was an increased willingness to reform the executive branch, to make the chief executive of government more like that of a corporation. These reforms included extending tenure, strengthening veto powers, and creating new state agencies to meet the demands of urban areas. Unlike many existing state agencies, the new agencies were more likely to be led by gubernatorial appointees than elected leaders.[5]

Such executive branch reforms gained particular importance in the 1970s, 1980s, and 1990s. Increasing federal budget deficits and a popular movement to push power away from the national government and back to the states (New Federalism), put governors in the spotlight. Broadly speaking, governors not only gained real executive authority, they faced a string of complex problems that required them to use that authority. Governors today are expected to do everything—keep property taxes down, improve the economy, make sure the roads get paved.

Governors don't just take care of business within their state borders. They also play an important political role nationally. The National Governors Association (NGA), an organization of governors designed to promote collective action on policy issues important to states, is judged by many experts to be one of the most powerful and influential lobbying organizations in Washington, D.C.[6]

Other executives have seen a similar rise in importance and influence. Lieutenant governors, for example, tend to have a much lower profile than governors, but they are next in line for the chief executive's job. In 2004 and 2005, Connecticut's Jodi Rell took over for Governor John Rowland, who stepped down rather than face impeachment in a corruption scandal, and Nebraska's Dave Heineman took over for Governor Mike Johanns, who left after President Bush selected him to run the Department of Agriculture. When such occasions arise, lieutenant governors are rewarded with all the powers, and responsibilities, that go with the chief executive's office.

Other executive offices have also grown in importance and influence. Spitzer is an example of the importance of state attorneys general, who can act collectively on issues of interest, like insurance rates, credit card fees, and deceptive business practices (see the latest news on the activities of attorneys general on the Web site of the National Association of Attorneys General, www.naag.org).

Highly competitive presidential elections in 2000 and 2004 highlighted the importance of secretaries of state. In most states, the secretary of state is the chief election official. He or she determines who is eligible to be on the ballot, canvasses the election returns, handles state-level recounts, and is responsible for approving the process and system of voting (punch card, electronic machine, and so on). These duties became an issue for national debate in 2000. At that time Kathleen Harris served as Florida's secretary of state, and thus had a central role in overseeing the hotly contested (and still debated) vote between Al Gore and George W. Bush. Harris was not only secretary of state, she was also a co-chair of Bush's Florida 2000 campaign. What had been a relatively low-profile state office became a central focus of the dispute over who was going to hold the most power executive office on the planet, and also the subject of a harsh debate about the role of partisanship in vote counting (for more on the duties and issues facing secretaries of state, visit the Web site of the National Association of Secretaries of State at www.nass.org/sos/sos.html).

The readings in this section consider some of these executives and the roles and challenges they face. The readings include profiles of people who hold two of the most visible state and local executive offices—the governor of California and the mayor of New York City (see the articles by Alan Greenblatt and Christopher Swope, respectively). Also profiled are a person who gave up being governor to head up a major federal agency (see the article by Jack Penchoff) and a lieutenant governor who stepped into the governor's job after the governor was forced out of office in a corruption scandal (see the article by Alan Greenblatt). Finally, Tom Arrandale's piece provides a glimpse into the increasing power and role of state attorneys general.

Notes

1. Sridhar Pappu, "The Crusader," *The Atlantic Monthly,* October 2004, 108–118.

2. The others were Ronald Reagan (former governor of California), Bill Clinton (former governor of Arkansas), and George W. Bush (former governor of Texas).

3. Larry Sabato, *Goodbye to Good-Time Charlie: The American Governorship Transformed,* 2nd ed. (Washington, D.C.: CQ Press, 1983).

4. Nelson C. Dometrius, "Governors: Their Heritage and Future," in *American State and Local Politics,* ed. Ronald E. Weber and Paul Brace (New York: Chatham House), 38–70.

5. Ibid, pp. 50–52.

6. National Governors Association, "What Is the National Governor's Association?" www.nga.org/nga/1,1169,C_FAQ^D_302,00.html (accessed May 3, 2005).

19

Strong Governor

Alan Greenblatt

Arnold Schwarzenegger may have been elected as a political novice, but he's outsmarting the pros at every turn.

O ne afternoon a few months ago, California legislators were sitting in a room in the capitol at Sacramento, arguing about workers' compensation. Their governor, Arnold Schwarzenegger, was hundreds of miles away, in Burbank, at a Costco warehouse store. He was gathering signatures for a petition to put a workers' comp initiative on the general election ballot. Schwarzenegger was happily signing just about any object offered to him: pieces of paper, books, even a $20 bill. He made sure the cameras had a good angle as he held up the clipboard with his signed petitions.

Some of the reporters on the scene wanted to know why Governor Schwarzenegger wasn't back at the capitol, engaged in the workers' comp negotiations. He batted the question right back to them. "This is what the people want to see," he declared. "They want to see an action governor—not someone who sits around the office in Sacramento, not doing anything."

The appearance at Costco had all the trappings of a publicity stunt. But anybody who saw it purely in those terms misunderstood the governor's strategy—and his cleverness. Schwarzenegger's real audience that day was the legislators at the capitol, the people he seemed to be ignoring. Schwarzenegger was, in fact, intimately involved in the backstage legislative bargaining. He handled much of the final negotiation himself, even getting down into minutiae about medical association guidelines for treating specific injuries. But he knew he needed to use the looming pressure of an initiative on the November ballot to force legislators to make a deal in April. And he succeeded.

Within days of the Costco event, Schwarzenegger had not only cut a deal but signed a new workers' comp bill into law. "They had

From *Governing*, July 2004.

gathered over a million signatures, were prepared to turn them in," says Steve Merksamer, a former Republican gubernatorial aide, "and miraculously, that's when the deal with the legislature happened."

It's the way the new governor of California likes to work. To no one's surprise, he frequently acts as if he were still in show business. He calls for "action, action, action" so often he sometimes reminds people of a manic movie director. But even those who were skeptical of the movie star-governor are forced to admit that Schwarzenegger isn't just demanding action: He's finding ways to get it. "The only people who are still laughing at Governor Schwarzenegger," says Claremont McKenna political scientist Jack Pitney, "are the people who don't know California."

A serious chess player, Schwarzenegger is demonstrating an ability both to read people and to get up to speed on complex issues in a hurry. Jim Brulte, until recently the state Senate Republican leader and the de facto leader of the California GOP, recalls that it was his job to show Schwarzenegger the ropes and tutor him in the ways of the capitol. "I realized after about five weeks," Brulte says, "that I was no longer the teacher."

In just his first few months in office, Schwarzenegger has won significant policy victories on tax, budget and policy issues: a car tax cut, a $15 billion bond to prop up the state's finances and a series of spending cuts worked out with interest groups, leading up to a budget package that was turned over to the legislature as a fait accompli. He campaigned for those victories with exquisite timing. On the budget, as he did with workers' comp, Schwarzenegger made deals in private and then announced them very publicly, one at a time, for maximum attention.

In virtually every case, the goal hasn't been publicity for its own sake; it's been publicity aimed at creating some movement in the state's legendarily gridlocked political system. Meanwhile, Schwarzenegger has focused attention on the governmental process in a way that hasn't been true in years. San Francisco and Los Angeles TV stations have set up Sacramento bureaus for the first time since the early 1990s. "When it comes to use of his per-

> *"History has yet to be written as to whether or not his obvious leadership skills actually result in long-term changes."*
>
> —Darrell Steinberg,
> Assembly budget chairman

sonal time in a very, very public way," says Brulte, "he understands that he can help focus public attention on a particular problem—and in so doing focus legislative attention on a particular issue."

In truth, though, the biggest trials lie ahead. Schwarzenegger's early deals have not resulted in any structural reform of the dysfunctional California budget process. Putting the state's fiscal house in order will require demands for real sacrifice, whether in the form of deep and permanent budget cuts that no constituent group would willingly agree to, or through the tax increases Schwarzenegger and California voters abhor. "I think history has yet to be written," says Democrat Darrell Steinberg, the Assembly budget chairman, "as to whether or not his obvious leadership skills, his force of personality, his smarts and his desire for change actually result in the long-term changes that are needed."

OUT AND ABOUT

It won't surprise anybody that Schwarzenegger brings show-business flair to his routine activities. Any working day during the spring saw lines of school kids waiting patiently outside the governor's office for a turn posing in front of the portrait of Schwarzenegger and his wife, Maria Shriver. One group argued among themselves whether he was famous "because he's an actor" or "because he's a senator." Those who were standing around when Schwarzenegger happened to pass by started screaming the way Beatles fans used to.

Deeply tanned and much shorter than he appeared on the screen as the Terminator or Conan the Barbarian, the 56-year-old governor can, in fact, regularly be seen walking around the capitol. Previous governors sat at their desks most of the time, waiting for people to come to them. Schwarzenegger gets out and about, appearing before groups that haven't seen a governor in the flesh in a long time and meeting with legislators in their own offices—even attending their birthday parties.

Voters and politicians alike felt that Schwarzenegger's ousted predecessor, Gray Davis, cared only for himself. Davis forever angered fellow Democrats in the legislature by saying publicly that their role was "to implement my vision." Schwarzenegger is not about to make any similar mistake. "Here's a guy who gets up from his desk to see legislators," says Fred Silva, of the Public Policy Institute of California. "It's a protocol change, which for public policy purposes is probably a good one"—and symbolic of Schwarzenegger's more active engagement in crafting legislation.

Democrats don't agree with Schwarzenegger on everything—and some of them say more critical things in private than they feel comfortable saying in public, since he is riding so high—but the new governor does seem approachable and willing to listen, and that alone is a change. (Both houses of the legislature are currently controlled by Democrats, as is every other statewide elected office.)

Schwarzenegger manages simultaneously to play both good cop and bad cop, calling for a part-time legislature that would send him fewer "strange bills" while opening up to Democratic Assembly members in a way they're not used to. He uses Bob Hertzberg, a former Democratic Assembly speaker, as an adviser and liaison to Democrats. But the governor may be his own best liaison. John Burton, the veteran Senate president pro tem, says that Schwarzenegger is "a lot looser than Gray" and recalls that during the workers' comp negotiations the two teased each other about personal image. "You're a great man," Schwarzenegger told Burton. "No," the senator assured him, "you're a great man."

NOT ANOTHER JESSE

The circumstances of California's 2003 recall election were, arguably, the most unusual surrounding any state campaign in recent times. Davis had been reelected in 2002 against a weak GOP opponent. As 2003 progressed, however, buyer's remorse set in among California voters, who disapproved of Davis' handling of the budget and remembered his tepid response to the energy-supply meltdown in 2001, when the lights literally went out in the state. A recall effort was launched by Republican activists and underwritten by a wealthy GOP congressman. Although the recall looked initially like an extended personal vendetta, it quickly gathered popular strength.

In retrospect, Davis was probably doomed by the time Schwarzenegger announced his candidacy on "The Tonight Show." Davis was recalled by a 54 percent majority, and Schwarzenegger easily led the field of 130 candidates who filed to succeed him.

Given Schwarzenegger's background, the obvious comparison at first was to Jesse Ventura, the ex-wrestler who was elected governor of Minnesota as a third-party candidate in 1998. Although Schwarzenegger ran as a Republican, he was, like Ventura, an outsider drawing mostly on show-business notoriety. Like Ventura, Schwarzenegger surprised skeptics in the early weeks by putting together a highly competent staff and cabinet.

But Ventura had the misleading luck of coming to office at a time of budgetary plenty, and he never really adjusted to the hard times that ensued. By 2001, Minnesota's fiscal surplus had evaporated, and Ventura's popularity had evaporated with it. In the closing months of his four-year term, Ventura was nearly irrelevant politically; the legislature passed a budget without his signature, overriding his veto within three hours of its issuance. "He had a tougher time dealing with the legislature when we were in a world of hurt," says Tim Penny, a former congressman and one-time Ventura adviser. Schwarzenegger, by contrast, came to office precisely because his state was "in a world of hurt." Voters were ready for a change, and anything he could do to improve the situation would look like a big win.

When he first took office, it looked as if Schwarzenegger might be content simply to remain a creature of the media, an outsider governor who appeared on TV to bash legislators. He often talked about taking his agenda directly to voters through the initiative process if the legislature wouldn't play ball, and kept political consultants on staff as if he were going to operate in permanent campaign mode.

It's now clear that Schwarzenegger had a more subtle strategy in mind, one that envisioned the initiative process less as a blunt instrument to get his way and more as a negotiating tool. "I like the idea of using deadlines," Schwarzenegger said at a news conference celebrating the workers' comp package. "Because why would we hang here for the next two years and negotiate and debate over this issue?"

The most frequent goal of the Schwarzenegger administration, it seems, is not to force movement in any foreordained policy direction but to close a deal that will have representatives from all sides standing together at the press conference to announce it. Schwarzenegger is a Republican committed to a no-tax-increase agenda, but beyond that he has been extremely flexible, working not only with a Democratic legislature but with lobbyists across the political spectrum to reach agreements that everybody can live with. Dianne Feinstein, California's senior U.S. senator and leading Democratic politician, calls the governor "a Republican with the body language of a Democrat."

"I realized after about five weeks, that I was no longer the teacher."

—Senator Jim Brulte, on tutoring Schwarzenegger on state politics

Not all the Democrats in the legislature feel that way; some of the budget deals have left them feeling shunted aside. But for the most part the administration has been open to them, and they have found Schwarzenegger to be someone they can make deals with, despite their partisan differences. "He understands the art of negotiation," says Steinberg, showing off a silver hamesh (a hand symbolizing protection), a religious gift Schwarzenegger brought him from a trip to Israel. "He's a pleasure to deal with," Steinberg insists. "He listens as much as he speaks."

BIPARTISAN MOVES

While maintaining his Republican credentials on taxes and most fiscal issues, Schwarzenegger has otherwise won points for pragmatism and kept his overall image moderate. When San Francisco began issuing marriage licenses to same-sex couples, Schwarzenegger complained that the move was against state law, but suggested he wouldn't be upset if that law were changed. He appointed an environmental activist to head the state EPA, has promoted the idea of building a "hydrogen highway," as well as a bill to allow hybrid vehicles to use HOV lanes, and has pledged to defend in court, if necessary, the state's pioneer law regulating the greenhouse gas emissions of cars and other vehicles. "On the environment, so far so good," says Assemblywoman Fran Pavley, author of the greenhouse gas bill.

Now politicians on both the right and the left are seeking out the center because, suddenly, that's were the action is. The governor's fondness for establishing consensus became apparent early in the game, in the way he handled the issue of driver's licenses for illegal immigrants. The legislature had passed a law last year establishing such licenses, and this quickly became a prime topic in the recall of Davis. Schwarzenegger's Republican allies argued that they should take the issue directly to voters.

Unlike a measure dealing with workers' compensation, an initiative to ban the driver's licenses was a sure winner. It would have passed overwhelmingly and been certain to fire up GOP partisans. Instead, Schwarzenegger worked with the original measure's sponsor, Democratic state Senator Gil Cedillo, to repeal the law through the legislative process. The governor promised that he would sign a compromise bill later on if it included tighter security provisions, although he and Cedillo have not yet been able to come to an agreement.

"A lot of Republicans were furious at him," says Tim Hodson, executive director of the Center for California Studies, at Sacramento State. "Arnold Schwarzenegger sacrificed the partisan interests of the Republican Party, in my view, to avoid a very racially divisive wedge issue election. It's a good example of what a governor does, as opposed to a campaign manager."

In the case of workers' comp, Schwarzenegger wanted agreement on a benefits package less costly to business than the one Davis had approved the previous year. The new governor warned legislators that a multimillion-dollar initiative campaign would go forward if they didn't cooperate on the workers' comp issue. He won near-unanimous approval on his final deal, even though he refused to give Democrats the rate regulation provisions they were hoping for.

Schwarzenegger has won over other potential antagonists by trying new approaches to their problems. Almost from the day of his inauguration, Schwarzenegger began wooing the lobbyists who represent California local governments. When he repealed Davis' car tax increase, he put at risk $4 billion in funds earmarked for cities and counties. Schwarzenegger made it up to them through use of an obscure budgetary mechanism called deficiency appropriations that had never been used nearly as expansively before.

When Schwarzenegger addressed the California State Association of Counties, he was the first governor to do so in 20 years. After the event, he sat down with CSAC leaders for nearly an hour to talk about their concerns that his initial budget proposal would, like previous state financial decisions, drain local treasuries. By the time they had finished talking, the governor had worked out the outlines of a deal. In the end, he persuaded cities, counties and special districts to take a $1.3 billion hit in each of the next two budget years, in exchange for his pledge to campaign for a constitutional amendment that the locals had long dreamed of, one that would make it much harder for the state to plunder local revenue sources in the future.

The localities won't get back any of the billions the state has claimed for itself over the years, but if the amendment passes—it would come in the form of another ballot initiative—any further legislative attempts to fiddle with local sales- or property-tax dollars would have to be approved by voters. "What he said to us," explains Chris McKenzie, of the League of California Cities, "was, 'I'll embrace your Number One priority if you embrace my Number One priority, which is to eliminate the budget deficit and get the state back in balance.' "

FEARS FOR THE FUTURE

The most serious question is whether Schwarzenegger has made much progress in addressing the long-term problem that he places first on his own priority list. For all the governor's efforts to distinguish his approach from that of Davis, the fact is that this year's budget, like last year's, will punt about $10 billion worth of debt into the following fiscal year. The $15 billion bond measure used to help balance the 2004 books was coupled with another that toughens balanced-budget requirements—but, conveniently, those new requirements don't apply this year.

Schwarzenegger has consistently maintained that it took years to create the budget mess in California and it will take years to solve it. The majority of state spending is mandated by law, and the governor has done nothing to address that underlying reality. And although the deals with constituencies such as teachers unions, university systems and local governments will help in the near term, the promises Schwarzenegger made to obtain those agreements involve future funding that will push

eventual solvency that much farther away. In the words of Pete Schaafsma, the Assembly's senior Republican budget adviser, the much-publicized agreements represent the exchange of "a little bit of pain now for eternal bliss later."

Will Schwarzenegger ultimately have the stomach to make the hardest choices—to raise taxes or impose spending cuts that will create real pain and discourage legislators and interest groups from sharing the stage with him? "Neither the legislature, the governor or the people of California are interested in facing the long-term fiscal problems of the state," warns Phil Isenberg, a lobbyist and former Democratic legislative leader.

Indeed, for all the goodwill Schwarzenegger has engendered, some in Sacramento are starting to wonder whether the governor isn't selling the same snake oil that has bedeviled the state in the past—short-term fixes that create longer-term problems—disguised by bright new packaging. "I've heard the talk about action, action, action, but I have not seen the courage," says state Treasurer Phil Angelides, a potential Schwarzenegger rival in 2006. "I don't sense from this governor any idea of where he wants to take the state other than making deals that calm the political waters. He's popular now, but he hasn't made people make the hard choices."

What's undeniable, however, is that Schwarzenegger has raised the stakes in California. A year ago legislators were debating bills on cross-dressing and baby-bird feeding while the state's budget shortfall was approaching $35 billion. Now, at the very least, there is a sense among voters that the state's toughest problems can be addressed and that they have elected someone willing to take them on. The governor may have punted, so far, on solving the long-term structural deficit, but he has tackled other issues that had long stalemated the capitol, such as workers' compensation. And he promises more to come. He is pushing the legislature and Public Utilities Commission, for example, to make changes in energy regulation—an issue both bodies had been afraid to touch—in order to allow the largest users of energy to negotiate their own purchases.

More dramatically, Schwarzenegger's California Performance Review threatens to "blow up the boxes of state government," as the governor says, with a mixture of agency consolidations—the state has nearly 20 agencies with tax responsibilities alone—and privatization of such services as real estate management. A prime target of the review panel, which is taking advice from a group of more than 250 state employees sworn to secrecy, will be the 300-odd state boards and independent commissions, whose appointed and well-compensated members are often former legislators or gubernatorial cronies.

The governor's Performance Review advisers have been given the broadest authorization to proceed, and the proposals that ultimately emerge from Schwarzenegger's office stand a fair chance of actually being adopted, because California has a government restructuring law that works like the federal procedure for closing military bases. Once a plan is submitted to the legislature, there must be an up-or-down vote on the entire package within 45 days. No amendments are permitted.

If he can update the state bureaucracy, which he has called "a mastodon frozen in time," Schwarzenegger will have accomplished a tremendous feat. Given his personal popularity and unforeseen talents as a negotiator, he continues to have enormous potential to change the way the state does business. But because the structural deficit is so enormous, even the most ambitious administrative shuffling can do little to solve it. "On the one hand, it's easy because you've got this guy who is so dynamic and unafraid to take on challenges," says Billy Hamilton, co-director of the performance review, "but on the other hand, you've got a budget problem that is in some respects more complex than the federal budget."

California could withdraw entirely from the business of funding roads, universities and parks—indeed, the governor could lay off every state employee—and the state might still have a deficit problem for years into the future. "To me, the jury's still out on whether he wants real, true structural reform," says Joe Canciamilla, an Assembly Democrat. "If he's not willing to take that step, with the popularity he's had, the independence he's had, the public statements he's made—if this governor isn't willing to go there, it ain't gonna happen for several generations."

20

Late Bloomer

Christopher Swope

New York's businessman-mayor is learning politics the hard way. But he's learning it.

A t 4:11 p.m. last August 14th, the lights flickered out across New York City, and Michael Bloomberg, who was drinking coffee in a Brooklyn diner at the time, turned on the most rousing performance of his mayoralty. Throughout the great blackout, Bloomberg was a ubiquitous and calming force. He was on CNN, coolly assuring everyone that the crisis was no act of terrorism; on the Brooklyn Bridge, cheering commuters walking home in the heat; on the radio, explaining the inner workings of the electric grid; in a darkened stairwell, trudging up 19 floors for a late-night hash-out with the head of the local power company.

The New York media, accustomed to beating up on Bloomberg, was suddenly impressed. "Bloomberg Shines in Outage Darkness," *Newsday* said.

Most politicians would have let the blackout story end then and happily ride the goodwill for as long as possible. But Mike Bloomberg is not like most politicians. As mayor, he is guided by the same contrarian instincts that helped him build Bloomberg L. P., the successful media empire that made him one of the richest men on the planet. And his business impulses tell him this: No matter how good a job he's done at something, it's always worth looking for weaknesses, in order to do better next time.

So, just three days after the lights came back on, Bloomberg asked a mixed group of people from the public, private and nonprofit sectors to perform a frank analysis of the city's blackout response. They uncovered all sorts of unseen management failures, in communications, transportation and planning. And there was Bloomberg, at a press conference in October, handing this work of self-criticism to a pack of reporters.

From *Governing,* August 2004.

103

Bloomberg acknowledged the risks of such brutal honesty. "Hopefully they won't criticize, but they'll take it in the manner that the study was done: We did a great job, can we do better?" Wishful thinking. The press took the bad news Bloomberg gave them and ran with it. "911 Blackout Chaos—Frantic Callers Were Left in the Dark," headlined the *New York Post*.

Such are the ups and downs of New York's "businessman mayor," a man who usually tries to do what strikes him as the rational thing, and almost always pays a political price for it. Bloomberg campaigned for office in 2001 on the basis of his private-sector credentials, arguing that what the city needed after September 11 was a successful businessman to turn it around. To show his freedom from special interests, he spent $73 million of his self-made fortune on his election. Three years later, it's clear that Bloomberg's business know-how, coupled with the independence he bought, is often an asset in his work as mayor. Just as often it is a liability.

Yet Bloomberg has learned a lot about politics since his early months as mayor, when he appeared at times to possess none of the most routine political instincts for his job. When the city's intake center for the homeless overflowed, Bloomberg suggested that an unused jail in the Bronx could be used as a backup. "He didn't understand the symbolism of it all—putting homeless families in a jail," says Arnold Cohen, director of the Partnership for the Homeless. "He was so politically tone deaf in the beginning that he was surprised by how vehement the opposition was."

NO RESPECT

The bottom line is that the city finds itself with both a successful mayor and a widely disliked one.

Bloomberg's accomplishments are many. He prevailed, where his predecessors failed, at persuading the state legislature to give him control of city schools. He steered the municipal government out of a deep fiscal crisis, turning a $6.4 billion budget gap in fiscal 2004 into a $1.9 billion surplus. He passed a controversial ban on smoking in bars and restaurants, setting a trend for cities around the country. All the while, crime on Bloomberg's watch continued its remarkable plunge—even with 4,000 fewer cops on the street and with the added pressures of protecting against terrorism. By the numbers, New York City is about as safe a place, the mayor likes to point out, as Port St. Lucie, Florida.

But for all the accomplishments, most New Yorkers continue to find Bloomberg aloof and out of touch. Much has been made about his frequent jaunts to his estate in Bermuda. More comfortable giving a Power-Point presentation than chatting up voters, Bloomberg is struggling to find a populist groove. His 24 percent approval rating in a *New York Times* poll last summer was the lowest for any mayor since that poll began in 1978.

It is the conservatives who are most upset with Bloomberg at the moment. They were not always enamored of his predecessor, Rudy Giuliani, but they did see him as a champion of tax cuts and privatization in City Hall. They hoped that Bloomberg, a lifelong Democrat running as a Republican, might be similarly inclined. Once in office, Bloomberg quickly alienated the Republican base in Staten Island and Queens by raising property taxes 18 percent. "They thought they were electing Rudy's choice of successor," says E. J. McMahon, of the Manhattan Institute. "Then he called for the largest property tax increase in the city's history."

> *"Bloomberg, who rides the subway each morning, purchased a $540 mountain bike when a transit strike loomed. The strike was averted, but Bloomberg's pricey "strike bike" is symbolic for those who think the billionaire mayor is out of touch."*

NEVER EXPLAIN

In some ways, Bloomberg's lack of political sensitivity should have been no surprise. Most successful executives who win high office promising to "run government like a business" find that is an impossible promise to keep: Business and government are two different enterprises. Moreover, unlike some widely publicized businessman-mayors of other cities in recent years—such as

Richard Riordan in Los Angeles or John Hickenlooper in Denver—Bloomberg had no experience in public life outside of his extensive philanthropy work. He was as close to a pure political novice as any city is likely to get.

Even in business, Bloomberg had no shareholders to answer to. He was beholden to no one but himself. In his 1997 memoir, *Bloomberg by Bloomberg,* he declared himself a member of the "never apologize, never explain" school of management. While he was free to practice that doctrine, CEOs of publicly-held companies aren't—let alone elected officials. "He's not a corporate guy," says Kathryn Wylde, president of the Partnership for New York City, a business group. "He's an entrepreneur."

An engineer by training, Bloomberg understood how technology could help financial firms to analyze market data quickly and smartly. When he left his equities trading job at Salomon Brothers in the early 1980s, he began building computer terminals, which came to be known as "Bloombergs," to do just that. By the early 1990s, Bloomberg terminals sat on nearly every desk on Wall Street, and in financial capitals around the world—available to clients who could afford the price (currently $1,700 a month). Bloomberg later added a business newswire to his media offerings, along with radio and TV programming and a few magazines. Since becoming mayor, Bloomberg no longer runs the company, but he still owns 72 percent of it, enough to rank him 36th on the *Forbes* list of wealthiest Americans, with a net worth of $4.9 billion.

Bloomberg's critics, especially conservatives disdainful of his tax increases, see unhealthy parallels between the wealthy entrepreneur's view of his product and the mayor's vision for his city. In a 2003 speech, Bloomberg described New York as a "luxury product"—a high-cost place to do business but also a place of such opportunity that people and companies would gladly pay extra to locate there. "He clearly thinks taxes matter very little to very few people," says McMahon. "It's a 'Tiffany city' vision that reflects a person who spent most of his career in a high-margin, price-insensitive business."

BULLPEN GOVERNMENT

Bloomberg brought a few physical trappings from Bloomberg L.P. into City Hall. The most obvious is his workspace without walls. Shunning a private office, Bloomberg had a large chunk of City Hall's second floor remodeled into a wide-open room of cubicles. The "bullpen," as this area is known, looks rather like a trading floor, or an old-fashioned newspaper city room. There is a fully stocked snack bar at one end—another import from Bloomberg L.P.—and some meeting tables out in the open. The mayor's desk sits in the center (with a Bloomberg terminal on it, of course), and he is surrounded by his deputy mayors, chiefs of staff and schedulers.

Bloomberg has always worked in a transparent environment like this, and he thinks it opens communication up and down the chain of command. Nobody needs to schedule meetings or leave messages to ask the mayor's opinion on something. They just stick their heads over the divider. "You don't have to peel back the layers to get into the inner sanctum," says Gino Menchini, Bloomberg's commissioner for information technology, who visits the bullpen frequently.

The denizens of the Bloomberg bullpen are meritocrats, with a broad range of backgrounds in business, government and nonprofit work. "If you look at the talent he's picked, they're not from political clubhouses or former candidates for office," says Mitchell Moss, director of the Taub Urban Research Center at New York University. "It's a very different team, picked for their knowledge and skills, not for their political party."

Bloomberg delegates tremendous authority to his managers, as he was known to do at his company, and lets commissioners take credit for their accomplishments. That helps explain why there's been almost no turnover in Bloomberg's upper-management ranks, which is unusual in the New York pressure-cooker. Bloomberg's style stands in stark contrast with that of Giuliani, a notorious micromanager who centralized decision making and

> *"If you look at the talent he's picked, they're not from political clubhouses. It's a team picked for their knowledge and skills."*
>
> —Mitchell Moss, urban affairs analyst at NYU

hogged the spotlight. Where Giuliani's ego battle with top cop Bill Bratton ended with Bratton's ouster, Bloomberg gives police commissioner Ray Kelly lots of leeway. "He does let his people run things," Kelly says of the mayor. "But he says clearly, 'Don't screw up.' "

Though Bloomberg prefers, as the saying goes, to let his managers manage, he does like the details: He can talk at length about trash collection or pothole repair. And he makes a point of prioritizing unsexy goals that are nevertheless crucial to the city's business climate. He settled scores of lawsuits filed against the city during the Giuliani years, saving on litigation costs and removing managers from the confines of court decrees. He's also quietly pushing an overhaul of the byzantine building code, in hopes of making it easier and less costly to construct housing, offices and retail space in New York.

Bloomberg's planning department, for instance, is conducting the most ambitious re-zoning of the city's land in a generation. Hoping to ease a severe housing crunch, planners are upzoning under-utilized land along the Brooklyn waterfront and around subway stations for high-density housing. At the same time, they are zoning for new mixed-use business districts in all five boroughs. The goal is to give Manhattan room to continue growing as a center of global commerce—while at the same time creating low-rent space for back-office businesses in Queens, Staten Island and the Bronx. Describing these changes, Planning Commissioner Amanda Burden sounds less like a bureaucrat than a corporate product development manager. "We're creating different products for different markets so the city can compete regionally and globally," Burden says.

CALL ANYTIME

Bloomberg's biggest import to government from the private sector has been an ethos of customer service. When selling data terminals, Bloomberg installed a button on the machines that his clients could push to request individualized service. His City Hall equivalent to that sort of pampering is the new 311 telephone hotline. New York has consolidated 16 city call centers down to one and trained its 500 call takers to answer nearly any question—or to know where to transfer the caller to if they can't answer. Streetlight out? Call 311. Not sure where to send your sewer bill? Call 311. Need directions to Yankee Stadium? Call 311.

Bloomberg isn't the first mayor to institute 311—Chicago and Baltimore have both had it for years—but New York's effort is stunning in its scope and complexity. A caller speaking Swahili is immediately transferred to a linguist who determines what part of the world she is from and then transfers her to a Swahili-speaking operator. Bloomberg himself frequently calls 311 (in English), and he promotes it relentlessly in press conferences and on his weekly radio show. The line gets 34,000 calls a day.

Call in a noise complaint, and it immediately dings the computer of the desk officer in the police precinct that handles it. Crime calls, obviously, take precedence, but at NYPD, word is out that quality-of-life calls matter. In many ways, what Bloomberg has instituted is a direct descendant of the much-publicized Compstat tracking system that revolutionized crime-fighting in New York and other cities in the 1990s. If a precinct is showing sluggish response to noise calls, the commander is likely to get a tongue-lashing.

In fact, 311 isn't just a complaint line but a powerful management tool. During the blackout, when 311 received 175,000 calls over two days, weary operators noticed that a lot of diabetics were calling to ask how long their unrefrigerated insulin would last. That information shot up the chain of command and before long, Bloomberg was on the radio telling New Yorkers what to do with medicine in their warming refrigerators. More recently, noticing that noise complaints are the top reason for calling 311 (there were 255,000 noise complaints last year), Bloomberg proposed an ordinance cracking down on barking dogs, loud air conditioners and other nuisances.

STRIKE BIKE

But Bloomberg's technocratic skills can be hard to separate from his flaws as a politician. New Yorkers tend to reward showman mayors, such as Giuliani or Edward I. Koch, who come off brash and kinetic as the city itself. Bloomberg rarely looks comfortable in public appearances, and often sounds like he is merely going through the motions.

One Friday in June, Bloomberg performed the annual rite of opening city pools for the summer. As he had the year before, the mayor jumped into the waist-deep water at a pool in Queens, hoping to demonstrate some solidarity with the common people. Mostly he managed to look uncomfortable in a soggy white polo shirt. Kids splashed and played with each other but not with the mayor. "If he didn't have to deal with the masses," says Doug Muzzio, a Baruch College political scientist, "I think he'd be perfectly happy."

For a man who ran a large media company, Bloomberg has a knack for flubbing his photo-ops. Late in 2002, transit workers threatened to go on strike, forcing New Yorkers to ponder how they'd get to work without subways or buses. Hoping to set an example, Bloomberg, who rides the subway each morning, purchased a bicycle and trotted it out for the cameras— a $540 mountain bike. The strike was averted, but Bloomberg's pricey "strike bike" endures as a lasting symbol for anyone who thinks the billionaire mayor is out of touch with the working classes.

The one trait that may have served Bloomberg best as an entrepreneur—decisiveness—tends to get him into trouble in politics. Bloomberg has shown a tendency to move without bringing interest groups on board, turning them into opponents rather than allies.

Last year, the Democrat-turned-Republican launched a personal crusade to take political parties out of city government altogether. He proposed a ballot initiative to create nonpartisan elections. Rather than trying to build grassroots support for the measure, Bloomberg spent $7 million of his own money on promotion. It wasn't just the city's powerful unions, entrenched in party politics, that came out against him. The League of Women Voters and other good-government groups opposed it on the grounds that it could harm minority representation. The measure was trounced by a 70 to 30 percent margin.

Another example, during the worst of the budget crisis, was the mayor's plan to begin levying tolls on the bridges connecting Brooklyn and Queens to Manhattan. For such a politically volatile proposal, one certain to spark an outcry in the outer boroughs, Bloomberg did little to prepare the public or political leaders. Instead, the plan came out as an obscure line slipped into his budget: congestion pricing—$800 million.

Gene Russianoff, senior attorney for the New York Public Interest Group, says that his group supported the idea but that Bloomberg botched the execution. Now it's

> *"The problem with Bloomberg owing nobody anything is that nobody owes him anything either."*

dead for the foreseeable future. "A different mayor," Russianoff says, "might've sat down with the Brooklyn borough president before announcing this, and said 'I know you'll hate this and probably attack it publicly, but if it happens, maybe we can get something for Brooklyn in return and you can pull your punches a little bit.'"

Bloomberg frequently boasts of his lack of political indebtedness to anyone as a crucial political virtue. Some think he carries that principle too far—and fails to realize that debts payable and receivable can be turned into genuine assets later. "He uses the word 'owing' as a negative," says Steven Cohen, a Columbia University political scientist. "But in government, it's not just a matter of owing. It's about relationship building, community building and consensus building—not about owing. That means going to Staten Island, a huge base of voters for him, but also Harlem and the Bronx and meeting with community leaders there, too."

Indeed, the problem with Bloomberg owing nobody anything is that nobody owes him anything either. "I get the feeling that he really believed he could govern as a businessman in the style of the progressive reformers who wanted the city governed as a city manager would with no reference to ideology," says Steven Malanga, of the Manhattan Institute. "It's impossible to govern New York City this way."

GETTING IT

As the 2005 election nears, however, Bloomberg the businessman is perhaps grudgingly turning into more of a politician. He doesn't jet off to Bermuda as much on weekends and has on several occasions pointed his private jet toward tropical islands that are important to more New York voters: Puerto Rico and the Dominican Republic. Closer to home, he's spending much more time than he used to in the Outer Boroughs, especially in neighborhoods that voted for him in 2001. Traditionally, New York mayors deliver their State of the City address in City Hall. Bloomberg gave his last one in Queens and the one before that in Brooklyn.

The businessman-mayor is also learning how to pander a bit. When the city recently projected a budget surplus for the fiscal year just ended, he suggested sending all homeowners checks for $400—a thank-you note reminding them of the upside of his property-tax increase. In another move, Bloomberg responded to anti-development sentiment in Staten Island and Queens by demanding downzoning in certain neighborhoods. That conflicts with his goal of building more housing in the city. But it is what these neighborhoods want, and Bloomberg is going to give it to them. People who watch Bloomberg closely say he seems more comfortable in his political skin. "He's growing into the ceremonial aspects of the job," says Fred Siegel, a veteran city observer and professor at Cooper Union.

One frequent target of City Hall, the bars and clubs represented by the New York Nightlife Association, has seen a turnaround in Bloomberg's style. Last November, the mayor proposed a change in licensing rules for establishments that want to stay open past 1 a.m. Complaining that bars and clubs weren't consulted about the changes, the association fought it, and the proposal was shelved. Eight months later, when Bloomberg proposed his noise ordinance, the administration specifically sought out the association's input. "They wanted us at the press conference announcing this," says Bob Zuckerman, executive director of the association. "It was a very different approach, and one that was extremely welcome."

Bloomberg's poll numbers are rising—his latest approval rating stands at 50 percent, according to a Quinnipiac University poll—but the electorate is still uneasy. Only 40 percent say that Bloomberg "cares about the needs and problems of people like you." Yet 64 percent say he is honest, and 65 percent say he has strong leadership abilities. In other words, New Yorkers may not like Mayor Mike but they admit the city is safe and the streets are clean. For Bloomberg, that may be just enough.

21

Fresh Start

Alan Greenblatt

After a series of scandals, Connecticut is taking ethics seriously. Governor Jodi Rell has a mandate to push for change.

R egime change in Connecticut has been less dramatic than in, say, Baghdad. But Jodi Rell, the state's new governor, is enjoying a lot of goodwill simply by presenting a different face.

In July, Rell succeeded fellow-Republican John Rowland, who finally stepped down when impeachment proceeding appeared imminent. Rowland's fault lay in accepting gifts from state contractors and running an administration in which rigging contracts became standard practice.

Although Rell served as his lieutenant governor for a decade, she was not part of his inner circle and appears to have clean hands. She has hired an ethics lawyer to work on proposals to restore trust in government and axed some of Rowland's more controversial appointees. She also set up a commission to revamp the way the state doles out contracts. "There's a golden opportunity here," says Rell, who insists that her moves to impose uniform rules on bidding amount to nothing more than "common sense."

Rell is lucky in her timing—the legislature won't meet again until January, allowing her plenty of opportunity to get her own team and proposals into shape. Income-tax receipts are curving up after a period of trending down (although the state lost 6,000 jobs in June). Rell will face an assortment of fights over health care, property tax relief and medical malpractice, but the budget is now in surplus.

A big question awaiting Rell is whether Democrats will want to cooperate with her, or whether they'll sense a political opening in Rowland's downfall. Democrats control both chambers of the legislature and are eager to win the governorship, something they haven't done since 1986.

From *Governing,* September 2004.

So far, everyone is making cooperative noises. "Democrats will seem small and petty unless they organize their opposition over something meaningful," says John DeStefano, New Haven's Democratic mayor. Nevertheless, he says that Rell will need to push a substantive agenda of her own if she wants to extend the current era of good feelings.

Rell had spent a decade as a state legislator when Rowland asked her to be his running mate in 1994. She had a reputation as a hard worker, trying to read every bill, and moved up into minor leadership positions by imposing "Rell's Rule," which held that Republicans could get more accomplished by sticking together as a caucus rather than letting their ideological rifts translate into split votes.

Rell kept a traditional low profile as lieutenant governor. (Referring to her suddenly "quadrupled" workload, she says, "I can see now why I got to do all those ribbon cuttings.") As governor, in addition to promoting ethics, she plans changes to the $57 million juvenile justice center that was at the center of the Rowland controversies. Built under questionable circumstances by cronies of the former governor, it was designed more as a prison than as a school, and is considered by many to be unacceptable for rehabilitating young people.

Rell takes the state's top job at a time when the legislative leadership is changing as well. The House speaker is retiring and the Senate president pro tem moved into the lieutenant governor's office. Jim Amann, expected

By the Numbers

Connecticut's New Governor

- Born Mary Carolyn Reavis in Norfolk, Virginia, 1946
- Studied at Old Dominion University and Western Connecticut State College; no degrees
- Honorary law doctorates from University of Hartford (2001), University of New Haven (2004)
- Married to Louis Rell, a retired airline pilot; two grown children
- State Representative, Town of Brookfield, 1984–1994
- Lieutenant Governor 1995–2004
- Sworn in as Governor July 2004

to be the new speaker, says the changing of the guard offers "a breath of fresh air" to a public convinced that too many decisions were made in back rooms.

With economists predicting a couple of smooth budget years ahead, that leaves ethics as Rell's main challenge. A former state treasurer is in prison for his part in a corruption scandal and two former mayors are doing time as well. "The way things operate in Connecticut right now allows people to exploit government for their own interests," says Andy Sauer, executive director of the state branch of Common Cause. "It won't be easy for her to restore the public trust, but she's committed to doing it."

22

Leavitt Ready for EPA

Jack Penchoff

Mike Leavitt stepped down as governor of Utah to lead the Environmental Protection Agency.

M ike Leavitt stepped down as governor of Utah in November and walked right in to one of the most controversial jobs in Washington, D.C.

As the nation's 10th EPA administrator, Leavitt told *State News* he had no illusions about what was in store for him when he arrived in Washington.

Assailed by environmental groups for not doing enough to protect the environment, and questioned by some industries for doing too much, the post of EPA administrator has been a balancing act between competing interests since William Ruckelshaus was appointed the nation's first environmental chief by President Nixon in December 1970.

"That's not going to change," said Leavitt. "It's part of the construct and we have to navigate in that."

A popular three-term governor, Leavitt championed states' rights in his 11 years as Utah's chief executive. In 1996 he served as president of The Council of State Governments. He also served as chair of the National Governors Association, Western Governors Association, and the Republican Governors Association.

During an interview with *State Government News* in 1996, Leavitt said it is up to the states to restore confidence in government.

"People feel that government a long ways away from the people is not to be trusted and not accountable," he said.

Leavitt did not leave that philosophy behind in Salt Lake City. The environment, Leavitt said in February, fits the basic federal system because it is a multistate issue.

"We need national standards, with neighborhood solutions," he said.

From *State News,*
April 2004.

111

It didn't take Leavitt long to put his philosophy into action.

SENSITIVE TO STATE ISSUES

"I was administrator for two weeks when I had to send a letter to 31 governors that they were not in compliance with ozone and fine particulate emission regulations," said Leavitt. "As a governor, I knew what that meant. It's like putting a sign around a community that says, 'Don't invest here.'"

Many of the 506 counties cited by the EPA for non-compliance, said Leavitt, had unhealthful air because they lay downwind from coal-burning power plants in other counties and in some cases other states.

Leavitt also knew that the states would need help meeting the air quality rules they were violating.

"It's unfair to give states regulations without the proper tools to solve problems," he said. "They can take all of the cars off the roads and close all the factories and still not be in compliance with interstate quality rules."

The solution Leavitt proposed was a set of rules that put the problem-solving in the hands of the states and the utility companies that own most of the nation's coal-burning power plants.

"The key is to reward results, not programs," Leavitt said.

Using the cap-and-trade model that was successful in reducing acid rain in the Northeast, the EPA is proposing to set the standards, but leave it up to the states and power plants to determine how the standards will be met.

"If the states and plants are successful, they will meet the requirements. If they exceed requirements, they will be rewarded with clean air credits. Those who don't meet the requirements will have to buy clean air credits," said Leavitt.

In December, the new administrator introduced two proposals designed to reduce air-polluting emissions from power plants, using the cap-and-trade model.

One proposal targets a reduction in sulfur dioxide emissions by 70 percent and nitrogen oxides by 65 percent.

The other, more controversial proposal, known as the Utility Mercury Reductions Rule, calls for a 70 percent reduction of mercury emissions following full implementation by 2018.

The proposed rules, said Leavitt, provide power plants incentives to comply with requirements.

"And they provide states more control and flexibility in developing their own plans to meet national standards," he said.

The mercury reduction proposal has drawn the most fire from environmental groups who contend that the emissions requirements are not as stringent as a finding by the Clinton administration EPA in 2000.

The electric utility industry, however, counters that there is no pollution control equipment specifically designed to reduce mercury emissions. According to the Edison Electric Institute, a trade association of electric utilities, 40 percent of the mercury emissions from power plants are reduced by the same equipment that reduces sulfur dioxide and nitrogen oxides.

COLLABORATION IMPORTANT

The cap-and-trade model satisfies Leavitt's underlying principle that collaboration is important in environmental protection.

In a speech to EPA employees in December, Leavitt said improvement in the environment will never be accomplished "under the slow, expensive and conflict-intense processes of the past."

He also believes in "markets before mandates." It's the impoverished countries in the world where there's the greatest lack of environmental protection.

"Environmental improvements stimulate the economy," said Leavitt. But, he adds, those improvements have to balance good intentions with the ability to pay for them.

"As governor, these complex dilemmas and the nature of the task are not new to me,"

—Mike Leavitt, EPA Administrator

"Collaboration does not eliminate litigation," he told EPA employees, "but it can minimize it."

One piece of litigation that hasn't been eliminated is a challenge to changes in the New Source Review permitting program that regulates installation of pollution control technology in power plants and other industrial facilities.

A coalition of 14 states, the District of Columbia and six local California pollution control boards won a delay in enforcing those changes in December when the U.S. Court of Appeals for the District of Columbia agreed that the proposed rules could cause irreparable harm to the environment if an injunction wasn't granted.

Supporting the EPA changes, however, are 11 other states that favor the increased flexibility they would have in enforcing the Clean Air Act with the regulation changes.

A final court ruling on the conflict is not expected until 2005.

Meanwhile, Leavitt vows to enforce the old rule pending a final outcome in the case. In January, the federal government sued an eastern Kentucky power cooperative for expanding two of its plants in violation of the older rules that the EPA is trying to change.

CONTENTIOUS CONFIRMATION

Leavitt became the center of controversy at EPA before he even assumed his new duties. During contentious Senate confirmation hearings, lawmakers critical of the Bush administration's environmental policies used the nomination process to voice their unhappiness.

Sen. Hillary Rodham Clinton of New York was particularly vocal about EPA reports released after the September 11 attacks on New York City. Her complaints led to an agreement in which the EPA promised more indoor air quality testing in Lower Manhattan and a review of the cleanup by government and nongovernment experts.

Other holds on Leavitt's nomination were placed, and then removed, by Sens. Frank R. Lautenberg of New Jersey and Barbara Boxer of California and three candidates for the Democratic presidential nomination: Sens. John Kerry of Massachusetts, John Edwards of North Carolina and Joseph Lieberman of Connecticut.

Leavitt also had to withstand verbal barbs during the process.

"You've got a lot of guts taking this job because you're in a big hole to start with," said Sen. Harry Reid, a Nevada Democrat.

But his supporters were equally demonstrative.

U.S. EPA Administrators

- Michael O. Leavitt
  Nov. 6, 2003–present
- Marianne L. Horinko (acting)
  July 12, 2003–Nov. 5, 2003
- Linda J. Fisher (acting)
  June 28, 2003–July 11, 2003
- Christine Todd Whitman
  Jan. 31, 2001–June 27, 2003
- W. Michael McCabe (acting)
  Jan. 20, 2001–Jan 30, 2001
- Carol M. Browner
  Jan. 22, 1993–Jan. 19, 2001
- William K. Reilly
  Feb. 6, 1989–Jan. 20, 1993
- John Moore (acting)
  Jan. 21, 1989–Feb. 5, 1989
- Lee M. Thomas
  Feb. 8, 1985–Jan. 20, 1989
- Lee M. Thomas (acting)
  Jan. 4, 1985–Feb. 7, 1985
- William D. Ruckelshaus
  May 5, 1983–Jan. 4, 1985
- Lee Verstandig (acting)
  March 10, 1983–May 17, 1983
- Anne M. Gorsuch [Burford]
  May 20, 1981–March 9, 1983
- Walter Barber, Jr. (acting)
  Jan. 26, 1981–May 19, 1981
- Steve Jellinek (acting)
  Jan. 21, 1981–Jan. 25, 1981
- Douglas M. Costle
  March 7, 1977–Jan. 20, 1981
- John Quarles, Jr. (acting)
  Jan. 21, 1977–March 6, 1977
- Russell E. Train
  Sept. 13, 1973–Jan. 20, 1977
- Robert Fri (acting)
  April 30, 1973–Sept. 12, 1973
- William D. Ruckelshaus
  Dec. 4, 1970–April 30, 1973

"President Bush and Mike Leavitt will lead us into a new era of environmental protection," Sen. James Inhofe of Oklahoma said during Capitol Hill hearings.

In the end, Leavitt was confirmed by the full Senate 88–8.

ENVIRONMENTAL POLICY PERVASIVE

Leavitt said he is sensitive to why environmental policy is a lightning rod for debate.

"It deals in issues very personal to people: their relationship to the earth reflects their values and aspirations. It touches so many aspects of society," he said.

It's that wide-ranging reach of environmental policy that attracted Leavitt to the job when President Bush asked him to take it.

"A unique quality of the EPA is that it regulates the other federal departments. It impacts not just state, local and private agencies, but all our colleagues at the federal level. Environmental policy is a pervasive part of our world," he said. "Energy policy is really environmental policy. Transportation, in a large measure, is environmental policy. Economic, social and international policies— environment questions are wrapped all through those. I'm in a lab where I see it played out every day."

Dealing with the broad span of policy issues at the state level, Leavitt believes, will help him address the challenges of his new post. "As governor, these complex dilemmas and the nature of the task are not new to me."

Nor is the nature of the federal bureaucracy a concern, despite a warning from Sen. Max Baucus of Montana, who during the confirmation hearings told Leavitt, "There's somewhat longer knives out here in Washington than in the capital city of your home state."

But the new EPA administrator is undaunted by the nation's capital.

"I checked and during my 11 years as governor, I averaged 16 trips a year to Washington, averaging two days a trip," he said. "This is a fascinating place to serve but I'm not unaware of the complexities, nor am I oblivious to the difficulties."

23

Attorneys general are taking the lead in trying to force a crackdown on power plants that pollute across state lines.

From *Governing,* February 2004.

Spitzer Attack

Tom Arrandale

Eliot Spitzer, New York's attorney general, shaped national securities policy when he took on Wall Street's unsavory anti-investor practices—federal regulators having dropped the ball. Now that Spitzer is turning his legal guns on federal pollution control programs, New York's chief lawyer could wind up taking charge of how the nation's air quality laws will be implemented.

That's hardly the ideal way for the federal system to work. But state officials are growing ever more impatient with the U.S. government's feckless performance in recent years in shying away from difficult choices on environmental threats that concern the entire country. Spitzer has led other attorneys general in neighboring Northeastern states in taking on the Bush administration and big coal-burning utilities in a series of lawsuits designed to force federal regulators to crack down on power plants that export harmful pollutants across state and regional boundaries. "Yes, it's the federal government's job," Spitzer says, "but it's also our job" to protect New York residents when Midwestern and Southern power plants release health-threatening pollutants that blow downwind in New York's direction. "We have standing to sue under the Clean Air Act, and we're using that standing to protect the quality of air for New Yorkers."

Because emissions drift in from coal-fired Ohio Valley generating stations far to the southwest, New York and other Eastern Seaboard states could shut down their own power plants and take all motor vehicles off the road and still not comply with federal Clean Air Act standards. Midwestern utility practices may keep electricity rates lower for Midwestern customers, but the consequences show up downwind in forests, lakes and lungs in Northeastern states.

The issue reveals a troublesome fault in the federal structure for regulating environmental threats. Northeastern states can't order cleanups outside their boundaries, but so far neither Congress nor the U.S. Environmental Protection Agency has made the tough calls required to settle the conflict. "The federal government has been basically abdicating the field across the board," says Peter H. Lehner, a former Natural Resources Defense Council attorney who leads Spitzer's environmental bureau.

State attorneys general are stepping into the breach, and Spitzer has been particularly aggressive, filing lawsuits against 17 coal-fired power plants in Indiana, Kentucky, Ohio, Virginia and West Virginia. Last spring, Spitzer and federal pollution-control lawyers settled one case with a Virginia utility that agreed to spend $1.2 billion over 12 years to cut sulfur dioxide and nitrogen oxide emissions from eight aging installations. In a separate August ruling, a federal judge found that the Ohio Edison Co. violated EPA rules by substantially modifying a 2,000-megawatt plant without installing state-of-the-art emission controls. Spitzer and other state attorneys general also have gone to court to block the Bush administration from easing new source review rules and to force EPA to start regulating carbon dioxide emissions.

The administration's "Clear Skies" initiative is built on the sensible concept of emissions trading. But state regulators read the fine print as delaying compliance too long while curtailing the opportunities the law now provides for states or citizens to prod federal action by petitioning EPA and the courts. There's reason to suspect that utilities will be content to keep outmoded facilities running several more years while legal and political skirmishing plays out. Spitzer's lawsuits have been winding through the courts since 1999, and "inevitably what litigation does is put off decisions at least five years or maybe 10 years," notes Kenneth A. Colburn, who directs an organization of air-quality regulators from New England, New York and New Jersey.

That makes it all the more important that state governments are now forging ahead to experiment with their own strategies to address global warming and other nationwide air-quality problems. California, for instance, is prodding auto manufacturers to curtail carbon dioxide from tailpipes, and New York Governor George Pataki invited Northeastern state governors to devise a region-wide cap-and-trade system to reduce CO_2 from power plants. As Utah's governor, new EPA Administrator Michael Leavitt was instrumental in negotiating a multi-state agreement to deal with regional haze across the West's scenic vistas.

These days, Congress doesn't seem up to its constitutional role of sorting out regional differences; so maybe Midwest and Northeastern governors should get the dialogue going themselves. Spitzer makes no secret that he'll run for New York governor two years from now, and he acknowledges that litigating case by case over how federal law should be applied may not be the best way to produce timely and predictable regulatory policy. "I am not one who says the Clean Air Act is the only answer," he says. "There are a lot of different approaches that are being discussed that might work better."

Courts

Sooner or later, all the big issues of politics end up in court. Desegregation, voting rights, abortion, school prayer, the death penalty, the powers of the legislature versus the powers of the executive—the more controversial the question, the more likely it is that somebody in a black robe will be asked to resolve the dispute.

Most of the small issues of politics also end up in court. Who gets Grandma's china in the divorce settlement might not be on par with resolving a multi-billion-dollar state budget dispute (see the article by Rich Jones and Brenda Erickson in this section), but it can be a pretty important (and very political) issue to the parties involved. Again, a judge is likely to end up resolving the dispute.

State court systems are possibly the most overburdened and underappreciated branch of state government. They tend to have lower profiles than their federal counterparts, yet they deal with equally weighty issues—as well a host of trivial ones—and their decisions often have broad social, economic, and political consequences. Judges in state courts have a say in the most intimate details of life. For example, they help decide whom you can (or cannot) have sex with, and whom you can (or cannot) marry.

In recent years exactly these sorts of issues have thrust state courts into high-profile controversies, most notably the question of whether homosexuals have the same marriage rights as heterosexuals. Legally speaking, marriage is a contract that is regulated by state law. Thus when gays seek the right to marry, the natural place to seek that right is in state court. State judges, like it or not, find themselves right in the middle of the debate over gay marriage. When the Massachusetts Supreme Judicial Court ruled in late 2003 that preventing same-sex marriage violated the equal protection rights guaranteed by the state constitution, it kicked off a nationwide struggle over how to define *marriage*.

By making such controversial decisions, courts become targets for criticism. Unlike federal court judges, however, most state court judges are not protected by lifetime appointments to the bench. After making their decisions, state court judges often have to go before the voters to retain their positions. Make a high-profile decision that rubs some powerful interests the wrong way, and you risk losing your career as a judge.

This section's readings explore some of the trends and issues facing court systems and highlight the critical role that state courts play within the broader political system.

THE STRUCTURE OF STATE COURTS AND THE SELECTION OF JUDGES

The United States is unusual in that it has a dual judicial system. This is a product of federalism, which makes the federal government and state governments (at least in theory) coequal partners. Broadly speaking, the federal courts are set up to deal with issues of federal law and interpretation of the U.S. Constitution. State courts are set up to deal with state law and state constitutions. The U.S. Supreme Court sits at the top of both systems, mainly to ensure that state courts stay within the confines of the U.S. Constitution, which as the supreme law of the land sets the boundaries of state lawmaking.

State courts, however, are not subordinate to federal courts; they constitute an independent system with their own jurisdiction. State criminal justice systems are structured by state constitutions and state law, which includes most criminal law (cases that involve violations of the law) and much civil law (cases that involve disputes between private parties). State courts thus handle everything from traffic tickets to murder and gay marriage to divorce. The state courts' caseload is staggering, with more than 100 million cases filed every year.[1]

Most state court systems are organized into a basic three-level hierarchy. At the bottom of this hierarchy are the trial courts, or courts of first instance. A trial court is where a case is initially heard: the parties involved in the case make arguments and present evidence to a judge and often a jury. It is the job of the judge and jury to decide what the facts are and which side the law favors. Trial courts are the most numerous type of state court, and they are the workhorses of the system. Roughly 30,000

judges, magistrates, and similar court officers serve in the state trial courts. Each year there are roughly 1,500 cases filed for every state trial court judge.[2]

Above trial courts are courts of appeal. The basic job of the appeals court is to examine whether the law and proper procedures were followed by the trial court—not to provide the losing party in a trial court with a "do-over," or an opportunity to have the entire case reheard. A successful appeal must be based on a claim that the trial court made some legal error that damaged the loser's chances of winning the case.

At the top of most state court systems is a state-level supreme court. This constitutes the highest legal authority within the state—the only place to appeal a state supreme court decision is to the U.S. Supreme Court. To do so requires making a federal case of a dispute through a credible argument that some element of the state court process or state law violates the U.S. Constitution. That's a tough argument to prove, and relatively few cases make it from a state supreme court to the U.S. Supreme Court.

Although this basic three-level system serves as a reasonably accurate description of state court systems, individual states have any number of variations. Some have courts specializing in criminal or civil cases. Some have specialized courts such as family courts or juvenile courts. Some have separate appellate courts for different parts of the state. A handful of states have only trial courts and a supreme court, with no intermediate appeals courts (these tend to be smaller and less populous states).

States also vary in how they select judges to staff their court systems. The process of selecting judges is important because it must reconcile two conflicting values. Most people are in favor of an independent judiciary; we want judges to make decisions based on an honest reading of the facts of a case and the applicable law, not on the basis of partisan or political interests. It is generally reckoned that judges are less likely to submit to political or partisan pressure if they are free to make rulings without worrying if their decisions will cost them the next election or prompt the legislature to remove them from the bench. Yet while most people see this as a good reason to support judicial independence, we also want judges to be accountable for their decisions. We don't want people who can legislate from the bench and never have to face the voters.

There is no objective way to decide whether independence or accountability should take precedence when it comes to selecting judges. At the federal level, independence is put above accountability. Once appointed, federal judges serve until they retire voluntarily, are impeached for flagrant misconduct, or die. In short, federal judges are insulated from the larger political process, the idea being that life terms will make them more likely to make the "right" decision even when it is unpopular to do so.

At the state-level, though, accountability is given more of a role. Some states elect rather than appoint judges. The argument for doing so is that judges who periodically have to face the voters are less likely to try to impose their own policy preferences from the bench. The downside, of course, is that elected judges may be tempted to do what is popular rather than what is legally proper, a fear some political scientists have argued is well founded.[3]

The extent to which judges are exposed to the ballot box varies from state to state, and sometimes even within a state. Roughly half the states use a form of popular election to select at least some judges. Many of these are non-partisan elections, but a few states still use partisan ballots for judges. Most of the other states use some form of appointment system. Some states use pure appointive systems where the governor or legislature selects judicial nominees. More states, though, use a hybrid appointment system called "merit selection." Under merit selection a nominating committee, typically a nonpartisan committee that often includes representatives from the court system and legal profession, is charged with drawing up a list of candidates who are highly qualified to serve as judges. The governor (usually) or the legislature (more rarely) picks judges from the list.[4]

Judges in appointive or merit selection systems may still have to face the voters. They often have to run in retention elections, where they run uncontested and voters are simply asked to vote whether they want to retain the judge in office.

The bewildering number of ways in which states select judges reflects the fact that there is no perfect compromise between the competing values of independence and accountability. Predictably, judicial selection comes in for scrutiny every time a controversial ruling upsets powerful interests (see the article by James C. Foster in this section).

ISSUE AND TRENDS

The process used to select judges is a perennial issue for state court systems. Other issues, however, tend to be products of their eras rather than products of the system itself. In the past five years or so, two of the bigger issues state courts have struggled to deal with are same-sex unions and when juveniles should be legally treated as adults.

The national debate over same-sex unions was ignited more than a decade ago by the Hawaii Supreme Court, which in 1993 ruled that denying homosexuals the same marriage rights as heterosexuals violated the equal protection rights guaranteed in the state constitution. Hawaii voters made this issue moot in 1998 by approving a constitutional amendment that, in effect, banned same-sex marriages. Regardless of the constitutional change, the 1993 ruling let this particular political genie out of the bottle. It seemed only a matter of time before some state supreme court granted same-sex couples the right to marry on equal protection grounds, and this is exactly what happened in 2003 in Massachusetts. This propelled the issue into the 2004 presidential election, and set off an ongoing national debate on marriage (see the article by Christi Goodman in this section).

Although not as high profile as the same-sex marriage issue, the question of how to deal with juvenile offenders has been an ongoing challenge for courts and state criminal justice systems. The issue boils down to a basic question: at what point does a child become an adult? Some states treat sixteen-year-olds as adults, sending young offenders into adult court to be tried and sentenced. There is a deterrent argument here—supporters claim that teenagers will think twice about committing a petty (or major) crime if they know they are going to face the consequences as an adult. On the other side of this issue are those who argue that teenagers are likely to engage in criminal activities based on impulse and emotion, without fully accounting for the consequences. They fear that sending teenagers into the adult criminal justice system at a young age is as likely to turn them into serial criminals as scare them straight.

There are no easy answers here. State criminal justice systems are left to deal with the vague gap between adolescence and adulthood as best they can and as the law allows. Two of the articles in this section, by Sarah Hammond and Sarah Wheaton, detail the challenges the situation presents and the impact it can have on young lives.

The final reading takes a look at how courts are used to resolve power struggles between state legislatures and governors. Sometimes when legislatures and governors disagree they end up suing each other. Rich Jones and Brenda Erickson look at how state supreme courts resolve those conflicts and the issues underlying the disputes.

Notes

1. National Center for State Courts, *Examining the Work of State Courts, 2003,* www.ncsconline.org/D_Research/CSP/2003_Files/2003_Overview.pdf (accessed April 20, 2005).

2. Ibid.

3. Melinda Gann Hall, "State Judicial Politics: Rules, Structures, and the Political Game," in *American State and Local Politics,* ed. Ronald E. Weber and Paul Brace (New York: Chatham House Publishers, 1999), 114–138.

4. For an overview of the selection systems see David Rottman et al., "Courts and Judges," in *State Court Organization 1998* (Washington, D.C.: Bureau of Justice Statistics, Department of Justice, 2000), NCJ 178932, www.ojp.usdoj.gov/bjs/pub/pdf/sco9801.pdf (accessed June 3, 2004).

24

State of the Unions

Christi Goodman

The debate to define marriage is raging around the country in the wake of Massachusetts' court decision.

The Massachusetts Supreme Judicial Court ruled in November that it is unconstitutional to bar same-sex couples from marrying, touching off a political maelstrom across the country. The mayor of San Francisco started performing same-sex marriages in February. A county clerk in New Mexico began issuing marriage licenses to same-sex couples one week later. The city of San Francisco is now suing the state, challenging the constitutionality of the California statute that prohibits recognition of marriage between same-sex couples.

Nationwide, legislatures have introduced dozens of proposals this session that run the gamut from defending marriage as a union between a man and a woman to creating civil unions to allowing gay couples to marry.

"This is a difficult issue for the country, and it is a difficult issue for state legislatures. We are doing the best we can," said Massachusetts Speaker Thomas Finneran, as his deeply divided legislature struggled with the issue.

The Massachusetts legislature has held two constitutional conventions in an attempt to find some resolution to this issue, but the conventions were not able to agree on any amendments. If lawmakers decide to amend the constitution, the proposal must be approved in two successive legislative sessions and then referred to the voters. The earliest any proposed amendment could make the ballot would be November 2006. By court decree, the first legally sanctioned same-sex weddings could take place in Massachusetts as early as May this year.

These are the latest developments in the larger public discussion of "marriage" and "family" that started in 1993 when the

From *State Legislatures,*
April 2004.

121

Hawaii Supreme Court ruled that laws denying same-sex couples the right to marry violated state constitutional equal protection rights unless the state could show a "compelling reason" for such discrimination. In 1996, a trial court ruled that the state had no such compelling reason, and the case headed back to the supreme court. Voters adopted a constitutional amendment in 1998, before the final ruling was issued, giving the Legislature the power to reserve marriage to opposite-sex couples and effectively ending the lawsuit.

Congress passed and President Clinton signed the Defense of Marriage Act (DOMA) in 1996, defining marriage as "a legal union between one man and one woman as husband and wife" for the purpose of federal law and benefits. The act also clarified that states are not required to recognize same-sex marriages from any other jurisdiction.

The Hawaii debate, similar cases in Alaska and Vermont, and passage of the federal act have spurred state action. Before 1996, only three states had language on the books defining marriage as between a man and a woman. Now 42 have such statutes.

Four of those states have added language defining marriage to their constitutions. This session, 16 states are considering legislation to enact or clarify defense of marriage statutes, and 18 have proposed constitutional amendments. Eight states have introduced bills that would legalize same-sex marriages or civil unions, and one would add registered domestic partners to the list of people who are allowed to make health care decisions. California, New Jersey and Vermont are currently the only states with laws establishing statewide domestic partnerships or civil unions.

Defense of marriage legislation proponents see these measures as protection for traditional marriage. They are concerned that judges may not respect long-standing state definitions of marriage. They contend that same-sex marriage subverts the belief that our society is based on marriage between a man and a woman, and weakens the idea that monogamy lies at the heart of marriage. They say that gay rights activists seek to enact laws based on the belief that all consensual sexual acts are morally equal. There also is concern that laws legalizing same-sex marriage could weaken laws against polygamy, group marriage and incest.

Ohio lawmakers have passed legislation that, in addition to defining marriage as only between one man and one woman, also limits state benefits to unmarried partners. Senator Bill Harris, one of the sponsors of the legislation, said that it was important to underscore the "strong public policy of the state that marriage between one man and one woman is the foundation of our society. We didn't want judges to determine the definition of marriage in our state, we wanted to do it in the legislature."

Proposed Laws and Amendments
(As of March 1)

3 States with language on the books before 1996 that defined marriage as between a man and a woman. Maryland (1973), New Hampshire (1987) and Wyoming (1957).

4 States that have added defense of marriage language to their constitutions. Alaska, Hawaii, Nebraska, and Nevada.

16 States that have introduced legislation this session to enact or clarify defense of marriage statues. Alabama, Maryland, Michigan, New Hampshire, New Jersey, New York, Oklahoma, Rhode Island, South Carolina, South Dakota, Tennessee, Utah, Vermont, Virginia, Wisconsin and Wyoming.

18 States that have proposed constitutional amendments. Alabama, Georgia, Idaho, Illinois, Indiana, Iowa, Kansas, Kentucky, Maryland, Massachusetts, Michigan, Mississippi, Missouri, Oklahoma, Utah, Vermont, Washington and Wisconsin.

8 States that have bills pending that would legalize same-sex marriages or civil unions. California, Colorado, Hawaii, Massachusetts, new York, Rhode Island, Vermont and Washington.

3 States that allow domestic partnerships or civil unions. California, New Jersey and Vermont.

Proponents of same-sex marriage argue that the government should treat all couples equally. They assert that gay marriage is beneficial to society because it promotes tolerance and officially clarifies that homosexuals are not second-class citizens.

Others argue that without the legal right to marry, same-sex couples do not have access to family health coverage, medical and bereavement leave, child custody, tax benefits and pension plans. Still others say this issue is about civil rights.

"For me, it is about one thing, the principle that one group of citizens cannot be 'almost' equal to

State Defense of Marriage Acts (DOMAs)

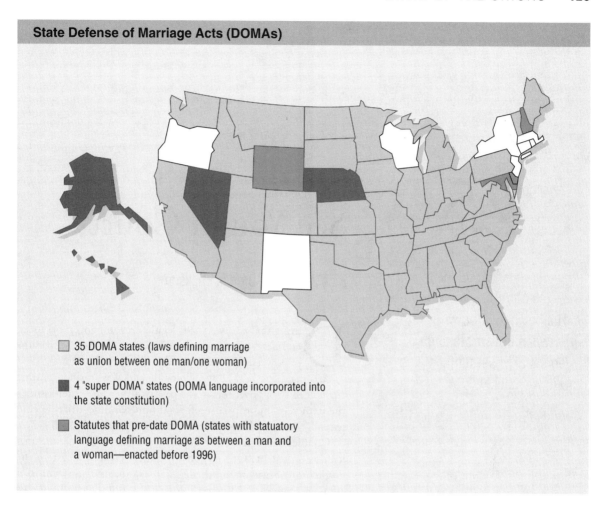

☐ 35 DOMA states (laws defining marriage as union between one man/one woman)

■ 4 "super DOMA" states (DOMA language incorporated into the state constitution)

▨ Statutes that pre-date DOMA (states with statuatory language defining marriage as between a man and a woman—enacted before 1996)

another," says Massachusetts Senator Dianne Wilkerson. "I was but one generation removed from an existence in slavery. I know the pain of being less than equal. I cannot and will not impose that status on anyone else."

There are several proposals before Congress to amend the U.S. Constitution, defining marriage as between a man and a woman and ensuring that states would not be required to recognize same-sex marriages from other jurisdictions.

President Bush has announced his support for such an amendment, however, he is receptive to allowing states to "define other arrangements." This could indicate that the president does not favor enacting a federal ban on civil union or domestic partnership laws. Opponents of the amendment cite federalism concerns in addition to support for same-sex marriages. A constitutional amendment requires ratification by two-thirds of the U.S. House and Senate and three-fourths of the state legislatures for enactment.

25

See You in Court

Rich Jones and Brenda Erickson

The balance of power between governors and legislatures sometimes gets out of whack.

During the past two years, legislatures and governors in several states have squared off in court. The issue? Separation of powers.

Arizona, New York, Iowa, Colorado and Wisconsin legislatures challenged their governors in the past two years over such issues as the item veto, appropriating federal funds and negotiating compacts. The rulings have so far favored the legislative branch 3-2.

Conflict between the two branches is a built-in feature of American government. Our nation's founders created a system that divides authority among the legislature, governor and courts to eliminate concentrated power in one place. But separation of powers is not absolute, and the conflicts that arise are usually resolved through the political process. Recently they have evolved into legal confrontations.

AN ARIZONA EXAMPLE

In June 2003, the Arizona Legislature passed the general appropriations bill for FY 2004 that contained line items entitled "lump sum reduction" for five state agencies.

The effect was to give the governor discretion over $4.7 million in cuts contained in these agencies' budgets. The governor vetoed the lump sum reduction lines, eliminating the budget cuts and, in effect, increasing the amounts appropriated by the Legislature.

The Legislature adjourned sine die without attempting to override the vetoes. But the Senate president, the House speaker and the majority leaders from each chamber filed suit in the Arizona Supreme Court challenging the governor's use of the line item veto.

From *State Legislatures*, July/August 2004.

Budget Battles

Legislatures and governors are most likely to clash over their respective budget and oversight powers because that is where executive and legislative powers intersect. It is understandable then that recent court cases involve aspects of each.

The legislature has the exclusive power to appropriate, but in most states the executive formulates and submits a budget for legislative consideration. In proposing the budget, the governor acts in some ways as an appropriator.

In addition to proposing the budget, governors in 44 states have veto powers that allow them to delete sections or items in appropriations bills without rejecting the entire bill. The item veto was proposed as a tool to prevent "log rolling" in which special interest spending was included in omnibus budget bills to secure votes. It gives the governor more power and flexibility than that granted under traditional all-or-nothing veto provisions that allow only the entire bill to be vetoed.

Thad Beyle, University of North Carolina professor of political science and nationally recognized expert on governors, says that the greatest increase in individual gubernatorial powers from 1960 to 2003 was in their veto powers as more governors gained the item veto.

"Governors like the item veto and extend it as far as they can," Beyle says. "The word is out among the governors, use the item veto or threaten to use it to get what you want."

It is not surprising then that three out of five of the recent court cases between governors and legislatures involved the item veto.

Most state budgets do more than appropriate funds. Many also contain substantive policy, as well as legislative directives, on how the appropriated funds are to be spent. By inserting language setting conditions on appropriations and recommending changes in programs based on oversight, legislatures come close to performing the administrative functions that are the exclusive province of the executive branch. Governors instinctively reject legislatively imposed restrictions on their ability to run state government.

We may be seeing more of these cases now because the likelihood of conflict increases when the governor and the legislative majority are from different parties. Currently the number of states with divided governments—governors and majority control of the legislature in the hands of different parties—is near an all-time high. In addition, the recent tough economies facing states have highlighted partisan and philosophical differences over approaches to balancing budgets. Sometimes these differences cannot be resolved politically, and the parties turn to the courts.

In Arizona, Iowa, New York and Wisconsin, the governor and at least one chamber of the legislature are controlled by different parties. And in Colorado, although both chambers and the governor's office are controlled by Republicans, the legislature sought to protect its considerable authority over the budget process.

Alan Rosenthal, legislative scholar at Rutgers University, finds that the differences among the states in the relative powers of the legislature and governor make it hard to generalize about trends. Governors may be gaining a bit more power because they can communicate their messages to the public better than legislatures with their numerous voices. He also finds that governors in the states with term limits have generally gained some power because of the increased turnover and lack of experience among legislators. "However, there is a rough balance of power between the legislature and governor in most states," says Rosenthal. "The separation of powers still holds, and it works."

—*Rich Jones, NCSL*

In December, the court ruled that the legislators lacked standing to bring the case and let the governor's vetoes stand.

"We stayed out of it," Arizona Chief Justice Charles E. Jones told the House Judiciary Committee in 2004. "It was strictly a political issue, an issue that should have been resolved by the branches."

But Jim Drake, rules attorney for the House, says the court neglected to consider examples of previous court cases. The decision leaves open the question of what the Legislature can do to enforce limits on the governor's line-item veto power, he says.

NEW YORK'S STRUGGLE

The New York Legislature has been sparring with the governor over the budget process and their respective powers for the past six years. Two cases currently ready for oral argument before the state's highest court may more clearly define these powers.

Working with the Governor

Partisan balance, legislative experience of the governor, regular and open communications, and respect for the institutional prerogatives of each branch help determine the nature of legislative-executive relations.

Oklahoma House Speaker Larry Adair has served with five governors in his 22 years in the Legislature. "It's a plus when the governor has previous legislative experience," he says. "They understand how the Legislature works and probably have more realistic expectations."

But while previous legislative experience can give the governor a better understanding of the process, familiarity also can breed contempt. Memories of past conduct can be a barrier to working with someone in a new position.

Most observers stress the importance of open, frank and regular communications in building solid working relationships between the legislature and the executive.

"Good interbranch communication can minimize misunderstandings regarding motives and goals," says Connecticut Senate Majority Leader Martin M. Looney. "This is especially important and difficult" in states like Connecticut with divided government.

"Honesty, integrity and trust bolster legislative-executive relations more than anything else," says Steven James, clerk of the Massachusetts House. He says that in the early 1990s Governor William Weld began meeting weekly with the Senate president and speaker, a tradition that continues today. These meetings help improve cooperation between the branches. "Even when the legislature disagrees with the governor, and they often do," says James, "it is at least helpful that the measures were discussed in a meeting among the legislative leaders and governor."

"Legislators need to treat the governor with respect, but must balance that with their responsibility to do what is best for the state," says Illinois Senator Donne Trotter.

"Friction occurs most often when the rules of engagement are not clearly defined, and the two branches are second guessing each other," says Kelly Skidmore, senior legislative aide to Florida Senate Minority Leader Ron Klein. "Or when the rules have been established, but are changed in the middle of the game or are totally disregarded for political expediency."

"Good legislative-executive relations must be based on a mutual recognition of the strengths and proper role of the branches," says Looney.

—*Brenda Erickson, NCSL*

The Legislature's role in budget preparation was significantly changed by a 1927 amendment to the constitution which gave the executive a strong role in the initiation of the state's budget. The amendment contains a "nonalteration" provision that states that the Legislature can alter appropriation bills only by striking or reducing an appropriation or proposing a new and different expenditure. However, the Legislature has challenged, in both cases, gubernatorial efforts to use the executive's appropriation-proposing authority to change or invalidate existing state laws.

The Legislature amended three of the governor's bills in the 1999 budget that did not involve appropriations, but contained policy directives relating to appropriations. Governor George Pataki used the item veto to remove the amendments. Assembly Speaker Sheldon Silver went to court arguing that the item veto only applies to appropriations.

In 2001, the governor's budget contained language that would have circumvented existing laws. In passing the budget, lawmakers deleted or revised this language. Pataki sued the Legislature claiming it had violated the "nonalteration" provision.

The state appellate court ruled in the governor's favor in both cases. It said that the governor can use the item veto to remove language in appropriations bills and that the Legislature can only make the adjustments described in the nonalteration provision. Both cases have been appealed.

The decisions "amount to a coronation of the governor," says Silver. "The only role left for the elected representatives of the Legislature would be to plead for the people of our state before the king's throne."

The Legislature and governor were at odds over the budget once again during the 2003 legislative session. This time they resolved their differences out of court.

The Legislature overrode all of Pataki's 119 vetoes—the first time since 1982 that it overrode a governor's veto.

IOWA'S POWER PLAY

A case before the Iowa Supreme Court involving the definition of appropriations bills and whether the governor can use the item veto to strike language in such bills was decided in the legislature's favor in June.

"This case is huge for us," says Speaker Christopher Rants. "It will forever change the relationship between the legislature and the executive."

In a 2003 special session, the General Assembly passed two bills promoting economic development. One created the Grow Iowa Values Fund and laid out its administrative structure. It included tax reductions and changes in workers' compensation and product liability laws—all favored by the legislative leadership, but opposed by the governor. The second law contained a $45 million appropriation for the fund.

The governor vetoed a number of provisions in the first bill, including many of those favored by legislative leaders. The speaker and the Senate majority leader filed suit to challenge the validity of the item vetoes.

A district court ruled in the governor's favor, upholding his item vetoes. The leaders appealed.

"This was a policy bill, not an appropriations bill," says Rants. "It contained policy objectives that we wanted and policy objectives the governor wanted. The only way to compromise was to meld the two together, but the governor tried to have it his way and leave the legislature out all together."

In its amicus brief filed with the Iowa Supreme Court, the National Conference of State Legislatures argued that the district court erred in its interpretation of case law to broaden the definition of appropriations. It also asserts that the governor can veto only "items of appropriation," a power that does not extend to policy language contained in appropriations bills. Without these limitations, the governor will be able to intrude on the general policymaking and appropriation powers that are the constitutional prerogatives of the legislature.

COLORADO'S CASE

The Colorado General Assembly recently asked the state supreme court to resolve a dispute over its authority to appropriate funds received under the federal Jobs and Growth Tax Relief Reconciliation Act of 2003. Governor Bill Owens allocated about $36 million received under the act to various programs with budget shortfalls and certain one-time capital projects.

At issue was whether the funds have significant restrictions on how they can be spent, making them custodial in nature and not subject to the legislature's appropriations powers. During the 2004 session, a bill defining the legislature's power to appropriate federal funds passed the House and passed the Senate on second reading. The legislature asked the Supreme Court to rule on the constitutionality of the bill.

"The most important power of the people's legislative body is the power of the purse," says Senate President John Andrews. "The joint legislative leadership felt strongly that we needed to protect the legislature's prerogatives in the budget process and develop a baseline for future actions."

The Colorado Supreme Court upheld the legislature's authority to appropriate the federal money received under the jobs program, finding that the limited restrictions on their use excluded them from being considered custodial funds.

"I am satisfied with the decision," Andrews says. "It is a good example of where the system worked—a dispute between two branches was refereed by the third branch as intended by the Constitution."

AND IN WISCONSIN

Wisconsin's Assembly speaker and Senate majority leader filed suit in the state supreme court in 2003, challenging the governor's authority to negotiate gaming compacts with Indian tribes that did not provide for periodic legislative renewal. The court ruled in favor of the Legislature, stating that the governor "exceeded his authority when he agreed unilaterally to a compact term that permanently removes the subject of Indian gaming from the Legislature's ability to establish policy and make law." The court also ruled that the governor did not have the power to negotiate a compact that waives the state's sovereign immunity because that is a policy decision that only the Legislature can make.

Generally, legislators want to work with the governor. Governors also recognize that their ability to get their programs passed will go a long way in determining whether the public views them as successful.

"Most governors can get much of what they want from the legislature," says Alan Rosenthal of Rutgers University, author of the new book *Heavy Lifting: The Job of the American Legislature.* "Governors who are willing to cut the legislature in on decision making and give it some power can be very effective in working with the legislature."

Institutional commitment on the part of legislators is important to maintaining a balance of powers between the branches, according to Rosenthal. This is a particular problem in states with term limits where lawmakers tend to have less of an appreciation for the legislature's institutional prerogatives.

Throughout American history there has been an ebb and flow of power and preeminence between the legislative and executive branches of government. While each branch has separate constitutional functions, the informal relationships that exist are important in maintaining the equilibrium over time. Occasionally the courts step in to sort out the differences.

26

Rethinking Politics and Judicial Selection During Contentious Times

James C. Foster*

Picking judges in the face of sharp ideological divisions is not easy. Is it time to rethink how we select judges?

S tudents of judicial selection are living through interesting times. Consider, for example, the continuing skirmishes on the same-sex marriage front in the culture wars. In November 2003 (and again in February 2004), the Massachusetts Supreme Judicial Court read that State's constitution as requiring state recognition of marital unions between gay and lesbian couples.[1] In his January 2004 State of the Union Address, President George W. Bush characterized such decisions as the result of "[a]ctivist judges . . . . forcing their arbitrary will upon the people" and warned that "the only alternative left to the people" might be a federal constitutional amendment to bulwark the 1996 federal Defense of Marriage Act.[2] Then, in February 2004, San Francisco Mayor Gavin Newsom, citing the California Constitution's equal protection clause, authorized City Hall officials to begin licensing and officiating at marriages of same-sex couples.[3] Two groups opposed to Mayor Newsom's action, the Proposition 22 Legal Defense and Education Fund—backed by the Alliance Defense Fund—and the Campaign for California Families, went to the California Superior Court, arguing that San Francisco was violating the California Family Code and California Ballot Measure 22, adopted in November 2000, that limit marriage to a man and a woman.[4] Everyone in this contest, it seems, has the law on their side. And politics abound.

In this highly charged environment, how are we to make sense of debates over the best way to select state judges? The question does

From *Albany Law Review,* 2004.

*The author appreciatively acknowledges the contributions of Sarah K. Delaney, Melinda B. Rickman, and Bob Ehrhart in the preparation of this essay.

not lend itself to any single definitive answer. Any answer will also be essentially contestable, because different people will define "best" differently. Nevertheless, amidst the comparatively tranquil precincts of academia, several salutary developments over the past decade serve as useful signposts indicating how we might think more clearly about the knotty issue of selecting state judges.

IT'S THE *SORT* OF POLITICS, STUPID

First and foremost, some students of judicial selection have sought to sophisticate (or one might say complicate) the concept of politics as that activity pertains to what judges do and how to select judges. Our key insight is comprehending that not all "politics" is the same. Scholars almost universally acknowledge that no selection procedure can be devoid of politics. "Merit selection" has a nice neutral ring, but such procedures turn out in practice to merely shift the locus of politics, rather than eliminate it. Elections to fill or to retain incumbents in judicial positions can be thoroughly political whether partisan or nonpartisan. So, for openers, there is wide awareness that judicial selection is the continuation of politics by other means.[5] It is simply delusional to attempt to purge politics from the process by which we select state jurists. Nor is it desirable to do so. In a republic that at least aspires to be based on popular sovereignty, many—including myself—believe that the judges who do the publics' business ought not to be removed from electoral politics. Here's the rub: What do we mean by "politics?"

IT'S THE CONTEXT THAT COUNTS

Politicization is one species of politics. However, the species is not coextensive with the genus. In certain contexts, the politics of judicial selection can become politicized. That is, under certain circumstances, state judicial elections occasionally can become metaphorical "crocodiles in the bathtub," as the late Judge Otto Kaus vividly pictured hotly contested judicial elections.[6] Politicization of judicial elections occurs via the infusion of large sums of cash, with all of the attendant media advertising, sound bites, and other trappings of contemporary American no-holds-barred electoral contests for executive and legislative posts. Not all judicial elections bite judges—in fact very few do so. Big spending on

judicial elections is driven by controversy over specific judicial decisions. What generates controversy?

The answer to this question comes from a second insight, derived from a methodological development within the judicial politics subfield of political science awkwardly dubbed "historical/interpretive 'new institutionalism.' "[7] This understanding is that politicization results from the specific social circumstances surrounding particular instances of judicial selection—not out of the form of selection per se. From this new vantage point, Alexis de Tocqueville's perceptive observation— "[s]carcely any political question arises in the United States that is not resolved, sooner or later, into a judicial question"[8]—is merely a point of departure. Although most questions of social choice indeed end up before courts in America, not all such questions are so controversial as to generate politicization. This insight does not render the mode of selecting state judges meaningless. It is not the case that one approach or another makes no difference. Rather, practitioners of the new institutionalism shift the analytical frame to emphasize that all means of selecting judges are embedded within a web of institutional circumstances.

For instance, returning to the storm over same-sex marriage described above, students of the new institutionalism are inclined to ask why same-sex marriage has risen to the front pages as a hot button issue in American politics. After all, it's not as though the political questions— the so-called cultural wars—that are resolved, sooner or later, into judicial questions arise out of thin air. Although this essay is not the place to develop the analysis, it is clear that several political, socio-cultural, and institutional factors are converging to generate the current dispute over how we are going to (re)define marriage.

Four salient factors occur to me: the gay rights movement, the post-New Deal constitutional regime, shifts in American electoral alignments, and insurgency within the Republican Party. One might summarize these developments with broad-brush-stroke, short-hand references to Stonewall, Stone, southern strategy, and social agenda.

The middle decades of the last century were the scene of resurgent social activism. The Civil Rights Movement, the Second Wave of Feminism, and groups advocating rights for, inter alios, farm workers, welfare recipients, disabled Americans, and illegal immigrants all flourished. On June 27, 1969, resistance to a routine police roust of the Stonewall Inn, a gay bar on Christopher Street in

Greenwich Village, turned into a germinal event that eventuated in the Gay Liberation Front.[9] Thirty-one years before Stonewall, Justice Harlan Fiske Stone wrote perhaps the most famous—or infamous—footnote in constitutional law.[10] In the course of narrowing the "scope for operation of the presumption of constitutionality," Stone specifically targeted for "more searching judicial inquiry" the issue of "whether prejudice against discrete and insular minorities may be a special condition, which tends seriously to curtail the operation of those political processes ordinarily to be relied upon to protect minorities."[11] It takes no imagination whatsoever to see that decisions such as *Loving v. Virginia*,[12] *Romer v. Evans*,[13] and *Lawrence v. Texas*[14] are Stone's spawn.

While gays and lesbians were organizing and state courts were following—and in some instances leading—the nation's highest courts in extending constitutional protection to homosexuals, the American electorate was undergoing realignment and the Republican Party was being remade. Gradually, throughout the mid-twentieth century, the solid Democratic South was becoming solidly Republican territory. By the time Kevin Phillips wrote *The Emerging Republican Majority* in 1969, he was synthesizing and mapping out the implications of macro demographic and cultural trends well under way.[15] Phillips's genius was discerning the writing on the wall, so to speak, and translating it into a game plan for Republican politicians. If support for gay and lesbian rights is traceable to social movements and constitutional interpretation, opposition is rooted in the shift in the center of American electoral gravity to the Sun Belt and to the capture of the Republican Party by social conservatives who define "being Republican" as being against a whole laundry list of behaviors—from receiving welfare or committing crimes, to homosexual relations or doing drugs—stigmatized as "licentious." By the time Ronald Reagan was elected president in 1980, the Party of Lincoln had become the party of Lee Atwater. It was not long in becoming the party of Karl Rove.

A JUDGE IS NOT A "POLITICIAN IN ROBES" . . .

In the present super-heated context, state judges who vote to protect the rights of gays and lesbians risk a politicized challenge. Like abortion and the death penalty, same-sex marriage has high "crocodile" potential—whatever the

particular mode of judicial selection. How can we keep the crocodiles at bay while assuring that judges are accountable to the public whose business they conduct? This question is usually phrased as the dilemma of balancing judicial independence with judicial accountability.

Here, as well, students of judicial selection have some constructive ideas to contribute. At bottom, these ideas rest on the argument that because judicial politics is different, the politics of judicial elections also must be different. A misconception exists in this country—widely shared among Americans as a cultural belief and among lawyers as a professional conceit—that law and politics are two separate realms. John Adams's 1780 line about ours being "a government of laws, and not of men"[16] may be both reassuring and flattering. It's also disingenuous. More to my point, this Kiplingesque view—law is law, and politics is politics, and never the twain shall meet[17]—frustrates a nuanced understanding of the *sort* of politics in which judges participate.

American judges engage in law-full politics: the currency of their exercise of power is rules and rights. In order to understand judicial politics it is helpful to recall to Max Weber's justly classic *Politics as a Vocation*.[18] For Weber, politics entails "striving to share power or striving to influence the distribution of power . . . among groups within a state."[19] Weber describes politics in terms of legitimate relations of domination and obedience. But for Weber—and here is his crucial move—not all bases (" 'pure' types"[20]) of political legitimacy are the same. In addition to " 'traditional' " and " 'charismatic' " legitimacy, there is " 'legality:' " obedience "by virtue of the belief in the validity of legal statute and functional 'competence' based on rationally created *rules*."[21] Students of judicial selection have "rediscovered" due process and republican government as the twin pillars of the legal rationality in this country, distinguishing our judicial politics. The argument is as elegant as it is complex. It is also controversial. The judicial function ought to be relatively insulated from popular will (and contests to (re)elect judges rid of politicization) because judges exercise power on behalf of those wise restraints that make men and women free. Wise restraints? Due process restraints on the arbitrary exercise of power by the executive and legislative branches; structural restraints (exemplified by the Guarantee Clause[22] and articulated in the political philosophy of *The Federalist*[23]) on untrammeled democratic majorities: judges are the care-takes of both. Returning to Weber, institutionally speaking, the political vocation of judges is to rule on the basis of restraints. Fundamental aspects of judicial politics—the socialization, roles, norms, settings, and M.O.—defining the judicial function differ decisively from what goes on in, say, a state assembly or the Oval Office.

It seems to me that the judicial vocation in the United States is an uneasy amalgam, residing on a continuum of Weber's civil servant and politician "pure types." The former engages in "impartial 'administration,' " ruling "*[s]ine ira et studio,* 'without scorn or bias.' "[24] The latter "take[s] a stand . . . [and is] passionate—*ira et studium.*"[25] Weber continues: "The honor of the civil servant is vested in his ability to execute conscientiously the order of the superior authorities, exactly as if the order agreed with his own conviction. . . . The honor of the political leader, of the leading statesman, however, lies precisely in an exclusive *personal* responsibility for what he does, a responsibility he cannot and must not reject or transfer."[26] As one moves higher up state and federal judicial hierarchies, from trial to appellate courts, the judicial vocation moves closer to this uneasy amalgam.

The amalgam is "uneasy" for a couple of reasons. First, although it is clear that judges are not strictly Weberian administrators, neither are they merely Weber's politicians. Perhaps the problem is the words Weber chooses: scorn and bias. No competent judge rules with contempt and prejudice. Still, every judge unavoidably rules "personally" in the sense that he or she brings his or her biography to the task of bringing the law to bear on resolving disputes. Judges are accountable to the rule of law—as they understand it. Second, "the exclusive *personal* responsibility for what [s]he does" that every appellate judge bears is an enormously complex blend of volition and constraint(s). Exercising judgment is a disciplined act of will. In other words, judges make choices, but not only as they see fit.

. . . AND AN ELECTION IS NOT AN ELECTION

The corollary to the view that judging is a distinct mode of politics is the insistence that judicial elections ought to be conducted differently that contests for legislative and executive office. A significant number of scholars of judicial selection—I'd venture a majority of us—reject the "unilocular" view of elections, a term used by Justice

Ginberg, dissenting in *Republican Party v. White.*[27] The five Justices in the *White* majority arguably did not adopt such a view, although they "obscur[ed]" important distinctions, as Justice Stevens argued in dissent.[28] However, the Eleventh Circuit Court of Appeals, in *Weaver v. Bonner,*[29] seems to have read *White* in unilocular terms: "[W]e believe that . . . *White* suggests that the standard for judicial elections should be the same as the standard for legislative and executive elections. . . . [T]he distinction between judicial elections and other types of elections has been greatly exaggerated. . . ."[30] Among many students of judicial selection, the *Weaver* opinion has been received like a fire bell in the night.

DIVERSE OPTIONS, DIVERSITY OF CHOICE

The dilemma of how to treat judges differently (assuring independence) while treating them the same (electing judges) will not be easily or definitively resolved. My sense from my own studies, from reading literature and listservs, and from listening to my colleagues debate, is that two frames of reference increasingly shape scholarly thinking about this dilemma: federalism and cross-national comparisons. How is this for a watchword: Let a thousand judicial selection flowers bloom—or at least fifty. There are lots of reform proposals in circulation, some more modest than others, vying for attention. The various combinations of training and credentialing, appointment, election, length of terms, and term limits are legion. The most credible of these acknowledge that politicization of judicial selection is a contemporary social reality. Mitigating politicization seems to be the name of the game. Toward that end, when it comes to the "best" mode of judicial selection for our tumultuous time, the twin recommendations that states should look around, and look different, are compelling.

Notes

1. *See* Fred Bayles & Richard Benedetto, *Mass. Debates Gay Marriage: Protesters on Both Sides Gather in Boston,* USA Today, Feb. 12, 2004, at A3.

2. President George W. Bush, State of the Union Address (Jan. 20, 2004), *available at* http://www.whitehouse.gov/news/resleases/2004/01/2004120-7.html (last visited Apr. 13, 2004).

3. *See* Harriet Chiang et. al., *Mad Dash to S.F. City Hall to Say 'I Do,'* S.F. CRON., Feb. 14, 2004, at A1.

4. *See* Proposition 22 Legal Def. & Educ. Fund v. City of San Francisco, No. 503943 (Cal. Super. Ct. filed Feb. 13, 2004); Thomasson v. Newsom, No. 428794 (Cal. Super. Ct. filed Feb. 11, 2004).

5. *Cf.* Carl von Clausewitz, *On War* 87 (Michael Howard & Peter Paret eds., Princeton Univ. Press 1976) (1832).

6. Paul Reidinger, *The Politics of Judging,* 73 A.B.A. J. 52, 58 (1987) (" 'There's no way a judge is going to be able to ignore the political consequences of certain decisions, especially if he or she has to make them near election time. That would be like ignoring a crocodile in your bathtub.' ") (quoting former California Supreme Court Justice Otto Kaus); *see* James C. Foster, *The Interplay of Legitimacy, Elections, and Crocodiles in the Bathtub: Making Sense of Politicization of Oregon's Appellate Courts,* 39 Willamette L. Rev. 1313 (2003).

7. Sue Davis, *The Chief Justice and Judicial Decision-Making: The Institutional Basis for Leadership in the Supreme Court, in* Supreme Court Decision-Making: New Institutionalist Approaches 135, 137 (Cornell W. Clayton & Howard Gillman eds., 1999).

8. Alexis de Tocqueville, *Democracy in America* 290 (Phillips Bradley ed., Vintage Books 1945) (1835).

9. *See* William N. Eskridge, Jr., *Challenging the Apartheid of the Closet: Establishing Conditions for Lesbian and Gay Intimacy, Nomos, and Citizenship, 1961–1981,* 25 Hofstra L. Rev. 817, 822–23 (1997).

10. *See* United States v. Carolene Products Co., 304 U.S. 144, 152 n.4 (1938).

11. *Id.*

12. 388 U.S. 1 (1967) (striking down a Virginia anti-miscegenation statute on the basis that such a statute violates the Equal Protection Clause and the Due Process Clause of the Fourteenth Amendment).

13. 517 U.S. 620, 624, 635 (1996) (holding that a Colorado amendment to its state constitution, which "prohibits all legislative, executive or judicial action at any level of state or local government designed to protect . . . homosexual persons," violates the Equal Protection Clause of the Fourteenth Amendment).

14. 123 S. Ct. 2472, 2476, 2484 (2003) (overruling *Bowers v. Hardwick,* 478 U.S. 186 (1986), and striking down a Texas statute that banned " 'deviate sexual intercourse with another individual of the same sex' ").

15. Kevin P. Phillips, *The Emerging Republic Majority* (1969).

16. John Adams, Novanglus No. 7 (1775), *available at* http://douglassarchives.org/adam_a50.thm (last visited Apr. 20, 2004).

17. Rudyard Kipling, *The Ballad of East and West, in* A Victorian Anthology, 1837–1895 (Edmund Clarence Stedman ed., 1895) ("Oh, East is East, and West is West, and never the twain shall meet. . . ."), *available at* http://bartleby.com/246/1129.html (last visited Apr. 20, 2004).

18. Max Weber, *Politics as a Vocation* (H. H. Gerth & C. Wright Mills trans., Oxford University Press 1958) (1919).

19. *Id.* at 78.

20. *Id.* at 79.

21. Id.

22. U.S. Const. art. IV, §4 ("The United States shall guarantee to every State in this Union a Republican Form of Government. . . .").

23. Alexander Hamilton et al., *The Federalist* (George W. Carey & James McClellan eds., Gideon ed. 2001).

24. Weber, *supra* note 18, at 95.

25. *Id.*

26. *Id.*

27. 536 U.S. 765, 805 (2002) (Ginsburg, J., dissenting).

28. *Id.* at 802 (Stevens, J., dissenting).

29. 309 F.3d 1312 (11th Cir. 2002).

30. *Id.* at 1321.

27 Downsizing Helps Delinquents

Sarah Hammond

Missouri has discovered that showering troubled teens with warmth, respect and concern works well in turning them around.

Thinking small has made a big difference for youth corrections in Missouri. The Missouri Division of Youth Services' (DYS) juvenile corrections system is gaining attention as a model for other states considering reforms favoring residential treatment over prison for kids who commit crimes.

Twenty years ago, Missouri, like many states, operated large state training schools. They were shut down and subsequently replaced when the state began to experiment with smaller correctional programs. During the 1980s, DYS divided the state into five regions and started using sites such as abandoned school houses, convents and large residential homes to house delinquent teens closer to their families.

Missouri's approach to youth corrections relies on personal treatment, rehabilitation and making internal changes within juveniles in positive small-scale settings rather than isolation, punishment and behavioral compliance.

The program's emphasis is on positive peer relationships and intense, consistent therapy coupled with a small and intimate group atmosphere. In this kind of a setting even the most violent of delinquent teens, preferably called "kids," not "prisoners" begin to share stories, discuss their emotions, and talk about their hopes and dreams for the future.

The staff consists of college educated "youth specialists" who do not wear uniforms and who work closely and are able to forge relationships with the kids.

Even the facilities' furnishings—goldfish tanks, couches, beanbags, potted plants, stuffed animals and handmade posters—are designed to make the kids comfortable and create a more family-type atmo-

From *State Legislatures,*
December 2004.

sphere. As a result of this warm, positive atmosphere, incidents of attacks on other juveniles or staff are rare. And there has not been a single suicide under DYS custody.

One of the key components of the program is the fostering of a positive relationship between each juvenile and a member of the staff. A young person entering a facility is assigned a service coordinator for his or her entire stay. The coordinator monitors the juvenile's progress by maintaining constant interaction and plays an important role in determining when the youth should be discharged. Stringent aftercare services also are provided. After the juvenile is released, the coordinator maintains the relationship by helping him find a job and adjust to life on the outside. "We become surrogate families to these kids . . . it makes all the difference" says Mark Steward, director of the department of youth services.

But the critical question is does this type of system work? Missouri's recidivism rate, which has been as low as 11 percent, is dramatically lower than the rest of the county. A 2003 study revealed that only 85 of 1,400 teens who were released in 1999 ended up in adult prisons. Another 2003 recidivism report compiled by the DYS found that 70 percent of the youths released in 1999 were not recommitted to a correctional program within three years.

Missouri's overall costs are lower when compared to what other states spend on youth corrections. The program costs approximately $94 per day for every youth between the ages of 10 and 17, while the cost per youth in surrounding states was $140, according to "Less Cost, More Safety: Guiding Lights for Reform in Juvenile Justice," a study by the American Youth Policy Forum.

"Our programs operate on less than other states because we are able to do many things internally, such as our health services and security," Seward says. "We don't have large perimeters with guards. And while we have high staff coverage, there is not a lot of support cost. We keep our overhead low."

Missouri's success has attracted criminal justice officials, policymakers, parents and juveniles from across the country to visit and leave surprised with the atmosphere and results that the youth program has achieved.

Alabama, Georgia, Illinois, Louisiana, Maryland and New Jersey are considering similar programs. Maryland has enacted legislation requiring the department of juvenile services to come up with a master plan of reform for their juvenile facilities—keeping things small, delivering services close to home while keeping the kids and community safe.

28

An Awkward Age

Sarah Wheaton

Runaway teens don't belong in adult court, but they're often too old for juvenile court. The law tends to ignore them.

Finding Makayla Korpinen didn't exactly require classic detective work. Technically, the 16-year-old was a "missing teenager," but dozens of people in her hometown of East Hampton, Connecticut, knew where she was. In April 2002, she left her mother's home and moved across town to stay with her boyfriend. Makayla's mother not only knew the girl's whereabouts—she picked her up and drove her to doctors' appointments. But she could not get Makayla to come home. Neither could the police. They offered to file a petition in juvenile court asking for her return, but the family declined. On May 18, three weeks after moving out, Makayla Korpinen died of an ecstasy overdose.

It was a simple tragedy, but one mired in endless legal complications. Connecticut is one of three states in the country where 16- and 17-year-olds are referred automatically to adult court. This change was made in the 1990s as part of a tougher stance on youth crime. But running away from home isn't a crime under state law, merely a "status offense," and adult court doesn't deal with those. So that wasn't an option in Makayla's case.

Just what leverage police did have was extremely murky under Connecticut's poorly drafted "Youth in Crisis" law, which had taken effect the previous year and which one child advocate calls "funny little legislation that nobody understands." The "Youth in Crisis" law, as it stood in early 2002, clearly allowed any runaway to be referred to juvenile court, but since that court's jurisdiction extended only through age 15, anything a judge did there would be only a suggestion, not a ruling.

The wording of the law was so vague that debates took place—and still do—over whether police had the authority to bring Makayla

From *Governing,* January 2004.

back home against her will. The officers on the scene did not think they were authorized to do that. Others think they were. Connecticut state Representative Gail Hamm, who has sponsored legislation to rewrite the Youth in Crisis law, says that when the law took effect in 2001, officers in her East Hampton district were "told to ignore it." One East Hampton police sergeant recalls that when officers were briefed on the legislation, they were told it was so flawed that it was "not even usable."

Even if police had been fully empowered to return Makayla, however, it's not clear they would have. Police are extremely reluctant to take such actions, both because they can be sued and because of the likelihood that she would only leave again. This is the so-called "revolving door problem" that authorities all over the country are familiar with.

MORE AUTHORITY

Makayla Korpinen's is an unusually graphic and depressing case, but it frames issues that quite a few states are confronting as they struggle to create a sensible approach to runaways and other teen-age offenders who primarily are a threat to themselves, rather than society. No state has found an ideal answer, and there may not be one. But tragedies such as Makayla's nearly always stimulate some action.

In Connecticut, where the details of the Korpinen case appeared on newspaper front pages for months, every recent legislative session has brought a new attempt to bring coherence to the law. "Makayla's death refocused a number of legislators who were frustrated that the gray area was getting worse and worse," says Gail Hamm. "The kids who hadn't broken laws had no authority [over them] anywhere. We needed to decide when we're going to treat kids as adults in Connecticut."

To resolve police uncertainty, the legislature passed a new law in 2002 granting immunity to officers who force teenage runaways to return to their parents, even if the teenager is past the juvenile age limit. This year, the law was changed again, spelling out a range of explicitly legal police tactics and in several sections replacing the word "may" with the word "shall."

State Senator Mary Ann Handley, one of the sponsors of the latest revision, acknowledges that there are civil liberties questions about it. But while some may be worried about infringing on teens' rights, Handley says, the main concern right now is to increase institutional authority.

The latest Youth in Crisis rewrite, passed during the 2003 session, also gives juvenile courts significant jurisdiction over 16- and 17-year-olds that it did not previously have. Juvenile court judges will now be able to direct the Department of Motor Vehicles to revoke the licenses of runaways and other teenage-status offenders, or order them to perform community service or get mental counseling.

The law does not go as far as many of its advocates would like: It does not allow the court to declare a youth who disobeys its orders to be declared delinquent, or even to be incarcerated. Nevertheless, some in Connecticut law enforcement see the system moving to a point where all offenders under 18 will be viewed as juveniles, reversing the course taken over the 1990s. The new law calls for a task force to look into the potential impact of extending full juvenile court jurisdiction to age 18. Grassroots parent groups and social service bureaus are supporting this idea. "In my estimation," says Sergeant Garritt Kelly of the East Hampton police department, "a lot of the stuff 16- to 18-year-olds get involved with are juvenile matters and should be treated as such."

But bringing more teens under the authority of juvenile court is no easy solution, either. Dissent against the idea is already coming from state prosecutors, who argue that adding so many new cases, without adding resources, would overburden the court. "Our juvenile prosecutors' offices wouldn't be able to handle it," says Ilana Cathcart, an assistant state's attorney. "They'd get buried." There is even doubt as to whether the physical court facilities could handle the extra load.

Hamm and other supporters of the juvenile court strategy acknowledge what she calls the "enormous fiscal cost" of expansion, and suggest that the process could be staggered—initially adding 16-year-olds and bringing in 17-year-olds later on, after the system has adjusted. "It's costing us so much money right now by not doing it right," argues Jeannie Milstein, who holds the appointed state position of Child Advocate. "I really believe we can actually save money in the long run" by classifying 16- and 17-year-olds as juveniles.

Most prosecutors would prefer a more modest reform, leaving 16- and 17-year-olds under the umbrella of adult court, but clarifying the rules so that status-offenders and violent criminals would not have to be treated identically.

"The court basically holds your hand" at the juvenile level, says Cathcart. "A lot of the kids know that they could basically hide behind their age."

FIXING PINS

The debate in Connecticut echoes one that took place three years ago in New York, which also sends 16- and 17-year-olds to adult court. New York's version of Youth in Crisis is a law that identifies "Persons in Need of Supervision," or PINS. For decades the law had provided for parents to petition a family court judge if they were having trouble keeping their teens under control. Parents could get help and counseling for boys under 16 and girls under 18. Three years ago, the legislature opted to expand the role of juvenile court by moving the maximum PINS age up to 18 for both sexes. As in Connecticut, there were arguments that opening the door for 16- and 17-year-olds under PINS would overwork the court, but the change was made anyway. "Parents feel empowered that they can go into family court and kind of scare their kids straight," says Maria Toro, of the Citizens Committee for Children of New York.

Child advocates in other states, however, continue to question whether an expanded juvenile court is likely to help much, even if adequate resources can be found. "If you need a lawyer to get your kids to come to breakfast, you're in trouble," says Al Singer, director of the Child Advocacy Commission in North Carolina. Singer argues that teen runaways are essentially a police matter, not a judicial matter. "Whether you change the laws or not,

"If you need a lawyer to get your kid to come to breakfast, you're in trouble."

police still have a problem with 16- and 17-year-old runaways," he says.

Yet some states have had success in giving law enforcement officers the powers they now feel they lack. That's what Louisiana did. One of the 10 states where adult court jurisdiction begins at 17, Louisiana has a long history of parental complaints that police would not respond to calls about runaways specifically. Even though the law allowed officers to pick up anyone 18 or under, police forces were reluctant to intervene out of fear of being sued by the families.

So in 2001, Louisiana changed the law to grant immunity from liability to police who assist or take into custody any runaway child at a parent's request. The law was sponsored by Representative Tony Perkins, who says he received at least five phone calls in 1999 and 2000 from parents complaining that when they reported their 17-year-olds had run away, the police refused to respond. Since the new law's inception, says an aide to Perkins, the office has "not had a single phone call. Obviously the parents that were having those problems are not having those problems anymore." The Louisiana approach is similar to what Connecticut has tried to do in its most recent rewrites of the Youth in Crisis law.

Meanwhile, as Connecticut struggles to find the right strategy, Makayla Korpinen's mother is suing the girl's boyfriend and his family. The boyfriend has been charged with first-degree manslaughter and narcotics offenses, and the Connecticut Child Fatality Review Panel is looking into the case to determine whether local and state agencies did enough to help at the time of crisis.

VII

Bureaucracy

Bureaucracy is sometimes called the fourth branch of government.[1] It's often called other things, many of which are not suitable for print. Forget about executives, legislatures, and courts—bureaucracy is the branch of government that people really love to hate.

The stereotype of bureaucracy is almost entirely negative. To most people, *bureaucracy* is synonymous with red tape, inefficiency, even malfeasance. It's big, it's bad, and if you want to do something about it, you'll have to wait in line and fill out a form in triplicate first. At least, that's the popular impression. Most professional scholars of the bureaucracy argue its reputation is mostly undeserved.[2]

The administrative arm of state and local governments is certainly big. Collectively, state and local public agencies constitute the single largest element of government in the United States. Of the roughly 21 million people employed in the public sector, more than 18 million work for state and local public agencies.[3]

When it comes to bad, however, the bureaucracy falls considerably short of its popular reputation. Most of the time, public agencies and public employees do a pretty good job (see the article by Ellen Perlman in this section). Take public schools, for example. In poll after poll, year after year, people express concerns about the poor performance of the public school system nationwide. Yet ask the same people for their opinion on their neighborhood school, and they will generally give it high marks. The data tend to support the more positive local view rather than the more gloomy national view; by most objective measures (graduation rates, test scores, and so on) public schools have shown steady improvement.[4]

The notion that public schools are generally doing well, and even improving, might come as a shock to some. This is understandable. Are there bad schools, bad school systems, and serious problems in public education? You bet—you've probably heard about them. They get the headlines. Yet those headline stories are rarely balanced with reports on the day-in, day-out success and progress in public schools. The public judges schools by the exceptions rather than the rule.

What goes for schools goes for bureaucracy generally. We tend to hear about public agencies when something goes wrong, which is actually not often. When things go right, we just take them for granted: schools, roads, parks, libraries, and safe drinking water, just for starters. What is something like clean water worth to you? This is a question very few people ever bother asking themselves—clean water is just there with a twist of the faucet. But what if it weren't?

In 1993 the residents of Milwaukee, Wis., got a painful lesson about the importance of clean drinking water. The city's public water supply got contaminated by the cryptosporidium parasite. Roughly 400,000 people ended up getting sick and more than 100 died.[5] Until then, the average citizen gave almost no thought to the agency overseeing the city's public water supply. It became topic number one only when things went drastically wrong.

The Milwaukee cryptosporidium outbreak shows that something most people consider trivial and mundane— a quick thirst-quenching stop at the water fountain— is trivial and mundane only because there is a public bureaucracy that makes it so. If the bureaucracy fails in its job or ceases to exist, the results can range from inconvenient to deadly. The fact that things like clean drinking water are taken for granted is testament to the notion that the administrative arm of the public sector is generally doing a good job.

The readings in this section examine the world of state and local bureaucracy, including the "shadow governments" of quasi-governmental authorities, the challenges of reorganizing and improving a public bureaucracy, and the question of what a good public administrator is really worth. The real world of bureaucracy turns out to be more complex—and much more interesting—than its stereotype.

WHAT BUREAUCRACY IS, AND WHAT BUREAUCRACY DOES

Broadly speaking, bureaucracy can be thought of as all public agencies and the programs and services they implement and manage. Most of these agencies are housed in the executive branches of state and local governments, and they run the gamut from police departments to schools, state health and welfare departments to public universities.

These agencies exist to implement and manage public programs and policies. In effect, bureaucracy is the "doer" of government. When a legislature passes a law to, say, set maximum speed limits on state highways, it expresses the will of the state. The law, however, will not catch speeders zipping down the highway. To translate the will of the state into concrete action requires some mechanism to enforce that will, such as the state highway patrol in the case of speeders on state highways. Virtually every purposive course of action that state and local governments decide to pursue requires a similar enforcement or management mechanism. Collectively these are public agencies and the people who work for them—the police, fire, and parks departments, schools, welfare agencies, libraries, and road crews. In short, the bureaucracy.

The bureaucracy is not just an agent of policy. In many cases bureaucracies and bureaucrats make policy. Public universities, for example, have broad leeway to set the required courses for their degree programs. Such policies affect the day-to-day lives of millions of college students, determining where they will be on certain days of the week and what they will be doing (maybe even studying state and local politics!).

Public agencies do not just shape the lives of college undergraduates—they have an effect on everyone who lives within the jurisdiction of state and local governments. Consider, for example, the role of state regulatory agencies, which, among other things, are responsible for licensing a broad variety of professional occupations. If you intend to be a doctor or a lawyer, or a barber or a bartender, you may require a state license. To get that license means at some point—and probably on an ongoing basis—you have to take the steps required and monitored by the relevant agency as a prerequisite to licensure.

THE DEVELOPMENT OF BUREAUCRACY

Recognizing the important role of public agencies in everything from getting an education to getting a haircut raises an obvious question: how did bureaucracy assume such a big role in our lives? It certainly wasn't always this way. For much of the first century of the republic's history there were no public schools. In many places there weren't even any roads. Libraries, public parks, and municipal water treatment programs were hit and miss—mostly missed altogether.

Bureaucracy grew primarily as a response to the growing complexity of society and the consequent demands made on government. For instance, the development of steam locomotives created a huge demand for railroads, which in turn created demand for regulation of the railroads, which a century-and-a-half ago were the hot new technology (think of them as the nineteenth-century equivalent of the Internet). The demand for regulation was driven by a number of issues, such as the freight charges railroads were levying on their customers. The Texas Railroad Commission (RRC), for example, was created in 1891 to regulate such issues.

The RRC still exists, even though the rail industry is not the dominant economic force it once was. Other industries also emerged in Texas, especially the energy industry. Drilling for oil and natural gas raised environmental issues, which created a demand for regulation of these sectors of the economy. As it turns out, these responsibilities were also handed over to the RRC. Texas is a big state, with a big energy industry and a lot of environmental issues. The RRC has thus become a big agency—it has a budget of $56 million and roughly 750 employees (check it out online at www.rrc.state.tx.us).[6]

It's not just technology, transportation, energy, and the environment. Citizens are placing more demands on their state and local governments than ever before. A public school is not enough—we want a school with high test scores, a good football team, a computer lab, AP courses, and so forth. That creates a set of complex administrative and logistical issues, and responding to all these citizen demands doesn't come cheap. In such fashion do public bureaucracies get bigger (but not necessarily badder).

Obviously, we want public agencies to do their assigned tasks well. But what are we willing to pay for them to do so? Nobody likes paying taxes, especially to feed the bureaucracy, and the high salaries paid to some top local-government executives are raising eyebrows. Consider that the chief executive officer of a billion-dollar corporation might earn millions of dollars per year. In contrast, the chief of the Los Angeles Police Department (LAPD), which has a budget of close to a billion dollars and roughly 12,000 employees, is paid about $250,000. And a bad day at the LAPD can be a lot worse than facing shareholders angry about a dividend drop (see the article on compensation by Jonathan Walters in this section).

Invariably, someone will always think that whatever public-sector employees are paid is too much. There is a widespread belief that private-sector companies could do a job better than public-sector bureaucracies, and do it cheaper.

REFORMING THE BUREAUCRACY

State and local governments, like the federal government, are always looking for ways to improve the bureaucracy. In some cases they try to figure out how to get rid of the bureaucracy altogether. In recent decades state and local governments have moved aggressively to privatize public services. Private corporations in some locales now run everything from public buses to prisons.

Although there are notable successes, most scholarly studies conclude that private companies perform no better—and sometimes do considerably worse—than traditional public agencies.[7] Even so, the mixed record, has done little to dampen the enthusiasm of state and local governments for trying to get rid of bureaucracy. One of the latest trends is to outsource bureaucratic jobs to private call centers. In this approach, rather than going to a public agency and talking with a public employee, you call a number much like you do when seeking technical help when your computer crashes. So, for example, if you have a problem with your welfare benefits, rather than visiting a caseworker, you dial a phone number and are connected with a call center run by the private sector.

Outsourcing represents a vast potential market for the private sector, with billions of dollars at stake. Critics, however, say the performance track record of outsourcing is poor. Driven by the bottom line, private companies have incentives to hire the least qualified (and thus cheapest) labor possible. In many cases, outsourcing isn't even cheaper. Once all the pros and cons are added up, it turns out that many programs are more cost effective when kept under the umbrella of a traditional public agency. The debate over outsourcing is fierce and ongoing, and it has the potential to affect a wide range of public programs (see the articles on privatization by Alan Greenblatt and Jonathan Walters in this section).

One form of privatization that has been around for some time is quasi-governmental authorities (sometimes called "quangos"), which occupy a vague area between the public and private sectors. These are typically specialized bureaucracies set up to handle the maintenance and governance of operations such as toll roads or ports. The idea behind quangos is that by mimicking some of the elements of a private corporation, they can operate more efficiently than a traditional public bureaucracy. There is certainly some truth to this. A quango that has the ability to levy fees or issue bonds without getting approval from a legislature or the voters can avoid the political bickering that inevitably accompanies such requests.

Yet this sort of independence raises questions of accountability. There are hundreds of quangos, called public authorities, in New York State, and they have little in the way of coordinated oversight and control. Indeed, it's not even clear exactly how many public authorities exist. They have been called "secret governments," operating outside the mainstream political process (see the article by Christopher Swope in this section). What quangos and outsourcing demonstrate is that getting rid of traditional bureaucracies is a perennially popular idea, but no one has come up with a surefire replacement that does an equally good job while remaining accountable to the democratic process.

Some of the readings in this section document the challenges of using alternatives to traditional bureaucracies to deliver public goods and services. Others show what traditional bureaucracies do, why they are important, and how they can do their jobs better. What they all demonstrate is that although we might not want bureaucracy, state and local governments seem to need it.

Notes

1. Kenneth J. Meier, *Politics and the Bureaucracy: Policymaking in the Fourth Branch of Government,* 3rd ed. (Pacific Grove, Calif.: Brooks/Cole, 1993).

2. Charles T. Goodsell, *The Case for Bureaucracy* (Chatham, N.J.: Chatham House, 1994).

3. U.S. Census Bureau, Table 454 in *Statistical Abstract of the United States: 2004–2005* (Washington, D.C.: U.S. Government Printing Office, 1994).

4. Julian L. Simon and Rebecca Boggs, "Trends in the Quantities of Education: A Pictorial Essay," *Economics of Education Review* 16 (February 1997): 69–80.

5. Dan Rutz, "Milwaukee Learned Its Water Lesson, But Many Other Cities Haven't," CNN.com, September 2, 1996, www.cnn.com/HEALTH/9609/02/nfm/water.quality/ (accessed April 20, 2005).

6. Railroad Commission of Texas, "Agency Overview" in "Appendix E–Workforce Plan" of the Commission's *Strategic Plan 05–09,* July 2, 2004, www.hr.state.tx.us/Workforce/Plans/2004/455-plan-2004.pdf (accessed April 29, 2005).

7. Elliot D. Sclar, *You Don't Always Get What You Pay For: The Economics of Privatization* (Ithaca, N.Y.: Cornell University Press, 2001).

29

Sweetheart Deals

Alan Greenblatt

States all over the country are eager to privatize services in the worst way. That's just how some of them are doing it.

Two years ago, as he took the oath of office for a second term as governor, Florida's Jeb Bush startled his audience at the capitol in Tallahassee by pointing to the surrounding complex of state office buildings and making a declaration. "There would be no greater tribute to our maturity as a society," he said, "than if we can make these buildings around us empty of workers."

There is still quite a bit of controversy over just what Bush meant that day. To some, he was merely expressing his vision of a future in which human betterment would make many government programs unnecessary. Others, however, believe he was making a subtle reference to privatization—to his preference for a system in which the state would serve more and more as a master contractor, removing programs from the public bureaucracy and bidding them out to the private sector, in his view a cheaper, more efficient alternative.

In any case, the latter interpretation reflects to a remarkable extent the Florida that Jeb Bush is creating. During his six years leading the state, 138 projects worth $1.6 billion have been outsourced to private contractors. In Florida as elsewhere, outsourcing has developed a bipartisan constituency, no longer restricted to conservatives who decry big government. Democrats as well as Republicans embrace it as a sensible expedient in lean economic times.

But if privatization has been a political success in Florida, it is turning out to be a substantial managerial embarrassment. The process of issuing contracts has led to an avalanche of stories about political favoritism and alleged sweetheart deals.

Take, for example, the Department of Children and Families, which has struggled for the past decade with inadequate and malfunctioning computer systems. Two years ago, following a scandal

From *Governing,*
December 2004.

in which the DCF lost track of a five-year-old girl, nominally in its care, for a period of 15 months, new leadership charged into the department, claiming it knew a better way. The idea was a contract that offered large incentives to a private vendor who could guarantee that a new system would finally be up and running within a year. The contractor would also get $21 million.

It sounded good, and all the relevant authorities signed off on the plan. But Ciber Inc., a vendor that didn't get the contract, claimed that AMS, the company that did, was given unfair advantages. The AMS bid, according to Ciber, was neither the lowest in price nor the most attractive, although the latter is more a matter of judgment than numbers. What was indisputable was the fact that an AMS board member had been the DCF secretary's boss and had recommended him for the job in Florida, while a former social services secretary served as a lobbyist for the company.

None of this constitutes proof of a conflict of interest, but Tom Hodgkins, director of state government relations for the newly merged CGI-AMS, says his company recognizes that perception is an especially tricky matter when working with taxpayer dollars. "There's a process that the state went through, and we as a company go out of our way to put together proposals that are responsive to the procurement policies," he says. "We followed the procurement process to the letter of the law." Nevertheless, DCF decided in November to rebid the contract rather than try to defend its decision in court.

As Florida pursues its aggressive program of privatization, it's running into this type of situation a lot. A bold new plan to save money and make government more efficient by turning to an outside contractor is alleged to have been tainted by favoritism. The number of state contracts that have offered significant benefits to well-connected individuals and companies is almost too large to tick off, although Florida media has made hay trying to do so. It's an especially big concern in a state now preparing to contract out the work of determining eligibility for food stamps, welfare and Medicaid—potentially the largest public procurement in the state's history.

That process has been put on hold, for the time being, because of scandals engulfing the Department of Children and Families. Members of the agency's top leadership, including Secretary Jerry Regier, have resigned in the wake of revelations that the agency had given more than $4 million worth of no-bid contracts to companies owned by or associated with the former head of social services for the state, accepting personal gifts and travel all along the way. "Doing business in Florida," suggests a senior marketing executive with a major software vendor, "is a lot like doing business in Chechnya. You come with your steel and your animals and your oil, and you barter it out."

This year, the state technology office canceled more than $250 million worth of contracts with Accenture and BearingPoint after the state auditor general found they were given an unfair leg up over their competitors. Shortly after signing off on the deals, Kim Bahrami, the state's chief information officer, took a job with BearingPoint. The auditor's office also has criticized a $350 million contract with Convergys to privatize the state's personnel management, having found evidence of illegal behavior among government officials and conflicts of interest.

Spokesm[e]n with all these companies deny any wrongdoing. John Di Renzo, who heads Bearing-Point's state and local government practice, says that his company saved Florida nearly $3 million during the 10 months its work was allowed to proceed, while apparently improving service. An Accenture spokesman notes that its contracts "were cancelled for convenience, not for cause." The vendors insist that many of the alleged sweetheart deals are actually sound and defensible decisions, victimized only by unsubstantiated suggestions of collusion.

ANGLING FOR PAYOFFS

The most familiar patronage abuses in American government used to involve public officials rewarding their friends with jobs in the public works department, or some equivalent. Now, in many places around the country, patronage abuse means something entirely different. It means friends and associates, campaign contributors and lobbyists angling for a payoff in the form of a multimillion-dollar contract with state government. Florida, of course, is hardly alone in this. Contracting scandals led directly to the resignation of Connecticut Governor John Rowland this summer and contributed to the downfall of Governor Gray Davis in California's recall election last year. Privatization is a growth industry at all levels of government, and investigations into ethical lapses and outright larceny are underway in virtually every corner of the country.

Throw a dart at the map and it won't land far from the scene of some contract-related investigation. Gary George, a long-time Wisconsin state senator, was sentenced in August to four years in prison for a kickback scheme that involved directing contracts to pals in construction and social services. Former Minnesota state Representative Loren Jennings was indicted in October on charges of steering $650,000 in state grants to a telephone pole recycling company in which he had an undisclosed interest.

Members of the Los Angeles City Council are reviewing a $540,000 contract given to a former port director who is the subject of a federal probe into contracting irregularities there. And the Wayne County Commission in Detroit has referred to prosecutors the case of county Treasurer Raymond Wojtowicz, who awarded $4 million in contracts to associates after circumventing a formal bidding process. "He threw the bids out and he just awarded the bid to his former employees," says Commissioner Sue Hubbard. "It's totally unprofessional and not in accordance with standard governmental processes of competitive bidding."

Privatization also has created many success stories. The private sector simply has more expertise than public bureaucracy in certain crucial areas—notably technology—where states and other governments need help in order to modernize. That has made contracting more necessary, no matter which party is in charge of government. But it also has made the entire process ethically trickier. Some contracts, such as hiring a company to pick up trash, or run the prison cafeteria, are relatively straightforward. Tech innovations are a lot more complex, and the steps involved can lead to abuses that were unknown even a decade ago.

Among other things, the standard sequence of procedures involved in bidding out a major contract has changed significantly. It used to be that states decided what work they needed done, figured out the terms they could afford and then let a contract out for bid. Now, more and more governments are turning to the private sector as a first step. They ask vendors for guidance in helping them find out about new and forthcoming innovations. While lending professional expertise and advice to states looking to create, say, a better child tracking system, private companies also come in and help craft solutions designed around their own products and services. Government managers across the country face the diffi-

cult challenge of cultivating vendors who have helpful ideas, while being careful to avoid the perception that their relationships with those vendors are too cozy.

As the movement toward outsourcing picks up speed, these same managers face an opposite challenge: how to put in place enough safeguards to ensure that abuses are rare and quickly caught, without imposing new layers of red tape that stifle innovation and undermine the benefits of speed and efficiency that privatization promises. For example, most states have some sort of "double-key" system requiring more than one sign-off on substantial contracts. Adding additional requirements for approval might mean greater ethical precaution but also could reduce savings and innovations.

TALLAHASSEE TRANSFER

In the past decade, as the arguments for privatization have begun to take hold nationwide, no political leader has been more supportive of them than Jeb Bush. And he has found himself in a position of political strength that allows him to try out many of the ideas. The first GOP governor to win a second term in Florida, he now enjoys control over a government and legislature that, following 120 years of Democratic dominance, are firmly in Republican control.

What's more, gubernatorial power has vastly increased during Bush's time in office. Florida shrunk the size of its cabinet and gave the governor more sway in that body's deliberations. Control of the machinery is now much more centralized in the governor's office, making for an executive branch that is committed to smaller government in general, and to outsourcing as a specific way of achieving that goal.

There is a lot of government to shrink. Over the past 40 years, Florida's government has grown even more dramatically than the Sunshine State itself. There were 31,000 state workers in 1957; by the time Governor Bush took office in 1999, the number was up to 207,000—more than a sixfold increase, compared with a tripling of the state's population as a whole. In 1977, a 22-story concrete monolith was completed and became the official capitol building, supplanting and miniaturizing its neighbor, the traditional domed structure that had served as the seat of government since the 19th century. The high-rise capitol overlooks a downtown of low-slung buildings filled almost exclusively with law firms and trade associations whose letterheads boast former state officials and senior gubernatorial aides. They are major players in lucrative and important work: the transfer of public functions to private contractors who need lobbying help in securing business.

Tallahassee still looks like a sleepy town, but it has become the dispensary for multimillion-dollar contracts, and the lobbyists who have the right connections have become less concerned with their traditional role of fighting regulation and more involved in the scramble to land money directly for their clients. "The gold in them thar hills are administrative dollars, available through the executive branch," says Jack Levine, a longtime children's advocate in Tallahassee. "When the stakes are so high and the dollars are so enormous, you can understand there's more power brought to bear."

In attempting to make the bidding process more fair and open, Bush this year created a new Center for Efficient Government within the state's Department of Management Services, charged with making procurement rules uniform and comprehensible across the maze of state agencies. The center provides training in contracting and contract management to agency officials, and has a board that is asked to sign off on all state contracts worth more than $10 million at every step of a five-part development-to-implementation process. "We have to close a lot of loopholes in our procurement laws," says DMS Secretary William Simon, who notes that he favors time limits before former state employees can start lobbying, with tough financial penalties for violations. "The potential PR impact is worse if we ignore some of the problems we have."

Additional efforts are taking place in the state treasurer's office. Like Simon, Treasurer Tom Gallagher argues that one of the important transitions in moving from bureaucratic management to largely privatized management is training people to negotiate and monitor contracts. In some ways, Gallagher says, it's harder to make sure a private operation is meeting performance goals than to manage a group of traditional in-house employees. In many cases, he believes, not enough time was allowed for making the switch. "There might have been a rush to privatization by some agencies without taking the time to see to it that there were the right rules and accountability," he says. "Anytime you have aggressive programs being pushed by leadership, you're going to have growing pains. I look at these as growing pains."

To others, however, cancellations and criminal investigation of contracts totaling in the hundreds of millions are more serious than mere growing pains. Critics of the Bush administration say its reforms are too little and too late, and claim the system is still too easily rigged in favor of well-connected friends of the most senior executive branch officials. "The biggest non-secret in this state is that this administration sees part of their business is giving business to their friends," says Mark Neimeiser, legislative director for AFSCME in Florida. "This administration is known to be the kind that does not tolerate whistle-blowers who say the emperor has no clothes, or the clothes are paid for by somebody else."

But it was, in fact, a whistleblower who drew attention to the contracting scandals that have led to the resignation and criminal investigation of the top leadership at the Florida Department of Children and Families. The social welfare agency funneled millions to Jim Bax, who had headed the social services department in earlier years and, until just before the probe began, ran a research institute at Florida State University, down the hill from the capitol. The state's universities can be granted contracts on a no-bid basis, which is how things were done for Bax. He then subcontracted work either to companies he owned or to others that paid him a fee in the process.

The fact that Bax had thrown a birthday party for Secretary Regier and invited him to stay as a guest in his waterfront home, coupled with the gifts Bax and other lobbyists gave to DCF officials, led to the resignation of Regier and two other top agency officials this past summer.

Ben Harris, the former DCF deputy secretary who has been at the center of the storm, contends, basically, that he was set up. He notes that he got prior approval for his sponsored trips from the state ethics commission. His argument is that the privatization program that he and Regier were pursuing was simply too threatening to a rearguard bureaucracy that saw its livelihood put at risk. He notes that the plan to outsource eligibility selections for public aid alone threatens the jobs of one-third of all DCF employees.

"Whenever you have rapid change, you have people who wonder where they'll fit in the new world," Harris says. "Just as in any other agency, there's a small group of people that want to preserve the status quo." (There are plenty of people in Tallahassee who are sympathetic to Harris' story—one state legislator says the DCF crew was a victim of "gotcha politics"—but his actions and contracting practices at DCF in general remain under criminal investigation.)

The best way to fight bureaucratic foot-dragging, says William Simon of the Department of Management Services, is not to rely on legal action but simply to make sure that contracts are done right and are aboveboard in the first place. "The only way to overcome some of the obstacles," he argues, "is to show that the contracts have worked the way they're supposed to and, by the way, saved money."

REFORM PACKAGE

That's the approach the new administration of Governor Jodi Rell is hoping to pursue in Connecticut. She took office in July, following Rowland's resignation in the wake of a scandal surrounding contracts awarded to his campaign contributors. Rell immediately ensconced an ethics czar in her office and appointed a task force to make recommendations to reform the state's contracting laws and processes.

The idea that Rowland was forced to resign because state contractors built a hot tub in his summer home has passed into political lore, but the root of the problem came with the awarding of healthy amounts of state business to those contractors in the first place. "People just didn't bother to bid because they didn't think they were going to get a fair shake," says James Fleming, Connecticut's commissioner of public works and co-chair of the Rell task force. "That hurt the private sector and it hurt us because we had less competition in our pricing."

The task force has released a detailed set of recommendations in anticipation of the upcoming 2005 legislative session. Among them are bans on gifts worth more than $10 to state employees, a uniform state code in bid evaluation and selection, and institutional changes to cut down on the number of times that the legislature signs off on "fast track" or sole-source contracts. There will be competing versions of reform legislation, but a bill of some kind seems certain to pass. "There's an old rule in politics, which is when you have the votes, you vote," says Fleming. Right now, he says, in the wake of the Rowland disgrace, the votes are there. "So this is the time to do it."

Whatever its final shape, Connecticut's package is likely to provide the most comprehensive changes in contracting rules anywhere in the nation. But other states are trying to change their rules to keep up with both the growth in contracting and the change in the nature of work contracted out. In New Jersey, Governor James McGreevey signed an executive order, shortly before resigning from office in November, that bans any state contracts from going to contributors to state or local candidates or political parties.

McGreevey had been hounded by accusations that his administration and fundraising team had engaged in just the sort of "pay-to-play" schemes that he ultimately banned. Similar accusations dogged former Governor Gray Davis of California and were among the complaints that led to his removal from office by recall vote last year. A no-bid $95 million contract that had been awarded to software giant Oracle led to the resignation of four top Davis aides; this past May, the state attorney general announced he was dropping the last remaining legal charges against Davis' former policy director.

A CLEAR VIEW

With so much potential for things to go wrong—and such a large political price to be paid when contracts are handled improperly—why are governments eagerly handing ever-increasing shares of their workload to private entities? The reason, suggests William Eggers, director of research at Deloitte, is that they have to. Today's public sector relies heavily on specialized expertise and services available most readily through private companies, often at a greatly reduced cost. "Much of what government does today gets done today through third parties, whether they're nonprofits or some form of contractors," says Eggers, himself a long-time advocate of privatization. "There's very little that would actually get done in most levels of government today without involving the private sector."

Despite the headlines, most government contracts are fulfilled in more or less the intended fashion. The Internet has created more transparency in the bidding process, and an open bidding process can prevent abuses in many cases. Vendors, such as Ciber, that feel they have been cheated are not hesitant to protest. Managerial problems that can be handled quietly in business-to-business transactions are more likely to reach the notice of the media when vast sums of public money are involved. "The nature of appearances—what something looks like to the person on the street—is something administrators are going to think about," says Levine, the children's advocate.

This is as true of Florida, and its Department of Children and Families, as it is of any government agency or contract in the country. Because of its long legacy of problems, DCF is falling under particular scrutiny from legislators and the media. Its mistakes, which involve the lives of children, naturally draw more attention than problems in, say, road maintenance. Even before the recent scandals broke out, state Representative Sandra Murman, who chairs a subcommittee that oversees the agency, inserted into the state budget a provision that blocks DCF from entering into any contract worth more than $100,000 without approval from the governor and the legislature. More restrictions of that sort may be imposed in the near future.

Murman says she shares Governor Bush's goal of contracting out an increased array of services, maintaining that there are plenty of private companies that can do at least as good a job determining welfare eligibility, for instance, as current state employees do, and probably at less cost. She says she just wants to make sure any major new deals meet her "comfort level" regarding conflicts of interest before the final deal is made. "Contracting management and oversight," Murman says, "need to be a little more well-defined." In the coming months and years, legislators and other public officials in much of the country are likely to be saying something similar.

30

Going Outside

Jonathan Walters

The push to privatize is expanding beyond service delivery into the areas of policy making and program design.

While governors and legislators scramble to deal with American jobs moving offshore, many of these same policy makers are creating anxiety about outsourcing within their own state's borders—among their own public employees.

Texas, for example, is poised to make a radical change in the way it administers welfare benefits. Anyone seeking public assistance will no longer visit a local government office but instead dial up a call center staffed by private-sector operators. Those corporate employees will be linked to a computer system that allows them fingertip access to a vast array of financial data. Using such information, the new-style eligibility workers will then tell callers whether or not they qualify to receive a variety of benefits—from food stamps and Temporary Assistance to Needy Families to child health insurance and Medicaid.

The "call center" approach to qualifying citizens for public benefits is the front edge of a wedge aimed at opening up a huge new area of traditional government work to the private sector. If it receives federal approval, the Texas privatization strategy could trigger a wave of state and local outsourcing nationwide worth billions of dollars, affecting millions of citizens and tens of thousands of state and local employees, while at the same time opening up whole new business lines for eager vendors. Frank Ambramcheck, who heads up public sector consulting for Unisys Corp., calls it the "the bow wave" of a private-sector push into government work, an expansion that is beginning to go beyond what has typically been privatized—service delivery to citizens—and into program design and decision making.

From *Governing,* May, 2004.

149

"If Texas gets its toe in the water," says Celia Hagert, an analyst with Progressive Policy Institute who has been tracking the issue, "then a whole lot of states will be diving in right behind it." Hagert, along with many health and social services advocates nationwide, is concerned about private companies deciding who ought to get government benefits, arguing that it has always been too sensitive a job to sell off.

> "I am a very strong proponent of free enterprise and private-sector solutions to meet the needs of government."
>
> —State Representative
> Arlene Wohlgemuth

The drive to privatize in Texas is part of a massive consolidation that will distill 12 health and human services agencies into four. The job of administering the four new departments falls to the Health and Human Services Commission, which formerly had more casual oversight over the sprawling bureaucracies. The law that engineered the consolidation also directs HHSC to turn as much other work as is practicable over to the private sector.

The commission already has sent out a request for proposals to run the human resource management function—not just payroll administration but a broad range of HR work, from recruitment of new employees to initial screening of job candidates. Other administrative basics such as procurement and information technology will also be on the table.

But that's not all. In keeping with the outsourcing theme of the overhaul, the reorganization itself is being quarterbacked by the private sector. Deloitte Consulting, Maximus and Accenture are doing everything from reengineering how work gets done, to ensuring that whatever system Texas ends up with squares with federal cost-accounting requirements.

As of this spring, the commission's "contracting opportunities" Web site had more than a dozen RFPs listed, ranging from such specific work as studying the closure or consolidation of certain facilities, to doing feasibility studies on community-based treatment for emotionally disturbed kids. What's more, vendors also are helping HSSC to do the analyses that will become part of the "business case" that the agency uses to evaluate the efficacy of contracting out.

The math and the mindset driving the privatization effort are straightforward: Texas is facing a $10 billion budget deficit and in the view of many influential Republicans there is only one way to deal with that number: Let the private sector in on state work to lower state costs. "I am a very strong proponent of free enterprise and private-sector solutions to meet the needs of government," says state Representative Arlene Wohlgemuth, who sponsored the consolidation bill. Through reorganization and consolidation, she says, the state is slated to save billions of dollars, in part through programmatic changes to such big-ticket items as Medicaid but also by turning work over to contractors. Under the Wohlgemuth plan, more than 2,500 state health and social services jobs are scheduled to be handed off to vendors in the next two years. Ultimately, the plan could directly impact the lives of thousands more state workers across Texas.

But if Texas is shaping up as a privatizer's dream come true, some who have been watching the process closely view it as an exercise in outsourcing gone amok. Patrick Bresette, executive director of the Austin-based Center for Public Policy Priorities, calls it the "the big-bang theory" applied to scaling back government service. There is scant evidence, according to the center's analysis of the consolidation plan and early outsourcing efforts, that it will actually result in improved services at lower costs.

Texas employees, meanwhile, express their own brand of skepticism. The state is "stepping over dollars to save dimes," says Gary Anderson, executive director of the Texas Public Employees Association. While he understands the cost-saving imperative, he believes the state isn't thinking much beyond a single budget cycle in assessing the actual value of outsourcing so much work. "In the short term, you may see some savings," he acknowledges. But in the long run, Anderson contends, the state loses valuable institutional knowledge along with the capacity to easily take work back if vendors don't pan out. That could saddle the state with huge down-the-road costs, for both rebuilding internal capacity and compensating for non-performance of basic work.

Anderson sees one other potential and ironic cost to the plan: If vendors are really going to save the state money, then they will probably have to do that by using low-wage, low-benefit workers, which means the very people taking over pieces of food stamps, TANF and Medicaid administration could end up qualifying for all those benefits themselves.

BRANCHING OUT

The issues of cost, performance and capacity have long been at the heart of what drives outsourcing—and the heated debates about it. "More (and better) for less" has been the longstanding rationale for using private contractors to do everything from mowing grass to placing kids in foster care. But recently privatization has been taking on a more ideological edge. A new generation of elected officials—top-level executives, in particular—is making no secret of its conviction that government should not only "be run like a business" but also, in many cases, be run by business. And that has led to a new aggressiveness in what states such as Texas are looking to contract out.

Adding heat to the simmering outsourcing debate is the current controversy over where, exactly, the privatized work is going. Offshore outsourcing began to capture the attention of lawmakers at the beginning of this year, fueled by a string of stories about private contractors sending state work—especially call-center work—to foreign countries. The image of employees in India handling Virginians' and Vermonters' queries about food-stamp benefits had governors and legislatures nationwide arguing all spring about whether they ought to limit state contracts to vendors who agree not to send jobs abroad.

But the issue of offshore outsourcing is clearly a sideshow to the main event: the increased interest in domestic outsourcing fueled by new, more market-friendly political leadership in combination with tough budget times. Faced with a $350 million budget deficit, South Carolina Governor Mark Sanford is among those identifying areas where the private sector might do the job better for less.

One of the items on Sanford's list—outsourcing inmate health care—has fallen to John Davis, the acting health services director for the Corrections Department. A veteran of past privatization efforts, Davis well under-

stands that coming up with a list of areas to consider for outsourcing is one thing, and actually doing the contracting in a way that delivers quality service at reasonable cost is quite another. In fact, the state had been contracting out part of its inmate health care prior to Sanford's election, and that experience wasn't altogether satisfactory. The state dropped its contract with a private health services provider working at 10 state facilities for a very simple reason: The company wanted more money, and the state didn't want to pay more.

Now health care for the *entire* corrections system is on the table, and Davis is wrestling with the RFP process. It is a daunting task. First, the state doesn't have a good handle on costs, so it's hard to judge if outsourcing will really be a better deal. "We break things down in large categories. What it costs for hospitalization, pharmaceuticals and personnel. But we don't know how much it costs to treat diabetics or cardiac patients," he says. Although the state is currently working on a cost-coding system that will help it to capture such data, for now it is negotiating RFPs absent such detailed breakouts. Cost, of course, is what makes the outsourcing world go around, and as part of the back-and-forth with potential vendors over the RFP, private-sector companies also are asking that liability for cost overruns be shared by the state. That has made for dicier negotiations.

Also complicating the contracting effort is the fact that the state operates on an annual budget, so it's hard to lock any company into a long-term contract. That raises the specter of a low-ball bid just to get the work, with ever-escalating contract requests to follow. The state may be particularly susceptible to such a syndrome in this case, Davis notes, because this contract involves outsourcing health care services at all 29 of its facilities, which would mean the state would lose the capacity to do the work itself. "Once you've dismantled the system, it's tough to put it back together," he says, "and vendors know that."

Still, the RFP process proceeds apace. Davis thinks that given the state's past experience, things are going a little smoother this time, and that the state is doing a better job of bargaining.

In all cases, though, whether it's outsourcing human resource management or inmate health care, the basic question is the same: Does it really add up to cheaper and better government? Organized labor challenges that notion, arguing that it frequently adds up to more expensive government and worse performance. Free marketeers, meanwhile, argue that privatization is the only way to break expensive government—and government employee—monopolies. Such a break wrings greater performance and productivity from government bureaucracies, argue proponents, while applying fresh ideas and strategies to government administration and programs.

With states and localities spending upwards of $400 billion a year on contracts, and with the recent incursions into new outsourcing territory, it's not an argument that's likely to ease up anytime soon. But even Adrian Moore, executive director of the pro-privatization Reason Foundation, admits contracting out is not a panacea. "Like all policy tools, it is neither good nor bad," he says, "It depends on whether or not you do it right."

THE CALCULUS

Stories and data abound illustrating how and where government does it wrong, say outsourcing critics. Joe Fox, vice president of the New York State Public Employees Federation, says he understands there are times when outsourcing makes sense—when a temporary spike in demand calls for some outside help or for certain kinds of seasonal work. But Fox argues that because of outsourcing, New York state government is currently paying more for a wide range of traditional government work and is getting lower quality service for the money.

According to PEF calculations, the state could save at least $160 million a year if it brought nursing, pharmaceutical, psychiatric, computer and engineering work back in-house. The federation's stand is bolstered by a March 2001 letter to the New York State Department of Transportation, in which the state comptroller declared, "It is generally less expensive for the department to design and inspect projects in-house rather than use consultants." For Fox, the game being played by New York and other states is obvious. "Politically, it looks good to say, 'I don't have this huge workforce.' But it's smoke and mirrors."

Outsourcing critics also say some politicians pursue privatization in order to offload difficult policy areas. In looking at the highly volatile area of child protective services and foster care, Richard Wexler, executive director of the National Coalition for Child Protection Reform,

says Florida is a national model of how outsourcing the administration of child protection is an effort to dump responsibility and accountability. "The only motivation for privatization of child welfare in Florida is that it is a political liability, and Governor Jeb Bush doesn't want that liability," says Wexler.

The governor's administration rejects that criticism out of hand. "If you look at that area, it's one where states have been outsourcing for 100 years," says Bill Simon, secretary of the Florida Department of Management Services. The whole concept of sending kids to foster homes instead of orphanages, Simon notes, is one where outsourcing has proved "wildly successful." And he adds, "It's not much of a step to then look at outsourcing its administration."

But Florida is a state that has come in for heavy criticism for its aggressive, big-ticket and low-accountability outsourcing efforts. In particular, the governor has been pounded over the state's high-profile and so far unhappy effort to outsource a significant portion of its human resources management function. A $280 million contract with Cincinnati-based Convergys Corp. to take over the job has bogged down badly, which means the state is spending millions of dollars keeping its old system up and running while Convergys tries to work out kinks in the new system.

Still, DMS secretary Simon believes that much of the criticism aimed at Bush is simply on account of the "blistering pace" with which the governor has pursued privatization. So far, state action on the outsourcing front has included everything from collecting tolls to investigating allegations of child abuse.

Not all of Florida's privatizing has gone badly. In several multi-million-dollar deals, the contractors have performed as advertised. But both the governor's own Inspector General and the legislature's Office of Program Policy Analysis and Government Accountability have released papers taking the state to task for its less-than-businesslike approach to contracting out. The legislative oversight office, for instance, said agencies need to make a better business case for privatization and look more at performance-based contracting. It also suggested the need for central oversight of contracting.

Florida has received enough official criticism about its privatization efforts that Governor Bush in March created a Center for Efficient Government in the state's Department of Management Services to oversee the state's outsourcing efforts. One of the center's main jobs will be to provide technical assistance to agencies not used to negotiating large contracts with experienced, savvy vendors. "We have state agencies that might do a $100 million contract every one or two years, whereas IBM does one a week," Simon says. The center will also be the central repository for information on cost and performance.

NEGOTIATING WITH THE FEDS

While Florida has received much attention for its outsourcing efforts, most eyes right now are on Texas and its decision to privatize eligibility determination—and whatever else it can—as part of its health and human services overhaul.

Texas is still negotiating with the feds for permission to outsource all the eligibility determination work that it would like to—particularly in the areas of food stamps and Medicaid. Gregg Phillips, a former consultant with Deloitte who is now HHSC's point man on reorganization and contracting out, is confident the state will be allowed to hand the work off to contractors. Other states are watching the action carefully.

Phillips is well aware of concerns about contracting out. But he says that Texas won't repeat the mistakes of other aggressive privatizers that have gone before it. Furthermore, he argues that the state already has been using the call-center approach in such areas as the child health insurance program and workers' compensation with no problems. "Right now with our CHIP program," he says, "every eligibility determination is being made by a private-sector company. Texans seeking service don't care who they're talking to as long as who they are talking to is courteous, accurate and performs well."

Furthermore, says Phillips, every outsourcing effort that HHSC undertakes has to be justified by a business case, and where contracting out is deemed cost effective—and he's confident there will be lots more cases—contractors will always be held to high standards of performance with clear penalties for failure to meet those standards. He also believes there are enough vendors around that are interested in picking up state work that HHSC will never be held hostage by any private-sector monopolizer.

Still, even the staunchest advocates of outsourcing, including Representative Wohlgemuth, understand that building that kind of contract-writing, administration and oversight capacity in state government is in and of itself a daunting task. But she has a ready answer for how to deal with any shortfall in state contracting capacity: "You can contract that out, too."

31

Techtonic Shift

Ellen Perlman

Delaware has reformatted the structure and operation of its technology agency.

Few things are more frightening in Delaware than an outbreak of avian flu. That's because chicken processing is a huge part of the state's economy. When the first cases were reported there this spring, chief information officer Tom Jarrett got a call from Delaware's agriculture secretary asking that a Web site be developed for providing information to the media and state agencies. By noon the next day, the IT staff had it up and running. "We've structured ourselves to operate like that," Jarrett says.

A few years ago, though, they wouldn't have had a prayer. The IT department "was a real mess," says Jarrett, who left a 30-year career at Verizon to accept the newly created CIO position offered by the governor in 2001—along with the challenge of completely revamping the state's technology operations.

It was a daunting assignment. No other state technology department has attempted a restructuring of this magnitude. The First State is home to the first IT agency to remove all of its employees from the civil service system, pay them as close as possible to competitive market salaries in the area, offer them bonuses for performance and at the same time keep systems running for users through the massive changeover. People in the department liken the feat to totally rebuilding an airplane while it's flying from New York to Los Angeles.

Although Delaware is a small state, its sweeping overhaul could have a big impact on how other states view their IT departments and personnel. Can a CIO with unique rules for compensating employees, paying for performance and in other ways rewarding workers create an agile organization positioned to attract and retain highly qualified people and make big strides with technology?

From *Governing,*
June 2004.

154

While it is too soon to reach a conclusion in Delaware, the state is out front at least on the basic premise. It has put a private-sector-style organization in place and is fine-tuning its operations. Policies and procedures "are ours and they're adaptable," says Richard Eakle, chief operating officer. "If something's not working, something else can be put in place." Other states have considered such an idea but gone nowhere with it.

The only other state IT department with a vaguely similar approach is the Georgia Technology Agency; its employees are exempt from civil service. But that's the case with all Georgia state employees. Moreover, GTA didn't experience the same struggle as Delaware did to make the change while continuing to run systems. And Georgia officials admit the agency cannot pay market-competitive salaries although they would like to.

While the Delaware department has taken the giant first step of setting up its structure and putting people in place, officials there agree it is still in its infancy and faces many more challenges. For example, although performance bonuses were promised when people agreed to leave the security of the civil service and sign on as exempt employees, the ailing state budget may preclude that right now.

A FRESH START

How was Delaware able to make such radical changes to the department? The key seems to be that the governor and the legislature were staunchly behind the concept. Governor Ruth Ann Minner in particular is a champion of using information technology to improve government service.

As Delaware's lieutenant governor for eight years, Minner had experience with the operations of the Office of Information Services, the previous technology department. She did not regard it very highly. "It was almost totally inoperable," she says. "It took weeks to get things and [the department] didn't have the ability to look at how to improve things." State employees would try to find ways not to have to work with OIS. As a result, the morale of department employees eroded. "They thought they were the dregs of state government," Minner says.

Within days of her inauguration in 2001, Minner issued Executive Order No. 2—second only to the one allowing her Cabinet to serve. It called for a task force to come up with recommendations on how the state could improve its management of information technology.

The task force reported back in May, saying that nearly everything about the IT department needed to be improved: leadership, project management, management of IT expenditures, employee recruitment and retention. It recommended that the state create a new Cabinet-level Department of Technology and Information, develop a new structure for managing and paying technology employees, establish a technology council to prioritize statewide IT spending and projects, redefine the role of the CIO and hire someone with the necessary skills to run the new organization.

State Representative Roger Roy, who chairs the House Telecommunications, Internet and Technology Committee and served on the task force, sponsored the legislation to make it all happen. Roy, too, was dissatisfied with the existing agency. "The old attitude was, 'Hey, this is what we're going to give you,' not 'What is it you need?' " he says.

Jarrett was the first exempt employee hired and was given two years to set up a department structure, design a compensation plan, create job titles and descriptions, hire people for leadership positions and get middle managers and staff in place. At the same time, he had to make sure two mainframes, 182 servers and all other technology equipment continued to operate smoothly.

When eight team-leader openings were announced, 900 resumes arrived at the department's offices. It was at a time when the private tech sector had tanked. "We were a little blown away," Jarrett says. He was also excited by the opportunity given to him to start fresh. "I hand-picked an entire department," he says. "We were charged with making a real significant change."

AWE AND ENVY

It's something his counterparts in other states have viewed with both awe and envy. Many have tried to get better salaries for their employees without much luck. "Most CIOs say, 'We would kill to be able to do what you've done,' " says Jarrett. "It's heard almost across the board."

Missouri tried about five years ago—not to get the technology department out from civil service but at least to pay employees along the lines of what similar positions in the private sector would earn. The idea didn't fly because other professionals in government, such as lawyers and accountants, could also claim rights to higher salaries based on the reasoning that the private

Slimming Down

Employment Pre- and Post-Restructuring at the
Delaware Department of Technology and Information

	Before	After
Employees	206	190
—Senior managers	11	6
—Middle managers	35	8
Civil service classifications	206	0
Pay grades	26	6*

*Includes 4 IT and 2 administrative salary bands

Source: Delaware Department of Technology and Information

sector is compensated better for those jobs, says CIO Gerry Wethington. "What Tom has done is the only way to do it," he says. "You would need support at the highest level."

Delaware's overhaul may have ancillary benefits. The department appears to be better positioned than a lot of other technology agencies for what most are going to struggle with soon—a wave of employee retirement. Higher salaries may encourage people to stay a little longer than they might have in traditional civil service, Missouri's Wethington notes. "There's a little better defense against people retiring at 55," he says. "When institutional knowledge goes out the door, we're at risk."

The enhanced pay scale enabled Jarrett to bring in an experienced chief operating officer, chief technology officer and a director for a new department of major projects under the CIO. All of them have had extensive private-sector experience.

Little by little, other employees were transitioned to the exempt status. For many months, Jarrett was running a hybrid organization, with civil service employees working alongside exempt employees. In the end, 80 percent of the employees from the old organization signed on with the new one. The other 20 percent retired, chose not to join the restructured department or were not invited on board. Jarrett finished getting everyone in place five months ahead of the two-year deadline.

The new department staff ended up being smaller than the old—especially in the managerial ranks. It might seem unlikely that a department comprising most of the

same people could turn itself into something head and shoulders above the previous one, but Delaware officials say they understand the dynamic. The IT ship, Minner says, essentially was rudderless. There were good people who were not managed well. "Those people hated to go to work," she says. "They didn't feel they were doing their job as efficiently and effectively as they could. They didn't have a leader helping them move in that direction. Now we have a vision where we might want to go."

STAYING COMPETITIVE

But not everything has gone according to plan. At the moment, officials are concerned that the state might not have the dollars promised to employees for performance pay. "We thought we had it made," says Eakle. "That was just the beginning. Now we have to keep them happy and challenged." They might not be as happy if the budget doesn't allow for the pay they had hoped and worked for. Just when the department is nearing the time to start rewarding people, the state is short on revenue. "The state budget may or may not have dollars to compete," Eakle says. "We have to be concerned about, cognizant of that. We have to stay competitive. Whether or not we can stay that way is an open question."

State employees might be inclined to jump to the private sector if the technology sector improves. In fact, Jarrett says, the new department may even drive such leaps because it has given employees a taste of what private-sector work is like—as well as made them more appealing workers for private industry to recruit. Neither the governor nor Jarrett admits to being worried, however. They don't expect the agency to implode if performance pay expectations aren't met.

As department head, Jarrett brought some unique strengths to the job. Having spent six years as a state lobbyist for the communications firm Verizon, he had gotten to know Delaware legislators, including those on the Joint Finance Committee who make the funding decisions. He still "lobbies" on behalf of his department, keeping the legislature informed about IT initiatives. While his technology people stay immersed in ever-changing technologies, his focus is on the forest, not the trees—setting standards and policies. He wanders the legislative halls wearing his "bat belt," as his assistant likes to call it, bearing two cell phones and two pagers, in case he's needed elsewhere.

State agencies are charged to work through the technology department, which gives it a lot of power. Some agencies have resisted that change with an attitude of "You can't tell us what to do," Jarrett says. The friction typically arises from people who were used to building their own systems their own way and want to be left to their own devices. It's hardly unusual in states. But with the governor and the legislature behind him, Jarrett has potent weapons for getting grousers into line.

The director of major projects, Lynn Hersey-Miller, has another tool for those fearful of or antagonistic toward technology transformations: a team of change-management specialists who are responsible for helping end users accept new technologies and ways of doing business. "I believe in cutting-edge change management," she says. "The easy part is the technology. The hard part is acceptance, the effect it has on people who use it."

SUSTAINABLE CHANGE

If change is good, in Delaware's case it was also essential. The data center was a real "rat's nest" two-and-a-half years ago, says Jarrett. The old IT agency had electrical problems and no back-up power. Agencies didn't want to house their servers there. The department had become simply a maintenance organization, rather than one seeking to solve agencies' business problems with the best use of technology.

Record keeping left something to be desired as well. Agencies and schools owed the department $1.8 million. The financial team in the new department has collected all of the delinquent payments and used the money for a mainframe computer upgrade.

There were disparate systems throughout state government and agencies weren't leveraging off other agencies' capabilities. Now, with new standards, agencies can share what they develop and save money all around. For instance, the information technology building has developed an electronic visitor-control system to let employees and guests in and out of the building. Others will adapt it to their buildings next.

Before, updates could be made to the state's portal once a week. Now, it's once a minute. And the department is saving $600,000 annually because it is doing the work in-house instead of contracting out. "If you didn't understand what we walked into, it's difficult to gauge how much change there's been," Jarrett says.

The department has already won national recognition for its Access Delaware project, a Web-enabled way for agencies to deliver information and services to citizens. Not only have citizens noticed good results but so have technology users in government. "We see a big, big difference in the response we get as users," says Representative Roy. "It's really oriented toward what the user needs."

The technology department now is able to quickly roll out e-government applications, as evidenced by the Web site developed for the avian flu outbreak, as well as offer hunting and fishing licenses online. "Under the old structure," Jarrett says, "it might have taken forever."

Over the next decade, the department plans to bring pockets of IT back into the fold. Currently, an agency might have a server in a closet and six IT people in a building where the only air-conditioning system is the one geared for the cooling of people, not the safe operations of computers. That is not a good environment, Eakle notes.

Top executives agree that the IT department is on track but not fully mature. Internal processes still need to be fine-tuned if the department is to become a "world-class IT organization," as the agency's principals hope. "Now's the hard part, living up to expectations," says Jarrett.

Some employees would like things to go even faster. But Jarrett reminds them that it's important to take steps that can be sustained in the long run. Governor Minner also is pleased with the results so far but knows the job is far from over. "We've come a long way," she says, "but there's still a lot more we can do."

32

The Phantom of New York

Christopher Swope

Quasi-governmental authorities spend billions of dollars of Empire State taxpayers' money every year. They don't have to answer many questions about it.

Every politico in New York State is familiar with the story of Robert Moses, even if few have finished reading all 1,100 pages of Robert Caro's biography of him. Moses, back in the 1930s, '40s and '50s, amassed the power to build roads, bridges, parks and housing projects in New York City and all over the state, pretty much however and wherever he wished, through his domination of public authorities—quasi-governmental agencies of which he controlled more than a dozen. Using the authorities, he could issue bonds to pay for public works and collect tolls or fees, all without seeking permission from any formal legislative body. He was able to exercise vast discretion with virtually no accountability at all.

Public authorities aren't quite as powerful today as they used to be, due in part to the backlash against Moses' abuse of them. But they remain very crucial, if little-noticed, institutions not just in New York but across the country. They manage an impressive array of America's infrastructure: airports, stadiums, convention centers, transit systems, turnpikes, bridges, tunnels, cargo facilities, sewer and water systems, public housing and even parking garages. These are critical functions. So it seemed like a reasonable request, given the authorities' significance and their checkered past, when Alan Hevesi, the comptroller of New York State, recently asked for a list of all of the state's public authorities. Surely a complete list must exist somewhere, Hevesi thought.

It didn't. So Hevesi's staff went on a public authority hunt. Flipping back and forth through volumes of state statutes, they recorded the names of hundreds of bureaucracies. Some were familiar to citizens, such as the New York State Thruway Authority and the Port Authority of New York and New Jersey. But many were obscure

From *Governing,*
November 2004.

entities that few have ever heard of: the Industrial Exhibit Authority; the Islip Resource Recovery Authority; the Overcoat Development Corp. The list went on and on. This past February, in a report that likened these bodies to a "secret government," Hevesi put the tally of state and local public authorities in New York at 640. Since then, his staff has "discovered" 70 more. They're still not sure they've found them all.

At the very least, it is a sign of weak oversight if a state government doesn't even know how many public authorities are acting in its behalf. But lately there have been other signs of poor management and questionable contracting. The Metropolitan Transit Authority, which runs the subways, buses and commuter trains in the New York City area, was accused of lying about its budget numbers in order to justify a fare hike. In another case, a subsidiary of the Thruway Authority known as the Canal Corp. offered lucrative development rights along the Erie Canal to a campaign contributor of Governor George Pataki's—for a paltry $30,000. Attorney General Eliot Spitzer put it bluntly when he said that "public authorities are becoming to New York what off-balance-sheet partnerships were to Enron."

A consensus is building that something about public authorities is broken in the Empire State—even if Pataki, Spitzer, Hevesi and the legislature don't agree on what to do about it. At the same time that the authorities are being attacked, however, more of them are being created. For example, a new state-local authority was just established to build a convention center in Albany. Discussions are underway to create an entertainment authority to manage sports and arts facilities in Greater Binghamton.

The biggest new entry, however, would be in the Big Apple, where the city and state are talking about forming a development corporation to redevelop the west side of Manhattan. "Public officials can cluck their tongues and say authorities are out of control," notes Steve Malanga, a senior fellow at the Manhattan Institute, a conservative think tank. "But when an issue comes up that they think can't win with the voters, they go back to using authorities."

ONE STEP REMOVED

Public authorities have been around since the 1920s, when good-government reformers suggested that quasi-independent agencies might perform certain tasks more efficiently than government could. There were good reasons to believe that, and there still are today. "Public authorities are pretty darned useful," says Kathryn Foster, a planning professor at SUNY Buffalo.

The original argument was essentially that authorities could remove politics from the delivery of basic services. Take sewers. If every rate hike had to go to a public referendum, long-term maintenance might never get done. Authorities are meant to circumvent such political messiness. They're typically set up one step removed from city, county or state government. They're supposed to enjoy the managerial freedoms of the private sector, while retaining some of the accountability that is so important in the public sector.

It's not easy to generalize about authorities. Not only do they perform vastly different functions but they're also structured quite differently from state to state. Some authority boards are elected, while others are appointed by governors or mayors. A few cross political boundaries, such as the Delaware River Port Authority, whose board is appointed by the governors of Pennsylvania and New Jersey. Some receive appropriations from legislatures, but most authorities can raise money on their own, from tolls, fares or user fees, and some can levy taxes on the public at large.

One thing that is clear about authorities is that their number is growing faster than that of any other slice of American government. It's difficult to pin down an exact figure for the whole country, precisely because they are so loosely defined from one state to the next. Nevertheless, the U.S. Census Bureau makes an effort. In 2002, it counted some 35,000 "special district governments"—a label that does not include school districts. By contrast, there were only 26,000 of these quasi-governmental institutions in 1977.

Much of this growth is in booming suburbs and exurbs, where development means that there are new water systems to manage, new parks to build, new bus systems to run. More often than not, a public authority is given these responsibilities. But some of the authorities' growth also reflects the changing needs of states and older cities. In Moses' day, many authorities literally paved the way to a new automobile era by building the first highways and bridges. These days, in urban areas, newly minted authorities are more likely to be building arenas and convention centers, or playing the role of lead developer in publicly financed real estate deals.

A new authority's strongest selling point is often its ability to stay focused on a single goal. For example, Washington, D.C., just created a new corporation to finance an $8 billion redevelopment plan along the Anacostia River. The job could have gone to the D.C. economic development department, or to an existing authority that does redevelopment work citywide. But planners didn't want to risk seeing the Anacostia program get lost in an overstuffed portfolio. They preferred to create a separate institution whose managers have one job—redeveloping the waterfront—rather than many.

Another reason why the number of authorities keeps growing is that old ones rarely seem to go away. Look at the Pittsburgh Stadium Authority, created in the 1960s to build and manage Three Rivers Stadium. Pittsburgh demolished that facility four years ago, replacing it with twin football and baseball stadiums—built by yet another authority. Still, the old Stadium Authority lives on, an oddity that nobody paid much attention to until charges hit this summer that an authority accountant had embezzled $193,000. The authority's ostensible raison d'etre is to pay off the bonds on Three Rivers, but Pennsylvania state Representative Jack Wagner thinks that's a bogus excuse. "There's no reason why that authority and the debt can't be merged into another authority," Wagner says. "This is nothing more than a duplication of government services."

CLOSED DOORS

A swell of complaints about alleged impropriety at authorities is what put reform on the agenda in New York. The MTA's budget scam and the canal land giveaway were only the beginning:

- The New York Racing Association, the quasi-governmental agency that runs three horse-racing tracks, was in-dicted as a body and many tellers were convicted of tax fraud and money laundering.
- The head of the New York State Bridge Authority, who was also the father-in-law of a close Pataki adviser, resigned when it was revealed that he had spent $25,000 of the authority's money on personal trips and rung up $80,000 worth of questionable credit card bills.
- Former U.S. Senator Alphonse D'Amato, now a lobbyist, received a $500,000 fee for a placing a phone call to the MTA and persuading the authority to help his client get a loan. (An investigation cleared D'Amato of any wrongdoing.)

"Here's the reality," says Hevesi, whose audits have turned up a few of the latest transgressions. "Some authorities are very effective and well run. But a lot are mismanaged and some are corrupt."

Pataki thinks that assessment is too negative. Like New York governors before him, Pataki, a Republican, influences many of the state authorities through his appointment power. His aides say he wants reform, but that much of the recent controversy is little more than political grandstanding. They insist that Spitzer, a Democrat, mostly wants Pataki's job, and another authorities critic, Democratic Assemblyman Richard Brodsky, wants Spitzer's job. Hevesi, too, is an elected Democrat. "We're proud of the work of our authorities," says Joe Conway, a Pataki spokesman.

But it is not just partisans who are calling for reform. Good-government groups have come to see the authorities as a subset of Albany's legendary governance problems (the state budget is typically decided in secret by three men, universally known as the "triumvirate": currently Pataki, Democratic Assembly Speaker Sheldon Silver, and

What Special Governments Do

Function	Percent
Natural resources	19.9%
Fire protection	16.2
Water supply	9.7
Housing and Community Development	9.7
Sewerage	5.7
Cemeteries	4.7
Libraries	4.4
Parks and recreation	3.7
Highways	2.2
Health	2.1
Hospitals	2.1
Education	1.5
Airports	1.4
Utilities (excluding water supply)	1.4
Other single functions	6.2
Multiple functions	9.0

Source: U.S. Census Bureau, 2002

the Senate's GOP Majority Leader Joseph Bruno). "Getting a handle on what the public authorities spend and how much money they raise is very difficult," says Diana Fortuna, president of the nonpartisan Citizens Budget Commission.

Authorities haven't had to report their finances in any consistent way, and their budgets don't show up on the state government's books. Authorities aren't subject to the same contracting or lobbying rules that state agencies are, even though they spend billions of dollars every year. If you want to know why an authority picked one vendor over another for a important contract, it is nearly impossible to find out. Nor is it easy to track how much lobbying contractors do, or how successful they are at it.

Top jobs at authorities are considered plum positions in New York, with salaries that often exceed six figures. Patronage is the prerogative of any governor, of course, but Albany insiders say that Pataki, more than his predecessors, has used the authorities to enrich his friends and campaign contributors. For example, a former mayor of the town of Peekskill, who is also a childhood friend of Pataki's, found his way to an executive vice president job at the New York Power Authority. Another friend, who had headed Pataki's security detail, also got a top job with the power authority. Blair Horner, a lobbyist with the New York Public Interest Research Group, argues that the conversion of authorities into patronage mills defeats their original purpose. "The idea that these authorities are semi-autonomous entities staffed by career civil service types who are divorced from politics has changed. They're now agents of the executive branch who are not subject to the same oversight."

BIG-TIME DEBT

Who are the authorities accountable to? That answer isn't always clear. Pataki is prone to issuing press releases anytime an authority generates good news, such as when the Lower Manhattan Development Corp. (LMDC) opened four reconstructed ball fields in a park on the East River. When events get politically dodgy, however, Pataki tends to emphasize the authorities' independence, keeping his own hands clean.

The messy debate over rebuilding the World Trade Center—detailed in Paul Goldberger's new book Up from Zero—is a good example of this. Pataki, more than any other public official, held great sway over Ground

Zero: His appointees led the Port Authority, which owned the land, as well as the LMDC, which ran the planning process. As early as the beginning of 2002, Pataki could have settled key questions regarding the lease on the Trade Center. But he was in the midst of a re-election campaign that year and might have offended voters who preferred one rebuilding plan over another. Rather than set clear terms for the planning process, he let the governmental, quasi-governmental and private parties involved squabble with each other. "Pataki talked about bringing consensus and public input to the process," Goldberger writes. "But he seemed often to be working to assure that the process would be slow, convoluted and more than a little bit opaque."

Finally, there is the huge amount of debt that New York's authorities have run up. The state is not allowed to borrow money without voter approval, but that rule doesn't apply when it's authorities that are doing the borrowing. Consequently, these entities are used like credit cards. State authorities are currently carrying approximately $114 billion in debt—28 times more than the $4 billion issued by New York State. Much of the authorities' debt is backed by highway tolls, subway fares or other fees. But a staggering amount of it—$43 billion—is supported by state government, meaning that if the authority that issued those bonds defaulted, taxpayers would be on the hook.

It is the job of an institution called the Public Authorities Control Board to ensure that that doesn't happen. But the operations of this board are even harder to decipher than those of the authorities. The PACB was created in 1976, when one of the largest state authorities, the Urban Development Corp., nearly collapsed. The control board must approve any debt issued by the 11 largest state authorities. There are three voting members—each a representative of the Pataki-Silver-Bruno triumvirate—and decisions must be made by consensus. What that means in practice is that the PACB makes its decisions the Albany way: behind closed doors.

Not that the PACB doesn't meet in public. It does, every month, in a vaulted pink room on the first floor of the Capitol. But by the time this happens, all the decisions have been worked out in advance. At its public hearing in September, the PACB zipped quickly through a lengthy agenda, approving $384 million worth of authority financing in exactly 20 minutes. All that remained for public consumption was a pro-forma flurry of motions, seconds and ayes.

Barbara Bartoletti, a lobbyist for the League of Women Voters, attends these meetings regularly, "just so that they know the public is watching." After five years of observing from the back of the room, Bartoletti says the PACB remains a mystery to her. "We're talking about billions of taxpayer dollars," Bartoletti says. "We can't crack why decisions are made the way they are. We don't have a clue about where the money is going and whom it's going to."

GROPING FOR SUNLIGHT

Exactly what can be done about the problems with authorities is open to argument. Pataki favors an approach that aims to do for authorities what the federal Sarbanes-Oxley law did for corporate governance. In February, Pataki's chief of staff issued a memo to the 31 state authorities most tightly under the governor's control. The memo called upon them to implement so-called "model governance principles," developed by corporate governance expert Ira Millstein. Pataki also asked Millstein to head a commission, whose June draft report fleshed these principles out further.

Millstein's suggestions include standardizing financial reporting among the authorities, and making more of it publicly available. He also would have each authority appoint an independent audit committee. The bulk of Millstein's recommendations, however, have to do with the authorities' boards. Many boards have developed reputations for rubber-stamping management decisions. Millstein thinks boards should be structured to have more independence. He also thinks that if board members went through extensive training, they might take the oversight part of their job more seriously. "Sunlight and active boards will be as much of a cure as we can get at this point," Millstein says.

Hevesi and Spitzer agree with most of Millstein's proposals, but don't think he goes far enough. They have joined together on more sweeping legislation that would, for the first time in 50 years, prune back the number of authorities in New York. The plan is to have a commission sort out those authorities that have outlived their usefulness, or whose duties can easily be handled elsewhere in government.

Hevesi and Spitzer would make other changes. Their proposal would rewrite lobbying and procurement rules so that authorities and state agencies are treated the same. That means the controller would get a veto over large authority contracts. It also means that anyone who lobbies an authority would have to register with the state lobbying commission. In September, Hevesi added another reform he would like to see: He wants authority spending to be considered "on budget" in the state's books.

Assemblyman Brodsky proposes a different approach, one that was passed by the Democratic Assembly in February, but died in the Senate. Brodsky would create new layers of oversight, including an inspector general's office for public authorities, as well as an independent budget officer. In September, Brodsky upped the ante, calling for a constitutional amendment that would abolish all public authorities, wrapping their functions back into state agencies. That was more a statement of principle than a realistic policy proposal. Still, Brodsky says, "anything authorities can do can be done directly by government on-budget, instead of hidden off-budget."

All the reform rhetoric makes officials at some authorities cringe, especially those that are widely acknowledged to be well run. In over-reacting to a few scandals, they warn, reformers might take away the independence that has allowed some authorities to thrive. Take the state Dormitory Authority, which started in the 1940s building dorms at teachers colleges, and has since become a well-regarded all-purpose builder of school and hospital facilities. Claudia Hutton, the authority's spokeswoman, cautions that a cookie-cutter reform package could cause more problems than it solves. "The New York Power Authority is a power company," Hutton says. "That's awfully different from what we do."

It's unlikely that she has much to fear. Talking about reform in Albany is easy. Doing it is another thing. Individual authorities such as the MTA and Canal Corp. have tweaked the practices that landed them in the headlines. But more sweeping reform of authorities isn't likely, if only because the desire to create more of them remains such a powerful force. Steve Malanga says the situation with authorities is a lot like New York's budget process in general. "It's broken, but it doesn't suit the people in power to fix it."

33

Worth the Money?

Jonathan Walters

The competition for top talent is producing a cadre of highly paid public executives.

From *Governing,*
July 2004.

L ike a baseball coach working his way up the organizational ladder, Rhoda Mae Kerr recently had to abandon her hometown team and make the move to a new city in order to take the top spot. Last January, Kerr took over as chief of the Little Rock fire department after a career in Fort Lauderdale that was capped by three years as deputy chief. Whereas the pattern in the old days was to stay in one place for an entire career, Kerr says, today it's typical to see executives in the fire service move around in order to move up. And for a handful of recognized achievers in her field, such moves bring with them something besides greater challenges and prestige: They bring increased salaries and perks along with a burgeoning reputation that, if nurtured, can put a public-sector career onto an all-star track.

While insisting that she has no plans to leave Little Rock, Kerr admits that some of her employees already have expressed concern that this might be just a short stop for her on the road to somewhere even bigger. That's because Kerr has now entered an elite corps of hired public-sector executives whose expertise makes them hot properties across the country. "There's been a confluence of forces," says Bob O'Neill, executive director of the International City/County Management Association. "There's this incredible pressure that's brought to bear between scarce resources, the demand for and focus on performance, and the political environment in which these people have to operate. People who are effective in that environment are worth their weight in gold."

Indeed, in this new world, hired-gun attorneys negotiate six-figure salaries on their behalf, headhunters make regular contact, and some even speculate that the day will come when the hottest

163

public officials will have agents to shop around for the most lucrative deal.

Some members of the "gold" club, such as Los Angeles Police Chief Bill Bratton and former New York City School Superintendent Rudy Crew, have managed to become household names. Robert Kiley, who is credited with rebuilding both the Boston and New York City subway systems, was recently the subject of a full-blown feature story in *The New Yorker* magazine, which chronicled his elevation to savior of the London Underground. Kiley was lured overseas by a compensation package estimated to be worth well over half a million dollars.

Because of the aggressive recruitment of top talent, members of the gold club can command heftier salaries and beefier benefits, whether it's big-ticket sweeteners such as generous contributions to pension funds, performance bonuses or help with housing costs, or littler treats, such as cars, cell phones and take-home computers. Meanwhile, the elite are increasingly opting out of traditional, at-will employment and insisting on multi-year contracts with clauses that ensure any falling out with their elected or appointed handlers will end up in a very soft landing.

Add to the dynamic a shortage of top people willing to take on what in many cases are considered impossible jobs and it makes for a lively, lucrative mix. "You have a lot of school districts chasing a few superintendents and that makes for a lot of churning and also for a significant increase in salaries and perks," says Paul Houston, a former school superintendent who is now executive director of the American Association of School Administrators. "In the past decade, it has really shifted from a buyer's market to a seller's market."

Eric Smith, the school superintendent in Anne Arundel County, Maryland, who reportedly was on the short list of candidates for the superintendent's job in Miami-Dade County (a position ultimately accepted by the aforementioned Rudy Crew), says it's the high profile and the high stakes, in particular, that require the combat pay. "It's an area that's covered intensely by the press and that is much analyzed and debated. And if you're trying to drive change, you'll draw a fair amount of fire."

Smith, who makes $200,000 a year, says that while these forces make for an improved salary picture, the downside is that peripatetic school officials can't draw upon the generous pension layouts afforded most state and local employees, who put in their 25 or 30 years in one place and then reap the benefits. Anne Arundel is contributing a decent sum to a 401(k)-style pension plan as part of his compensation package, says Smith, but he still lives in a world of defined contributions and not guaranteed benefits upon retirement. And Smith arguably is now on the modest end of the high-profile superintendent salary structure. Crew's compensation package in Miami-Dade is estimated to be around $550,000, including salary, bonuses and a housing allowance.

For public-sector superstars, goodbyes sometimes can be as lucrative as hellos. Interim District of Columbia School Superintendent Elfreda Massie, who was paid $75,000 to fill in for about six months last winter, was handed a bonus check for nearly $34,000 on her last day of work in April. Members of the city council and the mayor harshly criticized the bonus, but D.C. school board members saw it as much-deserved pay for a job well done. In recent months, D.C. Mayor Anthony Williams seems to have come around to a new way of thinking about compensating the city's chief education officer. A *Washington Post* article in May had the mayor's office speculating that the city might have to come up with as much as $600,000 to attract a top-flight candidate to fill the job. In mid-June, the city was attempting to lure Carl A. Cohn, former Long Beach, California, superintendent.

PERSONNEL PILFERING

While such remuneration indicates just how much of a seller's market it has become for some top executives, the lucrative talent trade can also be gauged by the amount of public-sector personnel larceny going on as governments jockey to secure the best and the brightest. "It's not unusual for any high-profile administrator to be contacted once a month and offered a job," says Professor George Frederickson, who has spent decades helping train future public managers at the University of Kansas. Rod Gould, city manager for San Rafael, California, say he is frequently on the receiving end of such queries. "I'm amazed at all the calls from recruiters." The 47-year-old Gould adds that part of what's driving demand is a rapidly aging and retiring cadre of experienced managers.

And it's not just high-profile players in traditionally high-profile jobs such as city manager, police chief or school superintendent who are being approached.

Planning directors, public works directors, chief information officers—those in the more utilitarian trenches of government—are also routinely recruited by other jurisdictions intent on a little personnel pilfering. "I get called every so often," says Bob Hunter, the long-serving executive director of the Regional Planning Commission in Hillsborough County, Florida.

Who Makes What	
■ Kerr	$102,000
■ Park	$115,008
■ Pataki	$179,000
■ Neff	$190,000
■ Wood	$250,000
■ Bratton	$256,155
■ Crew	$305,000
■ Bush	$400,000
■ Saban	$400,000

Hunter says he's happy to stay put for now, but as one of the most respected planners in the country, he could probably write his ticket on any given day.

And while few lay people have probably ever heard of Peter Park, the city of Denver knows him as one of the top urban planners in the field. "The reason that I just about killed myself to get Peter Park is that planning is as important as anything else when it comes to what a city does," says Denver Mayor John Hickenlooper, who spent weeks wooing Park. "Park is not just a New Urbanist, he's one of the national and international leaders in urban planning." And probably a significant bargain to Denver at $115,000 a year.

Michael Armstrong has been the assistant city manager for information technology in Des Moines for the past six years. He knows that there aren't very many people with his level of technical skill and knowledge who can also work cooperatively on large projects that span departments citywide. If he wanted to, Armstrong could no doubt move to a bigger municipality on either coast. According to the International City/County Management Association's 2004 salary survey, Prince William County, Virginia, pays its IT director around $130,000 a year; San Diego County pays $160,000; Phoenix pays almost $145,000. But Armstrong says his salary of $125,000 goes a nice distance in the Midwest, which is one of the reasons he has stayed put; salaries may be higher elsewhere, he says, but so is the cost of living. As for being contacted by headhunters, Armstrong says, "It's nothing like two or three times a week, but every once in a while."

Jerry Newfarmer, who finished his city manager's career in Cincinnati after stints in Fresno and San Jose, says that the job has always paid pretty well. But clearly things have gotten better in the past couple of decades as competition for top talent has warmed up. For example, when Newfarmer took over as San Jose's city manager in 1983, the salary was $90,000; the job now pays $209,000. And whereas the big perk for Newfarmer was having the city contribute to a 401(k)-style retirement plan, employment packages in numerous California jurisdictions now include the ability to tap into the state pension system, CalPERS, as well as housing allowances and generous severance packages.

Rod Wood, who at $250,000 a year may be the highest-paid city or county manager in the country, worked out an arrangement with his new employer—the city of Beverly Hills—whereby the city subsidizes his annual housing costs to the tune of $70,000. Wood, who made his name in other cities by thinking up creative ways to finance sewage expansion and affordable housing projects, is also a pioneer in fashioning creative financial packages to attract top talent to public service in a high housing-cost environment. He believes he was the first to work out an equity-sharing deal with a city when he became manager of Indian Wells, California, back in 1989. "I think Indian Wells may have the second-highest per capita income of any city in the country and it costs a ton of money to live there." So he proposed an arrangement whereby the city helped subsidize his mortgage but also profited from the sale of his house when he moved on.

LOCAL LARGESSE

In analyzing who pays how much, it's clear that high pressure and high stakes are only part of what drives salaries. ICMA's salary survey shows that big cities and wealthy suburbs are where the money is. Bratton makes upwards of $250,000 in L.A.; the chief financial officer for Washington, D.C., rakes in more than $170,000. Meanwhile, the fire chief in the well-heeled Boston suburb of Needham earns more than $110,000. Rod Wood's old haunt, Indian Wells (population 3,816), pays its public works director $114,000. Greenwich, Connecticut, pays its police chief more than $110,000. The economic development director in Lake Forest, Illinois, makes around $112,000.

If it sounds like the big-salary and generous perks action is all at the local government level, that's because with a few exceptions— notably state university presidents, athletic directors and football or basketball coaches—it is. "Our experience is that there are fewer restrictions on pay for local officials," says Bob Lavigna, the former head of recruitment and selection for the state of Wisconsin who now works for CPS Human Resources Services, a Sacramento-based human resources consulting firm. "In many cases, by law or by tradition, state officials can't make more than the governor." (New York's George Pataki is the highest-paid governor, at $179,000.) It's a quirky restriction that in some places even extends to municipalities. For example, when CPS was asked to help Minneapolis find a public works director, Lavigna says, the task was made much trickier by the fact that state law caps municipal salaries at 90 percent of the governor's annual $120,000 salary. Minneapolis recently sought and got a waiver from the state legislature in order to hire a police chief at $128,000.

There may be other reasons that local governments offer salaries more commensurate with the market—not to mention actual job responsibilities. "It's a riddle that always perplexed me," says Alisoun Moore, who left her $101,000 job as chief information officer for the state of Maryland to take the $155,000 CIO job in Montgomery County, Maryland. "But I think that county legislators and executives know that their primary job is to deliver very direct services, so they're willing to pay competitive wages to attract good folks, whether it's firefighters or executives."

Despite all the talk about big bucks and generous perquisites, one point needs to be made clear, say those who follow issues of pay and benefits for public officials: Given the incredible responsibilities heaped on upper-level public-sector executives and the frequently volatile political environments in which they're asked to operate, they are still arguably underpaid. Whether it's taming the streets of Los Angeles, raising student test scores in Miami-Dade, or trying to pull Denver's disparate districts

> *"Given the incredible responsibilities heaped on upper-level public executives, they are still arguably underpaid."*

and neighborhoods together into a cohesive, economically dynamic metropolitan whole, lots of upper-level public executives are atop gigantic, sprawling organizations that are charged with accomplishing nearly impossible tasks. Kevin Baum, assistant fire chief in Austin, Texas, and a rising star in his field, says that he is probably paid one-third of what one of his organizational counterparts at Austin-based Dell Computer makes, "minus the stock options," he adds wryly. And it hardly needs stating that the Dell executive's job is sandbox play compared to what Baum faces every day.

Baum says he could move up a salary notch if he listened to any of the headhunters who he says call every so often trying to woo him out of Texas hill country. Baum's next logical move, he says, would be to chief in a mid-size city, which would set him up for the jump to the big league—a Chicago, Boston or Seattle. And certainly there are plenty of six-figure jobs in smaller cities around the country, from Birmingham, Alabama, to Downers Grove, Illinois, to Costa Mesa, California, which pay $115,000, $102,000 and $140,000, respectively, according to the ICMA salary survey. But the politics of fire chief have become more volatile and the job strains more pronounced since 9/11, he says. In fact, he's seeing a lot of longtime chiefs getting out altogether, with fewer and fewer experienced candidates willing to step up. That, along with the fact that average tenure of larger city fire chiefs is getting ever shorter, says Baum, has him thinking twice about the whole idea of pulling up stakes. "I have to ask myself if I really want to move to another city and be chief."

It's a sentiment that's expressed by others who find themselves at the edge of superstar status, not sure if it's worth the extra money to step into the frequently unforgiving limelight that is populated by the public sector's executive movers and shakers. Kevin Duggan, city manager for Mountain View, California, says he could certainly be making more money working somewhere else. But he adds that many of those jobs are in "meat grinder" cities, and he's just not sure he's ready for the blades to swirl his way, regardless of pay.

LURE OF THE LIMELIGHT

But for others, the prospect of taking on seemingly impossible high-level jobs is an enormous part of the appeal. "It's an interesting combination between a really true and altruistic sense of public service, on the one hand, and enormous ego, on the other," says the school administrators' Paul Houston. "It's the adrenaline buzz. There's a lot of pressure, but a lot of people thrive on that and become addicted to it."

When Oakland City Manager Robert Bobb, who had co-existed for five years with the famously egotistical Mayor Jerry Brown, was finally ousted last summer, he received a $275,000 severance package. But rather than riding off into the sunset or choosing some easy assignment, Bobb soon headed for Washington, D.C.—a city with comparable problems and egos. As the District of Columbia's top administrator, Bobb now earns $185,000. That's a step down from the $224,400 and generous benefits he had negotiated with Oakland but $50,000 more than D.C. paid his predecessor.

But even given the potential for high-visibility failure or feuding, the money and the personal satisfaction of doing a hard job that matters make it all worthwhile, says San Rafael's Rod Gould. "If you've got the chops for it, there are few things better than taking on the variety and challenge of being a city manager."

And of course it's not always a jungle out there. Just ask Rod Wood, who was actually contemplating a switch to the private sector before a headhunter talked him into giving Beverly Hills a try. Shortly after taking the job, he was at one of the many after-hour events that city managers view as obligatory. "There was a band," says Wood, "but nobody was dancing. Well, they started playing a particular song, and I just couldn't resist and so I started to sort of move my feet a little." As he got into his groove, an attractive young woman who just happened to be wandering by joined him.

For any public officials out there looking for signs that they have hit the big time: It has arrived when a city gets down on bended knee to offer a compensation package worth a quarter-million dollars. Or, as in the case of Rod Wood, when the job includes taking a quick twirl on the dance floor with Britney Spears.

VIII

Local Government

There is a lot of government below state government. Actually, there are a lot of *governments*—close to 90,000 of them by one count.[1] These governments provide many of the basic services that society has come to take for granted: law enforcement, public schools, fire protection, and libraries, as well as basic infrastructure operations such as water, sewer, and local road systems.

There are so many local governments, so many forms of local governments, and so many different programs and services that they provide, that it is difficult to make general statements about local governments with any degree of accuracy. Consider that both the municipality of Los Angeles, Calif. (population roughly 4 million), and the town of Strang, Neb. (population something less than 40), fit under the umbrella of local government. The term *local government* covers everything from general municipalities responsible for hundreds of programs and services to mosquito-control districts that exist for the sole purpose of killing bugs.

Thus, if the articles in this section seem to cover very different subjects (such as sewers and schools), it is not without good reason. To provide a representative sample of all the things local governments do, and all the forms local governments take, would require a volume the size of an encyclopedia. A single section's worth of readings cannot cover all of that ground, but it can convey a basic notion of the breadth of what local governments are and how they differ.

WHAT LOCAL GOVERNMENTS ARE

Local governments come in three basic forms: counties, municipalities, and special districts. Counties originated as, and to a considerable extent still are, local outposts of state government. For governing purposes, states subdivided themselves into smaller political jurisdictions called counties, and turned over to these counties basic local functions such as road maintenance and law enforcement.

Municipalities are public corporations, created to provide basic governance to defined geographic jurisdictions. Municipalities include familiar political entities such as towns, villages, and cities. They differ from counties in that municipalities tend to be more compact geographically and more urban, and they legally exist as independent corporations rather than being the local offices of state government.

Special districts, something of a miscellaneous category, include everything else—and when it comes to local government, there is a lot of everything else. Unlike counties and municipalities, which are general governance units that provide a broad range of programs and services, special districts are created to provide specific programs or services. School districts are the most common form of special district—they exist solely to provide public education. Other examples include water treatment and sewage management districts.

Keep in mind that these definitions are fairly loose. For example, what constitutes a town, a village, or a city is governed by state law, and the powers and policy responsibilities of these different categories of municipality may vary considerably. Municipalities, counties, and special districts are not even clearly separated by geography—they are piled on top of each other, which can be confusing to citizens and can create coordination and control problems for public officials. A county may be almost completely covered by a municipality or a series of municipalities. There may be several school districts crossing over county and city boundaries. Fitted across these jurisdictions may be other special districts. Local governments fit together like some sort of three-dimensional jigsaw puzzle that is missing some pieces. Given this, it should not be surprising to hear that local governments sometimes get into arguments about who should be doing what.

Although local governments can seem to be a confusing jumble, there is a fairly clear difference between the vast majority of local governments and state governments. Generally speaking, state governments are sovereign governments and local governments are not. What

this means is that state governments get their powers and legal authority directly from citizens—this power and authority is codified in state constitutions.

Most local governments get their power from state governments, not directly from citizens. Their powers and legal authority are mostly set by state laws, which is to say by state legislatures. And what the legislatures give, they can take away. So unlike the relationship between the federal and state governments, which at least in theory is a relationship of equals, the relationship between state governments and local governments is legally a superior-subordinate relationship. Some states grant local governments broad powers, whereas others reserve many of these powers to themselves and delegate comparatively little authority. Even in the states that grant local governments considerable independence, however, the state is still the sovereign government.

This hierarchy is codified legally in what is known as Dillon's Rule, which is the legal principle that local governments can only exercise the powers granted to them by state governments. The independence and power of local governments thus varies enormously not just from state to state, but from locality to locality within states. Some municipalities are virtually city-states, powerful political jurisdictions with a high degree of self-rule. Others are little more than local extensions of state governments.

The most independent local governments are those with home rule, which in effect grants localities the right of self-government and is most commonly expressed in the form of a city charter. Such a charter is basically a mini-constitution that specifies the powers, organization, and responsibilities of a local government. City charters and the basis for granting home rule vary from state to state.

DIFFERENCES AMONG LOCAL GOVERNMENTS

State governments, for all their variety, follow a roughly similar organizational blueprint, which bears a strong resemblance to that of the federal government. There are three branches of state government (executive, legislative, and judicial) that share power through a system of differing responsibilities and checks and balances. But there is no basic blueprint for local governments. All forms of local government frequently mix and match executive and legislative functions and responsibilities in a manner completely alien to what is taken for granted at the state and federal levels. In addition, counties and many municipalities (especially larger cities) typically have a judicial branch. District attorneys, for example, are often a county-level office. Special districts, however, have no real judicial component.

Local governments, in short, not only differ by geography, responsibilities, and power, they also differ organizationally. This isn't just a difference between school districts and county governments. The same types of functional governments can have radically different forms. Take cities, for example, which often govern using variations of the mayor-council, council-manager, and commission systems.

The mayor-council system is a fairly generic organizational plan for city government that includes an elected legislature (a city council) and an elected executive (a mayor). The separation of powers between the legislature and the executive, however, are not always as clear-cut as it is at the state and federal levels. Under strong mayor systems, the executive wields veto power, is independently elected, and sits as the chief bureaucrat over all city departments. But there are also weak mayor systems, and weak mayors do not have true executive powers—no veto over council decisions, no ability to appoint department heads. In weak mayor systems, the council wields most of the executive power.

The mayor-council system is not the most common type of municipal government. Roughly half of all cities use a council-manager system. In this system the council makes major policy decisions, but leaves the implementation to an appointed administrator called a city manager. Political power is vested in the council, which makes major decisions such as setting the budget, deciding tax rates, and formulating the major goals for city government. The professional manager handles the day-to-day job of translating the council's decisions into action.[2]

Some cities have commission forms of government. City commissions are elected bodies, and each commissioner is the head of an executive department. Commissioners do not run for office as general legislators; they are elected to be the police commissioner or pub-lic works commissioner, for example. The commissioners typically elect one of themselves to head the board of commissioners, but this individual usually has no real executive power.

Each form of government has its supporters and detractors. Fans of the strong mayor system like the notion of a strong executive. In effect, a strong mayor can act as an equivalent to a state governor—he or she can get things done because he or she has the tools a chief executive needs. Supporters of the council-manager system like its attempt to separate politics and administration. The chief bureaucrat in a council-manager system is a professional administrator, not a politician who makes decisions with an eye on the next election. The pros and cons of different systems are periodically debated when local governments consider organizational reforms, and some municipalities occasionally shift from one system to another (see the article by Alan Ehrenhalt in this section).

To keep things interesting, counties and special districts can, and often do, have different governance structures than municipalities even though they might all share the same geographic space. Thus in a local election you might vote for a city councilor, a county commissioner, and a slate of school board candidates whose primary job will be to hire a professional manager to run the school district (i.e., a school superintendent).

The articles in this section focus on how these different types of local governments and local officials go about getting their jobs done. Three of the articles deal with the nitty-gritty issues that local governments typically face. One piece by Rob Gurwitt details the politics of improving infrastructure in Atlanta, where Mayor Shirley Franklin has had to reach out and forge coalitions with unlikely partners to deal with a sewer system in disrepair. A second article by Rob Gurwitt examines the increasing trend of school-related sprawl. Many school districts are choosing to build new schools rather than renovate old ones, and this often means relocating schools from the heart of a community to its edge. At stake in these decisions are not just millions (even billions) of dollars, but also a reshaping of the public school's role in community life. Elizabeth Daigneau's article deals with what appears to be a mundane aspect of local politics—sidewalks. They are mundane . . . unless they are not there at all.

Christopher Swope's piece focuses on an issue you might not immediately link with local politics—the tough times of the airline industry. Air carriers, however, are the reason major air hubs exist. Local governments with large airports within their jurisdictions cannot escape the sometimes worrying implications of a shakeout in the airline industry. Finally Alan Ehrenhalt takes a look at El Paso's experiment in government reform. The remote Texas city recently shifted from a strong mayor system to a city manager system. As the article details, the shift left the city's chief executive with little to execute.

Notes

1. U.S. Census Bureau, "Census Bureau Reports Number of Local Governments Nears 88,000," January 3, 2003, www.census.gov/Press-Release/www/2003/cb03-10.html (accessed May 5, 2005).

2. International City/County Management Association, "The Council-Manager Form of Government: Answers to Your Questions," 2002, www2.icma.org/upload/library/IQ/114238.pdf (accessed May 6, 2005).

34

How to Win Friends and Repair a City

Rob Gurwitt

Atlanta needs all the help it can get. Luckily, it has a mayor who knows where to get it.

L ast fall, the president of the Georgia Senate, Eric Johnson, published a letter in the *Atlanta Journal-Constitution*. It was polite, as public rebukes go, but just barely.

The subject was Atlanta's sewers, or, more precisely, Atlanta's desperate need for help in fixing its sewers. After four decades of deferred maintenance and a federal consent decree that city officials had ignored for years, the bill had come due. Under its new mayor, Shirley Franklin, Atlanta was embarking on a $3 billion overhaul, but it was also staring at astronomical water and sewer rate increases for residents. The new rates promised much hardship for Atlanta's large population of poor people—who in a few years might be paying a total of $100 a month—and for its businesses, especially hotels, which in this convention-dependent city could be paying $100,000 a month by 2008. Not surprisingly, Franklin wanted help from the state and the federal government in defraying the cost.

Johnson's letter was his way of saying "forget it." Atlanta had repeatedly shrugged off its responsibilities, he said, and now had to pay the price. "I will fight any effort to shift the costs of Atlanta's sewer repairs onto the taxpayers of our state," Johnson wrote. "And I will not participate in any effort to ask that America's taxpayers share in your costs, either. . . . Atlanta is already costing Georgia's taxpayers plenty. I will not ask them for any more."

As unsympathetic as the letter might have been, its symbolism was even more barbed: a white Republican from Savannah lecturing the black Democratic mayor of a majority-black city on its spendthrift ways. It's not hard to imagine a disastrous chain of events: fury in political circles, an angry press conference at City Hall and shattered relations between the state and its capital city.

From *Governing*, April 2004.

173

And that makes what actually happened all the more interesting. Franklin and Johnson had a private meeting. Shortly afterward, the Republican governor, Sonny Perdue, stepped forward with a commitment to put together a $500 million loan package. Then the GOP-controlled Senate agreed to Atlanta's request that it be allowed to vote on a sales tax increase to defray the repair costs. That bill's sponsor was Eric Johnson himself. A *Journal-Constitution* reporter called these events "the biggest pre-Christmas happy hour since Tiny Tim and Scrooge patched things up."

Actually, a lot of people are getting along surprisingly well with the city of Atlanta and its mayor these days. Since taking office in January 2002, Franklin has engineered a remarkable turnaround in the city's credibility and public demeanor. She is on friendly terms with the state's leaders. She has plunged into regional efforts to deal with metropolitan transportation, economic development and watershed dilemmas. She meets regularly with officials from the fast-growing suburban counties that surround her jurisdiction. And she has cajoled members of Atlanta's powerful corporate community into serving on task forces that deal with everything from expanding the city's park system to revising its ethics code to exploring the problems of the homeless. "She and I talk every week," says Sam Williams, president of the Metro Atlanta Chamber of Commerce. "If my phone rings at 7 in the morning, I know it's Shirley."

All this bonhomie is in large part the result of Franklin's political candor, nuts-and-bolts understanding of what makes her city tick and willingness to tackle Atlanta's problems head-on. "Before her," says Eric Johnson, "Atlanta hadn't been taking leadership, they were viewed as corrupt, no one trusted them. I think she has the highest integrity personally, but she has also gone out of her way to make everybody know there's a new atmosphere."

Yet what makes the 58-year-old Franklin one of America's most intriguing mayors isn't just her persona, it's her determination to master the trickiest balancing act in urban politics today. Franklin has decided that making progress on her city's challenges means working with everyone from the governor to suburban county commissioners to regional business leaders and nonprofit executives—as she says, "I'm looking for friends for Atlanta." At the same time, she admits it's far easier to enlist their help if the city can show it's willing to take responsibility for straightening out its own messes.

As reasonable as this may sound, it's a daunting task. To build the trust she needs among state officials and business leaders, Franklin has to bolster the political will within the city to make hard choices The state sewer deal, for instance, could not have been put together without the stunning rate increases Atlanta has asked residents and businesses to pay. Yet to sustain political support for such burdens, Franklin needs to show measurable progress in improving their lives—which she can only do with the help of people who want to see her city step up to the plate first. Franklin has juggled these demands with aplomb so far; the trick will be to continue doing so as the cost of putting Atlanta on a solid footing takes an ever bigger bite out of citizens' wallets.

CHANGING DIRECTION

There was a time, of course, when a big-city mayor in search of "friends" generally looked in only one direction: toward Washington. Chasing federal largesse for everything from highways and sewers to anti-poverty funding was a way of life. In 1982, an uproar ensued when E. S. Savas, an aide to President Reagan, drafted a report taking cities to task for relying too heavily on federal programs. Support from Washington, Savas concluded, had transformed mayors "from leaders of self-reliant cities [into] wily stalkers of federal funds. All too often the promise of such guaranties has created a crippling dependency rather than initiative and independence." The report generated such a storm of protest that Reagan publicly distanced himself from it. He also, however, began the process of cutting and reshaping federal aid.

By the 1990s, it was becoming increasingly clear that pinning a city's fortunes on substantial money from Washington was a fool's game, and a different attitude began to take hold among many mayors: the sense that in effect Savas had been right, and they could do just fine on their own.

Milwaukee Mayor John O. Norquist argued that federal policies had actually hurt cities more than they had helped, and he pulled out of the U.S. Conference of Mayors, which he believed paid too much attention to Washington. "You can't build a city on pity," Norquist insisted. Meanwhile, in New York, Rudolph Giuliani was demonstrating that a mayor who focused on issues such as safety and clean streets could create a sense of dynamism and give urban life a chance to reassert itself.

In a sense, Franklin is amalgamating the two approaches, except that rather than looking to the federal government for help, she's looking everywhere else. This is a strategy that big-city mayors across the country may have little choice but to adopt, whether they recognize it or not.

In part, it's a simple function of money. Atlanta is hardly the only city facing extraordinary infrastructure costs, as local governments in every region confront deferred maintenance on bridges, roads and transit systems and federal environmental mandates on sewers. Indianapolis, Cleveland and Providence are all raising water and sewer rates as they struggle to come up with the hundreds of millions, if not billions, of dollars they each need to bring their sewer systems into compliance with environmental regulations.

So, too, with the costs of meeting demands for better public schools and for boosting homeland security—federal mandates may be plentiful, but federal money is not—and with the costs of improving parks, neighborhoods and other amenities that urban fortunes depend on these days. Finding the resources to meet all those needs demands creativity and an ability to build partnerships at every turn.

At the same time, it's more evident than it used to be that cities' fortunes are tied inextricably to the fortunes of the communities around them. Their economies are linked, their watersheds acknowledge no political boundaries, they inherit one another's air-quality problems, their residents' cars jam one another's streets. This is hardly news, but metropolitan political leaders haven't exactly built a strong track record of taking it to heart.

"For too long, the various counties and cities in the metro region spent all their time on their own governance issues and insufficient time on how their actions affected their neighbors," says Sam Olins, chairman of the commission government in Cobb County, the huge suburban jurisdiction to Atlanta's northwest. "This doesn't take a

---

Atlanta and Its Environs

City of Atlanta: Mayor and 15-member council

- Area in square miles_____132
- Population_____423,400
- Average household income _____$51,328

Metro Atlanta: 28 counties and 110 municipalities

- Area in square miles _____6,208
- Population _____4,262,584
- Average household income _____$58,568

Sources: Metro Atlanta Chamber of Commerce, *Atlanta Journal-Constitution*

---

degree in public administration. It just takes common sense."

OUT OF THE RED

That may be, but in the years before Franklin took office, there wasn't a great deal of common sense on display in Atlanta City Hall. Franklin's predecessor, Bill Campbell, was smart, articulate and impressive in person, but his two terms were also calamitous for the reputation of city government. In addition to possessing an argumentative and thin-skinned nature, Campbell paid attention to the wrong details: He micro-managed personnel decisions but ignored major budget issues. He got into constant spats with the business community, disregarded the city's regional profile and engendered a deep pool of ill will toward Atlanta among politicians around the state.

By the time Franklin took over, the city was on the fiscal ropes, although not many people knew it. One of the new mayor's first moves was to bring in several teams of consultants—some of them paid for by the Metro Chamber of Commerce—to get a handle on finances and to help reorganize the human resources, procurement and information technology systems. A group from Bain & Co., working pro bono on the city's finances, discovered that, instead of the $21 million surplus Campbell's last budget had shown, the city was actually deep in the red.

"It was a very intense process," says Franklin, "with a dozen people doing a 20-year analysis of the city's budget, revenues, expenditures. In the previous years, it had spent well over its revenue. So while the city was holding property taxes low, in fact we were spending ourselves into a hole." Franklin's team eventually announced a gap of $82 million for 2002—"because at some point you just had to settle on a figure," Franklin says—although it probably amounted to more than $90 million, or over a fifth of operating expenditures.

Franklin's response was to tell residents that in order for things to be fixed they were going to have to share the pain. She persuaded the city council to raise property taxes, cut nearly 1,000 jobs from the city payroll and, in announcing a series of other budget cuts, began by slicing her own salary. Since then, she has set out to overhaul everything from yard waste collection to the municipal courts and corrections systems.

Through all of this, Franklin has mastered the political art of appearing to be non-political. It is an art she learned over two decades as an aide to previous Atlanta mayors. Franklin was commissioner for cultural affairs under Maynard Jackson in the 1970s, then chief administrator for Jackson and his successor, Andrew Young, in the 1980s. Later, she spent five years helping to organize Atlanta's 1996 Olympic Games. In each job, she managed to maintain credibility among widely disparate interests and factions. She also benefited from a tendency of those in power to underestimate her.

"I always thought she was little and cute, but I'd say 'Beware!' that first impression," warns longtime Atlanta political figure Michael Lomax, who is now head of the United Negro College Fund. "She's a powerful intellect, a tough personality and a person of extraordinary integrity. She's become formidable in her mature years."

Franklin insists that in forging coalitions with unexpected partners, she is merely responding to what voters told her they wanted during the 2001 campaign. "They wanted a mayor," she says, "who could relate to the state leadership and relate to the region." But Franklin is also responding to reality: Without allies, it would be difficult to solve any of Atlanta's significant problems. "There is no issue the city faces that can be solved alone," says Bill Bolling, a longtime civic leader.

MEETING THE CRITICS

There's no better example than the sewer crisis, which has forced the active involvement of an astounding array of players. At heart, the problem dates to several decades of infrastructure neglect, but the immediate catalyst was a pair of consent decrees, in 1997 and 1998, which the city agreed to after it was sued for violating the federal Clean Water Act. As is true in many other cities, the century-old sewer system in Atlanta combines sewage from households and businesses with runoff from the streets, and it has a tendency to overflow during heavy rainstorms, dumping raw sewage into the South and Chattahoochee rivers.

The consent decrees imposed deadlines for fixing the system, but very little had been done when Franklin took office, even though failure to meet the deadlines carried with it the threat of fines, contempt of court citations, and the very real possibility of a ban on new sewer hookups, which would effectively halt all development in Atlanta. Franklin created a task force, headed by Georgia Tech President Wayne Clough, to look at the city's options, then based the $3 billion overhaul plan on its work.

The challenge, of course, was how to pay for it. With the state and federal governments in fiscal distress, it became clear that help from those quarters would be limited, and the city's water and sewer rates would have to rise dramatically, if only to forestall court action. At the same time, the resulting rate increases were unsustainable for either the city's businesses or its residents, and the only way for the city to roll them back even in part was to get help from somewhere on the outside to underwrite the repairs.

For much of 2003, nothing seemed to be happening. A majority on the city council, worried about constituent anger, refused to pass the rate increase that Franklin was proposing. Governor Perdue and Senate leader Johnson ruled out any state grants, while other Republicans at the state capitol suggested that Atlanta ought to sell its international airport and use the proceeds for sewer repairs. Perdue did eventually offer a $100 million loan, but Franklin rejected it. "Though a generous offer compared to the zero we'd gotten before," she says, "$100 million wasn't going to significantly help the people or the ratepayers." And the Fulton County Commission, which had to approve any sales tax increase for Atlanta, voted against one three times.

Behind the scenes, however, progress was being made on two fronts. The Metro Chamber of Commerce, worried by the prospect of Atlanta failing to fix its sewers and appalled at the possibility that a federal court would shut down development, created a task force on the problem, headed by Lee Thomas, president of Georgia Pacific and EPA administrator under Reagan from 1985 to '89. And Franklin hired a lobbyist to represent the city at the state capitol: Linda Hamrick, an influential white Republican who was a friend of Eric Johnson's and a board member of the state's Christian Coalition.

The key breakthrough came after Johnson sent his letter to the newspaper, rebuking Franklin and the city's demands for money. Hamrick called to tell him he really ought to sit down with Franklin, that they would actually like one another. Johnson called Franklin, and she accepted his offer. "Her attitude is if people say nasty things about you, apparently they don't understand, so you better meet with them," says the Chamber's Sam Williams.

What had rankled Johnson most was that Franklin sent out a letter to close to 200,000 Atlantans recommending that they get in touch with everyone from President George W. Bush to state legislators asking for financial help for the city. "His complaint," Franklin recalls, "was that I didn't give him a heads up—I should have called him. I explained that the element of surprise was part of our plan, but I appreciated that he didn't like it. Then I said that just because it was part of our plan didn't make it right. So he and I began to talk about what it was we really needed."

Meanwhile, Lee Thomas was serving as a broker between Franklin and Governor Perdue. Once the governor had been convinced that the state had to act somehow, he settled on amending a loan program for localities so that Atlanta could qualify for the $500 million Franklin had been hoping for, albeit over a 10-year period. Senator Johnson, for his part, agreed to help Atlanta make an end-run around the Fulton County Commission and vote on its own local-option sales tax. And in January, the city council finally agreed to pass Franklin's rate increases.

"Once the governor said, 'I understand this is a Georgia problem and I'll step into it,' Lee Thomas explains, "he communicated with legislators to say, 'We have to step up.' But they had to see the city was going to pass the rate increase. At the same time, the governor coming in was probably the big thing in helping us with the city council." For her part, Franklin happily gives credit for the arrangement to everyone else. "All I did," she told local business leaders in January, "was hold on by my fingernails until everybody else realized I was about to fall off a cliff."

RICHER AND POORER

With the sewer crisis largely behind her—"to say it's been smooth sailing is an overstatement," she confides, "but at least we're not bailing water"—Franklin has turned her attention to the broader issues facing Atlanta. Close to a quarter of the city's population lives below the poverty line, and although there are signs of gentrification dotted throughout the city's southern (read African-American) neighborhoods, there are still many places that look as though no one with any influence has

paid attention to them for years. The city's overall population has been growing larger, wealthier and whiter. Demographic forecasts predict a metro region increase of 2 million people over the next 25 years, but not everyone is confident this will benefit the inner-city black community. Atlanta seems fated to endure a whole new round of stresses as it figures out how to apportion the benefits of its growth.

For a mayor who entered office facing a budget deficit, infrastructure crisis and economic downturn, Franklin provoked little overt opposition during her first year. But frustration is beginning to surface. The mayor's willingness to take uncomfortable measures to improve the city's image among outside power-brokers has raised questions in the poorer neighborhoods. Although the property tax increase, the water and sewer rate increases and a recent rise in property values haven't yet generated angry protests, they are becoming political issues. "She made a lot of people unhappy with some of the decisions she made," says Sandra Robertson, a longtime anti-poverty activist who runs the Georgia Coalition on Hunger, which sits in a depressed neighborhood in south Atlanta. Robertson is quick to add, however, that Franklin still enjoys not only her support but that of the people with whom her agency works.

For her part, Franklin has begun to talk about wealth-and-poverty issues. She has asked a cross-section of the community to advise her on homelessness, and on how the city ought to pursue a living wage for its residents. While the specifics haven't taken shape yet, she insists that they will. "The city of Atlanta's interactions with people of low income around issues of poverty are [limited to] law enforcement," she says. "That's how we interact with them. Well, we've got to shift that model." She is also looking for advice on persuading companies that fled to the suburbs to return to the city.

These are long-term strategies, and whether they'll pay off in time to forestall unrest among key portions of Franklin's constituency is anyone's guess. "The problem she faces is that Atlanta is a poor city," says Robertson. "It has this image as a prospering, glitter city, but it is a poor city. She does not have a large tax base to support the government. And then, there's a very strong, organized corporate community she has to deal with. So far, she's gotten a bye from the citizens, but it's not everlasting. Shirley is going to have to handle that, and that's why I keep her in my prayers."

35

Edge-ucation

Rob Gurwitt

What compels communities to build schools in the middle of nowhere?

There can't be many people in Ohio who have heard of Henry Linn. But they're certainly becoming familiar with his work.

Ohio is four years into a massive $10.5 billion school-building program, which is expected to leave very few communities untouched. For many school districts, the prospect of millions of dollars in state aid has been enormously appealing; faced with the question of whether to renovate existing schools, or to abandon them and build anew—often out on the edge of town—they're opting for the new.

There's a reason for this, and that's where Linn comes in. A half-century ago, the Columbia University education professor wrote an article for a trade magazine, *American School and University,* in which he suggested that if the cost of renovating a school was more than half what it cost to build new, school districts should swallow the extra expense and build new. It's unclear how Linn arrived at this disdain for the old, but until recently, his thinking appeared to hold the force of scripture within school facilities circles. "If you track the literature," says Royce Yeater, the Midwest director for the National Trust for Historic Preservation, "it starts to appear in foot-notes, then one study refers back to another. . . . But still, it all comes back to one man's opinion. If you look at the original arti-cle, there's no studies, there's no nothin' behind this. It is clearly an old wives' tale."

Perhaps, but it's an old wives' tale with legs. Many states, Ohio included, use what's now known as the "percentage rule" in decid-ing whether schools should be renovated or replaced. The actual percentages vary from state to state, but the rules all amount to the

From *Governing,* March 2004.

178

same thing: a preference for creating new schools over preserving old ones. In Ohio's case, until a few years ago, a school district couldn't get state money for renovation if it cost more than two-thirds of building new. These days, the "two-thirds rule" is just a guideline, but many school districts, with the encouragement of the state, follow it anyway. Officially, the Ohio School Facilities Commission is neutral on the question. Still, it has a clear, if unstated, preference. "There are a lot of advantages in building new," says spokesman Rick Savors. "You can get into situations when you try to renovate where you have no clue what the actual costs will be; just ask anyone who has renovated a kitchen or bathroom." Which is a part of the reason why, of the 1,300 schools the commission has looked at so far, 790 will be abandoned.

Six of these are in the town of Galion, Ohio, which is giving up its four neighborhood elementary schools, its middle school and its high school, built in 1917 and housing a pipe organ believed to be one of only two of its kind left in the world. An old industrial town about 60 miles north of Columbus, Galion is crawling back from a series of plant closures that began in the 1970s and, by the mid-1990s, had left its downtown largely vacant. In recent years, a revitalization program has generated new life there. But although most storefronts are occupied, the future is still tenuous. As Pauline Eaton, a member of the city council, puts it, "We still have a long way to go, because we were in really bad shape."

Now downtown Galion is about to lose the high school and middle school that sit at its very heart. "Renovation," says school board president Ken Green, "is completely out of the question." The school board has come to this conclusion, he says, in part because the state encouraged it to do so, and in part because of a sense of "what we had versus what we could have." The board is hoping it can build the new schools on 29 acres not far from downtown that were given to the school district last year, but the site presents some challenges, so there is also a strong possibility that the schools will end up outside of town, at one of two new highway interchanges planned for Galion. That prospect galls Eaton. "Our whole revitalization program is built around smart growth and historic preservation," she says. "We also know that the area around the interchanges will become our sprawl area. So we've tried to come up with a plan for how the growth will take place, so that it doesn't suck everything out of downtown again." The problem, Eaton notes, is that where schools go up development inevitably follows.

This seems an obvious point, but it has been only within the past few years that the issue has taken wing around the country. Driven in part by concerns about stemming urban sprawl, in part by movements promoting smaller, neighborhood schools as antidotes to ailing educational quality, and in part by burgeoning concern over keeping community cores intact, many people are asking whether it makes sense to keep putting up large new schools on the edge of town.

It would be a stretch to say that this "anti-school-sprawl" movement has swept the nation. "I would bet that 60 or 70 percent of the time," says the National Trust's Yeater, "we find the bureaucracy and prevailing attitude immovable; we're losing more schools than we're saving." Yet the issue is picking up steam, from local planning boards to legislatures and governors' offices, and the attention has had two notable effects: It has turned a spotlight on the assumptions that are embedded in state school-building guidelines; and it is beginning to call into question the relatively free hand that school systems have enjoyed in shaping community development patterns.

BIPARTISAN CONCERN

If the national effort to get a handle on school sprawl had a single catalyst, it was the publication in 2000 of a report by the National Trust called *Why Johnny Can't Walk to School*. "We were getting more and more desperate requests for help from community groups who were finding that due to state policies, as well as misperceptions about what they could do with older buildings, they were losing neighborhood schools," says Constance Beaumont, its author.

The report was careful to cast the issue as reaching far beyond preservation for preservation's sake. "Schools that hold the memories of generations are disappearing," it commented. "Handsome school buildings—landmarks that inspire community pride—are being discarded for plain, nondescript boxes that resemble factories. Increasingly, a stressful drive through congested traffic separates parents and children from ever-more distant schools. Like the movement of post offices and other public buildings from downtowns to outlying commercial strips, the migration of schools from settled neighborhoods to middle-of-nowhere locations is one more factor weakening the ties that once brought people together."

The report served its purpose, drawing national attention to the issue, and winding up in the hands of countless citizens standing up before school-board meetings called to consider plans for a new school. Yet even without the Trust's report, it's likely that the growing size and on-the-fringe location of schools would have become an issue. For what's striking about the various state and local efforts to address school sprawl is they were not sparked by a single set of political concerns.

In Michigan, for instance, the matter is being spurred by a growing understanding that even while the state's economy and population are holding steady, land is being eaten up at a ferocious rate. "What's happening," says Mac McLelland, of the Michigan Land Use Institute, "is parents move to good-quality school districts around urban areas, they expand and grow and then have to expand more to meet the demand. At that point, they can take an incremental approach and add on, or they can build a new facility because they figure they'll need the space in the future, so they hopscotch development out toward the rural area. And then people say, 'Hey! They've got a nice new school, let's move there.'"

In response, Democratic Governor Jennifer Granholm has launched an initiative to promote denser development and preserve open space, and MLUI and the state's Chamber of Commerce have joined forces to tackle school sprawl. The two organizations don't always see eye to eye, but in this case, the Chamber's concern with how tax dollars are being spent and MLUI's focus on land use have brought them together. Indeed, says Bill Rustem, senior vice president of Public Sector Consultants in Lansing, the very breadth of the political ground covered by the two groups makes it likely that their proposals—which were due out last month—will get attention. "Anytime you get a group on one end of the spectrum and one on the other saying, 'This is a problem,' the inclination of legislators and agencies is going to be to deal with it," he says.

In South Carolina, the matter has gone beyond the talking point—and has led to the most far-reaching legislative effort in the country. The issue first surfaced in a 1998 study of how difficult it was for children to walk to school, sponsored by the South Carolina Coastal Conservation League. The study found that schools built before 1973 had far larger percentages of children able to walk to them than schools built later, simply because they were placed within neighborhoods or other central locations.

For a few years, only the League seemed to care much, but then, in 2002, Republican Mark Sanford won the governor's race. Before taking office, Sanford convened a task force to examine quality-of-life issues in the state;

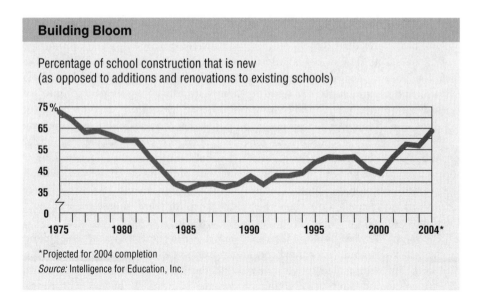

Building Bloom

Percentage of school construction that is new
(as opposed to additions and renovations to existing schools)

*Projected for 2004 completion
Source: Intelligence for Education, Inc.

its members found themselves agreeing that school-building decisions needed attention. "What they said," recalls Michelle Sinkler, director of the League's land-use program, "was that they were all seeing an alarming trend of mega-schools built far from population centers, and because of that they were seeing a degradation in the quality of education as well as exacerbation of growth-management issues."

Sanford didn't wait long to respond. In his State of the State address last year, he launched a campaign to promote smaller, neighborhood schools, decrying the "construction of massive, isolated schools" and their tendency to "accelerate developmental sprawl into our rural areas and what comes with it—increased car trips, lengthened bus routes and a disappearing countryside." Sanford and a small, bipartisan group of legislators worked together to come up with a bill to attend to several of the forces driving school sprawl: the state's requirement that new schools sit on large lots; a variety of building codes that made it difficult to convert existing commercial sites into school buildings; and a lack of limits on how large schools would be allowed to grow. In the end, only the first two were addressed in last year's legislative session; Sanford's bid to cap school size died in committee.

Even so, eliminating the so-called "acreage standard" is a significant step. Like Henry Linn's percentage rule, it's a longstanding part of the armature of school-building regulations that push school districts to consider older schools outmoded, since they tend to sit on smaller parcels; instead, minimum-acreage standards encourage districts to look for new-school sites outside settled areas. And like the percentage rule, these standards have no clear roots. "We never could find a definitive answer as to where those acreage standards came from," says Constance Beaumont. Many states have simply adopted the standards established by the Council of Educational Facilities Planners International, which suggests 10 acres for elementary schools, 20 for middle schools, and 30 for high schools, plus additional acreage depending on the number of students at the school. These numbers were developed in an era when most school building was taking place on suburban sites, where land is more plentiful.

BIG VS. SMALL

The truth is, there are any number of guidelines, regulations and concerns that convince school districts they're better off building large new schools on large sites. In the Cincinnati suburb of Glendale, for instance, school administrators are considering abandoning the town's 1901, Spanish-style elementary school, which sits in the heart of the village, despite clear opposition from residents and a school board that seems to prefer renovation. Glendale is a wealthy community, so the state isn't contributing any money; instead, the issue seems to be coming down to school design.

"The big thing now is 'adjacencies,'" says Albert Slap, the PTA president and a local lawyer. "We've gotten past the fact that there's enough square footage on the current site—they can build behind the school. But now they're talking about the 'important adjacency' of the gym, the lunchroom, the music room and the playground. The argument goes that it's important for kids to be able to do all these things grouped in one area and not have to go through the building, with all the noise and the disruption and how far it might be for them to walk."

Similarly, school districts often make the argument that, given their financial pressures, they can offer the full range of educational opportunities to students only if they can build large schools on large parcels in order to reap the benefits of economies of scale. This is one of the reasons it's not unusual to find high schools and even middle schools—such as the one containing 4,000 7th- and 8th-graders that recently opened in Cicero, Illinois—that are larger than many colleges.

For proponents of renovation or those who favor the construction of smaller, more centrally located schools, these various arguments all have counter-arguments. Is putting the lunchroom next to the gym, for instance, really more important than holding on to a school that has defined its community for more than a century? As for size, "Small alone doesn't make for a good school," says Michael Klonsky, who runs the Small Schools Workshop at the University of Illinois in Chicago, "but in a big school you can't do the things that good research shows are needed: personalization; building a professional community among the educators; making the curriculum relevant to the lives of the students and the teachers; making the school safe. These big schools have 10 to 20 times the level of serious violent incidents as smaller schools."

Indeed, driven by these considerations and others, some school districts are opting for smaller, centrally located schools. This is the thinking behind one of the more striking neighborhood schools efforts in the country—the ambitious school-building program launched by the Los Angeles Unified School District. Facing the prospect of a 200,000-seat shortfall over the next 10 years, L.A. Unified has two phases of construction underway—the first, costing $3.8 billion, will deliver 78,000 new seats in 80 new schools and 60 major additions; the second, approved by voters last November, will add another $1.5 billion to build or expand some 40 schools. A third bond measure is on the ballot this month; it would add another $1.7 billion for new construction.

Many of the first-phase schools, which were planned three or four years ago, will be large, albeit in neighborhoods with a lot of students. But in the past few years, led by school superintendent Roy Romer, the former governor of Colorado, L.A. Unified has rethought its plans, and now intends to build smaller schools, although some will share a campus with others. "When the program started," says Jim McConnell, the district's chief facilities executive, "we were facing a compelling imperative to get seats built. But now, we have a small-school philosophy. We gained confidence that we would satisfy the most severe overcrowding, and Governor Romer came to believe that he needed to improve secondary education, and the way to do that was to move away from huge high schools to smaller learning academies."

CATALYST FOR RENEWAL

Just as schools going up on the periphery of a community can promote sprawl, so a decision to build or renovate in the central city can generate revitalization. In Omaha, Nebraska, the public school system will open a 650-student elementary school on the edge of downtown, which Omaha Public Schools decided was warranted because of the number of students living in the area. Students who will go to the school are already in temporary space nearby, and the impact on the neighborhood has been dramatic, notes Mark Warneke, the public schools' director of buildings and grounds. "There's been more involvement of parents around that school now," he says, "and fewer problems in that community because parents are walking their children to school and there are more activities in the evening. Also, now that the school is being built, you're seeing more renovation going on around it."

Downtown Spokane, Washington, saw a similar impact after officials decided to renovate Lewis and Clark High School. The school system bought the entire block next to the high school in order to give it room for expansion, and the renovation—finished in 2001—has been so successful that the school's population has grown since it reopened, as students from other areas opt to go there instead of their local school. Just as important, says Michael Edwards, president of the Downtown Spokane Partnership, the renovation has stabilized a part of town that badly needed the help. "If LC had left downtown," he says, "I don't know what would be going on down at that end. It would eventually be eaten up by [the nearby] hospital, but in the meantime it would just be parking lots and derelict buildings. LC showed a certain commitment to downtown, and it's been part of the renaissance going on here."

COORDINATED PLANNING

For all the debate over percentage rules and acreage guidelines, adjacency requirements and economies of scale, cases such as Galion, Glendale, Omaha and Spokane serve as strong reminders of one overriding fact: School building decisions have an impact that stretches far beyond the education of a community's students. Which is why those concerned about stemming school sprawl are beginning to focus on one key consideration: Not *how* decisions get made, but *who* makes them. They're questioning the freedom that school boards and administrators have had to weigh their own criteria separately from the wishes of other public bodies.

You might take as an example a high school built about four years ago in Mount Pleasant, South Carolina, a suburb of Charleston. The 3,000-student school went up at the edge of town, within walking distance of none of its students, on land that developers made available to the school district in anticipation that the school's presence would spark demand for development. Which is exactly what the county recently approved. As the Coastal Conservation League's Michelle Sinkler puts it, "Those 2,000 acres around the school, it's going to be big-box nightmare hell."

What's most striking about all this, though, is that the school is there despite the fact that Mount Pleasant imposed an urban growth boundary designed to limit growth precisely where the school sits and the new development has been approved. In other words, the school district simply ignored the town's effort to get a grip on how it develops.

That has sparked a bill in this year's legislative session by the local state representative, Republican Ben Hagood, that would require contiguous municipalities, local transportation authorities and school districts to coordinate their land-use planning. "Growth is happening, and I'm not anti-growth," says Hagood. "But I'm for better planning of the growth. The idea is to plan where you build and build where you plan."

The state that has gone furthest in encouraging school districts to pay attention to overall planning priorities is Maryland, where former Governor Parris N. Glendening's "Smart Growth" initiative made it hard for districts to get state support for building projects that would promote sprawl. These days, although schools no longer have to be in a so-called "priority funding area" to get state financing—a move the state made in an effort to help out rural schools—proposed projects do score higher on the

> *"Our position is very clear," says North Carolina's Ed Dunlap. "It is the responsibility of the local board of education to make decisions about where schools are sited. Period."*

state's point system if they're in established neighborhoods or within corporate limits.

Elsewhere, getting school districts to play ball with other public agencies is likely to be difficult. The attitude of many state school board associations is pretty well summed up by Ed Dunlap, who runs the North Carolina School Board Association. "Our position is very clear," he says. "It is the responsibility of the local board of education to make decisions about where schools are sited. Period."

Even so, in states such as South Carolina and Michigan, where policy makers are starting to take a hard look at school sprawl, it may just be a matter of time before school districts' planning independence comes up for review. "I think there is increased understanding that much of this whole land-use issue relates back to government decision making," says Michigan's Bill Rustem. "The rules of the game are set by public agencies. And, of course, school boards are public agencies."

36

Sidewalk Cachet

Elizabeth Daigneau

Cracked concrete and calls
for walkability are pushing
cities to focus on long-
neglected pavement.

I t's a common phenomenon in Houston: a sidewalk suddenly
ends, sometimes to resume a block or two later. Continuous
stretches of pavement are rare, and where sidewalks do exist,
they often are in terrible condition—cracked and rising at awk-
ward angles out of the ground.

Houston's sea-level location, with its soft and shifting soil, doesn't
help matters. But the real issue is that for the past century this sprawling metropolis of 2 million people has focused on building more and
better roads; little thought or money has been poured into either the
construction or maintenance of sidewalks for pedestrian use. "It's
not a priority," laments Glenn Gadbois, of Just Transportation
Alliances, a nonprofit advocacy group based in Austin, Texas.

In fact, that's the case for many fast-growing cities and suburbs
nationwide, where the car culture has driven urban design and development. But change is afoot. The combination of crumbling infrastructure, which can result in injury lawsuits and lower property
values, and the recent trend toward creating "walkable communities"
is causing local officials to take sidewalks seriously.

Not that the situation is dire everywhere. In some cities, sidewalks are especially well maintained. Unlike most municipalities
that hold property owners responsible for fixing cracks and holes,
Chicago pays for both installations and repairs as part of a multi-
faceted approach to enhancing pedestrian life.

In 2004, Mayor Richard M. Daley and the city council budgeted
$136 million for the Capital Improvement Program, which includes
sidewalk improvements along with curb and gutter replacement,
street resurfacing, lighting and traffic-signal modernization. Since
1989, CIP has funded 3,500 blocks of new and repaired sidewalks.

From *Governing*,
January 2005.

184

This year, the Chicago Department of Transportation plans to build or repair 300 additional blocks of sidewalks.

The also city runs the 50/50 Sidewalk Program, which encourages citizens to be proactive. If a sidewalk in a residential neighborhood needs repair, rather than waiting for the city to get around to it, residents can arrange to have it fixed privately and then split the cost with the city. This significantly reduces the backlog of projects.

Finally, Chicago has a streetscape program that has improved and updated more than 75 neighborhood commercial districts. The program installs new sidewalks, lighting, community identifiers and street furniture. "We invest so much into non-vehicle related infrastructure through so many different programs," says Brian Steele, assistant commissioner of CDOT. "More than sidewalks, which is the first and foremost thing you can do to promote walking, we invest in our entire pedestrian program."

THE MISSING LINK

The problem in many suburban areas isn't that sidewalks are in bad shape but that they simply don't exist. Over the years, building codes evolved to the point that developers either were not required to construct them or could easily get out of doing it. Increasingly, though, residents are demanding sidewalks—especially around neighborhood schools and parks.

In Clive, Iowa, a town of about 13,000 just outside of Des Moines, this issue spurred the city council to authorize a massive sidewalk installation. In 2002, the city created the Sidewalk Safety Program. "Sidewalks have really been an issue for 20 years," says Doug Ollendike, Clive's community development director. "There was just never a big effort to get it done. We decided to put our money where our mouths were." The city was lacking more than 25 miles of public sidewalk, and some of the missing pavement fell within the walk zone of the community's schools. Residents also lobbied for sidewalk connections to city parks and a bike trail. Over a three-year period, Clive will install 134,000 feet of sidewalk. The price tag is expected to be $1.7 million, down from the original estimate of $2.7 million, because most property owners have agreed to pay half the cost.

Although the expense is much greater, a number of big, sprawling cities are also making sidewalks a priority and reincorporating them into their budgets. In Los Angeles, residents regularly navigate sidewalks that are broken up by seismic movements and tree roots. Problems from the latter started back in the 1950s and '60s, when the city planted ficus trees to help keep urban neighborhoods cool. Although California's 1911 Improvement Act makes property owners responsible for repairs, the city amended the code to pick up the tab for sidewalks damaged by trees. The Department of Public Works runs an $8 million-a-year sidewalk repair program. Since 2001, the program has saved 7,000 trees that would otherwise have been destroyed and repaired 262 miles of sidewalks.

Separately, 324 miles of public sidewalks suffering from longtime neglect have been repaired over the past four years, at a cost of $64.8 million. Last March, despite a projected $300 million shortfall for the coming fiscal year, the Los Angeles City Council not only rejected a proposal to eliminate funding for sidewalk repairs but voted to spend an emergency $2.2 million to fix 23 miles of cracked and potentially dangerous sidewalks promised to residents and businesses. Nevertheless, a 40-year backlog of 4,300 miles remains.

Atlanta, one of the nation's fastest-growing metropolitan areas, has its eye on being a "walkable city." Through a public campaign complete with a mascot, Sidewalk Sam, the city seeks to help property owners understand that the responsibility for maintaining sidewalks lies with them. Holding a "Walk for Sidewalks," city officials urged compliance and put residents on notice that they intend to enforce it the standard way: inspect, notify and fix. "We are trying to get people out of their cars," says David E. Scott, commissioner of Public Works, "and we need to make sure it's safe first."

FAR TO GO

Houston has yet to embrace that philosophy. But calls for a culture change with regard to the use of vehicles are increasing all across the Lone Star State. "We need to examine how livable our cities are," says Glenn Gadbois, an advocate for equitable transportation policies. "If we don't start with that, we will never prioritize sidewalks."

Currently, Houston spends a paltry $4.5 million a year on its Capital Improvement Plan for design, construction and repair of about 52 miles of sidewalks. Houston also funds a Safe Sidewalk Program to repair sidewalks near schools, major thoroughfares or to assist the disabled. But the small percentage of residents who qualify under the program can expect to wait up to two years for sidewalk repairs once approved.

Ironically, given its long-time emphasis on streets and highways, the loudest voice for sidewalk maintenance and construction in Texas is the state Department of Transportation. Since the mid-1990s, TxDOT has been encouraging the construction of sidewalks. In 2003, the agency sent out a memo providing additional design guidance on when it would be appropriate to include the construction of new sidewalks as part of any particular project. TxDOT spent $20 million in FY2004 to fund sidewalk construction. The department earmarked $5 million, some of which was spent on sidewalk improvements, to enhance safety around schools for children who walk or bike to class. The agency also spends money on sidewalk improvements and construction through its Americans with Disabilities program and its "Partnership for Walkable Texas," a grant given to groups of community representatives who have identified pedestrian safety issues in their area.

"It's big challenge," Gadbois says. "We're talking about a lot of communities with no sidewalks or sidewalks that are dilapidated. But once cities start spending a lot of money on sidewalks, it's a clear indicator a city's trying to create better places."

37

Wing and a Prayer

Christopher Swope

A shakeout in the airline industry is creating major turbulence for hub-and-spoke cities and their airports. At the same time, some other localities are getting a lift.

I t's 9:15 in the evening at Pittsburgh International Airport and the lights from US Airways' planes are streaking in from Los Angeles, Nashville and Watertown, New York. One by one, the planes nose up to their gates and discharge their passengers, filling the terminal with businessmen in tailored suits and retirees in sweat suits, many wheeling carry-on bags behind them. The majority of these people aren't staying in Pittsburgh. They're connecting to flights headed somewhere else. In about 45 minutes, the great in-migration will turn into an exodus and all the blue-and-gray planes will load up and take off as rapidly as they came in.

This is the kind of activity Allegheny County expected to see when it opened this sleek airport on the grounds of its old one just 11 years ago. Pittsburgh International was the nation's first true hub airport, custom-made to the centralized route networks the airlines wanted. "Hub and spoke" was the name of the game, and Pittsburgh figured that life as a hub, with nonstop flights to dozens of cities, surely beat being a spoke. So Pittsburgh built the perfect hub airport, specially designed to move passengers and planes quickly from one flight to the next. The features have since been widely copied: moving walkways and a compact X-shaped terminal for fast connections, as well as a retail mall in the center so people can shop during longer layovers.

Allegheny County built the new facility primarily with one airline in mind: US Airways. The airline, then known as USAir and before that as Allegheny Airlines, was the hometown carrier and a big local employer with grand expansion plans. By 2000, US Airways predicted, it would be moving 30 million passengers through Pittsburgh, creating one of the nation's busiest airports. "No airport

From *Governing*, January 2004.

or community in their right mind would turn down an airline that comes and says it wants to make your facility a hub," says Kent George, executive director of the Allegheny County Airport Authority.

So there was a high spirit of public-private partnership when Allegheny County and USAir agreed in 1988 to share the cost of building a new $1 billion airport. All of the airlines using Pittsburgh International would pay that off through landing fees and rents over a 30-year lease, but as the dominant carrier, USAir would pay the bulk of it. The setup seemed to work well for both sides. US Airways built up a schedule of 542 departures a day. Local business travelers, meanwhile, enjoyed the convenience of well over 100 nonstop destinations—far more than Pittsburgh could support without the hub.

But a couple of years ago, the airline industry as Pittsburgh knew it turned upside down. The economy tanked, sending droves of business travelers to lower-cost airlines such as Southwest. The events of September 11, 2001 and all the security hassles since then put a damper on air travel nationwide. And US Airways was forced to make an emergency landing in Chapter 11 bankruptcy, where it used court protection to reorganize its finances. Today, US Airways' daily flights from Pittsburgh are down to 379. It's enough to keep the terminal bustling, but the commotion isn't quite what it used to be.

In fact, there's a chance those connecting crowds may vanish from Pittsburgh altogether. US Airways is still in such bad fiscal shape that it no longer wants to pay its original share of the cost of the airport. If Allegheny County and the state of Pennsylvania don't find a way to wipe clean $500 million worth of airport debt, the airline says it will shut down its hub as soon as this summer, taking 80 percent of Pittsburgh's air traffic with it.

State and local officials, their loyalties spurned, say they won't cave in to the demands. Even if they do, US Airways may not survive. Depending on how things play out, it's possible that Pittsburgh will wind up stuck with a white elephant—a custom-built hub airport with an entire concourse of gates, maybe two, in mothballs. "Who could have foreseen what would happen?" says Dan Onorato, Allegheny County's newly elected executive. The deal with US Airways "made sense at a time when the airlines were strong. But in 2004, that industry doesn't exist anymore."

LOSERS AND WINNERS

Pittsburgh isn't the only place that's experiencing a bumpy ride from the airlines these days. Air carriers are now in the midst of their biggest shakeout since Congress deregulated the industry in 1978. All airports—hub cities and spoke cities alike—are struggling to sort out the new rules of the business. The stakes are huge. In the past two years, dozens of small airports have lost air service entirely. Meanwhile, several big cities that invested heavily in airline hubs, believing they would become magnets for jobs and economic development, stand to lose them.

The news isn't all bad, however. Even as the airlines put jets into storage in the dry air of the Mojave Desert, cities such as Oakland and Long Beach, California, and Akron, Ohio, actually gained new flights to new destinations. The growth is mostly attributable to the rise of a few fast-growing low-cost carriers. JetBlue Airways alone has added 24 departures to Long Beach since 2001. As a result, the airport's total passenger count soared from 1.4 million in 2002 to 2.4 million through the first 10 months of 2003.

Meanwhile, some localities are benefiting from another recent airline trend: the increasing use of small regional jets. The planes, with 30 to 90 seats, are opening up new long-distance routes that never were economical before. Delta Air Lines, for example, recently began nonstop service between Atlanta and Appleton, Wisconsin, using a 50-seat Bombardier jet—a trip that previously required a layover in a Midwest hub such as Chicago, Detroit or Cincinnati. "We wouldn't be able to support that market using a larger airplane," says Jeff Mulder, director of the Outagamie County Airport in Appleton.

In short, airline upheaval is creating a new set of winners and losers among localities and their airports. "If you shake it all up in your hands and throw it down on a map, you find some airports are doing rather well, many are doing about the same and a lot are not doing well," says Stephen Van Beek, a senior vice president at the Airports Council International-North America.

The vulnerable places with the most to lose in this new travel market are second-tier cities with lots of connecting traffic. No city knows this better than St. Louis, where American Airlines downsized a hub in November. America West Airlines last summer ditched a hub in Columbus, slashing its departures from 49 to four. Industry analysts say more consolidation of the airlines and their hubs is inevitable. Leo Mullin, the retiring head of Delta, predicted in October that a number of hubs are soon to become spokes. "The hub-and-spoke system will continue, but it will not remain the same," Mullin told a conference of economic development officials. "We have too many hubs in this country, especially in the Midwest."

The country's six so-called "network" airlines—American, Continental, Delta, Northwest, United and US Airways—are in financial turmoil. All of them operate vast and costly hub-and-spoke systems and have significantly cut back flight schedules since 9/11. Still they're struggling to get their flying costs down. Although business has picked up a bit recently, Delta, United and US Airways are all losing money and American is just barely breaking even. They aren't interested in flying to new cities unless they're certain they can make a profit on them.

While the mainline carriers falter, low-cost carriers are gaining ground. Airlines such as Southwest, JetBlue, AirTran and ATA are still relatively small, but they are growing fast (Southwest's value on Wall Street exceeds that of the six network carriers combined). They're making money by cherry-picking the big boys' profitable routes. They're also building service at small, uncrowded airports near major metro areas. Southwest won't fly to Boston, with its notorious delays. But it's doing a brisk business in both Providence, Rhode Island, and Manchester, New Hampshire.

The trend toward regional jets adds another new dynamic. Communities that used to enjoy air service using wide-body jets are frequently seeing it replaced by the smaller aircraft. Delta's Cincinnati hub is actually seeing more plane traffic now than it used to, but two-thirds of the aircraft are regional jets flown by a Delta partner. In Denver, where last summer United threatened to pull its hub, the city agreed to add a $40 million regional jet facility to an airport it built only nine years ago.

Smaller jets are a boon to some cities and a bust to others. Places such as Appleton love them. But large, busy airports such as New York's LaGuardia don't. For one thing, airports earn lower landing fees on lighter planes. And the small planes create just as much traffic without helping to relieve airport congestion. "Regional jets take just as much time on the runway and taxiways and in the airspace around the airport, but they're carrying fewer people," says Hank Dittmar, a transportation expert who heads the nonprofit group Reconnecting America.

The case of Port Angeles, Washington, shows another downside to the airlines' fast-shuffling fleet mix. Horizon Air is the only airline in Port Angeles, and it used to fly 18-seat turboprops to Seattle six times a day. The small city on the Olympic Peninsula could usually fill up the small planes. But then Horizon replaced all of its turboprops with 37-seat regional jets. To compensate for the larger aircraft, Horizon cut its schedule to four flights a day, creating longer layovers in Seattle for connecting passengers. That inconvenience persuaded some travelers to make the three-hour drive to Seattle instead. Passenger counts dropped and finally Horizon decided to delete Port Angeles from its route map altogether. The last commercial flight out of Port Angeles is January 6. "The turboprop was ideal for this market," says Jeff Robb, the airport manager. "When they doubled the seats, it became difficult to fill that airplane up."

COST IS EVERYTHING

All of these crosscurrents mean that cities and counties need to adjust their thinking. Local officials tend to regard their airports as something like a utility, an essential service such as water or sewers that provides a gateway to the community. The airlines, meanwhile, are more focused than ever on controlling costs so they can turn a profit. "Cost is everything," says aviation consultant Michael Boyd. "A lot of airports want to put artwork up, as a front door to the community. The level of artwork most airlines are comfortable with now is a second coat of latex."

The cost equation looms particularly large at hub airports. In the past, the big airlines didn't care much about airport cost because it added up to only about 5 percent of their overhead. But now that some are fighting for survival, airlines are wringing costs out of every source they can find: labor unions, suppliers and also the airports. In tense negotiations with Denver last summer, United used the cover of Chapter 11 protection to insist that the city cut its rent. After much haggling, Denver finally agreed in November to use cash from airport concessions and rental cars to lower United's costs by $7 million a year. (Denver gave the other airlines a rent cut, too.) "Every airline is very focused on cutting costs in every arena," says Vicki Braunagel, Denver's co-manager of aviation. "That includes airport leases."

This shift is fundamentally changing the relationship between the airlines and airports. It may also change the way airport expansions are financed in the future. Airlines used to be willing partners when it came to financing new facilities. Not anymore. Denver's deal with United and the unfolding drama with US Airways in Pittsburgh indicate that communities may have to take on more of the costs and risks of airport construction themselves. "The days of building an airport and passing the cost along to somebody else are over," Boyd says.

In the new airline world, cities may have to reconsider their loyalties. That's one lesson St. Louis learned from the demise of its hometown carrier, TWA. St. Louis repeatedly propped up TWA through the 1990s as it struggled financially. In 1993, the city bought the airline's gates at Lambert Field, a bailout package worth $70 million. Later, the local business community primed TWA with cash by buying up millions of dollars' worth of advance tickets. Still TWA struggled, and in 2001 American Airlines bought it out. American promised to keep the St. Louis hub open, but then it, too, found itself on the verge of bankruptcy last year. In November, American slashed daily departures at Lambert in half, a crushing blow to civic leaders who had worked so hard to keep the hub. "In the past, if you had a hub airline at your airport, you could assume that what was good for the airline was also good for the community," says Van Beek. "You can't make that assumption anymore."

Small spoke airports hoping to woo the airlines these days have a different challenge. They need to focus on building a large enough base of passengers to make flying there profitable. Increasingly, small cities are doing this by helping airlines with local marketing. Some are even bringing cash to the table. One popular strategy to get the airlines' attention is to open a so-called "travel bank" account. The idea is to raise funds from likely fliers, which are set aside for the purpose of buying tickets on a certain airline—if it comes to town. The setup gives the airlines some assurance that the route will make money. It also gets travelers, who must use their "deposits" or lose them, in the habit of flying the carrier.

Pensacola, Florida, used this strategy to lure AirTran in 2001. Local businesses travel-banked $2.1 million, which was enough to persuade the low-cost carrier to compete with Delta on an Atlanta route. Similarly, Wichita, Kansas, used travel banks to attract AirTran and Frontier, another low-cost carrier. "These don't work in every market," says Mike Boggs, a consultant who has helped several communities set up travel banks.

"If the market can't generate passengers, travel banks won't work."

PITTSBURGH'S PLIGHT

When it comes to adapting to the new realities of the airline industry, airport managers around the country view Pittsburgh as a critical test, just as it was a harbinger of the hub heyday a decade ago.

Then, cities across the country envied the airport Allegheny County built. Travelers found layovers in Pittsburgh more comfortable than at other hubs. The airport's design also saved USAir about $12 million a year in fuel costs. Unaware of how starkly the industry would change in just 10 years, both the county and the airline boasted in ways that seem ironic today. One county official bragged that "any other airline would snap this up in a minute if USAir went out of business tomorrow." A spokesman for the airline said USAir didn't mind paying big fees to use the facility. "$35 million in the grand scheme of things is not that big an amount," he said.

US Airways never came close to moving 30 million passengers through Pittsburgh as it had promised (total passengers at the airport peaked in 1997 at 21 million).

Troubled Hubs

Large hub airports ranked by percentage reduction in weekly flights, Oct. 2001–Oct. 2003

	Weekly Flights Lost	Percent Flights Lost
Washington Dulles	–877	–29.0%
Boston	–1,165	–28.7%
Los Angeles	–1,674	–27.3%
Pittsburgh	–1,047	–25.5%
San Francisco	–820	–25.4%
St. Louis	–973	–22.0%
Miami	–358	–20.8%
Honolulu	–315	–20.8%
Newark	–723	–19.6%
New York JFK	–344	–19.6%

Source: Analysis of Official Airline Guide (OAG) data by James Debettencourt and Hank Dittmar for Reconnecting America, December 2003.

The booming economy of the late 1990s hid flaws in US Airways' cost structure, but when business travel slacked in early 2001 the airline's deep problems became clear. Then 9/11 happened and within a year, US Airways filed for Chapter 11 bankruptcy. Under new management (the Alabama retirees pension fund bought a large stake in the airline), it restructured its debts and negotiated new labor pacts with its unions. Then, in a last minute move before coming out of Chapter 11 last March, it attempted to get out of the cost-sharing deal with Allegheny County. With a bankruptcy judge's blessing, US Airways prospectively rejected its lease in Pittsburgh, as of January 5, 2004.

US Airways wants the county, or the state, to eliminate $500 million of the $673 million debt outstanding on the airport—and it has suggested a range of tax hikes they could use to do it. What the airline wants is for its per-passenger costs at Pittsburgh, currently more than $9, to fall in line with the $2-per-passenger cost at Charlotte, another of its hubs. "We simply can't afford to continue operating at Pittsburgh with the existing cost structure," says US Airways spokesman David Castelveter. "We're faced with more and more aggressive low-fare competition. The only way for us to compete is to control costs."

SHIFTING FOCUS

Allegheny County officials are livid. As one person involved in negotiations with US Airways puts it, "we can't just snap our fingers and make $500 million in debt go away." Negotiations are continuing. A lot of people in Pittsburgh think US Airways is bluffing, but with 7,700 local jobs in the balance, that's a tough call to make. "US Airways is looking at any place they can to save money," says airport director Kent George. "If they can turn around and cram down some debt and get a better deal,

they're going to do it. It's just a plain business approach." Some sort of arrangement to lower costs at the airport will likely emerge, but airport officials want any help for US Airways to benefit other airlines, too.

That's because the county's approach to the airline game is evolving. The initial thought in Pittsburgh was that state and local governments might have to find a way to bail out US Airways. But more and more, civic leaders are pondering a world without Pittsburgh's hometown carrier. They are preparing for the prospect that US Airways may vanish entirely—even as they hope it won't. "We don't have the wherewithal to save them," says Glenn Mahone, a corporate lawyer who chairs the airport authority's board. "We can relieve all the debt service and still see them go down the toilet."

Pittsburgh's biggest mistake was to hitch its fate so thoroughly to one airline. Now the airport is trying to diversify. In the past couple of years, George has bagged a few new carriers to soften the blow should US Airways go belly-up. AirTran is now flying in from Atlanta. America West has a flight from Phoenix. ATA is flying to Chicago. And a small airline called USA 3000 runs a couple of routes to the Caribbean. Pittsburgh also has high hopes for an upstart low-cost airline, known only as "Project Roam." If investors can line up private financing, the new carrier plans to base itself in Pittsburgh later this year.

Clearly, Pittsburgh International is an airport in transition—even if US Airways remains in business. It has given up its dreams of 30 million short-term passengers, and is instead fashioning itself as an airport focused more on the 5 million people who actually start and end their trips each year in Pittsburgh. "We may not end up with the same frequency of flights as we've had with US Airways," says Mahone. "But someone will come into Pittsburgh and fly these folks where they want to go."

38

The Mayor-Manager Conundrum

Alan Ehrenhalt

Reform advocates want the same thing—a local government that operates like a successful business. But they have different plans for achieving that goal.

From *Governing*, October 2004.

El Paso has always been a little bit eccentric. When the state university campus was built there, in the 1920s, the local leaders chose Bhutanese architecture, based on an obscure style used in the Himalayas in medieval times. For the administration building, they made a replica of a dzong—a 12th-century Nepalese fortress. Nothing like it existed in the United States at the time, and nothing does now.

There's a reason why El Paso frequently bucks common trends: It's too isolated to worry much about them, or sometimes even to know about them. El Paso is an outpost of 700,000 people on the Mexican border, wedged between the Rio Grande and the lonely Texas plains, remote from any other city of significant size. It isn't even in the same time zone as the state capital.

So perhaps it shouldn't come as too much of a surprise that El Paso's civic establishment, dissatisfied with the way local government had been operating, recently decided to try something brand new: Put a city manager in charge. With all due respect to the many virtues of the city manager system, it is not exactly a hot innovation. In the past few years, many cities around the country have been debating whether to dispense with managers and move to strong-mayor governments, in which administrative responsibility and political accountability are combined in a single elected leader. Switching to a city manager is an unusual decision for any large municipality these days. Nevertheless, that is what El Paso chose to do.

To a large extent, this move is the personal project of the city's current mayor, Joe Wardy, a trucking company executive who unseated his predecessor last year on a platform featuring his argument that city manager government was an idea whose time had come in El Paso. Once in office, he pushed for a referendum to make the change, and the measure was approved decisively earlier this year. Last month, Joyce Wilson arrived from Arlington County, Virginia, to become the city's first appointed manager.

And Wardy became a chief executive without anything much to execute. He no longer has managerial control over any of the city's 32 departments and 6,000 employees, and he doesn't have a vote on the city council. He can veto legislation, but a majority on the council can override him. He does get to keep his staff of six, but it is not entirely clear what they will do. The mayor will effectively be reduced, as mayors in manager-run cities often are, to the role of cheerleader and external promoter of his city's image and interests.

The one significant new perquisite of mayoral office is a four-year term; Wardy wanted longer terms for both the mayor and the eight council members, and the electorate went along with this. The longer terms are an important part of the story, and go a long way toward explaining El Paso's restlessness with its previous form of government. More than almost any big city in the United States, El Paso has been addicted to changing leadership. Between 1969 and 1979, it had eight different mayors; then, after a brief period of stability in the following decade, it has had six mayors in the past 15 years, three of whom served one short term and then left.

In a city-manager government where the manager remains in place through succeeding administrations, this might not have been a serious problem. In a government where the mayor is the chief administrator, musical chairs is a dangerous game. "The way it's been," Wardy argued earlier this year, "the mayor and city council change every two years, so the direction changes can really be drastic."

At least as important as the issue of turnover, though, was the common perception that El Paso's way of operating was unbusinesslike—inefficient, undisciplined and unsuited to a modern, rapidly growing metropolis. Wardy made this argument, and so did the citizens committee that formed to lobby in favor of the charter revision. Times were changing, and the city needed to be run more like a business.

Sooner or later, this argument turns up in virtually every debate over what form of government any city should have. It was central to the initial growth of the city manager system early in the 20th century, promoted largely by urban chambers of commerce and other corporate interests. Replace the partisan strong mayor with a nonpartisan manager, they argued, and cities would conduct themselves efficiently—the way private corporations do.

Curiously, this same argument is being raised elsewhere in the country right now in cities that are pondering whether to make the opposite move: Junk their nonpartisan managers and go back to an old-fashioned strong mayor. San Diego will vote next month on a proposed switch to strong-mayor government; Dallas is expected to have a referendum on the subject next spring. And in both cases, it is the business community that is leading the charge, arguing that city manager regimes are unsuited to the realities of 21st-century urban politics.

In San Diego, which has had a city manager since 1931, the Chamber of Commerce, the City Club and a committee of financial and media CEOs have joined Mayor Dick Murphy in blaming the manager-run system for the current huge budget shortfall and the fact that the city pension plan is seriously underfunded. They claim that recent city managers have lacked the political strength or mandate to deal effectively with excessive demands from public employee unions. "Giving additional authority to the mayor and the council is something the business community wants," Chamber of Commerce vice-president Mitch Mitchell said recently. "That will make it definitive who is operating the city."

The issues are a little different in Dallas, but the lineup is similar. Downtown business leaders argue that the current form of municipal government, with 15 city council members nearly all representing parochial neighborhood interests, and a mayor with little power other than a single council vote, leaves no one responsible for the interests of downtown or the city as a whole. Local newspaper columnist Jim Schutze calls Dallas a "weak mayor, weak council, weak manager" form of government. "We're a football team with no coach," he complained recently.

In fairness to city managers, it is appropriate to point out some numbers that portray their situation a little more positively. About half of all American municipalities with populations over 2,500 currently use the city manager system, and that represents a substantial increase compared with 20 years ago. In 2000, when *Governing* graded the 35 largest cities in the country on their management practices, the two top performers, Phoenix and Austin, both happened to be long-time bastions of city manager government.

On the other hand, you have to pay attention to momentum, which is clearly moving in the other direction. If San Diego and Dallas decide to trade in their city managers for strong mayors, they will join a rather extensive list of large places that have gone that way in the past decade: Oakland, Cincinnati, Hartford, St. Petersburg, Richmond, Sioux Falls and Spokane, to name the most prominent ones. A list of major cities that have moved the other way—to a city manager system—is quite a bit shorter.

What's clear from all the recent charter reform developments—and especially those in El Paso, San Diego and Dallas—is that the disparate advocates of urban charter reform are pleading for the same thing: a local government with the virtues of a successful modern private enterprise. The paradox is that they offer wildly different schemes for how to create it.

But there's a reason for that paradox, and you can get at it by asking a simple but crucial question: What is it that people admire about successful corporate management, anyway? Primarily, it's two things—efficiency and accountability. We respect companies that get their work done with a minimum of wasted effort and resources, and we admire companies where the top executives are held firmly responsible for their performance and results. Ideally, a corporation can aspire to both of these virtues, at least for a while.

But a city really can't. It can hire a manager to replace wasteful political patronage with non-partisan administration, but in doing that it gives up the benefits of having highly visible political leadership. Or it can choose a strong mayor, and get the leader it is looking for. But as often as not, that brings in an element of managerial cronyism and politically tainted policy decisions. Either way, something seems amiss.

These points are made extremely well in a recent article in the *Public Administration Review* by three prominent scholars: H. George Frederickson, Gary Johnson and Curtis Wood. They portray trends in local government as being essentially cyclical. In some places at some moments, partisanship and waste seem to be damaging local public life and a consensus develops that what's needed is a good dose of efficiency. In other places, government may be running smoothly but there's no public figure with the credibility and the clout to make tough decisions and get them accepted. So a powerhouse mayor begins to look pretty good. Sometimes a city will react to these frustrations by making a 180-degree turn in its rules. In other cases, it will split the difference and try to blend the two systems, creating what Frederickson and his colleagues call a "Type 3" city. The results of these experiments have been mixed.

The truth is there is no perfect system for all cities and all seasons. Almost any set of rules can work under the right circumstances. Phoenix has done extraordinarily well under a rather strict system of city-manager government. Chicago has prospered under the relatively benign political autocracy of the Daley family.

Political problems being largely problems of human nature, no arrangement of duties is going to solve them all. In a great many cities, "reform" is always going to consist of whatever system hasn't been tried there lately. "What you really need," says Terrell Blodgett, an eminent public administration scholar and an adviser to El Paso, "is a strong mayor, a strong council and a strong city manager. But that's easier said than done."

Budgets and Taxes

There is an old saying that goes, "May you live in interesting times." It's meant as a curse rather than a blessing. Anyone connected with state budgets can relate. Those responsible for, or dependent on, state budgets have been living in very interesting times during the past few years. They have also been doing quite a bit of cursing.

How "interesting" has it been? According to the National Association of State Budget Officers (NASBO), nearly every state has been in a fiscal crisis at some point during the past few years. In fiscal 2003, states faced a collective budget shortfall of $80 billion. Fiscal 2004 looked a little brighter, but NASBO warned that "as states fight to balance their budgets, the choices available to them are increasingly difficult, and some of the most difficult decisions have yet to be made."[1] Not exactly comforting sentiments for those running K–12 school districts, universities, welfare and health care offices, and other programs funded with state dollars.

States are still suffering financial hangovers from the heady days of the 1990s, when a rocket-propelled economy flooded government coffers with cash and provided a brief era of political manna. For a short period, state legislatures across the country cut tax rates and still increased spending. It seemed too good to last—and it was. The economy fizzled and drained state government treasuries of all their excess cash. After the economy receded, states found themselves committed to spending a lot of money without collecting much revenue. That resulted in a tough choice: cut spending or raise taxes.

They first tried to cut spending. In the late 1990s state governments were increasing their expenditures roughly 4 percent per year after accounting for inflation. However, in 2002 and 2003 state budgets shrank in real terms, and in 2004 growth was flat.[2] Most people believe the government can get along with less money—or at least less of their money—and in the past few years many state governments have been struggling to do exactly that. The result? Among other things, education spending went down while college tuition went up, and less funding was available for health care programs even as medical costs rose.

Cutting spending, though, wasn't always enough to balance the books. States had to increase taxes. In 2004 and early 2005 there were signs that state governments were emerging from the genuine fiscal crisis of the previous few years as state revenues began to increase. This was due to the fact that many states bit the bullet and took a little more from taxpayers. The tax and fee increases proposed by governors for 2005 were in the neighborhood of $5.4 billion (see the article by Nick Samuels in this section).

The readings in this section examine how states are dealing with their often grim financial realities. Their responses have ranged from being creative with taxes to simply breaking promises when it comes to spending. Many of these choices make everyone involved unhappy. Unfortunately, state governments may be making such choices for at least the near future.

RAISING AND SPENDING MONEY

According to the most recent estimate, state and local government spending totals roughly $1.89 trillion (that's $1,890,000,000,000),[3] which is a lot of money by anyone's reckoning. Where does it all come from?

State and local governments rely on six major sources of revenue: sales taxes, property taxes, income taxes, motor vehicle taxes, estate and gift taxes, and grants and transfers from the federal government. Of the taxes levied by state and local governments, the biggest moneymakers are sales taxes (about $320 billion), property taxes (about $263 billion), and individual income taxes (about $226 billion). Money from the federal government adds roughly another $324 billion.[4] Other sources of revenue include fees for hunting, fishing, and wedding licenses and interest earned on bank deposits. There is enormous variation from state to state—and even locality to locality—in how governments raise their money. Some states—such as Alaska, Florida, and Texas—have no individual income tax and rely more heavily on sales taxes.

There are pros and cons to employing different forms of taxation. Property taxes, for instance, are one of the most hated forms of taxation. They are levied as a portion of the assessed valuation of property such as a house. They are typically paid in a lump sum once or twice a year and thus are very visible to taxpayers. For most people property taxes work out to approximately 1.55 percent of the value of a home. So if you own a house worth $200,000, you pay $3,100 per year in property tax. Writing that check can be painful and will make it abundantly clear that the government is taking a big chunk of your change.

While property owners are never going to be enthusiastic about them, property taxes have clear advantages for state and local governments. Most importantly, property taxes are a relatively stable from of income. Sales and income taxes may fall pretty dramatically during an economic downturn. Property values might fall too, but generally they don't fall by a whole lot. In short, property taxes are a reliable source of income that is less prone to unpredictable fluctuations.

Much of the controversy that surrounds state and local taxes comes from issues of fairness and who pays. Sales taxes, for example, are a flat tax. It doesn't matter who you are, when you buy a book, a television, or a car, you pay the same sales tax as everyone else. This strikes some as fair—as a flat tax, sales tax treats everyone equally.

Critics of sales taxes say that's exactly the problem: they treat everyone equally when clearly not everyone is equal. If you and Bill Gates were to buy the same television in the same city, you would pay the same sales tax. This strikes some as regressive, because sales tax doesn't take into account the ability to pay taxes. In contrast to sales taxes, income taxes are more likely to consider comparative economic standing. States with income taxes generally have differing tax rates based on individual earnings. The logic is that richer people pay higher tax rates because they can afford to. Arguments over the advantages and disadvantages of various taxes, and the issues of fairness and who pays, have been worked out in different ways in different states and localities. Thus, it might be less expensive to buy that television in another city.

There is another prominent source of revenue: borrowing. The federal government covers a significant chunk of its spending with deficit financing. In effect, the feds use the equivalent of a credit card to cover their bills—they spend more than they take in by borrowing.

State and local governments also borrow, primarily by issuing bonds. Bonds are essentially IOUs, certificates stating that the issuing government promises to pay the buyers of the bond a specified interest rate for a specified period of time and to return the principal when the bond reaches maturity.

State and local governments, however, have considerably more constraints on their ability to engage in deficit financing than does the federal government. Most notable is the fact that forty-nine states are legally bound to enact balanced budgets, or budgets in which expenditures are equal to or less than revenues. Only Vermont is free to run itself into debt in a similar fashion as the federal government. This means most states have less wiggle room to deal with a drop in revenues during an economic downturn.[5]

States and localities obviously raise a lot of money. What do they do with it all? If you are the typical property owner, what do you get for the $3,100 you fork over in property taxes? Some of the biggest users of property taxes are local rather than state governments. Counties, municipalities, and special districts often rely heavily on property taxes as a major source of revenue. So, if you have kids in public school you can think of that $3,100 as covering 180 days or so of education. That's about $17.20 a day, which isn't bad—and it's less expensive than most baby sitters. If you don't have kids, think of roads, libraries, parks, and all the other stuff that local governments do. It might not take the sting out of writing the check, but at least you'll know you really do get something back.

Education is the single largest expenditure of state government. More than twenty cents of every dollar taken in by the state goes toward K–12 schools. Another eleven cents goes to state-supported colleges and universities. After education, the biggest expenditure is Medicaid, which accounts for more that 20 percent of state spending. As these three things alone account for more than half of state spending, basic math dictates the policy result: fiscal stress means schools and health care programs are going to suffer.

THE POLITICS OF BUDGETS

The basic problem that states have faced during the past few years is that the demand for programs and services has grown, along with costs, while revenues have remained flat or even declined. The readings in this section show how states and localities have responded to this problem, and detail how some states dug their deep financial holes in the first place. Nick Samuels's article provides a basic overview of the most recent trends in state budgets. The news is still not good, but recent history shows it could be a whole lot worse.

The article by Chris Frates details Colorado's financial difficulties, which at least in part are of its own making. Through ballot initiatives, Colorado's voters have placed tight constraints on the revenue that the state government can raise and spend. The idea was to rein in the growth of government spending. The result has been to precipitate a fiscal crisis.

The remaining three readings consider the different ways in which states have responded to the basic imbalance between revenues and expenditures. One option is to simply renege on spending promises, which a number of states have done, as detailed in Janet M. Kelly's article. In response to voters' anger over property taxes, some states capped property tax rates—in effect limiting the primary revenue source of local governments. State governments promised to make up the difference, which seemed doable during the economic good times. After the economy went sour, however, states backed away from those promises, leaving local governments fiscally strapped.

Other approaches include getting creative with revenue sources, as detailed in Bert Waisanen's article. Utah has levied a tax on adult entertainment. Many states are increasing taxes on other "sins" such as smoking, drinking, and gambling. Alan Greenblatt's article shows that states are also gingerly looking to corporations. Whereas states once raced to cut corporate taxes in an effort to lure jobs and economic opportunity, they are now looking to roll back business tax breaks.

Taxing and spending always create political conflict because there is a basic imbalance between what people want from government (a lot) and what they want to pay for it (not much). In times of fiscal stress, those conflicts are more over who gets to lose rather than who gets to win. That makes for interesting times. Not particularly pleasant, but definitely interesting.

Notes

1. National Association of State Budget Officers, *Budgeting Amid Fiscal Uncertainty,* 2004, www.nasbo.

org/Publications/budgetstabilityFeb2004.pdf (accessed May 9, 2005).

2. National Governors Association and National Association of State Budget Officers, *The Fiscal Survey of States,* December 2004, www.nasbo.org/Publications/fiscalsurvey/fsfall2004.pdf (accessed May 8, 2005).

3. U.S. Census Bureau, Table 428 in *Statistical Abstract of the United States: 2004–2005,* 2004, www.census. gov/prod/2004pubs/04statab/stlocgov.pdf (accessed May 9, 2005).

4. Ibid.

5. For a basic primer on balanced budget restraints on state governments, see National Conference of State Legislatures, "State Balanced Budget Requirements," April 12, 1999, www.ncsl.org/programs/fiscal/balreqs. htm (accessed May 9, 2005).

39

Trends in State Budgets: Surviving the Recovery and Future Challenges

Nick Samuels

States are recovering from fiscal crisis, but they still face tough choices.

After a brutal beating that started in 2000 and continued at a harsh pace through the next three years, many state budgets have recovered notably. While several states still struggled to pass a budget on the last day of the 2004 fiscal year, most no longer must scramble to plug gaping holes between revenues and spending. However, even amid rebounding revenue, some gaps still exist, and states face enormous post-downturn challenges. Spending pressures are immense, structural revenue concerns are serious, the effects of one-time budget balancing measures will come to bear, and long-term demographic changes with dire budgeting consequences loom.

THE CURRENT FISCAL SITUATION: GOOD . . . AND BAD

As the national economy continues to improve, state budgets likewise have brightened. Recent data from the Fiscal Studies Program of the Rockefeller Institute of Government illustrate an improving state revenue picture. In the January–March quarter of 2004, the Rockefeller data show that total nominal state revenue increased by 8.1 percent compared to the same quarter in the previous year, and total real revenue grew by 5.5 percent. The revenue data obviously are good news comparatively and indicate that states have turned a corner. At the same time, it must be kept in mind that improved revenues should be expected considering that they performed so poorly for so many preceding quarters. Indeed, other budgetary indicators help paint the full state fiscal picture, which is still blurry.

From *Spectrum: The Journal of State Government*, Summer 2004.

States Still Were Cutting Budgets This Spring

The most recent examination of state general funds by the National Association of State Budget Officers (NASBO) illustrates cautiously optimistic fiscal conditions. The data in NASBO's April 2004 *Fiscal Survey of States* contrast sharply with those presented in editions of the report from the previous three years. Exemplifying just how grim the state budget situation was and how little it left unscathed, 37 states in both fiscal 2002 and fiscal 2003 cut their enacted budgets by $12.6 billion and $14.5 billion, respectively. Recently, even as the fiscal picture brightened and recovery took hold during the first half of fiscal 2004, 18 states still were forced to make post-enactment budget cuts that totaled $4.8 billion.

Revenue is Improving, but it Had Been Performing Miserably, and Tax Increases Play a Role

As with budget cuts, some state revenue observations are mixed. Based on the January–April period that data were collected for the April *Fiscal Survey,* 11 states reported that revenues were not meeting budgeted projections, 17 states said they were coming in on target, while 22 states said revenues exceeded projections. It is important to note that those figures refer to budgeted revenue estimates, not comparisons of actual year-to-year revenue collections. How a state's revenue performs relative to the estimates settled on in its budget may mean (along with spending levels) a budget shortfall, as it did for nearly every state between 2000 and now. As the fiscal crunch continued to flatten state finances, most of them lowered their revenue expectations (several times); as revenues recover, states with a cautious outlook are better able to meet their targets and less likely to require mid-year budget adjustments.

States also looked to tax and fee increases when preparing their fiscal 2005 budgets, as they have each year since fiscal 2002. Governors proposed $5.4 billion in net tax and fee increases for fiscal 2005, following enacted increases of $9.6 billion in fiscal 2004, $8.3 billion in fiscal 2003, and $0.3 billion in fiscal 2002 (NASBO will publish data on enacted fiscal 2005 budgets in the fall). States continue to focus on user fees rather than broadbased tax increases as a politically-acceptable means to enhance revenue, proposing to increase them by $1.5 billion in fiscal 2005. Other proposed increases were in sales taxes ($1.4 billion), cigarette and tobacco taxes ($1.4 billion), "other" taxes ($525 million), corporate income taxes ($400 million), and personal income taxes ($64 million).

Spending Growth is Below Average

State spending data also paint a mixed budget picture. As fiscal crisis gripped states and they cut budgets, spending stayed virtually flat. Needing to maintain an array of government services, trying to hold elementary and secondary education harmless, and facing ever-mounting Medicaid pressure, nominal state general fund spending increased by only 1.3 percent in fiscal 2002 and 0.6 percent in fiscal 2003. When adjusted for inflation, the fiscal 2003 figure reflects a 2.5 percent decrease in general fund spending. Fiscal 2004 spending ticked upwards slightly, growing by 2.8 percent and based on the budgets that governors proposed in the spring, it will do the same in fiscal 2005. However, *Fiscal Survey* data indicate that both years still amount to small real spending decreases and each year falls far short of the 1979–2005 average nominal growth rate of 6.2 percent. Indeed, the governors of 10 states proposed budgets that are smaller than the previous years' in nominal terms for fiscal 2005.

Medicaid Crowds Out Other Categories of State Spending

While net state spending has flattened, one category of state expenditure in particular has swelled: Medicaid. The means-tested entitlement program financed by the states and the federal government consumes more than 21 percent of total state spending, second only to K-12 education, based on data from the forthcoming edition of NASBO's *State Expenditure Report.* Indeed, Medicaid is the monster under the bed of state budgets. Even during a time of fiscal crisis when states cut wide, across-the-board swaths through most programs, when total state spending decreased in real terms, Medicaid continued to grow. In fiscal 2003 (when 37 states were forced to cut their previously enacted budgets) state funds for Medicaid increased by 6 percent according to the April 2004 *Fiscal Survey,* and increased by 4.6 percent in fiscal 2004 (when 18 states cut their budgets). The increasingly large bite of state budget pie taken by Medicaid could have been even more dramatic: the growth of state funds in those two years was mitigated by temporary changes in the federal Medicaid matching rate that, as part of the Jobs and Growth Tax Relief Reconciliation Act of 2003, provided $10 billion in fiscal relief. With those changes expiring, recommended fiscal 2005 budgets suggest state funds for Medicaid will balloon, growing by 12.1 percent. Besides the temporary federal relief, the growth in Medicaid also comes despite a variety of cost-containment actions states have taken to control the budget-busting program, including increasing co-payments, reducing benefits, freezing provider payments, and implementing prescription drug controls. Still, Medicaid exceeded budgeted amounts in 23 states in fiscal 2003 by an average of 4.6 percent, while as of April, it was over budget in 18 states, by a net $2.3 billion. Adding further pressure, the Kaiser Commission on Medicaid and the Uninsured forecasts that 2004 Medicaid enrollment will grow by more than 5 percent.

Reserves Funds are Stable, but Too Low

Following a steep drop after 2001, reserve funds—on which states relied heavily to weather the worst of the fiscal storm—have stabilized, but at insecurely low levels.

During the boom years of the late 1990s, states bolstered their reserve funds (or "total balances," defined as their annual ending balances plus the amounts in their budget stabilization or "rainy day" funds) substantially. While those total balances amounted to only $3.1 billion or 1.1 percent of expenditures in fiscal 1991, by 2000 states had built them to $48.8 billion or 10.4 percent of expenditures. As the economy soured and fiscal crisis took hold, states looked to their reserves as an important tool to mitigate budgetary pain. Early in the state fiscal crisis, drawing on available reserves allowed states to attempt to protect services from cuts such as K-12 education and Medicaid. As the fiscal slump continued, states used their reserves more directly to balance their budgets. As a result, total balances fell significantly, dropping by more than 66 percent between fiscal 2000 and recommended fiscal 2005.

While total balances have fallen so far so quickly, at least they have stabilized somewhat. Total year-end

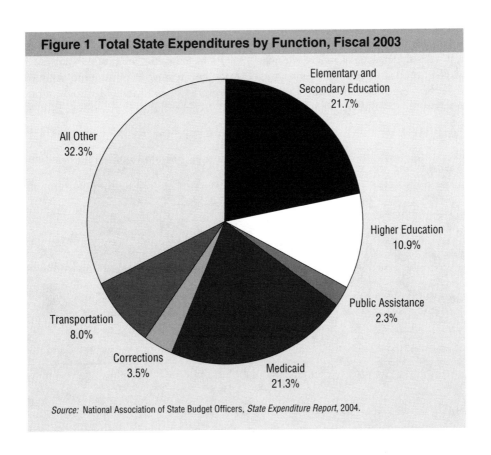

Figure 1 Total State Expenditures by Function, Fiscal 2003

Elementary and Secondary Education 21.7%

All Other 32.3%

Higher Education 10.9%

Public Assistance 2.3%

Transportation 8.0%

Corrections 3.5%

Medicaid 21.3%

Source: National Association of State Budget Officers, *State Expenditure Report*, 2004.

balances were $17.1 billion or 3.4 percent of expenditures in fiscal 2003, $19.1 billion or 3.7 percent in fiscal 2004, and $16.5 billion or 3.1 percent of expenditures based on recommended fiscal 2005 budgets. However, those reserve levels may not be healthy enough to provide states with an adequate cushion should the economy slump again soon or if they find themselves in unforeseen circumstances. Many budget observers consider 5 percent of expenditures to be the minimum acceptable reserve level. Based on fiscal 2005 recommended budgets, only 11 states estimated balances as a percentage of expenditures of 5 percent or more.

With little cash available, states leaned heavily on the debt market to help weather the fiscal downturn. Just as states could afford a pay-as-you-go approach to capital spending during the boom years, state debt issuance has soared more recently. According to Moody's Investors Service, net state tax supported debt has increased more than 44 percent since 2000, when it totaled $211.5 billion, to 2004, so far totaling $305.2 billion. The growth of state debt was particularly strong in the last year, increasing by nearly 17 percent between 2003 ($261.3 billion) and 2004. At the same time, with weak state finances and state leaders left in a decision making quandary, the quality of state credit has suffered. While many states with the highest rated debt recently have been able to maintain their credit status, several other states have not fared

as well. Between 2001 and mid-2004, Moody's says, there were 14 downgrades to the debt of 10 states.

CONCLUSION: TOUGH CHALLENGES LAY AHEAD FOR STATES

As states move forward out of a time of fiscal crisis into a time of fiscal recovery, the decisions that they must now make do not necessarily become any easier. Some decisions are short term ones. After several years of budget cuts and lean spending, significant pent up demand exists for funding to not only be restored, but increased. Functions that were particularly subject to budget cuts such as higher education will look to states to restore funds that were used to balance the budget in other areas. But states have not recovered from the fiscal downturn: they are in the process of recovering and cannot yet afford to restore every dollar that was cut from every program. Demand for state spending precedes available funding. Additionally, states used a variety of one-time measures to balance their budgets and may have only deferred difficult spending and taxing decisions into the current fiscal year.

In the long term, many of the choices states must now make are ones that will impact the severity of future fiscal downturns. Not only will Medicaid continue to pressure state budgets, how states provide health care to their

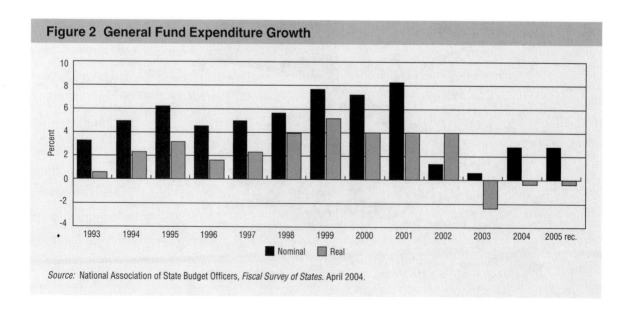

Figure 2 General Fund Expenditure Growth

Source: National Association of State Budget Officers, *Fiscal Survey of States.* April 2004.

employees and retirees will also. Average annual health care costs will increase by 12.3 percent in 2004, forecasts Hewitt Associates, and states must examine carefully what health benefits they can provide and how much of the cost individual employees must themselves bear. States also must soon turn to their pension systems. According to Robert Borden of the Louisiana State Employees' Retirement System, in 2002 nearly 80 percent of state pension plans were underfunded. As the population ages and more employees retire, the burden on those systems and state budgets become more severe in tandem. The statistics regarding that aging population and the choices states face in light of them are perhaps the most daunting of all and will have the gravest consequences on state budgets. According to Bureau of the Census figures, the age 55+ population will increase from just more than 66 million in 2005 to nearly 130 million in 2055, an increase of more than 96 percent.

40

Fiscal Folly?

Chris Frates

Does a Taxpayer's Bill of Rights mean the end of commonsense budgeting? Colorado legislators are finding out.

From *State Legislatures*, January 2005.

Three years after Colorado's budget began to sink, revenues have started to come back bigger than expected. That should be good news. But in Colorado, budgeting has little to do with logic, thanks to two conflicting constitutional amendments that have hamstrung state spending.

Over the last four years, officials have slashed about $1.1 billion from the state budget and are facing an additional $263 million in cuts when they return to Denver this month.

Legislators have a number of options to balance the budget, none of them pleasant. They include removing some elderly patients from nursing homes, closing state parks or imposing huge college tuition hikes. Lawmakers could also try to generate cash using methods like selling state buildings and leasing them back. But that kind of Band-Aid solution would leave the underlying reasons for the shortfall untouched.

Like most states, Colorado's economy took a hit during the recession. In March 2001, Colorado's economic growth was second in the nation only to Nevada. In 2004, Nevada still topped the list, but Colorado dropped to No. 40, according to the June issue of *State Policy Reports*.

The topple from a top performer to barrel bottom wreaked havoc on the state's budget as lawmakers desperately plugged holes caused by sinking revenue. This was exacerbated by the permanent tax cuts the legislature made in the booming years of the late '90s. Economists estimate those cuts alone cost the state $480 million this budget year.

But by late 2004, state economists released figures that would, at first blush, seem to indicate Colorado's fiscal recovery—larger than expected growth in state tax collections. But that doesn't mean the state can spend the money. In fact, Colorado will refund more than $459 million to taxpayers while it will likely cut $263 million in programs and services.

Sound strange? Welcome to The TABOR Zone.

TABOR, or the Taxpayer's Bill of Rights, is a voter-approved, constitutionally imposed tax limitation that, among other things, prevents state revenue from bouncing back after a recession. Instead, it can create situations where lawmakers are forced to make cuts while giving money back to taxpayers.

ALONG CAME AMENDMENT 23

The state's fiscal crunch is further complicated by another voter-passed constitutional provision—Amendment 23, which requires annual spending increases in primary and secondary education. So while TABOR has locked in recession-level spending, Amendment 23 requires lawmakers to spend an increasingly larger share of available money on education.

Lawmakers are left to balance the budget on the backs of programs not protected by constitutional requirements, like public colleges and universities and Medicaid.

The crunch had gotten bad enough by 2003 that four college presidents warned leaders that expected state funding would be so insignificant by 2009 that public colleges and universities would either be forced to close or privatize.

"If something is not done through legislation or creation of a new funding mechanism, public higher education as we know it today in Colorado will become an endangered species," University of Colorado President Betsy Hoffman said at the time.

During the 2004 legislative session, lawmakers passed a plan that allows colleges and universities to raise tuition to cover expenses, something they were unable to do under TABOR. But, the law doesn't provide more money for higher education. In the words of the bill's prime sponsor, it just "keeps our higher-ed system alive."

The collision of TABOR and Amendment 23 has lawmakers in both parties worried. In July, Republican Governor Bill Owens called it "the most critical challenge facing us fiscally." Republican state Treasurer Mike Coffman and a bipartisan group of legislative leaders have talked of impending fiscal disaster.

Republicans, who tend to favor TABOR, and Democrats, who generally support Amendment 23, spent much

of 2004 trying to find a solution that would garner support from two-thirds of the state's lawmakers—the requirement needed to put constitutional reform on the ballot. But state leaders failed to find a compromise for myriad reasons including philosophically entrenched partisans, a factious Republican Party and a lack of leadership.

DEMOCRATS TO TAKEOVER

But those power dynamics were shattered on Election Day when Colorado voters gave Democrats the majority in both chambers for the first time since 1960. Both House Speaker-elect Andrew Romanoff and Senate President-elect Joan Fitz-Gerald have said mending the state's budget problem is important.

"Our top priority is restoring Colorado's leadership in job growth. To do that you need to rescue higher education from the brink of financial extinction and shore up our crumbling transportation infrastructure," Romanoff said. "To do either of those things . . . you need to solve this fiscal crisis."

How they do that is an open question. Both Democratic leaders and Governor Owens have suggested using a provision of TABOR to ask voters to allow the state to keep some of the money that would otherwise be refunded to taxpayers—a move that would take a simple majority to put on the ballot.

Lawmakers may also consider putting constitutional reform in front of voters, which would require approval from two-thirds of each chamber. But it's unclear whether the constitution allows a reform measure to be voted on in an odd-numbered year.

VOTERS FINALLY SAID YES

To understand where the state is now, it's important to better understand TABOR and how it came to be the fiscal force it is today.

Coloradans had voted against at least seven tax-limitation measures over almost three decades before TABOR passed in 1992. But the organized push for TABOR-like reform started in 1986 with Amendment 4, which would have required voter approval of any tax increase. The proposal died after getting only about 37 percent of the vote.

The Amendment 4 campaign introduced California transplant and anti-tax maven Douglas Bruce to

Colorado's tax limitation crowd. Bruce would become the face of TABOR and architect of three campaigns.

During the campaigns, Bruce, a relative unknown, faced opposition from then-high profile politicians including Republican U.S. Senator Bill Armstrong and state Senate President Ted Strickland as well as Democratic Governor Roy Romer and U.S. Senator Tim Wirth. Four ex-governors also opposed the measure.

But it wasn't just politicians opposing Bruce's plan. The education and business communities were also firmly against it including Coors Brewing Company, the now defunct telecommunications provider U.S. West and the state's largest business group, the Colorado Association of Commerce and Industry (CACI).

George Dibble, CACI president from 1985–1998, chaired the opposition to three tax limitation proposals between 1986 and 1990. The organization opposed Bruce's proposals and its predecessor because, Dibble said, it "strangleholds" state and local governments.

"If you looked at it from a business standpoint, it was essential that we have flexibility in government to address infrastructure needs, address the need to maybe offer some incentives—tax incentives—to companies to relocate here," he said. "You can sell the scenery all day long, but you've got to have something more to attract investment."

Real or threatened cuts to public colleges and universities, public safety and Medicaid services aren't attractive, he said.

The broad coalition, however, could not beat back Bruce's third attempt to pass TABOR in 1992. Dibble said he thought the measure passed because the roaring 1990s were just starting and economic growth appeared to be never ending.

The Tax-inator

Douglas Bruce. Mention the name in Colorado political circles and you're likely to get one of two reactions—swear words or accolades.

Bruce is the author of the state's constitutional tax-limitation measure, the Taxpayer's Bill of Rights or, as it's known in these parts, TABOR. Among other things, the limitation prevents Colorado from bouncing back from a recession.

This means that state lawmakers in 2005 will be forced to cut about $263 million in programs and services while they refund about $459 million back to taxpayers because that money exceeds the spending limits set by TABOR.

Depending on whom you're talking to, Bruce is either an anarchist who doesn't understand the role of government or the taxpayers' best friend.

For his part, Bruce said that any tax money that directly benefits individuals and not the general public is "stealing."

"I can't go to you and pick your pocket and take $20 to buy a meal. But I hire a politician to pick your pocket, take the $20 and then he spends $10 on a bureaucratic overhead and gives me $10 for a meal," he said. "That is stealing."

If this was Bruce's world, government would not fund programs like higher education or Medicaid. Instead, he would leave those services to the market and charities.

"We could cut at least half or more of government spending and 95 percent of the people wouldn't miss it. They wouldn't notice the impact on their lives," he said.

Bruce doesn't like people to use the word "cut" to describe what's happening to state programs. They can't be cuts, he argues, if state revenue is growing. He doesn't view things like caseload increases as a "need."

If legislators want to keep more money, Bruce said, they can exercise a provision of TABOR and ask voters for permission.

Former Republican Senate President and County Commissioner Ted Strickland said he has "a difficult time assigning any credibility to Douglas Bruce. The man does not understand that there are necessary services that have to be provided by government."

Bruce's new role as a county commissioner, Strickland said, could be the best exposure for TABOR's "insidious ramifications."

"Let him address the needs of those citizens with his attitude, 'Well, they don't need those services; we can cut taxes.' He'll understand in the wink of any eye what his brainchild has done to local government and state government," he said.

One of Strickland's successors, former Republican Senate President John Andrews, however, praises Bruce and TABOR.

"Douglas Bruce is the best friend Colorado taxpayers have ever had. Like many other gifted individuals, he can be personally difficult but in the conservative movement for Colorado, or any state of the last several decades, he's just one of the real heroes."

For his part, Bruce said he thought it passed because people finally realized government would not limit itself.

TABOR DOES ITS JOB

Since that time, the state has refunded about $3.4 billion to taxpayers under TABOR's requirements. Between 1998 and 2002, the average taxpayer received an annual refund of between $56 and $269. Other groups, like farmers and businesses', also received tax breaks.

TABOR champions laud the amendment for keeping a check on spending during the booming '90s and preventing the kind of hangover California recently faced after years of spending growth.

"When you look at the decade since TABOR and compare it with the previous decade, clearly the goal of limiting the growth of government has been achieved," said outgoing Republican Senate President John Andrews. "Colorado has had its troubles but they have been very manageable compared to the deep hole that California ended up in."

But Rocky Scott, president of the Greater Colorado Springs Economic Development Corporation, said the state's "fiscal mess" is hurting its ability to provide "economic infrastructure," like good roads and colleges, and is going to put Colorado at a competitive disadvantage.

Critics especially criticize the TABOR provision that prevents the state from recovering from an economic downturn. Instead of returning to pre-recession spending levels if revenues allow, TABOR limits spending increases to a formula that includes population growth plus inflation.

Think of it, for example, like a reservoir that falls by half during a drought. When the rains return, the basin can't refill to its pre-drought capacity. Instead, the amount of water the reservoir can keep is based on drought levels.

TABOR sets the state's revenue limit in a similar way. Any money that comes in above the limit must be returned to taxpayers.

That frustrates lawmakers on both sides of the aisle who want to restore service and program cuts, but must refund hundreds of millions of dollars to taxpayers while they continue to cut programs.

"We've cut to the point now that every cut we do is going to cause . . . elimination of some service that's been provided in the past," Republican Representative Brad Young, former chairman of the legislature's budget-writing committee, has said. "You can't just do things more efficiently. We're beyond that."

Young, a conservative Republican, is one of TABOR's biggest critics. And while he has said he believes in tax limitations, TABOR's limits just aren't practical because they shrink government relative to the economy.

Last session, Young introduced a proposal that would have changed the state's revenue limit from inflation plus population growth to a percentage of the state's total personal income—a limit many believed better reflected the economy. The measure was killed in the Senate.

Young's proposal was one of at least a dozen the General Assembly considered last year. There was also a citizen's initiative to reform TABOR that supporters had planned to put on the ballot before pulling the plug at the last minute.

In order to get a two-thirds majority to reform TABOR and Amendment 23, Republicans and Democrats had to compromise. And while Senate Democrats played the spoiler once, it was often the Republican Party that couldn't get its members in line.

Republicans, who controlled both the legislative and executive branches in 2004, were split into three camps when it came to constitutional reform, said Republican Senator Norma Anderson, an 18-year veteran lawmaker:

- TABOR-lovers such as outgoing Senate President Andrews, who believed the amendment was fine.
- Outgoing House Majority Leader Keith King and his supporters, who were willing to change TABOR if it was done on their terms.
- And Governor Owens, who is waiting on lawmakers to devise a solution.

"When you've got one party in control, you need somebody who . . . can pull everybody together," Anderson has said. "We're divided as a party, Republicans are; it's as simple as that. And neither side gives," Anderson said.

During the 2004 legislative session, a closely divided Senate became the killing field of constitutional reform. The more conservative House passed a number of proposals that were promptly killed in the upper chamber. Critics charged that the proposals either changed too much of TABOR or Amendment 23 or too little.

The other dynamic in play was a planned citizens' initiative. The initiative was similar to budget committee chairman Young's plan, which proposed tying the state's revenue limit to a percentage of total state personal income.

Senate Democrats favored Young's plan, but many Republicans thought it went too far. Republican Senate President Andrews sent Young's plan to an unfriendly committee where it was promptly killed. Supporters tried to resurrect the measure by including it in another bill, but failed.

Democrats were unwilling to vote for anything that strayed much from Young's plan. If they couldn't get what they wanted through the legislature, they reasoned they could get it through the initiative.

The session ended without reform, but Republican and Democratic leaders continued to negotiate throughout the summer. Those talks reached a breaking point in July when House leadership did not poll its members on the latest proposal. Lola Spradley, then Republican House speaker, said her leaders never agreed to count. Other players in both parties thought otherwise.

Aside from a few more sputtering efforts, the talks were dead. But the summer's greatest surprise was yet to come.

NOTHING ON THE BALLOT

In July, supporters of the citizens' initiative to reform TABOR decided at the last minute to pull the plug. The group didn't have the money and support needed to educate voters about such a complex issue.

A poll done earlier that month for initiative supporters showed almost a tie between those who would change TABOR and those who wouldn't. According to the poll results, 48 percent of those polled believed school districts—not state government—were the hardest hit by the recession. Supporters said the finding means K12 funding, and by extension Amendment 23, will be untouchable in the future.

No Choice But Higher Ed

Colorado's public colleges and universities have taken a beating since the economy began to tank in 2001. Since then, lawmakers have cut more than $150 million from higher education.

Those cuts are largely due to two conflicting constitutional amendments that have choked state spending. The Taxpayer's Bill of Rights, known as TABOR, limits state revenue while Amendment 23 mandates annual spending increases in primary and secondary education.

When the recession hit and revenues sank, the state was still forced to increase K-12 funding. And now, as state economists predict larger than expected revenue gains, lawmakers are still chopping because TABOR limits how much of that money Colorado can keep.

With such strict constitutional budgeting requirements, lawmakers were forced to balance the budget on the backs of programs like higher education, which are not constitutionally protected.

That led college presidents in 2003 to warn that state funding for higher education would be so insignificant by 2009 that institutions would be forced to privatize or close their doors.

Faced with such dire consequences, and without the political will for constitutional reform, lawmakers passed an escape hatch for higher education—college vouchers.

The voucher or stipend sends state money directly to students instead of to the institutions. In the first year, students will receive $2,400 to attend any state school and $1,200 to attend several private schools.

Before the stipend, the state sent money directly to schools, which meant tuition was subject to TABOR's revenue limits. But by sending state money through the students, college tuition is no longer capped by TABOR.

Even with its controversial funding of private school tuition, the plan passed, in large part, because it allows state schools to raise tuition to cover expenses. College and university presidents supported the plan.

Critics argue that the stipend provides no new money for higher education—and in fact much less to the bigger schools such as The University of Colorado and Colorado State University. So in effect, students and their families will be paying higher tuition.

The bill's prime sponsor, Republican Senator Norma Anderson, said while the stipend helps in the short-term, there has to be constitutional reform. Without it, the stipend's $2,400 value will fall.

"We're using it to bridge the gap on TABOR," Anderson said of the stipend. "If we don't reform TABOR, this state's in big trouble at some point, particularly higher education."

With no reform to vote on, citizens will have to rely on lawmakers to try and salvage funding for programs and maybe, just maybe, offer them a solution to consider next election. Meanwhile, initiative supporters say their plans are not dead.

Former Republican Senate President and County Commissioner Ted Strickland offers this advice to states contemplating a TABOR-like measure.

"Think very hard before you try it," he said, adding that the effect of TABOR isn't felt until an economic downturn, when flexibility is most needed.

And don't, Strickland said, constitutionalize the measure. The constitution is far too rigid to allow policymakers to respond to emergency needs.

A lesson Colorado leaders have learned from experience.

41

The Perils of Property Tax

Janet M. Kelly

State legislatures capped property taxes and promised to help local governments make up the fiscal loss. Their broken promises mean local governments must scramble for revenue.

S tate-local fiscal relations deserve another look in the wake of the economic recession that produced the deepest state deficits in 50 years.

When coffers were brimming during the 1990s, states created new programs and services (and new benefit constituencies for them) in health and social services, education and the arts.

Overall, state spending increased by 28 percent, adjusted for inflation and population growth, according to Donald Boyd of the Rockefeller Institute of Government.

Many states also were able to cut their own taxes during this period. They took steps to reduce local property taxes, supplanting the revenue lost to localities with state revenue from sales or income taxes.

Supplanting local property taxes with state revenues is problematic for a number of reasons, however.

First, from an intergovernmental perspective, the line between state taxes and local taxes becomes blurred when states pay localities for forgiven taxes. From a financial perspective, a stable source of revenue at the local level (property tax) has been replaced with state revenues (income and sales taxes) that may or may not be stable.

When the bottom dropped out in the third quarter of 2001, states did not respond by raising taxes. They cut discretionary spending and used one-time or short-term money, like the tobacco settlement, to fund ongoing programs. Predictably, the targets of state cuts were the fastest growing budget items (Medicaid and to a lesser extent K-12 education) and the two "balance wheels" of state budgeting, higher education and state aid to local governments.

From *State Legislatures,*
October/November 2004.

State reimbursement for local property tax relief granted to homeowners falls squarely into the category of state aid to local governments, and is a favorite target for budget cutters when state revenues are stretched thin. That is the danger of fiscal centralization, or the tendency toward states assuming a larger share in the provision and financing of government services. When states need revenue, history demonstrates that revenue shared with localities is an attractive target.

Steven D. Gold and Sarah Ritchey wrote about this when they were studying state actions affecting cities and counties in the early '90s. They demonstrated a propensity for states to target shared revenue and higher education first as a source of budget cuts during fiscal downturns.

The Wisconsin experience is instructive. The Shared Revenue Fund was created in 1911 (when the state income tax was enacted) to reimburse cities and counties for lost property tax revenue on personal and intangible property. At its outset, 70 percent of the income tax revenue went to municipalities, 20 percent to counties and 10 percent to the state for administrative costs.

The Shared Revenue Fund was expanded over the 30-year period prior to the recession of 2001 as the state offered localities property tax relief and some fiscal equalization, especially for schools. Despite historically harmonious state-local relations, Wisconsin Governor Scott McCallum recommended eliminating the Shared Revenue Fund in his 2002 budget, along with strict local property tax controls. The Legislature gave the localities a temporary reprieve by using funds from the tobacco settlement, but the fund remains a target for spending cuts next year.

The moral: In the face of budget crises, fiscal centralization can handcuff the same localities it intends to help even when state-local relations are healthy.

The dilemma: Without access to revenue alternatives and with their own tax domain constricted, local governments in Wisconsin and other states are practicing their own form of cutback budgeting.

LIMITS ON PROPERTY TAXES: 1992–2000

Measures to limit local property taxes have been a sticking point in state-local relations since the late 1970s. After Proposition 13 passed in California, legislatures began to cap local tax rates or slow the rate of growth in property values.

In the 1980s, restrictions on property taxes sometimes came with access to other revenue sources like sales and income taxes. Local governments often preferred alternative revenue sources to the unpopular property tax, not only because they were more acceptable, but also more efficient and elastic.

The changes in property tax law in the 1990s were different in that local governments were typically not given greater access to alternate revenues, but promised reimbursement for "forgiven" property taxes.

A few changes in local property tax law were the product of initiatives or constitutional amendments. Michigan's Proposal A (1994) limited the annual increase in taxable value of property by a formula tied to consumer inflation. Oregon's Measure 50 cut assessed values to 1995–96 levels, capped annual growth at 3 percent and required voter approval on new levies. Colorado's Referendum A created a new homestead exemption for senior citizens with a 50 percent exemption on the first $200,000 of assessed value.

The most sweeping changes came from legislatures. Over a three-year period, Iowa's legislature offered an $85 million property tax cut for homeowners by increasing state-funded school aid, created a property tax relief fund for county expenditures relating to mental health and required the state to fund the homestead property tax credit.

South Carolina extended the homestead exemption in 1995 to all homeowners (it was previously restricted to the elderly and disabled), increased the exemption and shifted school property taxes from local governments to the state for the first $100,000 in assessed value.

South Dakota's Legislature froze owner-occupied and agricultural property in 1996 and gave taxpayers a 20 percent credit on their tax bills. In 1998, it mandated an additional 5 percent cut in property taxes. Missouri completely exempted older people from property taxes on their primary residence in 1999.

SHARED REVENUE: 1992–2000

We can get a sense of the extent to which local property tax laws were changed in the 1990s by looking at the variety of legislation adopted.

During the boom years between 1992 and 2000, 21 states restricted growth in tax rates, tax bases or property values. Thirteen states began property tax relief programs.

Sixteen states expanded their homestead exemption (Ohio twice). Seven states made their circuit breaker programs more generous. Many states pursued property tax relief on multiple fronts. Very few states did nothing.

Unfortunately, state-by state comparisons don't reveal the financial impact of the changes on either state or local budgets. For an estimate of the cost of fiscal centralization of local property taxes, an analyst would typically turn to the Census of Government Finance for data on intergovernmental transfers. Though it seems counterintuitive, the Census Bureau counts reimbursements to localities for forgiven property taxes as state aid to local government, mingling property tax reimbursements with other forms of state aid. Of course, they are actually reimbursements for tax expenditures, or property taxes forgiven by the state that localities otherwise have a right to collect.

The result is that the casual observer might conclude that state aid to local governments has increased dramatically over the period when, in fact, localities did not receive any more revenue than they would have if they had applied the tax, nor were they able to reap any efficiencies in the administration of the tax.

Local Property Taxes as a Percent of Local Taxes, FY 2000

Local dependence on the property tax varies from 39 percent of local tax collections in Alabama to nearly 99 percent in Connecticut.

Rank	State	Percent	Rank	State	Percent
1	Connecticut	98.7%	27	Nebraska	77.5
2	Rhode Island	98.6	28	Kansas	76.8
3	New Jersey	98.3	29	Wyoming	76.0
4	New Hampshire	98.2	30	North Carolina	75.2
5	Maine	97.9	31	United States	72.1
6	Massachusetts	96.9	32	Virginia	70.6
7	Vermont	96.2	33	Pennsylvania	70.5
8	Montana	95.6	43	Arizona	69.0
9	Idaho	94.6	44	Utah	68.8
10	Minnesota	94.2	35	Ohio	65.4
11	Wisconsin	93.8	36	Nevada	63.8
12	Mississippi	92.0	37	California	63.2
13	Iowa	89.5	38	Washington	61.5
14	Michigan	89.4	39	Tennessee	61.5
15	Indiana	88.6	40	Georgia	60.4
16	North Dakota	88.1	41	Colorado	59.9
17	South Carolina	84.4	42	Missouri	59.0
18	West Virginia	83.6	43	Maryland	57.4
19	Illinois	82.8	44	New York	55.8
20	Alaska	80.7	45	New Mexico	55.4
21	Oregon	80.5	46	Oklahoma	54.0
22	Texas	79.9	47	Kentucky	53.8
23	Delaware	78.6	48	Arkansas	44.4
24	Hawaii	78.6	49	Louisiana	39.3
25	South Dakota	78.2	50	Alabama	39.0
26	Florida	77.9			

Note: Taken from "A Guide to Property Taxes: The Role of Property Taxes in State and Local Finances," an NCSL report by Judy Zelio. To order call (303) 364-7812.

Source: State Policy Reports, no.21; (Washington, D.C.: Federal Funds Information for States, Nov. 2002); based on U.S. Census Bureau data, 2002.

Property Tax Is Leading Source of Local Revenues

State and local government revenues include not only taxes, but also charges and fees, interest and federal aid, among others. Although the state-local general revenue picture in the past 30 years has changed, particularly with respect to the property tax, the property tax has continued as the mainstay of local taxes. Local governments collected $354 billion in taxes in FY 2001. Property taxes amounted to $253 billion, or 71 percent, of the total. More than $100 billion came from other taxes, including $62 billion in local sales and gross receipts taxes and $22 billion in local income taxes.

Clearly, the property tax remains the most important source of tax revenue for municipalities, counties and school districts, even though it is declining in importance as other revenue sources gain.

—*Judy Zelio, NCSL*

According to the Census Bureau, per capita state aid to local governments grew a whopping 30 percent from 1992 to 1996 and 21 percent from 1996 to 2000, the two periods corresponding to the economic boom. This is one piece of evidence that makes the case for fiscal centralization of property tax revenue. A look at the own-source and property tax revenue for the same period also suggests a story of fiscal centralization.

There was significant and practically identical growth in both state and local own-source revenue for the 1992 to 1996 period, as we would expect. But from 1996 to 2000, state own-source revenues grew by 14 percent while local own-source revenue grew by only 8.65 percent.

Moreover, local property tax revenues grew by 24 percent during the 1992 to 1996 period, but by only 7 percent in the 1996 to 2000 period. State-imposed limits on property tax revenue growth can account for some of the drop in revenues realized, but not all of it, and certainly not a 17-point drop in revenue growth.

One could reasonably conclude that local property tax revenues were growing by a much smaller proportion because states were rebating property tax relief programs to local governments.

A National Conference of State Legislatures report in 1997 noted slightly increasing fiscal centralization from 1970 to 1994, so the trend did not start during the period examined here—it intensified. The benefit of centralization for states is the capacity to equalize fiscal disparities, say in the area of education or social services. There is little evidence, however, that states actually have used this tool to equalize. For localities, state centralization means loss of local control and accountability and a set of one-size-fits-all services that leave some citizens paying for services they do not want or need. Conversely, centralization may also leave some localities unable to afford services their residents want or need because the primary means to finance them has been restricted.

THINKING AHEAD

States are, by necessity, economic opportunists, and they are helped along by localities that do not protest loss of fiscal autonomy because it may have a political cost.

We have known for more than 20 years that state-imposed restrictions on local taxing, spending and fiscal administration decisions are the greatest barriers to local autonomy.

No Money in Colorado

Colorado voters approved Referendum A in 2000, an amendment to the state's constitution that reduced property taxes on primary residences for citizens over 65 years of age. This new homestead exemption was more generous than most, reducing the taxable value of a home by one-half of the first $200,000 in assessed value. The referendum, which went into effect in 2002, required the state to fully reimburse local governments for the loss of the property tax revenue.

It also contained a clause that let the legislature suspend the program during times of budgetary difficulty.

The day after Colorado's treasurer made the first payment to local governments in the amount of $61.5 million, that's what the legislature did. The program was suspended until the 2006 tax year.

"We therefore find ourselves in the ironic situation of suspending the program, at least for the time being, during the same week in which the first reimbursements to counties were made," said Treasurer Mike Coffman.

We did not worry because devolution seemed to come slowly, and with reimbursement, in the 1980s. The cyclical recession of the early 1990s was not sufficiently prolonged to call local capacity into question. The relatively rapid economic recovery left few to worry about intergovernmental fiscal relations in general or fiscal centralization in particular.

If there is a bright note to this perilous forecast for local government tax revenues, it is that the recent state budget difficulties have concentrated the minds of many state elected officials toward comprehensive tax reform.

If states were experiencing cyclical rather than structural deficits, we might take the same position as we did a decade ago—philosophizing on local fiscal autonomy as we wait for the storm to pass. Structural deficits are our signal that the storm will not pass. The consequences for intergovernmental fiscal relations, and for governing, will be realized soon enough.

42

Taxing Behavior

Bert Waisanen

Personal vices have been around a long time. But the price for those habits and other controversial behaviors is about to go up.

What do individual behaviors and state tax policy have in common? Plenty, as it turns out. People who smoke or chew pay excise taxes on tobacco.

The same is true for people who quaff a beer, drink a martini or sip a glass of wine instead of a Shirley Temple. Included in the price of their purchases are excise taxes on alcohol.

Is this news? No. But alcohol and tobacco taxes are only part of the story of an emerging trend in states: the use of tax policy as a means to change personal behavior and choices.

Taxes on beer and cigarettes have existed through much of American history, either to curb what may be considered a vice or to finance outlays, such as war spending. These targeted taxes are usually imposed at higher rates than a general sales tax on other retail items. But recently the states are taking aim at other behaviors and trying to change them through the tax code. In their sights: Promoting healthy lifestyles and safer driving or discouraging adult entertainment.

XXX TAXES

The most novel idea passed in Utah this session. The Sexually Explicit Business and Escort Service Tax imposes a 10 percent excise tax on the escort and adult entertainment industry. The language was carefully designed to target the sexual nature of escort services and nude dance clubs, rather than other organizations that provide companionship or services that clearly are not of a sexual nature. The funds raised by the tax will be dedicated to a special fund for treatment programs for sex offenders.

From *State Legislatures,* June 2004.

215

NUTRITION AND EXERCISE

Obesity, particularly in children, is on everyone's radar screen. New federal research attributes $75 billion in annual medical costs to obesity, so there is significant activity this year to address its risks. Several initiatives seek to encourage better nutrition or more exercise through the tax code.

Legislation in New York would fund the state's childhood obesity prevention program by a quarter-cent sales tax increase on video game and movie rentals, sweets and snacks. They were targeted because they promote the couch potato syndrome among kids that can lead to childhood obesity and future health costs to the state.

Another proposal to boost healthier living would provide incentives to exercise. That bill gives a tax credit for certain purchases of exercise equipment, gym memberships or other sports or activities related to fitness and healthy living. The credit limit is $1,000. Neither proposal had been acted on as of this writing.

Representative Jerry Ellis introduced a bill in Oklahoma that would have imposed just under a 2-cent excise tax on a can of pop. He said the bill, which did not come out of committee, was designed to provide funding for important budget priorities such as bridge repair, Medicaid and education. It would have brought in some matching funds, as well.

"It was less than 2 cents per can," Ellis says. "That's not going to stop anyone from buying a soft drink. And it's a better avenue than going to a property tax or a higher fuel tax, which is a killer tax in my opinion."

The Maryland Senate unsuccessfully tried to reinstate a snack food tax in the budget reconciliation bill. It would have removed the sales tax exemption for potato chips, corn chips and pretzels, among other snacks. The proposal, which was a substitute for another health revenue raiser, passed the Senate, but was not included in the final budget bill approved by the General Assembly.

Meanwhile, some interesting policy questions remain about special food taxes. How should nutritional value be measured and then put into policy? Should targeted items include foods that are high in calories or sugar or "bad" carbohydrates? How about saturated fat? Or should a common sense test regarding "junk foods" be sufficient? Differentiating can be challenging from a policy standpoint, particularly for snack foods, which have undergone periods of on-again off-again state taxation and exemption.

TRADITIONAL VICES

On the traditional "sin tax" front, at least 11 states have proposed tobacco tax increases this session. Michigan is one of several states with a projected budget shortfall in FY 2005. A proposed 75-cent increase in the tobacco tax would be earmarked for health care programs. When polled, 75 percent of Michigan residents supported it. One legislator was quoted as saying that the higher tax would also discourage children from smoking, because the higher price would be a greater drain on the average kid's pocket change.

Legislators in Kansas, Missouri and South Dakota looked at increasing alcohol taxes this session, but none of the proposals passed. The bills would have earmarked funds for alcoholism treatment programs, at-risk youths and aid to local governments, in addition to money for the general fund.

"We're convinced that substantial tax increases on alcohol, particularly beer, will dramatically reduce heavy and frequent drinking by underage kids," says George Hacker, alcohol policies project director at the Center for Science in the Public Interest. "There is a lot of credible evidence to support this."

Hacker cites a new study from the National Research Council on underage drinking that says price does affect alcohol use, and that higher prices tend to reduce con-

7 Taxes for 7 Sins	
Target	**What's Taxed**
Child obesity	Soft drinks, snack foods, video rentals
Smoking	Tobacco products
Excessive drinking	Alcoholic beverages
Gambling	Casinos and other gaming venues
Unsafe driving	Surcharges on licenses
Sex offenders	Sexually explicit entertainment venues
Animal neglect	Pet food

State Tobacco Tax Actions

Year	Number of States	Revenue Raised
2003	19	$891 million
2002	20	3 billion
2001	6	215.5 million
2000	2	335 million
1999	3	125 million

sumption. A higher alcohol tax at both the federal and state levels was one of the study's recommendations.

ROAD RESPONSIBILITY

Another idea in at least two states is penalizing irresponsible drivers. New Jersey is looking at increasing surcharges in its existing unsafe driver law. Florida is considering a $1,000 surcharge on licensed drivers who have DUI offenses. Anyone who accumulates seven or more violation points against their license within the preceding three years will face a $100 surcharge each year and $25 more for each additional point above seven. The Florida Driver Responsibility Law was approved by the House Transportation Committee. The funds would be earmarked for certified trauma centers, brain and spinal injury programs, highway patrol officer recruitment and transportation projects.

PALATABLE TAXES

It seems clear that legislators and the public like taxing unhealthy or controversial behavior to balance the budget or support specific programs. The duality of purpose is appealing. Because vices impose public costs across communities, citizens aren't concerned that excise taxes don't broadly distribute the tax burden for public services or raise substantial revenues.

Excise taxes are apparently evolving into a blended policy intent—one based on revenue needs and social goals. In any case, a growing trend toward taxing behavior by increasing the consumer's cost of consumption or otherwise discouraging controversial activities continues in 2004.

43

Taking Back a Tax

Alan Greenblatt

With their bottom lines still troubled, states are trying to regain the revenue corporations owe them.

When he took office two years ago, New Jersey Governor James McGreevey noticed that many of the companies doing business in his state were not paying much in the way of taxes. More than 75 percent of New Jersey companies, in fact, were paying only $200 apiece in state income taxes—the bare minimum allowed by law. These included 30 of the 50 largest payroll companies, and their total contribution to state revenue was less, McGreevey liked to point out, than the amount paid by the janitors who mopped up their offices.

It took a special session, but McGreevey persuaded the legislature to close a number of loopholes. As a result, New Jersey corporations paid more than twice as much in state income tax last year than they had in 2002.

Not surprisingly, the state's business community tagged McGreevey's plan a jobs-killer and warned that the extra billion in tax dollars it was going to have to pony up would result in economic stagnation. But it hasn't worked out that way. More than 70,000 new companies opened for business last year, and New Jersey gained jobs.

That's a story other states are eager to hear. As they continue to struggle with difficult budgets, states are looking around for untapped sources of revenue, and corporate income taxes are an obvious target. Twenty-five years ago, corporate income taxes accounted for more than 10 percent of all state revenue. Today, without legislation purposely reducing that burden, the corporate share is less than 6 percent. The cost of the erosion is high. According to the Multistate Tax Commission, the tab for corporate tax shelters in 2001 was $12.4 billion, which is more than one-third the amount that corporations actually paid that year. The loopholes,

From *Governing,*
May 2004.

of course, may serve a public purpose. Some states may be keeping their corporate income tax laws on the books as an economic development ploy: They can waive the tax when trying to attract new companies.

But much of the lost revenue from corporate taxes has less to do with incentives offered in the name of job creation than with outright, if legal, evasion. And that is why, in the past few years, revenue officers in several states have been working to persuade state legislators to give them additional powers to make sure that income corporations generate within a state is counted as income in that state.

In some places, revenue departments have been emboldened by court decisions. In Maryland, for instance, the court of appeals ruled last year that a clothing retailer and a packaging manufacturer were skirting state law by sending their profits to holding companies in Delaware.

MOVING MONEY AROUND

The problem for most revenue departments is that corporate income is not nearly as straightforward as personal income. It's easier for a company to reallocate income among different subsidiaries than it is for a state to prove that income was generated in a specific place. That's why many state legislatures are focusing on the holding-company tactic. The way this works is that companies transfer a portion of their profits to a holding company in a jurisdiction with lax corporate income taxes, such as Delaware or Nevada—or, increasingly, a foreign country, such as Barbados. Out-of-state holding companies might not have any employees or sales in the tax-sheltering state. The corporate presence may be nothing more than a plaque on a door in an office building. But what the holding companies do have are valuable company trademarks that subsidiaries pay royalties to use—royalties that can appear to eat up a subsidiary's profits. "It's a simple but high-profile tax sheltering technique that companies are using to shift income away from where states believe the income was earned to a tax-haven situation," says Dan Bucks, executive director of the Multistate Tax Commission.

Tax collectors often refer to this issue as the "Geoffrey problem." Toys 'R' Us, the toy retailer, has set up a subsidiary in Delaware called Geoffrey Inc., named for its iconic giraffe, that charges state affiliates a fee for use of its "intangible assets," such as trademarked characters

and names. The fees, in effect, transfer the profits the toy seller makes in other states to Delaware, which does not tax intangible assets.

Over and above Geoffrey, states are having an increasingly tough time solving the riddle of exactly where a company that does business in multiple states should declare its profits. For instance, a company in one state might rely on an affiliate in another state to do its accounting work or manage its real estate—and deduct those expenses from its corporate tax liability. Because such services are intangible, it becomes hard to draw a definitive line between what is a legitimate business deduction and what is an attempt to transfer income to an out-of-state tax haven.

Dan Navin of the Ohio Chamber of Commerce sees this as a lawful means for a firm to take a deduction for real intercompany expenses, just as though it had hired an in-state CPA or Realtor to do the job. "Transactions between affiliated companies are a convenient target," he says, "particularly where they can trot out the term 'Delaware holding company' and tar all intercompany transactions with that brush."

Many elected officials agree with him and want to head off efforts to stop the deductions. "The bottom line is that there are certain individuals who would like to do away with those legitimate business expenses, and we're not going to do it," says Shannon Cooper, who chairs the Missouri House Tax Policy Committee. He is sponsoring a bill that would put the burden of proof on the state revenue department to show that companies were using such expenses merely as a means to avoid paying state taxes.

Corporate tax-collection woes don't stop there. Federal law governing state taxation of multistate companies has not been changed for more than 40 years and so does not take into account the enormous shift in business activity away from purely tangible property to the kind of intangible services and trademarks that are now in dispute. If he gets his way, Congressman Robert Goodlatte of Virginia would put an end to states' ability to collect taxes from many of the corporations that conduct business within their borders under the umbrella of a holding company set up safely outside a state's borders. He has introduced legislation in the U.S. House to that effect and, if passed, it could be devastating to state collections. "Companies would have to be physically present to be subject to a corporate income tax," explains Dan Bucks. "Because holding companies are not present, they would escape taxation in that state."

Business Losses

States ranked by percentage change in corporate income tax revenue, July–March FY 2002–FY 2003

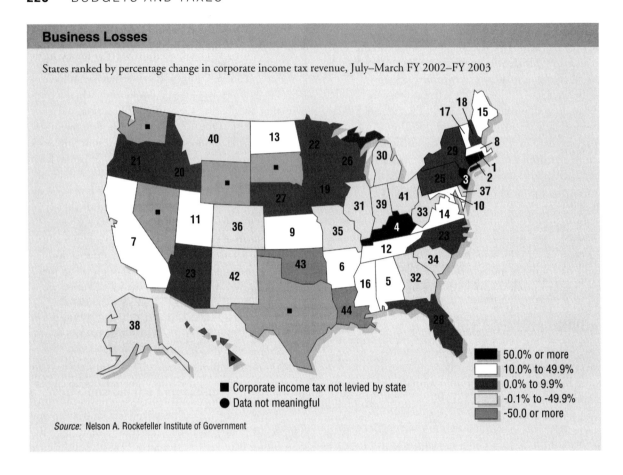

■ Corporate income tax not levied by state
● Data not meaningful

■	50.0% or more
□	10.0% to 49.9%
▦	0.0% to 9.9%
▨	-0.1% to -49.9%
▩	-50.0 or more

Source: Nelson A. Rockefeller Institute of Government

THE ADDING MACHINE

Several states that are attempting to close the holding-company loophole are trying to do so by varying the way they handle deductions allowed under the federal tax code. Most states, for instance, allow all the deductions that the federal government allows. More specifically, that means that a royalty paid to a Delaware holding company is deductible under federal law. What several states now want to do is require that the amount of the royalty payment be added back when calculating gross state income. It is not a precedent-shattering move. There are many other expenses deductible for federal tax purposes that states insist on adding back in when state income taxes are calculated—the most common one being the deduction for state income taxes themselves.

Last year, Maryland Governor Robert L. Ehrlich Jr. vetoed a bill that would have addressed the problem of companies shifting profits to Delaware holding companies, arguing that it would put the state at a competitive disadvantage. He also said he wanted the judiciary to rule on the matter. Now that the state Court of Appeals has said the holding companies are a means of circumventing state laws, Ehrlich has signaled he would sign a narrow bill addressing the Delaware problem. But some legislators in Annapolis want to go further. They argue that corporate tax lawyers and accountants can find ways to make income-shifting look like legitimate intercompany expense payments, so they want to adopt another method of collecting money from multistate companies, known as combined reporting.

Under combined reporting, all corporate income taxpayers in a state list the total profits of all their related subsidiaries and affiliates, regardless of location. The state then uses an allocation formula to determine how much of those profits were generated within its borders. Combined reporting was pioneered by California back in the 1930s when state legislators became incensed that movie studios were shifting profits across the border to Nevada. The combined approach is now the law in 16 states. Richard Pomp, a University of Connecticut law professor, sees combined reporting as providing a better and fairer account of a company's activities than add-back provisions, which are easier to manipulate. But he recognizes that it's a tough sell politically. "The business community," he says, "will tell you that this combined-reporting nonsense will destroy the economy of the community."

Changing corporate tax law is always hard. During a recession, businesses argue that any change to the code will cost even more jobs. When times are good, they warn against killing the golden goose. Moreover, corporate tax law is abstruse. "Really the only people who pay attention to corporate taxes and corporate tax loopholes are the businesses who take advantage of them," says Steve Hill of the Maryland Budget and Tax Policy Institute. "It's more difficult to rally the general public around closing them."

Nevertheless, with budgets as tight as they are and corporate scofflaws a staple of news broadcasts, legislators—and even the general public—are upset that businesses are paying a smaller share of state taxes than they used to. In March, 38 states signed a pact to help each other fight illegal tax schemes to carry profits across state lines, including coordinated enforcement actions, joint audits and swapping documents and information about cases. "Legislators know their pockets are being picked," says Pomp. "They may not be able to explain it the way a tax lawyer can, but they know there's a problem out there."

PART

X

Policy Challenges

One of the consistent messages emerging from the readings in this book is that state and local governments are expected to do a great deal. Education, health care, roads, parks, libraries, professional licensing, airports, utilities, information technology—there's virtually no aspect of social and economic life that is not touched in some way by state and local government policy.

Given that, there is a fairly all-encompassing view of what the most important policy challenges are for state and local governments: everything. You name it, it's probably on the agenda in some form or another at a council meeting, a legislative committee, a governor's policy team, or before a state judge.

Governments, though, are like people in general—they have a limited amount of attention, time, and money. So while state and local governments in a broad sense deal with just about everything, there is a much smaller spectrum of issues that attract a disproportionate share of government interest and resources. What's at the top of the agenda these days?

As we saw in Part 9, finances are probably issue number one. It's important to keep in mind that budgets are not just accounting tools—they represent policy. A good way to figure out what state and local governments consider most important is to follow the money: who is getting it, and who isn't? By that yardstick, education and health care rank up there as two of the most important issues on the public agenda. They consume the most state and local tax dollars and are considered primary responsibilities of those two levels of government. Conflicts over education policy and health care policy are also central components of state politics these days.

Money, however, is an imperfect indicator of key policy challenges. The National Guard, for example, claims a small part of most state budgets compared with big-ticket items like education and health care. Nonetheless, the National Guard is a major component of the nation's armed services and makes up a significant portion of the forces serving in Iraq, Afghanistan, and various active-duty assignments in the United States.

The readings in this section focus on these three key policy challenges: education, health care, and the new role of the National Guard. These are far from the only challenges state and local governments face, but they are three issues that are likely to have the attention of policymakers for the next couple of years.

EDUCATION

State and local authorities fund, govern, and regulate K–12 schools and public colleges and universities. States often set grade school curricular requirements and teacher certification standards. Local school districts hire and fire teachers and handle a mind-boggling array of logistical and administrative duties—they determine particular teaching approaches, provide lunches, and field a football team. Both state and local governments raise the revenue to run schools.

Increasingly, the federal government has been encroaching on what historically has been state and local government turf. The most prominent example of this is the No Child Left Behind (NCLB) Act. This is the signature education initiative of the Bush administration, which was passed with overwhelming bipartisan support in 2002.

The basic thrust of NCLB is to shift standards and accountability in primary and secondary education away from state and local governments and toward the federal government. NCLB sets down a series of annual testing requirements and mandates that states set and achieve ambitious performance standards. A school's failure to meet those standards can give parents the right to remove their children and transfer them to other schools that receive federal aid.[1] The law has received mixed grades from schools and state governments.

While most policymakers and citizens are supportive of the general intent behind NCLB, its implementation and its costs are problematic. There are three basic objections to NCLB, and each of these objections has created

controversies and heightened tensions over the federal government's new role in public education.

One objection is simply its cost. NCLB requires states to implement new standards for testing and teacher quality, which is proving to be an expensive proposition. The federal government promised to help cover some of those costs, although many NCLB critics believe the federal government has severely underestimated the bill and already reneged on its promised portion. Some argue that implementing NCLB will cost states about ten times more than the support they receive from the federal government.[2]

A second objection is that NCLB requirements are needlessly complicated and so stringent they are counterproductive. For example, the bill requires that states define a "proficient" level of academic performance and hold schools accountable for getting at least 95 percent of students to achieve that level. The difficulty, however, is not just getting 95 percent of the student body to a proficient level; the law requires that it be 95 percent in each of a range of subgroups (e.g., racial minorities and low-income students). Thus if a school has forty students in a particular subgroup and three of these do not meet the proficient standards—or are absent from school on the day the key accountability test is taken—the whole school is labeled as failing. By the standards of NCLB, nearly 90 percent of public schools in Florida were judged not to be making adequate yearly progress.[3]

The third key objection is that NCLB distorts the entire process of public education by overemphasizing standardized tests. Critics assert that standardized tests are dictating what is taught and how, at the expense of the creativity of teachers and the nurturing of intellectual curiosity in students. This is not just the fault of NCLB, but reflects a broader shift in education toward more reliance on standardized testing. Some states, for example, now require exit tests to get a high school diploma. Or even to get into fourth grade (see the article by Jane Carroll Andrade in this section).

Dealing with these issues is going to be a long-term project for state governments and school districts. Proposed solutions run the gamut from more federal funding, to major modifications of NCLB, to scrapping the law altogether and returning the governance of education to what some see as its rightful owners—states and localities. Unfortunately, this is a political battle so there's no test to determine which answer is the best solution.

HEALTH CARE

Health care is a major concern of state governments for two reasons. Reason one is cost. Reason two is access—many Americans have limited access to health care because of reason one.

This issue is front and center for state governments because they bear a major portion of the responsibility for ensuring adequate access to health care for their citizens. The program most identified with this responsibility is Medicaid, which helps pay medical costs for millions of low-income people. This is a joint federal-state program: the federal government establishes broad guidelines and covers half of the costs, and the states determine specific eligibility criteria and cover the remainder of the costs.

Financially speaking, Medicaid is one of the fastest growing programs for state governments. Fifteen years ago, Medicaid accounted for roughly a dime of every dollar in state spending. Today it accounts for twice that, and it will undoubtedly continue to increase even more as health care costs outpace inflation and more Americans go uninsured.

Medicaid's voracious appetite for state government dollars would be cause enough for concern during times of financial plenty. Given the fiscal stress that states have struggled with during the past few years, containing Medicaid's costs has become an urgent priority for state policymakers. The problem with Medicaid is that there are no easy choices, and scrapping the program is a political nonstarter.

Rather than giving up on Medicaid, states are considering a variety of reforms that range from ratcheting up eligibility requirements—in other words, taking away health care coverage from some poor people—to emphasizing primary care based on the philosophy that an ounce of prevention is worth a pound of cure. States have also begun cracking down on abuse of Medicaid; the system is so large and sprawling that fraud is not uncommon (see the article by Martha King and Dianna Gordon in this section).

Medicaid simply reflects a larger problem with the escalating costs of health care. Several factors combine to drive up the costs of health care. New medical technology and drug therapies are expensive. The nation is aging, increasing demand for long-term health care. The rising costs in turn raise the question of who will pay them. And that is the real political issue.

The United States has historically relied on the private sector to provide health care insurance, with many of the premiums being paid by employers as part of workers' benefits packages. That system is showing cracks. Job growth in the economy has primarily been in low-benefit sectors such as retail. The economic downturn of recent years has also meant that many people lost their jobs, and their health care benefits.

The end result is that the number of uninsured Americans is increasing by about 15 percent per year; in 2003, there were 45 million citizens without health insurance. The most at-risk group is poor children—one in five children living in poverty have no health insurance.[4]

This in turn puts pressure on the programs designed to ensure that the neediest in society have access to health care programs like Medicaid. Health care is a complex issue that resists easy solutions, and state governments have little choice but to deal with the problem. This means that health care is likely to be a priority issue on the agenda of state policymakers for the foreseeable future (see the article by Katherine Barrett, Richard Green, and Michele Mariani in this section).

NATIONAL DEFENSE

National defense is traditionally thought of as a responsibility of the federal government. The U.S. Constitution designates the president as commander in chief of the armed forces and reserves to Congress the right to declare war.

A significant portion of the nation's military power, however, spends most of its time under state rather than federal control: the National Guard. Traditionally, National Guard units have served within their own states, often taking lead roles in responding to natural disasters or maintaining order during other times of emergency. But state Guard units are also part of the nation's armed forces, and if called up by the federal government, they must serve.

Many National Guard units are being called to serve these days, often in combat zones in Iraq and Afghanistan. The National Guard took on a newly prominent role almost immediately following the terrorist attacks of September 11, 2001. Initially, Guard units were used for airport security and to safeguard other facilities viewed as probable targets for terrorists. With the invasions of Afghanistan and Iraq, Guard units were sent to war, with tens of thousands of Guard members currently serving active duty tours of a year or even longer.

Guard deployments on that scale and for that duration have not been seen since World War II and the Korean War, and they have created a number of problems for state and local governments. One of the problems is simple absence—a Guard unit cannot be called out to deal with the impact of a storm or to control a civil disturbance if it is on the other side of the globe combating Iraqi insurgents. Many Guard members are also public employees, and the long tours of duty have sometimes left police and fire departments, as well as other public agencies like schools, shorthanded.

Roughly one third of the National Guard is on active duty these days, and with demands in Iraq and Afghanistan stretching the regular military thin, it seems likely that significant numbers of Guard units will continue to be called up. This situation not only leaves governors with fewer assets to deal with major emergencies and public agencies with fewer key employees (especially first responders such as police officers and paramedics), it is also taking a toll on the Guard itself. The prospect of being taken out of civilian life for a year or more, leaving jobs, families, and friends behind, and being shipped to a combat zone has had a significant impact on Guard recruiting.

The National Guard has a "weekend warrior" image no more. The fact that Guard members are becoming warriors, period, raises a number of issues state and local government are going to have to deal with for the foreseeable future (see the article by Karen Imas in this section).

TRENDS

The readings in this section provide insights into the three policy areas discussed above. Jane Carroll Andrade's article examines statewide student testing and finds advantages and disadvantages. Most agree NCLB's goals of accountability and raising achievement levels are worthy, and that standardized tests can play a role in achieving those goals. Many educators, however, believe the focus on testing is obscuring—and perhaps even harming—other important issues in education.

The articles by Martha King and Dianna Gordon and by Katherine Barrett, Richard Greene, and Michele Mariani provide two perspectives on the health care policy challenges faced by states. The former explores Medicaid and a range of potential reforms that could ease the pressure this program puts on state budgets. The latter takes a broader look at health insurance coverage, its implications for state policy, and what state policymakers can and are doing to deal with those implications.

Finally, Karen Imas's article focuses on the new role of the National Guard and how states are moving to implement programs to support Guard members.

Notes

1. National Education Association, "No Child Left Behind?" *NEA Today,* May 2003, www.nea.org/neatoday/0305/cover.html (accessed May 5, 2005).

2. William J. Mathis, "No Child Left Behind Act: What Will It Cost States?" *Spectrum: The Journal of State Government* 77 (Spring 2004): 8–14.

3. Dewayne Matthews, "No Child Left Behind: The Challenge of Implementation," *Spectrum: The Journal of State Government* 77 (Spring 2004): 11–14.

4. DeNavas-Walt, Carmen, Proctor, Bernadette D., and Robert J. Mills, *Income, Poverty and Health Insurance Coverage in the United States: 2003,* U.S. Census Bureau Current Population Reports, P60-226, August 2004, www.census.gov/prod/2004pubs/p60-226.pdf (accessed May 10, 2005).

44

Statewide Student Tests

Jane Carroll Andrade

Standardized testing gets a failing grade from critics.

I
t's the last week in April, and more than 1,000 sixth, seventh and eighth graders crowd into the gym at De Leon Middle School in McAllen, Texas. They whisper excitedly as the school band begins to play the fight song. Cheerleaders cheer. Kids perform skits and sing songs. It is a pep rally of Texas-size proportions.

But this particular pep rally is not about gearing up for a football game or a fund-raiser. It is about academics. The students and teachers at De Leon are getting revved up for the annual Texas Assessment of Knowledge and Skills test (TAKS).

You know something's changed when schools in Texas are holding rallies for tests. Although standardized testing has been a reality in many states for decades, a flurry of activity in recent years has resulted in a much higher profile—and plenty of controversy—for state assessment programs. Now, not only are students being tested, their teachers, schools and districts are being held accountable, as well. And the stakes are high.

"Testing for accountability has been with us in various forms probably for the last 40 to 50 years," says Joan Herman, co-director of the Center for Research on Evaluation, Standards and Student Testing (CRESST) in Los Angeles. "In the last 10 to 12 years, it's the consequences attached to performance that have been growing pretty drastically."

THE CONSEQUENCES

Indeed, more states are beginning to withhold high school diplomas and retain third graders for failing to pass state tests, igniting strong emotions in parents, students and even some school districts.

From *State Legislatures,*
February 2004.

227

In Massachusetts last year, several school districts threatened to defy the state by issuing diplomas to seniors who failed to earn a competency determination as required under the Massachusetts Comprehensive Assessment System (MCAS). Phone calls from Education Commissioner David P. Driscoll eventually quelled the rebellion, and a student-filed injunction to stop the graduation requirement was denied by state and federal courts.

Statewide, 92 percent of Massachusetts high school seniors passed the MCAS test. Even with remediation classes and retesting opportunities, however, 4,800 students didn't get their diplomas.

The stakes will continue to grow as states implement the complex requirements of the federal No Child Left Behind Act (NCLB) over the next decade. The new law requires states to test all students annually in math and reading in grades three through eight and at least once in math and reading in grades 10, 11 or 12, beginning in 2005–06.

Schools must use state-defined performance standards to show continuous gains—or adequate yearly progress (AYP)—in achievement for all students, including those with disabilities and limited English proficiency. Schools failing to illustrate adequate progress must offer school choice or supplemental services and may eventually face corrective action, which could include replacing staff, receiving technical assistance or even being turned into a charter school.

Advocates of high-stakes testing maintain that tough consequences are necessary to achieve the goals of education reform, which are that students and schools be held to a high standard, that students be tested on and measured against those standards, and ultimately that public school students be better prepared for higher education and the workforce. The goal of No Child Left Behind is unambiguous: that every student in America be deemed proficient or better by 2014.

States with fairly rigorous assessment systems already in place point to increasingly better test results as proof that high-stakes testing works.

"MCAS holds the whole system accountable, starting with the students," says Sylvia M. Smith, chief of staff for Senator Robert A. Antonioni of Massachusetts. She cites progress made by the class of 2003 as an example.

"Between the class of 2002 and the class of 2003, there was a significant increase in the number of students who passed the English language arts and the math test, because that class was being held to the graduation requirement," she says. Seniors who failed the test in 2003 were allowed to take it again, however.

Florida Governor Jeb Bush announced in May that more students met or surpassed the proficient level in 2003 than ever before on the Florida Comprehensive Assessment Test (FCAT). Progress was particularly dramatic for minority students, with 51 percent of Hispanic fourth graders scoring at or above grade level in 2003, compared with 38 percent in 1998.

Despite the dramatic progress announced by the governor, about 2,500 protesters gathered outside his office in May to demand he suspend FCAT. Requirements for 2003 were that high school seniors pass the 10th grade exam to graduate.

"We've seen tremendous results," says Ohio Senator Robert A. Gardner, the "father" of that state's assessment program. There has been a dramatic drop in the number of schools on academic emergency or academic watch, while more schools have jumped to the excellent category.

"We had 71 schools last year that were in the excellent category. This year, we have 109," he says.

THE UNINTENDED CONSEQUENCES

But critics point to predictions that harsh consequences for failing to show annual progress will tempt states to lower their standards in order to meet the federal act's proficiency targets, and that the federal formula will end up labeling perfectly good schools as failing. Officials in Iowa and Nebraska are concerned because their students already perform well on tests, so schools in those states may have trouble showing improvement in the annual increments required by NCLB.

In fact, three school districts in Connecticut turned down Title 1 funding under NCLB because of fears of "too much federal intervention" and the sanctions on "failing" schools imposed by the federal law.

And some question whether high-stakes testing actually motivates students and schools to perform better. Although studies to try to prove it remain controversial, the National Education Association maintains that high-stakes testing does not improve student achievement and that it may in fact produce more dropouts.

Michael Pons, policy analyst for the NEA, says that even though teachers welcome the emphasis on greater clarity in standards and expectations for students, the federal act's across-the-board requirement for adequate yearly progress is unachievable.

"It's the equivalent of saying every kid should be three feet six when they're in fourth grade," he says.

Representative K. Mark Takai of Hawaii also believes that while schools and students must perform better and make progress every year, the requirements of NCLB are a recipe for failure.

"The surprising element of this law is that it makes no distinction between a school in a well-educated and very affluent community and a school in an impoverished community," he says.

ONE SIZE CAN'T FIT ALL

Representative Takai says there is a strong, predictable correlation between a school's performance on assessment tests and factors that are beyond the control of the school and its staff. Those factors include attendance rate, percentage of disadvantaged students, percentage of limited English proficiency students, percentage of special education students and other factors.

"The federal government is dreaming if they expect those student groups to perform at the level being required by the federal law," he says.

Lynn Stockley, a seventh and eighth grade counselor at Carver Middle School in Tulsa, Okla., agrees. Even though students at Carver, a magnet school, do well on tests, Stockley contends that comparing urban and suburban schools is like comparing apples and oranges.

"It's really not fair to judge a school whose kids come without having ever read a book, and compare it to a school where kids go to the library and have libraries in their home," she says. "It's rather discouraging when you're one of those schools. You know you're working very, very hard and yet your scores are consistently low."

Critics of high-stakes testing also point out that simply scoring well on tests doesn't necessarily mean that students are learning what they need to know to be better prepared for the future. Common complaints are that some students simply don't test well (especially on timed tests), and that such tests force teachers to spend too much time teaching to the test.

"I am completely opposed to the notion that the school's job is to prepare for the test," says Scott Hollinger, principal at McAuliffe Elementary School in McAllen, Texas. "My belief is that the school's job is to teach a well-rounded curriculum and the test is to tell how well we're doing."

Current assessment programs, however, do not encourage a broad curriculum, he says. Many of his col-

---

Where's the Money?

New Hampshire's Experience

Finding the money to pay for mandated tests is a challenge facing most states. In New Hampshire, it became a real issue. The legislature wanted the state Department of Education to use money from the No Child Left Behind law to cover all testing. But federal money, argued the agency, cannot be used to pay for tests already required by the state, only to expand them to additional grades.

Convinced that federal money should be available, budget writers in September cut the $2.7 million appropriated for state testing in each of the next two years to $1 to force the issue. State officials argued they were getting mixed messages from the federal government on exactly what would be covered by federal funds.

The tests must be given for the state to comply with NCLB—or it risks losing $60 million in federal aid.

The situation has prompted the state to look at trimming some of the current state tests in an effort to save money. State Education Commissioner Nicholas Donohue proposed a plan in November that sets aside $2.4 million for next year's tests. Two thirds—or $1.6 million—would come from federal money through No Child Left Behind. The remaining $800,000 would be from state money, primarily an unspent portion of a special education grant received from the federal government. The proposal would eliminate testing in science and social studies this year and the language arts tests would no longer include a writing sample. The changes are expected to save about $600,000.

—Scott Young, NCSL

leagues focus too heavily on reading and math, for example, because their students will be tested only in those subjects. Furthermore, he says, many schools are waiting until fifth grade to begin teaching science, because students aren't tested in science until then.

Barbara Provenzano, a fourth grade teacher at Forest Hill Elementary in West Palm Beach, Fla., maintains that the pressure to perform well on the FCAT drives out opportunities for creativity.

"We don't like the fact that everything is so assessment driven," she says. "As teachers, we have less energy to put toward projects, fun activities, activities that are more geared toward getting the students interested and involved."

Provenzano used to organize an end-of-unit region feast, during which her students would bring in different dishes from various regions they had studied. But that popular activity has fallen by the wayside, a victim of the prevalence of testing.

Senator Gardner of Ohio, an educator for more than 28 years, argues that there is nothing wrong with teaching to the test. "During the week I gave the kids information, and at the end of the week I tested them on it," he says. "So if that's what I wanted them to know, then that's teaching to the test."

> *"We don't like the fact that everything is so assessment driven."*
>
> —Fourth Grade Teacher Barbara Provenzano

DRIVEN BY STANDARDS

As the consequences become more severe, the tests themselves are growing more rigorous. Most experts agree—and No Child Left Behind requires-that states develop challenging standards and align their tests with those standards. As such, many states have spent considerable time developing their standards with input from educators, parents, and business and political leaders. Then they've developed customized tests to accurately reflect and measure those standards.

"We took a few years to develop our standards, then took a couple of years to make sure our tests were aligned with them," reports Mike O'Farrell, staff director for the Florida Senate Education Committee. "Florida has

done an excellent job of aligning tests with standards."

President Bush's home state of Texas did much the same. The TAKS program is the most recent incarnation of an assessment system that has been evolving since 1978.

"Now we have a uniform curriculum and a way of testing that uniform curriculum," says Adrienne Sobolak, deputy director of communications at the Texas Education Agency.

With higher standards come more complex tests. Before the 1990s, large-scale assessments consisted primarily of multiple-choice tests, according to CRESST's Herman.

Since then, tests with more open-ended questions were developed to paint a more accurate picture of a student's knowledge and skills. Today, many state tests include writing assignments. And some states have experimented with portfolios, hands-on activities, teamwork skills and the like.

"Part of the impetus for all this performance assessment was trying to get at these more complex skills," Joan Herman says, "and understanding the problem-solving skills that we think are important for kids to know and be able to do."

But Herman says there has been somewhat of a retrenchment from the more open-ended tests because of the expenses associated with them.

THE COST FACTOR

A May 2003 report by the United States General Accounting Office (GAO) found that, in general, tests that are hand scored—those with essay questions, for example—are more time and labor intensive and more expensive than tests that are machine scored, such as multiple-choice tests. The GAO estimates that between FY 2002 and FY 2008, total state expenditures would be about $1.9 billion if states used multiple-choice tests. That figure jumps to $5.3 billion if states use a mix of multiple-choice questions and open-ended questions requiring written responses.

In light of the huge budget shortfalls being faced by almost all states, policymakers are concerned about their ability to adequately finance assessment programs. No Child Left Behind does provide states with additional money ($387 million in FY 2002), but questions remain about whether federal funds will cover states' costs. Policymakers wishing to incorporate more thorough, open-ended tests must find a way to finance them, or face compromising their standards in order to meet all the federal requirements within the fiscal constraints of the federal law.

Budget shortfalls are also threatening other aspects of assessment programs. Besides paying for tests, state funds are typically directed to high-performing schools as part of rewards and incentives programs, low-rated schools that need help in raising their performance, programs for improving teacher quality, and myriad other school improvement efforts.

In Texas, for example, a program that rewards schools for excellence is no longer being financed, and legislators were looking at cutting funds for math and reading academies for teachers. In Ohio, Senator Gardner is struggling to find a way to restore teachers' professional development money, a victim of budget shortfalls.

A PRESSURE COOKER

While policymakers and administrators grapple with assessment systems at the state level, teachers and students are facing their own challenges in the classroom.

Testing is "a necessary evil," says Christena Southwick, a fourth grade teacher at Kendrick Lakes Elementary School in Lakewood, Colo. "There needs to be standards, some sort of leveling so that the teachers are all on the same page, kids get all of the same skills covered,

and there's no unevenness in their skill development. That's part of not leaving any child behind."

On the other hand, she says, standardized assessments force all students to be tested the same way even though they learn in different ways and at different rates.

School testing also tends to raise the anxiety level in the classroom.

"The kids are nervous," says Provenzano. "We do our best to try and keep it low key, but on the other hand we can't afford to let it be too low key. We have to communicate how important it is."

Southwick agrees. "There's so much pressure on the teachers who in turn put pressure on the kids to do their best."

Back at De Leon Middle School in McAllen, Texas, Principal Jodie Ellis says that after "blowing off steam" at the pep rally, the TAKS test itself was a serious, but positive, experience. The kids know what to expect, she says, because the state has done a good job of communicating the standards to schools and providing resources, such as workbooks, for students who need extra help.

And students seem to be rising to the occasion. Nearly 90 percent of the members of the Texas Elementary Principals and Supervisors Association say that the Texas system is helping more children succeed, according to Executive Director Sandi Borden.

"So many more children—and that's real children—are learning at higher levels than they ever were before," she says. "We've narrowed the gap in a state whose children have become increasingly poorer. It shows policymakers that, indeed, their investments are paying off."

45

Medicaid: 10 Fixes That Work

Martha King and Dianna Gordon

State governments are prescribing lots of reforms for health care programs. Some of them actually work.

The national economy hit states hard. Most cut their budgets, and Medicaid wasn't spared. States have trimmed services, cut provider payments and taken people off the rolls. Yet Medicaid continues to consume a larger and larger slice of revenues.

Over the past 15 years, Medicaid's piece of the budget has doubled from about 10 percent to 20 percent of spending.

State budgets grew an average of 1.2 percent in 2002, but Medicaid costs increased by 12.8 percent. The 2003 increase was 9.3 percent. And experts see no relief in sight. The Congressional Budget Office anticipates Medicaid costs will keep growing by at least 8 percent a year.

All 50 states and the District of Columbia have worked to contain costs and slow growth over the past couple of years, specifically by targeting provider payments and drug expenditures. In addition, nearly half the states have restricted eligibility, reduced benefits and increased copayments.

These approaches may be necessary in the short term. But many quick fixes could trigger costly consequences:

- Patients denied certain services may get sicker and ultimately seek more expensive treatments (e.g., people with diabetes or mental illness may need hospitalization if they cannot get needed medications.)
- Shifting costs to providers could cause them to drop out of the program. Or they may charge insured patients more, driving up private insurance premiums.

From *State Legislatures,* March 2004.

Dick Cauchi, Allison Cook, Donna Folkemer, Karmen Hanson, Joy Johnson Wilson and Laura Tobler also contributed to this piece.

Important to the Big Picture

However costly, states aren't ready to scrap their Medicaid programs entirely, even if they could. Medicaid contributes substantially to every state economy. According to the Kaiser Commission on Medicaid and the Uninsured, it accounts nationally for:

- 17 percent of total personal health care.
- 48 percent of nursing home care.
- 17 percent of prescription drug payments.
- 17 percent of hospital care.

Medicaid—at least 50 percent of each state's spending is paid by the federal government—pays for about 35 percent of the nation's births. It also funds services to nearly one third of all Americans over the age of 85, including prescription drugs and long-term care not covered by Medicare.

So states keep searching for longer term reforms to meet the needs of their most vulnerable citizens. Below are the top 10 fixes:

1. REFORM LONG-TERM CARE

States can save a lot by fixing expensive long-term care for low-income people with serious medical needs. Up to 40 percent of a state's medicaid spending can go to long term care.

In just a few years, Maine cut the time Medicaid clients stay in nursing homes by 44 percent. The state also reduced the percentage of long-term care clients who live in nursing homes. And the total per person spending on Medicaid-funded long-term care has dropped by 12 percent.

Maine tightened medical eligibility standards, substantially increased service capacity in the community and controlled administrative costs and per person expenditures. Because home care and assisted living generally cost less than institutional care, Maine has been able to serve more people with only modest increases in total spending. The number of people using long-term care services has increased by 30 per-

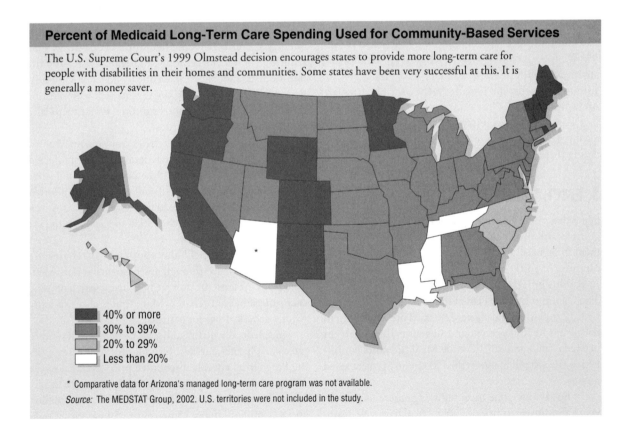

Percent of Medicaid Long-Term Care Spending Used for Community-Based Services

The U.S. Supreme Court's 1999 Olmstead decision encourages states to provide more long-term care for people with disabilities in their homes and communities. Some states have been very successful at this. It is generally a money saver.

- 40% or more
- 30% to 39%
- 20% to 29%
- Less than 20%

* Comparative data for Arizona's managed long-term care program was not available.

Source: The MEDSTAT Group, 2002. U.S. territories were not included in the study.

cent since 1995, while total spending has increased only 17 percent.

"It's not often you have the opportunity both to save money, and respond to consumer preferences," says Christine Gianopoulos, Maine's director of Elder and Adult Services.

2. FOCUS ON THE SICKEST PEOPLE

People who are seriously and chronically ill account for a significant amount of Medicaid spending, even though they are a small percent of all Medicaid patients. By giving patients more intensive ongoing services, states can prevent or reduce serious problems later and save money.

At least 21 states have programs to manage diseases—mainly asthma and diabetes—of chronically ill Medicaid beneficiaries. The goal is to improve their health and control costs. The jury is still out on how much is saved, but the theory is that the initial investment will pay off down the road.

Florida, one of the first states to experiment with disease management, had hopes of saving $112.7 million over four years. Although that proved too ambitious, the state did realize $42.2 million in savings over five years.

"We tried a number of approaches and programs, and are pleased with the results so far," says Heidi Fox, an administrator for the Florida Agency for Health Care Administration.

Despite the mixed results on savings, other states are testing new approaches to disease management and evaluating them.

3. EMPHASIZE PREVENTION

States that invest in keeping people healthy can avoid more costly health problems down the road. How? An investment in prenatal care, well-child visits and immunizations can prevent costly illnesses among Medicaid patients.

A pilot program in North Carolina is one example. The Community Care Plan of Pitt County, which started with 12,000 Medicaid clients, increased preventive health check-ups by 330 percent and sick visits by 60 percent between 2000 and 2001. While Medicaid costs continued to rise around the state, the Pitt County project saved money.

"The savings came from reducing emergency room visits and hospitalizations," says Dr. Charles Willson,

president of the state's chapter of the American Academy of Pediatrics.

The physicians focused on health and safety, making sure children were immunized and their parents were aware of such things as using car seats, locking cabinets and having kids wear bike helmets. The project also offered an after-hours pediatric clinic and worked with a local hospital to provide a 24-hour nurse hotline.

"By focusing on prevention and giving our patients an after-hours option, we saw a 20 percent decline in ER visits our first year," says Willson. Today, the pilot has expanded to become Community Care of Eastern North Carolina, serving more than 50,000 children and youths.

4. REDUCE PRESCRIPTION DRUG COSTS

States have saved millions of dollars by implementing prior authorization, preferred drug lists and supplemental rebates, and by requiring generic drugs.

And that's important when prescription drug costs now account for 11 percent of Medicaid spending with annual increases of 18.8 percent through 2002.

Maine is saving $15 million a year after adding 70 frequently prescribed medicines to its list of drugs that require prior authorization. Michigan saved $44 million from an annual pharmaceutical budget of $540 million in 2002 by requiring doctors to seek prior authorization for any medications not on a list of medically sound and cost-effective drugs.

Some states have sought rebates from manufacturers. These are in addition to the federal rebates established in 1990 that return nearly 20 percent of the total price back to Medicaid (about $4.9 billion in 2000). Florida and Michigan were convinced they could negotiate even better prices if increased rebates led to a spot on the list of preferred products.

Courts have upheld the approach, if rebates are approved in advance through amendments to state Medicaid plans. At least 20 states are now investigating or using such supplemental rebates. Many states also explicitly require generic drugs for patients.

Since federally qualified health centers are allowed to purchase pharmaceuticals through the 340B Drug Pricing Program at a deeply discounted price (even below the Medicaid price), states may save by expanding their use. Massachusetts estimates a savings of between $15 million and $27 million, if just 25 percent to 50 percent of their

Preferred Drug Lists Aim at Medicaid Savings

Prescription drug costs have risen dramatically over the past several years and now account for at least 11 percent of Medicaid spending—an estimated annual increase of 18.8 percent. To save money, states have developed by law or regulation lists of less expensive, medically sound medications from which physicians can choose for their patients.

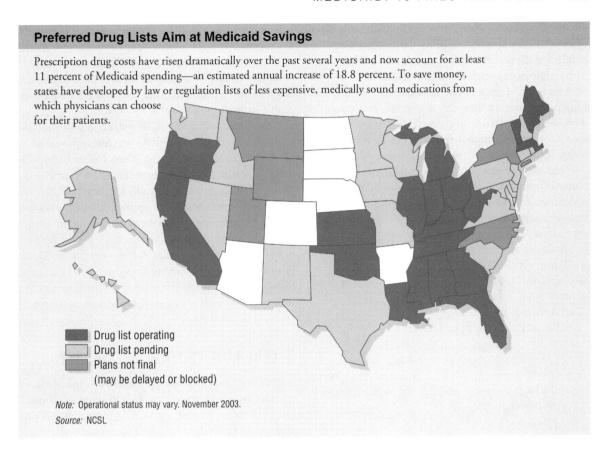

■ Drug list operating
□ Drug list pending
▨ Plans not final
(may be delayed or blocked)

Note: Operational status may vary. November 2003.
Source: NCSL

current Medicaid prescriptions are filled by qualified health centers.

Some states have hired management firms to help them trim the cost of medicines. Virginia and California, for example, just signed on with AmeriHealth Mercy, which has managed to keep its average Medicaid pharmacy increases to 8.8 percent compared to the national trend of 18.8 percent. They call their program PerformRx.

5. INVESTIGATE FRAUD AND ABUSE

Florida was losing $1 billion a year before lawmakers began to crack down on fraud.

"The pressure on Medicaid is to receive bills and pay them as quickly as possible because providers need the cash flow," says Senator Burt Saunders. Unfortunately, that makes it hard to investigate possible fraud.

So the Legislature authorized hiring specialists to design a Medicaid fraud software program that analyzes medical bills. More enforcement staff were hired, adding

"a hundred people to find fraud, investigate and prosecute" he says.

The beefed-up investigative and enforcement policies led to the discovery of a number of fake Miami clinics that had billed Medicaid $25 million over a year's time. "We found out there were no clinics, no doctors, no patients. Some smart person had rented a P.O. box and simply started billing Medicaid," the senator says. Now an on-site inspection is conducted before any Medicaid license is issued.

Saunders says that, so far, fraud has been cut in half. "That's a huge savings."

6. USE ELECTRONIC RECORDS

Arkansas saved an estimated $30 million over 17 months by creating an integrated electronic billing, eligibility verification, payment, data collection and analysis system.

"Medicaid cannot continue to grow by double digit funding without deep cuts," says former state Medicaid director Ray Hanley who now works for Electronic Data Systems Corporation, a private firm that designs electronic billing and data collection systems. He says getting smart with technology can help avoid those cuts.

Arkansas developed one of the country's first "decision support systems. That's a data warehouse that can hold three to five years' worth of claims," Hanley says. "A staff member can sit down and do reports far faster from the computerized database than the old ledger system."

The state now runs an e-business system that includes photo ID cards with patient information on their magnetic strips. At a doctor's office, the patient's card is swiped through a computer terminal, and eligibility and benefits are verified. The system also confirms payment and electronically deposits it in the physician's bank account.

Other firms such as First Health Services and ACS also offer this technology and are competing for these lucrative state contracts.

In Arkansas, the technology has:

- Reduced the time for processing claims from 15 days to 3.5.
- Cut collection expenses for Medicaid claims.
- Dropped claim denials from 12 percent to 1 percent at a large children's hospital due to more efficient processing.

7. GET THE MOST OUT OF FEDERAL FUNDING

States have tapped additional federal funds by identifying services they already pay for that qualify for matching money.

In the past, states have used creative financing schemes, such as taxing providers and tapping intergovernmental transfers, to "draw down" additional federal funds. In recent years, however, Congress has made it tougher for states to be creative. Other state approaches to leveraging additional funds have been limited.

So by identifying matching programs, states can save more. For example, some special education programs, services for foster care children or substance abuse treatments may qualify for federal Medicaid reimbursement if the people served meet certain criteria. Oregon recently converted its state-funded insurance program for low-income families to Medicaid to take advantage of federal funding to help finance it.

A new Medicaid 1115 Pharmacy Plus waiver allows states that run pharmaceutical subsidy programs to gain federal matching funds for people age 65 or older with incomes between 100 percent and 200 percent of federal poverty guidelines ($12,120 to $24,240 for a family of two). Depending on the size of the state, this option can save millions in pharmaceutical costs and allow additional people to be covered.

Florida, Illinois, Indiana, Maryland, South Carolina and Wisconsin have received waiver approval as of November 2003. At least nine others have filed applications. However, new budget neutrality requirements make it more difficult for states to qualify for these 1115 waivers.

Rhode Island, which has applied for such a waiver, plans to combine three existing state-funded groups and get a 55 percent federal match. "This waiver program should be a win-win for the people of Rhode Island," says former Senate President William Irons. However, the new Medicare law puts the future of this program into question, and the status of existing programs is under review.

8. LEVERAGE FEDERAL FLEXIBILITY

States have never had more flexibility to craft Medicaid reforms, especially in covering additional people through the 1115 waiver process. Expanding the number of people covered by Medicaid can save state, local and provider contributions that go toward other programs to cover the uninsured.

Utah received a first-of-its-kind federal waiver in March 2002 to cover up to 25,000 additional low-income adults. The "firsts" are a benefit package for new enrollees limited to primary and preventive services financed in part by savings from a reduction in benefits to the already enrolled Medicaid population.

Rod Betit, former director of the Utah Department of Health, described the program as an investment in "front-end" services with the potential to save the state money on hospitalizations and emergencies down the road. "The state wanted to meet the day-to-day needs for uninsured adults, provide access to primary care providers and encourage them to use the health care system more appropriately," he said.

Another potential way to gain funds by expanding coverage is to define eligibility for the federal category known as "aged, blind and disabled" to include people with incomes up to 100 percent of federal poverty. Since a high percentage of these individuals have Medicare

Stop-Gap Solutions 2002–2003

	Eligibility Limits	Optional Services	Reimbursement Rates	Cost-Sharing
Alabama				
Alaska	•	•	•	
Arizona	•		•	•
Arkansas				
California	•	•	•	
Colorado	•	•	•	•
Connecticut	•	•	•	•
Delaware		•	•	•
Florida	•	•	•	•
Georgia	•	•	•	
Hawaii			•	
Idaho		•	•	
Illinois			•	•
Indiana		•	•	•
Iowa		•	•	•
Kansas		•	•	•
Kentucky		•	•	
Louisiana		•		
Maine				•
Maryland	•		•	•
Massachusetts	•	•	•	
Michigan		•	•	•
Minnesota	•	•	•	•
Mississippi		•	•	•
Missouri	•	•	•	•
Montana		•	•	•
Nebraska	•	•	•	•
Nevada		•	•	•
New Hampshire				
New Jersey	•	•	•	•
New Mexico		•		
New York	•			
North Carolina	•			
North Dakota		•	•	•
Ohio		•	•	•
Oklahoma	•	•	•	•
Oregon	•	•	•	•
Pennsylvania		•	•	
Rhode Island			•	
South Carolina			•	•
South Dakota		•	•	
Tennessee			•	
Texas	•	•	•	•
Utah		•	•	•

(continued)

Stop-Gap Solutions 2002–2003 (Continued)

	Eligibility Limits	Optional Services	Reimbursement Rates	Cost-Sharing
Virginia		•	•	•
Vermont		•		•
Washington	•	•	•	•
West Virginia				
Wisconsin		•	•	•
Wyoming				•

Source: Health Policy Tracking Service

coverage for most primary and catastrophic illnesses, this change mostly allows access to pharmaceuticals, reimbursable by the full federal matching funds. At least 20 states have adopted the 100 percent standard ($8,980 per year for an individual in 2003).

9. EVALUATE THE PROGRAM

Seeing rising costs and plummeting resources, South Carolina lawmakers asked the Legislative Audit Council to examine the Medicaid program for the state Department of Health and Human Services. The result: $22.9 million in potential savings that included using a preferred drug list ($12.8 million) and starting a Medicaid enrollment fee ($1.4 million).

Many of the council recommendations have passed the House and are now before the Senate Committee on Medical Affairs. Representative Adam Taylor says House members spent more time debating Medicaid reform than the budget.

"We passed this bill with one purpose in mind: Clean up the Medicaid system," he says. One of the major provisions of the bill is tightening eligibility for recipients, says Taylor, "which is key."

He also wants accountability. "Before I put any more money in this program, I wanted an audit of the [health and human services] department."

10. MAKE MEDICAID THE PAYER OF LAST RESORT

By law, Medicaid can pay only for services not covered by other public or private insurance or other payers. Sometimes states have to be creative in maximizing the role of other payers.

In crafting its long-term care reforms, Maine was able to shift more of the state's nursing home costs from Medicaid to Medicare. Since Medicare's funding comes from the federal government, Maine was able to save state money. "Requiring nursing homes to certify beds for both Medicaid and Medicare payment ensures that residents use their Medicare skilled nursing facility benefit for the initial part of the nursing facility stay, rather than having Medicaid pay from Day 1," said Christine Gianopoulos. The result: The number of admissions Medicare paid for increased 559 percent between 1993 and 2001, while the number of Medicaid admissions increased only 40 percent.

Fresh Approaches

You cannot reform your Medicaid programs overnight. But if you can assess the current situation, learn from other states, determine how you may improve people's health while achieving efficiencies, you may accomplish reforms that will save money over time.

46

Access Denied

Katherine Barrett, Richard Greene and Michele Mariana

Nearly 44 million Americans lack health insurance. It's a serious and chronic problem for those who can't afford care and for both the private sector and the states, which are left picking up the tab.

DIAGNOSIS

Health insurance, and the growing lack of access to it, is a daunting national issue, one that congressional committees, presidents and presidents' wives have wrestled with—to no avail. Meanwhile, the situation continues to deteriorate. In 1992, there were 35.4 million uninsured people in the United States; a decade later, there were 43.6 million, with the biggest jump coming in 2001–02 when the rate rose 5.8 percent in that one year alone.

States want to reduce the ranks of the uninsured within their borders, and they keep trying—with very little success. Right now a bad situation is growing markedly worse in 18 states, with a small statistical improvement in only one. The rest have stayed stable, but stable is not exactly a good place to be. "The best thing we can say we've done for the uninsured is that we haven't created more of them," says Barbara Edwards, Medicaid director in Ohio, one of the states where the rates haven't changed.

The basic problem is systemic: The United States relies on the private sector to insure its citizenry, but that arrangement is being undermined by changes in the economy. There's been a migration of workers from benefit-rich manufacturing jobs to benefit-poor service jobs, and to small businesses, many of which do not provide any coverage at all. On top of that, the economic downturn that started in 2001 tore yet more holes in the net of coverage: Many people lost their insurance when they lost their jobs. Although the economy is recovering, job growth has not been impressive, and many employers continue to rely on temporary employees, who usually do not qualify for health benefits.

From *Governing,* February 2004.

"Employer-based coverage is eroding at the edges, and that erosion is contributing to the growth in our uninsured population," says Diane Rowland, executive director of the Kaiser Commission on Medicaid and the Uninsured. In 2002 alone, the number of U.S. residents insured by their employers dropped by 1.3 million to 61.3 percent of the total population.

Lack of insurance translates into unfortunate outcomes for those without it: higher mortality rates, lost productivity, increased personal bankruptcies and the need for more expensive care when early signs of illness are ignored. "You see many more people coming in through the emergency room or with poorly managed conditions or later-stage diseases," says Benjamin Chu, president of the New York City Health and Hospitals Corp., the largest municipal hospital system in the country. The bottom line, Chu says, is that "the uninsured ultimately get care somewhere. They come to our system, and they contribute to a large bad-debt pool, and someone has to pay that."

Medical costs for the uninsured were about $60 billion in 2001. Of that, $35 billion was "uncompensated care," which means it was care not paid for by the patients.

Who foots the bill? State-financed public hospitals or charity hospital systems as well as nonprofits provide care to needy patients. That pressure on a hospital's balance sheet, however, translates into higher prices for paying patients, which in turn helps push up the cost of insurance premiums—making health insurance more expensive and putting a financial squeeze on the companies that provide it.

To defray some of the uncompensated-care costs, the federal government and the states chip in with special Medicaid payments for hospitals that serve large numbers of poor people. These are called "disproportionate share" payments simply because those hospitals serve a disproportionate share of the poor population. Hospitals also seek donations, and states and localities provide tax exemptions or credits, as well as indigent-care grants.

This patchwork of funding is a poor way to support a medical system. Medicaid's contribution through its disproportionate share program, for example, compensates hospitals but not necessarily in direct proportion to the number of uninsured they serve. "It's grossly inefficient. The distribution of these dollars across the states is very uneven," says John Holahan, director of the Urban Institute's Health Policy Center. "There are a lot of inequities and a lot of problems with it."

There are also administrative expenses. Lower-income individuals in particular may go off and on insurance several times during any given year. "If they fall off insurance, we send in a claim and the claim is denied," says New York Hospital System's Chu. "Then we spend a lot of time and manpower working on the denied claims. It's an administrative nightmare."

CASE HISTORY

Employer-based health care insurance was introduced in this country during World War II, when wage and price controls were in place and health insurance was a great fringe benefit that helped employers attract employees. Coverage expanded for 25 years. Then, in the 1980s, a slow contraction set in. Since foreign competitors didn't have the same obligation to their employees, U.S. firms found themselves at a disadvantage in a global economy. "The general economic pressures of a world market made it more difficult for firms to continue the unabated growth of private, employer-based insurance," says Allen Koop, visiting history professor at Dartmouth University.

In the past decade, medical advances have continued pushing health costs higher, and these increased costs have made insurance increasingly unaffordable to businesses and individuals.

To lower their health care expenses, companies have begun forcing their employees to shoulder more of the load. The Kaiser Foundation's Annual Employer Health Benefit Survey for 2003 found that 65 percent of companies hiked the employee's share of the health premium in 2003, and 79 percent of large firms planned to do so in 2004. By 2003, employees reported paying 50 percent more for both individual and family coverage than they did in 2000. Some employees, particularly low-income workers and young adults, decided they couldn't afford to pay, or didn't want to, and dropped their health insurance.

COMPLICATIONS

One of the biggest obstacles states face in expanding employer-based health insurance is ERISA. Passed by the U.S. Congress in 1974, the Employee Retirement Income Security Act was primarily intended to protect employees' pensions. But it also put employee benefits under the

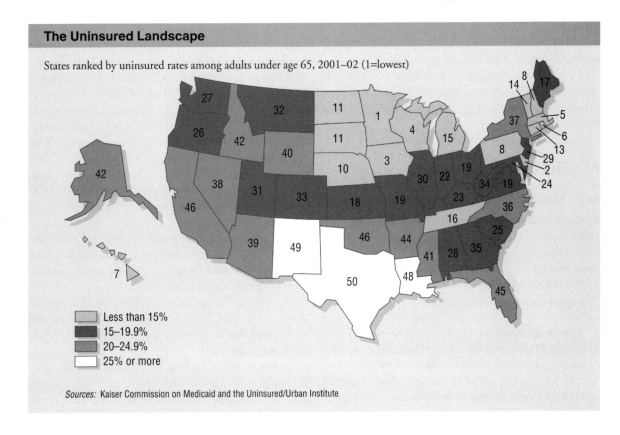

The Uninsured Landscape

States ranked by uninsured rates among adults under age 65, 2001–02 (1=lowest)

Less than 15%
15–19.9%
20–24.9%
25% or more

Sources: Kaiser Commission on Medicaid and the Uninsured/Urban Institute

jurisdiction of the federal government and not the states. That meant a state could not mandate that all companies provide their employees with coverage, even if the political will to do so were there. "ERISA was enacted for a totally different set of purposes," says Kaiser's Rowland. "But it's become a fundamental barrier for states in dealing equitably with insurance plans and employers."

The only state exempted from ERISA's health care clauses is Hawaii, which passed its Prepaid Health Care Act a few months before ERISA was enacted and was, therefore, grandfathered in. Hawaii's law mandates that employers provide coverage for any employee who works more than 20 hours a week. Not surprisingly, Hawaii's uninsured rate is among the lowest in the country. California passed a law this fall that also has mandates for employee coverage, but employers are challenging it in court, arguing that it is out of compliance with ERISA.

While employers have played the ERISA card in every state that has toyed with legislating coverage, people in general support the idea of employer mandates. A recent poll taken by Stony Brook University on Long Island found that 71 percent of respondents were in favor of the government requiring businesses to provide health insurance. Of course, that support would likely erode if businesses perceived the idea as a genuine threat and started to lobby heavily against it.

In any case, the current situation is putting pressure on small businesses and self-employed individuals to find bargain insurance plans. That demand is creating an opportunity for con artists who have flooded the market with fraudulent policies that charge very low premiums but have no intent of actually paying anything but small claims. Recently, Mila Kofman, an assistant research professor at the health policy institute at Georgetown University, looked at four health plans that were shut down by states or the federal government and found $85 million in unpaid claims for 100,000 individuals. "When you have a demand for affordable alternatives and there aren't any, you'll always have a criminal element providing the supply," she says. The U.S. General Accounting Office has been asked to do a study on this issue. The results are expected early this year.

REMEDIES

Small Business Boost

The weakest links in employer-based coverage are small and very small businesses. Among uninsured workers, 14 percent are self-employed and 49 percent come from businesses with fewer than 100 employees. Many states have tried to encourage small businesses to provide their workers with health insurance, with only limited success.

The latest—and arguably most ambitious—effort in the field is Maine's recently enacted Dirigo (the Latin for "I lead"). The plan, which begins implementation in July, is the "last best test of an employer-based system," says Trish Riley, director of the Governor's Office of Health Policy and Finance in Maine.

A key element of the multi-layered system is state-administered health plans for small businesses and the self-employed. Private insurers will provide the health coverage, with the state regulating rates. The state will also help with enrollment, eligibility determination, wellness programs and disease management. The assistance with administrative details, which will help eliminate employer hassle, is a vital element, Riley says. "They work through us. If we have to change insurers every year, it will be invisible to them."

Riley sees this as an important part of the program's appeal to a small business. She ran her own small enterprise for 15 years and says her problem with health insurance "wasn't just the high cost of the increases. It was the unpredictability."

The program also includes state subsidies to help with the purchase of private insurance, through employers, for those whose incomes would otherwise qualify them for public help. Those with incomes below 300 percent of the poverty level, and who don't have employer insurance, will still qualify for Maine Care, the state's Medicaid and Children's Health Insurance Program.

In an effort to control health care costs and thus keep insurance premiums affordable, the state imposed a temporary moratorium on capital expenditures for such things as new hospitals, enforced through its certificate-of-need program. When that moratorium ends in May, the state will explicitly limit the capital expenditures it is willing to finance on the public side. Meanwhile, the state has sought voluntary cooperation from the private side—both providers and insurers—to limit operating profits for a year and publicly post both prices and quality measures. A forum has been set up to monitor quality issues and act as a clearinghouse for evidence-based medicine.

This drive to erase the problem of the uninsured was a key campaign issue for Governor John Baldacci, who was elected in 2002. While the private sector, particularly hospitals, had muted enthusiasm for a number of Dirigo's elements, there's been a major effort to include diverse representation on the study commissions and task forces that are moving the program from idea to implementation.

In its first year of funding, the plan will be bolstered by $53 million in one-time state money. In the future, the state plans to use an assessment of up to 4 percent assessment on gross revenues of insurance companies. Eventually, this assessment may be reduced—"offset" by the elimination of bad debt and charity care, as well as other cost-containment activities. All payments—from employees, employers and insurers—will stream into the Dirigo Health Fund where the state hopes to use some of them to match Medicaid dollars.

Pooled Purchasing

Several states have set up purchasing cooperatives for small businesses with the idea that these organizations could eliminate some of the administrative hassle and improve bargaining power, thereby increasing rates of employee coverage. But states often find that their own regulations provide huge obstacles to negotiating good deals. In Florida, for example, state insurance rules prohibited the cooperatives from negotiating with insurers based on price, except for administrative costs. The latter just didn't make enough of a dent in the financial terms to persuade businesses to sign up.

Texas also attempted to establish cooperative plans that would be marketed by the state centrally, thereby skirting the expense of insurance agents. But it turned

Tapping Into Health Benefits

Health insurance coverage, by type of provider, for adults under age 65, 2001–02

	PRIVATE		PUBLIC		UNINSURED
	Employer	Individual	Medicaid	Other*	
Alabama	67.8%	4.3%	7.0%¹	3.9%	17.1%
Alaska	62.4%	3.7%	6.8%	4.8%	22.2%
Arizona	61.1%	7.1%	6.8%	3.7%	21.3%
Arkansas	58.8%	6.6%	6.5%	5.7%	22.5%
California	59.7%	7.0%	8.0%	1.8%	23.5%
Colorado	66.9%	7.2%	3.6%	3.1%	19.2%
Connecticut	73.5%	5.4%	5.2%	2.0%	13.8%
Delaware	74.1%	4.8%	6.5%	2.9%	11.6%
Florida	60.9%	7.3%	5.8%	3.2%	22.8%
Georgia	67.2%	5.5%	4.3%	3.3%	19.7%
Hawaii	71.4%	5.1%	7.1%	3.9%	12.6%
Idaho	63.2%	5.5%	6.7%	2.4%	22.2%
Illinois	69.4%	5.2%	5.7%	2.2%	17.6%
Indiana	73.1%	5.0%	3.7%	2.3%	15.9%
Iowa	72.4%	8.7%	5.3%	1.8%	11.7%
Kansas	69.9%	7.5%	4.3%	3.2%	15.1%
Kentucky	68.3%	4.4%	6.2%	4.8%	16.4%
Louisiana	57.9%	5.8%	6.7%	4.1%	25.6%
Maine	66.6%	4.7%	10.6%	3.0%	15.0%
Maryland	73.4%	5.1%	3.4%	1.5%	16.6%
Massachusetts	71.7%	4.9%	9.8%	1.4%	12.1%
Michigan	72.4%	4.3%	7.0%	1.9%	14.4%
Minnesota	75.5%	6.9%	6.3%	1.4%	10.0%
Mississippi	58.7%	4.2%	11.9%	3.1%	22.1%
Missouri	69.5%	6.5%	6.3%	2.2%	15.4%
Montana	56.7%	12.7%	6.7%	5.3%	18.6%
Nebraska	68.3%	10.9%	4.8%	2.8%	13.3%
Nevada	68.9%	4.1%	3.1%	2.7%	21.2%
New Hampshire	78.1%	3.5%	2.9%	2.4%	13.1%
New Jersey	71.8%	3.2%	6.1%	1.5%	17.4%
New Mexico	55.0%	5.1%	7.4%	4.3%	28.3%
New York	63.4%	4.1%	10.0%	1.5%	21.0%
North Carolina	64.7%	4.7%	6.0%	4.3%	20.3%
North Dakota	65.3%	11.6%	5.7%	3.7%	13.7%
Ohio	72.3%	4.5%	5.9%	1.9%	15.4%
Oklahoma	61.4%	5.4%	5.4%	4.4%	23.5%
Oregon	63.3%	8.2%	9.4%	2.2%	16.9%
Pennsylvania	72.8%	5.5%	6.9%	1.6%	13.1%
Rhode Island	70.5%	5.4%	10.4%	1.4%	12.3%
South Carolina	66.1%	4.9%	8.3%	4.0%	16.7%
South Dakota	67.5%	11.0%	4.8%	3.0%	13.7 %

(continued)

Tapping Into Health Benefits (Continued)

Health insurance coverage, by type of provider, for adults under age 65, 2001–02

	PRIVATE		PUBLIC		UNINSURED
	Employer	Individual	Medicaid	Other*	
Tennessee	63.2%	5.6%	13.8%	2.8%	14.6%
Texas	58.6%	5.5%	4.3%	1.9%	29.7%
Utah	69.2%	6.4%	4.6%	1.7%	18.1%
Vermont	67.1%	6.5%	11.1%	1.5%	13.9%
Virginia	70.3%	5.4%	4.2%	4.6%	15.4%
Washington	66.3%	6.6%	7.5%	2.5%	17.0%
West Virginia	61.6%	3.4%	10.3%	5.3%	19.3%
Wisconsin	73.1%	6.8%	6.2%	1.9%	12.0%
Wyoming	65.0%	5.6%	4.5%	3.2%	21.7%

*Medicare and military-related

Source: Kaiser Commission on Medicaid and the Uninsured

out that agents are tied in to small businesses for a variety of financial services. Once bypassed, "they turned out to be a formidable adversary," says Linda Blumberg, senior research associate at the Urban Institute. One problem, she notes, was that alienated agents worked against the purchasing cooperatives by sending them high-risk individuals—the most expensive to cover. Eventually, the state decided it had to work with the agents, but as soon as it did, the cost savings went away, and there weren't real financial incentives for businesses to join the plans.

California probably has the most successful cooperative insurance program for small businesses. The program was started in the public sector and was subsequently privatized. Initially, the state set rules and negotiated contracts to provide businesses with two to 50 employees with up to 20 health plan choices and two levels of benefits. The actual operation of the program was left to private-sector vendors and health plans. Employers who participated loved it, but market share remained small. At its peak, only about 2 percent of small businesses that purchased insurance did it through this program.

In spite of good programs, California has seen an increase in the number of uninsured over the past two

years and ranks a lowly 46th in the country on this measure.

The Subsidy Approach

If states can't mandate universal coverage, they can help lower the rates of the uninsured by helping those in need pay the premiums for health insurance.

In Massachusetts, one innovative effort requires employers to pay into a fund that helps the recently unemployed buy their former employers' coverage through COBRA. The federal Consolidated Omnibus Budget Reconciliation Act requires many employers to offer continued health benefits to terminated employees. The former employees, however, must pay the premiums themselves—not necessarily affordable for someone who has just lost a job. Massachusetts will kick in with supplementary payments, so individuals—even those with incomes as high as 400 percent above the poverty level—will have to pay only 25 percent of the COBRA premium.

Rhode Island and Massachusetts also are trying to promote the use of private insurance through subsidies. Rhode Island has had moderate success with Rite Share, its premium-assistance program. The program has iden-

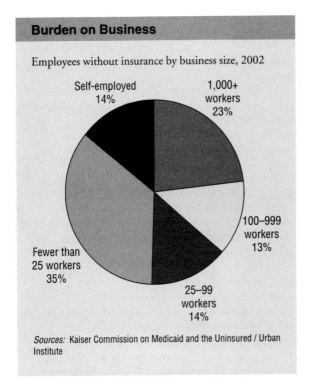

Burden on Business

Employees without insurance by business size, 2002

- Self-employed 14%
- 1,000+ workers 23%
- 100–999 workers 13%
- 25–99 workers 14%
- Fewer than 25 workers 35%

Sources: Kaiser Commission on Medicaid and the Uninsured / Urban Institute

tified about 5,300 people who have qualified for public insurance but who work for employers who offer private coverage. The state pays the employees' share of the premium so they can afford the private plan. This reduces the costs of coverage by about half. In Massachusetts, the premium-assistance program covers 10,000 to 12,000 individuals—substantially less than the 60,000 once anticipated. But the program, which provides subsidies to both employer and employee, is regarded as a qualified success and has continued a steady, if slow, growth.

A New Tool

For several years, states have been able to use waivers to shift SCHIP dollars that were not spent on children to cover their parents. CMS is now approving a second generation of waivers that allows this money to go to childless adults as well. Money for hospitals that serve the poor—disproportionate share dollars—also can be shifted by states to expand insurance coverage for adults.

The waivers appeal to states because they provide more freedom to cut back on benefits and increase cost sharing as long as the individuals affected are not among the groups mandated to receive coverage. A few states, notably Arizona, Illinois and Maine, have taken advantage of this new opportunity with vigorous coverage expansions. But overall, the new waivers have had far less impact than was hoped, according to a December 2003 study from the Kaiser Commission on Medicaid and the Uninsured.

One of the big problems is that the new waiver program was introduced just as the economic downturn clicked in. California, which intended to add coverage for 275,000 people by the waiver's third year of operation, never implemented the program. Colorado, which was going to cover 13,000 over a four-year period, had 253 enrollees by September 2003. Faced with budget problems, it closed its enrollment, as did New Jersey. While federal officials ballyhooed coverage of 2.7 million more Americans when the waivers were designed in 2001, the actual net impact has been fewer than 202,000.

Some experts worry that the waiver contains a big risk: In a strained budget climate, states could take advantage of the permission to cut back on benefits but limit the expanded-coverage part of the equation.

Meanwhile, the new waiver-based flexibility provided by CMS can also be used to focus on premium assistance. This approach removes some of the regulations that have made these efforts administrative nightmares in the past. It's too soon to know how effective this will be, although state officials say they are optimistic.

PROGNOSIS

The Bush administration has provided grants to 30 states over the past several years to study the issues of the uninsured within their borders and to develop policy decisions. And that fits in with the current public mood. "When you ask the public what government should do about the problem, most people would like to see it do something," says Leonie Huddy, director of the Center for Survey Research at Stony Brook University on Long Island. "Everyone realizes that this is a major problem. But the problems rise when you get to specifics."

Two Grand Experiments

Tennessee and Oregon both expanded coverage for the uninsured dramatically in the 1990s by remaking their Medicaid programs—and winning federal waivers to experiment with their approaches.

Tennessee moved most of its Medicaid system to managed care in one fell swoop in 1994. The idea behind TennCare was to use managed-care savings to provide enough money to expand Medicaid to cover Tennesseans whose incomes reached as high as 400 percent of poverty—a level of coverage way beyond what any other state had attempted.

Initially, TennCare appeared to be a national model as the number of uninsured Tennessee residents plummeted. But TennCare had managerial problems from its early days. A change in governors a year after the program's inception, unrealistic assumptions about cost and a very high rate of managerial turnover led to ongoing difficulties.

The major issue was the state's reliance on unstable and untried managed care organizations. At the basis of the program's philosophy was the use of capped fees, but following negotiations with the federal government in 2000, Tennessee leaders reverted to a partial fee-for-service system. Expenditures escalated by 15 percent in both 2001 and 2002 and 13 percent in 2003. A study by McKinsey & Co. in December 2003 concluded that on its current course, TennCare would eat up 91 percent of all new state tax appropriations by 2008. Even with improvement efforts and solid management, "TennCare as it is constructed today will not be financially viable," the study concluded.

Oregon took a very different tack. Rather than relying totally on controlling provider costs through managed care, it designed a plan to control costs by limiting types of care. The state set up a list of benefits in priority order—treatment for a heart attack was near the top of the list; surgery for back pain was much further down. When dollars ran short, the state would eliminate benefits from the bottom of the list, instead of cutting back on the number of people insured, which is one of the basic ways most Medicaid programs control costs when budgets are squeezed.

This bold plan provided coverage to adults age 19 to 64 who wouldn't otherwise be eligible for Medicaid. The federal government, however, was uneasy about overt rationing of health services—as opposed to the covert way of rationing through access to insurance. When Oregon needed to cut lower-priority benefits, the feds occasionally agreed but more often refused permission.

Currently, the state is awaiting approval from the Centers for Medicare and Medicaid Services to drop 30 lines of coverage, including treatment for earaches, incontinence and arthritis. "This will be a real test to see if CMS is willing to let us use that tool," says Lynn Read, Oregon's Medicaid director. If CMS denies Oregon's request, the underlying structure of the state's approach will be compromised. Meanwhile, faced with gigantic budget problems, Oregon has gotten tough about its requirement that adults who don't qualify for the traditional Medicaid program pay a modest monthly premium. If a payment is missed, the person loses coverage. As a result, enrollment of this group has dropped by about 45,000 individuals.

One specific in particular: It costs money to insure people. Innovation and experimentation can certainly help. But most states simply don't have the financial resources they need to come anywhere near a full solution to this problem.

Within government circles, there is great frustration, even among wealthier states with greater resources. Mary Kennedy is the Medicaid director for Minnesota. She's worked under three governors and observed three different health-cost containment commissions attempt a variety of innovations. Today, Minnesota has one of the highest levels of public coverage in the country and the

lowest rate of uninsured people. But segments of the population continue to be beyond the grasp of the state's substantial efforts. Meanwhile, escalating costs are dimming the luster of past programs that looked successful for a while, such as the state's reform of the insurance market for small businesses.

"I think it's very difficult for an individual state," she says. "People will say that individual states can be incubators of new ideas, but employers have to be competitive across all states. Even our public programs can't be dramatically different from our border states, or we wouldn't be able to afford it."

The Age Question

Nonelderly adults without insurance by age group, 2002

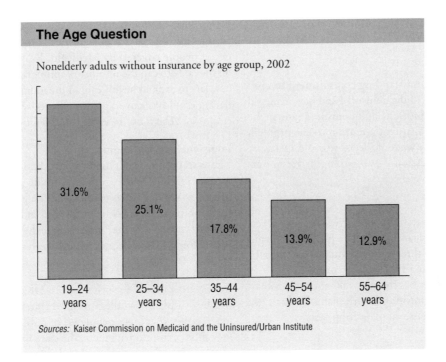

31.6%	25.1%	17.8%	13.9%	12.9%
19–24 years	25–34 years	35–44 years	45–54 years	55–64 years

Sources: Kaiser Commission on Medicaid and the Uninsured/Urban Institute

From the states' point of view, only Uncle Sam has deep-enough pockets, or the authority, to help them come anywhere near a broad-based solution. But waiting for Uncle Sam to arrive is like waiting for Godot. Everybody can talk endlessly about him, but it's not likely that he's going to show up anytime soon.

STATES THAT STAND OUT

Success Stories

Delaware and Iowa

Both states have a long-standing commitment to confronting the problem of the uninsured and have achieved the second- and third-lowest adult uninsured rates in the U.S. In Delaware, consistent attention to the problem has come through the work of the 14-year-old Delaware Health Care Commission. Iowa's strengths are in outreach and education.

Maine

This is the state to watch this year. New legislation sets the stage for universal coverage, with a phase-in to begin in July. Maine has a three-pronged attack on the problem, focusing on quality and cost control as well as access. A key element has the state taking on the role of purchaser for small business health plans, with an eye toward eliminating hassle and lowering costs.

Minnesota

With only 10 percent of non-elderly adults uninsured, Minnesota has the most successful insurance record of the 50 states. It has the second highest rate of employer coverage, the most generous public coverage for parents, and a state-funded program for childless adults, though this was cut back some last year. A strong safety net is also in place for the people who still fall through the cracks.

New York

Despite having a low rate of employer coverage, New York's expansive public programs, including one for childless adults, have helped the state make headway in covering low-income, non-elderly adults. In addition, a new program will make insurance more affordable for small businesses that employ low-income employees by shifting risk to the state for high-cost cases.

Rhode Island, Vermont and Wisconsin

All three states emphasize full family coverage, providing insurance to parents at higher levels of income than most states. One bonus to this approach: When parents are insured, children also end up getting better preventive medical care.

Trouble Spots

California

The state's extreme budget problems are making a bad situation worse. With the rates of uninsured already higher than in 45 other states, California made several changes last year that will dramatically reduce the number of people covered by Medicaid. Proposals are also on the table to cap the number of immigrants covered. A new law to expand health care to the uninsured by mandating employer coverage was signed by former Governor Gray Davis but faces legal and political challenges.

Louisiana and Oklahoma

These states cover parents only at the very lowest of income levels. Their bare-bones public coverage contributes to very high rates of uninsured adults. Oklahoma's situation particularly is likely to worsen because it has dropped coverage for the "medically needy"—people who qualify for Medicaid because of high health bills.

Oregon

A long-time model for other states, Oregon's innovative health plan has fallen on hard times. With a get-tough policy that kicks people off of public insurance if they miss premium payments, the state has reduced the numbers of adults covered by about a third. It also ended its inclusion of the "medically needy," which had covered selected population groups. If last year's tax increase is repealed, the Governor says the Oregon Health Plan, which tried to expand the number of people covered by setting limits on benefits, will cease to exist in its current form.

Tennessee

An adult uninsured rate of 14.6 percent, the lowest in the South, shows the Volunteer State did something right in TennCare. But the beleaguered program provides other states with many lessons of what not to do. The state plunged into a near-total managed care environment without a solid infrastructure of managed care organizations. A restructuring of the program led to vastly weakened cost controls. A major study recently concluded that TennCare is unsustainable in its current form.

Texas

The state dropped into 50th place in its rate of insured adults last year. Texas has low rates of employer coverage, covers parents only at very low income levels and has no coverage for childless adults. Cutbacks in Medicaid eligibility and the elimination of the state's medically needy program in 2003 will only compound the problem.

47

New Roles for Civilian Soldiers

Karen Imas

What happens when the National Guard goes to war?

National defense is a mission often associated with the federal government, yet increasingly states are playing a vital role, overseas and at home, in providing troops, technology and manpower.

When they are deployed, troops in the Guard must put their civilian lives on hold. The concerns about job security, diminished income, and time away from loved ones put great pressure on these troops and their families.

"The increasing frequency of call-ups is becoming a hardship for some members of the guard who make considerably less in military pay than in their civilian jobs," said Rhode Island Lt. Gov. Charles Fogarty. "This has left some of our guard families in tight financial situations, forcing them to struggle to pay bills while their loved ones fight on behalf of our country."

"One third of our Guard members make less in the military than at their civilian jobs and they are worrying about making ends meet," Fogarty said.

In a survey of 481 Army National Guard members from six states, the GAO found that 450 of them had experienced pay problems. Families state-side bear the burden.

In the war on terror, record numbers of National Guard members are being called up for longer deployments. Since Sept. 11, 2001, half the nation's Army National Guard and 30 percent of the Air National Guard units have been activated to meet the national requirements of the war on terrorism, according to a report by the General Accounting Office based on the congressional testimony of Janet A. St. Laurent, the GAO's director of defense capabilities and management.

From *State News,*
August 2004.

Deployments of this size, which have not occurred since the Korean War, are bringing attention to the challenges faced by "civilian solders" and their families.

DEPLOYMENT SINCE SEPT. 11 AND THE FEDERAL OUTLOOK

The National Guard is composed primarily of civilians who serve their country, state and community part-time (usually one weekend each month and two weeks during the summer.) Each state, territory and the District of Columbia has its own Army and Air Force National Guard units. The Army National Guard has 350,000 troops—38 percent of the Army's force structure. The Air National Guard has about 107,000 troops—34 percent of the total Air Force.

For state missions, the governor, through the state adjutant general, commands Guard forces. The governor can call the National Guard into action during local or statewide emergencies, such as storms, fires, earthquakes or civil disturbances. In addition, the president can activate the Guard for participation in federal missions.

More soldiers were called up and served in support of this nation in 2003 than in any year in the past 50 years. According to the Department of Defense, approximately 140,000 Army and Air Force National Guard and Reserve troops were on duty as of June 30, 2004. While the Guard is under the joint jurisdiction of the states and the military, Reservists are strictly under the control of the U.S. Department of Defense.

Since the Gulf War, the active military has downsized some 35 to 40 percent. Consequently, there is greater reliance on the National Guard and on the Reserve. Guard units with certain specialties—especially military police, transportation and engineering—are in high demand.

> "In the war on terror, record numbers of National Guard members being called up for longer deployments. The Pentagon projects that over the next three to five years, it will require between 100,000 and 150,000 Guard and Reserve forces to support ongoing military operations."

The Pentagon projects that over the next three to five years, it will require between 100,000 and 150,000 Guard and Reserve forces to support ongoing military operations. The Department of Defense also expects that mobilizations of up to one year or more will be the norm for Guard components during that time.

CHALLENGES FOR STATES

Some state officials are concerned that with longer deployments, the Guard's absence may put states at risk if there is a terrorist attack or natural disaster. New York Gov. George Pataki appeared in Congress recently urging lawmakers to support a plan that would ensure that at least half of all Guard troops would remain available for use by states in the event of emergencies or natural disasters. As [o]f the end of March, 41 percent of New York's National Guard troops were deployed.

Another concern about large Guard deployments is that small communities may lose first responders, including police officers and firefighters—popular professions among National Guard members.

Some states feel the squeeze more than others. Many state officials say they have enough Guard members available to deal with local emergencies. Thirteen percent of Vermont's Guard members are on federal active duty, for example, well below the national average of 30 percent.

While national retention is currently on par with 2003, the stresses of long deployments and fear of injury or casualty may have a negative impact on retention and recruitment rates. Between October 2003 and February 2004, the Rhode Island National Guard was running 20 percent below its 10-year average for enlistments. As one of the state's largest employers, the National Guard's contribution to the local economy is significant.

In addition to staffing shortages, the Guard faces equipment shortages, at home and abroad. Air and Army Guard units have reported that they are shorthanded with equipment overseas and that some of the equipment is outdated. Some Guard troops expressed concern that the active Army receives the most current equipment and technologies.

According to the GAO report, 22,000 pieces of equipment belonging to the National Guard had to be transferred from non-deploying units to deploying units to meet the demand overseas. In the event of a domestic emergency, "equipment and personnel may not be available to the states when they are needed because they have been deployed overseas," the report concluded.

THE GUARD RESTRUCTURES FOR INCREASED RESPONSIBILITIES

In response to the Guard's increased responsibilities, National Guard Bureau Chief Lt. Gen. H. Steven Blum outlined a plan last year to streamline the state military bureaus, the Army Guard's state area commands, and the Air Guard's state headquarters into single joint headquarters. Last summer, the National Guard Bureau began functioning as a joint headquarters and the state and territorial headquarters began functioning as provisional joint commands in October. The intent is to have the 54 joint force headquarters fully operational by October 2005.

"This will ensure a rapid and coordinated response to any emergency, making the National Guard more versatile, relevant, and able to meet our national security challenges," said Blum in congressional testimony.

The reorganization will also make it easier to implement one of the Guard's homeland security pilot programs. Twelve states have been selected to field enhanced chemical, biological and incident response task forces. The states in the pilot program are California, Colorado, Florida, Hawaii, Illinois,

Massachusetts, Missouri, New York, Pennsylvania, Texas, Washington and West Virginia.

Many of the concerns about longer and increased deployments have been bolstered by the April GAO report, which called for further restructuring of the Guard. The report, *Reserve Forces: Observations on Recent National Guard Use in Overseas and Homeland Missions and Future Challenges,* says that the Defense Department, the states and Congress face three major challenges with regard to balancing the Guard's future role in overseas and domestic missions:

- the eroding readiness of Army Guard units that may be mobilized for overseas operations within the next few years;
- the need to determine how the Army National Guard should be structured and funded to support federal missions in the longer term; and
- how to balance homeland and overseas requirements.

Although the report commends Blum's restructuring efforts, it recommends that the National Guard be restructured further to reflect its expanded role in defense. In order for Blum's reforms to work, it adds, they must be backed up by federal funding and by increased cooperation among the Defense Department, Congress and the states.

"The way ahead includes making sure that no more than 50 percent of any state's Guard force is involved in the nation's war fighting effort at any given time so that between 50 and 75 percent of the force can be available on a no-notice, immediate basis for missions on their home turf," Blum said during a speech at a recent National Governors Association meeting.

STATE INITIATIVES TO SUPPORT THE GUARD

While decisions on restructuring the Guard will come from the federal level, state officials have been working to ease the strain on activated troops.

Many lieutenant governors across the country are taking the lead in ensuring that

> "There are **311,951 dependents** of citizen soldiers who have plenty to worry about when their **loved ones** are stationed on the frontlines in the **fight against terrorism.**"
>
> —Illinois Lt. Gov. Pat Quinn

National Guard troops and their families are provided for during deployment and upon their return. Lieutenant governors are also working to guarantee that state needs, whether homeland security or natural disaster response, are met during periods of high National Guard deployment.

The National Lieutenant Governor's Association, a CSG affiliate, has passed two resolutions supporting these goals—one urging state legislatures to pass military relief funds to support Guard members' families, and another urging balance between the Guard's state and federal roles (visit www.nlga.us to read the resolutions).

"Having the resolutions passed by NLGA has brought increased attention to the issue, leading to more initiatives among state officials to support the National Guard," said Julia Hurst, executive director of the association.

Military relief funds are part of a national effort to provide grants of $500 to $2,000 to families of National Guard members and reservists. The first military relief fund law came into effect in Illinois in February 2003. More than $1.3 million in grants has been distributed to more than 2,500 families in the state to help with rent, utility bills and other expenses. Individuals can donate to the fund by checking a box on their state tax forms.

"There are 311,951 dependents of citizen soldiers who have plenty to worry about when their loved ones are stationed on the frontlines in the fight against terrorism," said Illinois Lt. Gov. Pat Quinn.

He has launched Operation Home Front, a Web site dedicated to offering services to National Guard members and reservists and informing them about their rights under the Soldiers' and Sailors' Civil Relief Act.

Maine Gov. John Baldacci and Wyoming Gov. Dave Freudenthal also recently signed into law military relief fund legislation, and South Carolina's bill was awaiting Gov. Mark Sanford's signature as of this writing. Similar bills are pending in California, Connecticut, Iowa, Michigan, Minnesota, New York, North Carolina, Pennsylvania, Rhode Island and Washington. Delaware Gov. Ruth Ann Minner set up a military relief fund in April 2003 through executive order. Delaware also has pending legislation for a check-off box to appear on state tax forms that would allow individuals to donate to the fund.

The recently passed and pending military relief fund bills will not take effect until taxes are collected for 2004. In the meantime, state officials have responded quickly to other Guard needs, particularly equipment and supply shortages. They have done so through care package drives, working with corporations for donations of supplies, and lobbying on the federal level.

In Delaware, Gov. Minner appointed Lt. Gov. John Carney to lead a comprehensive program to help part-time troops in the state. One initiative would extend state health insurance benefits for Guard member families up to two years from the current six months.

Rhode Island Lt. Gov Charles Fogarty, House Majority Leader Gordon D. Fox and Senate Majority Leader Teresa Paiva-Weed are leading the "Strong Families, Strong Troops" campaign, advocating for tax credits, education assistance, health care and financial protection for National Guard members and their families. There are 21 pending bills in the Legislature related to the initiative.

To bolster retention and recruitment, one of the Rhode Island bills would authorize the National Guard to

Federal Legislation

Addresses Concerns

In late June, the House and Senate passed their FY 2005 defense authorization bills, which addressed some of the Guard and Reserve readiness issues. As this article went to press, conference negotiations were about to begin. The Senate authorized the establishment of a commission to study Guard and Reserve roles and missions, including the pay and benefit process. The commissions report would be due at the end of 2005.

Both the House and Senate set aside funds for body armor and Humvees in response to equipment shortages faced by Guard members and reservists. The bills also seek to extend greater health benefits to Guard members and Reservists through Tricare, the health care program for active duty and retired members of the uniformed services. The Senate bill goes further by offering National Guard and reserves access to Tricare even when they are not deployed.

establish a three-year program to pay a recruitment finder's fee for persons referring enlistees who complete basic training. Two related bills would provide free tuition to public universities in the state to the spouse and children of members of the Guard or reservists who die on active duty.

In the Commonwealth of Puerto Rico, the government passed a law in April 2003 ensuring that university students in the reserves and the Puerto Rico National Guard are not academically or financially penalized when called to duty. There are 6,000 Guard members and reservists enrolled in Puerto Rico's universities and advanced academic institutions.

As these initiatives show, although state officials can't control foreign policy or natural disasters, they can help support Guard members and their families adjust to the new reality.